W9-ARO-162

How To...

IIS 4 and Proxy Server 2

IIS 4 and Proxy Server 2

seven

M. Shane Stigler
Mark A. Linsenbardt

NETWORK® PRESS
SYBEX

San Francisco Paris Düsseldorf Soest London

Associate Publisher: Guy Hart-Davis
Contracts and Licensing Manager: Kristine O'Callaghan
Acquisitions & Developmental Editor: Maureen Adams
Editors: Raquel Baker, Susan Berge
Project Editor: Susan Berge
Technical Editors: Robert Gradante, Donald Fuller
Book Designer: Bill Gibson
Graphic Illustrators: Tony Jonick, Jerry Williams
Electronic Publishing Specialist: Adrian Woolhouse
Project Team Leader: Jennifer Durning
Proofreaders: Ruth Flaxman, Rich Ganis
Indexer:
Cover Designer: Ingalls + Associates
Cover Illustrator/Photographer: Ingalls + Associates

SYBEX, Network Press, and the Network Press logo are registered trademarks of SYBEX Inc.
24seven and the 24seven logo are trademarks of SYBEX Inc.

Screen reproductions produced with Collage Complete.
Collage Complete is a trademark of Inner Media Inc.

TRADEMARKS: SYBEX has attempted throughout this book to distinguish proprietary trademarks from descriptive terms by following the capitalization style used by the manufacturer.

The author and publisher have made their best efforts to prepare this book, and the content is based upon final release software whenever possible. Portions of the manuscript may be based upon pre-release versions supplied by software manufacturer(s). The author and the publisher make no representation or warranties of any kind with regard to the completeness or accuracy of the contents herein and accept no liability of any kind, including but not limited to performance, merchantability, fitness for any particular purpose, or any losses or damages of any kind caused or alleged to be caused directly or indirectly from this book.

Library of Congress Card Number: 99-64123
ISBN: 0-7821-2530-1

Manufactured in the United States of America

10 9 8 7 6 5 4 3 2

I dedicate this book and all my love to my wife Sue.
Shane

To my mother, I dedicate my efforts, my work, and my life.
I love you, Mom.
Mark

Acknowledgments

When people ask what I do for a living, I tell them I'm a writer. It's hard to believe how many of those people tell me how they dream of being a writer. Sometimes they tell me about book ideas they have and ask if I can help get them started. Most of the time, they are somewhat disappointed when I tell them that I write technical books and I can't help them at all. But the one thing I find most is that these people have no idea how hard it is to write a book. That's why the acknowledgments are so important. This is the writer's one chance to thank the people behind the scenes who make the book possible—not just the people who work for the publisher, but also those individuals who have inspired or helped the writer's success.

That being said, I would like to thank Lars Klander for helping out in many ways during the writing of this book. I want to thank Maureen Adams from Sybex. Maureen, you were really patient (most of the time), and I truly appreciate your efforts to keep this book going. I also want to thank John Dierzewski for doing some important research on this project. I want to thank Julian Mallin for giving me something to shoot for, and the following individuals for numerous reasons: Jerry Raymond, Wes Jones, Jamie Morrison, Connie Morrison, Robin and Terry Dunlap, Ben and Paul Liebrand, Jim Parris, the whole Samuelson clan, Don and Debbie Stigler, and Sharon and Christi Stigler.

I also want to thank my partner Mark Linsenbardt for tying the rope tight, getting a good footing, and never letting me fall.

There is one more person I want to thank—someone who taught me more than I ever realized. This person taught me pride in a job well done, that hard work is the only kind, and that there is honor in working on small pieces of a much larger project. This person didn't teach me these things by sitting down and explaining them, he taught me by doing them for thirty years. To my grandfather, Tom Morrison, thank you.

Shane

The more books that you write, the more people you get to thank for making you look good. Each book is an effort that the author plays less a part in than you may know. This book, for example, would not have been created without the efforts of Shane Stigler, Lars Klander, the editors Raquel Baker and Susan Berge, the production staff at Sybex (Jennifer Durning and Adrian Woolhouse), and countless other people whose efforts are somehow always left unrecognized. Thanks to all of you for your time and hard work. I appreciate what you do very much.

Chief among the benefits of being a writer is the fact that we get to thank people for all kinds of things. Each book is an opportunity to grant recognition to an individual for things that may not have directly affected the book, but that helped to form the author's views so that the work itself is possible. This opportunity is, perhaps, the best thing about being an author. With that in mind, I would like to thank Greg Darden for teaching me to play Zork. There in that tiny office, a friendship grew and a path began that had an outcome that neither of us could have ever guessed.

Additionally, I would like to relate something very personal. My middle name is Anton. I have this name in honor of my grandfather Anton Dubravic, whose name was changed to Dubrick when he immigrated to this country and began working for the Chicago Transit Authority in 1912. Anton retired in 1955, which was the same year that the Chicago Street Cars were retired. Of the many accomplishments of his life, the one that means the most to me is the shaping of the woman who would later become my mother. It's hard to put into words the awe that I feel when I am in the presence of my mother. It's hard to accurately describe a respect and admiration for a woman who is always there, whose caring seems endless, and whose love has brought me through the most difficult moments of my life. She has been my champion when my choices left little to brag about, my advisor, my teacher, and my guide.

Mark

Contents at a Glance

Table of Contents

Introduction

Welcome to the *IIS 4 and Proxy Server 2 24seven* administrator's guide. As the demand for Web-based commerce continues to grow, more and more companies are finding the need to implement in-house Internet, or intranet, servers. With the growth of the Internet, companies also need to control user access to Web sites more than ever before. As well, protecting internal systems within their networks from outside encroachment is a growing concern. The widespread growth of the TCP/IP protocol—the backbone of the Internet and therefore, the default networking protocol for many—with its distributed and unsecure nature, has also created issues for network administrators that weren't considered even five years ago.

The 24seven series is designed specifically for you, the modern system administrator. Because basic network administration, databases, and messaging systems are so prevalent today, the system administrator's job duties are expanding every year. In today's information-based society, the need for quick reference materials is substantial and ongoing, especially for the system administrator. At most companies, once they realize how much you already know, they force you to learn even more.

This book covers all aspects of IIS and Proxy Server administration. You will find it to be an invaluable administrative asset, covering topics from basic installations to more complex topics, such as Web security. It also includes coverage of existing technologies, such as Certificate Server, that are becoming common in many installations. Our discussions and case studies provide you with the tools you need to take advantage of these complex new technologies. *IIS 4 and Proxy Server 2 24seven* was written by seasoned, professional system administrators with real-world, hands-on experience. Both authors are MCSE MCTs with years of experience in the field. Shane Stigler owned and operated an Internet Presence Provider (IPP) as well as a retail computer store. Mark Linsenbardt was the Director of Engineering for a computer manufacturer and frequently travels out of the country to consult on Internet sites. With this kind of experience behind us, you can count on getting the information that you care about, without any of the heavy concept chapters associated with books written for beginners.

About This Book

During the initial development of this book, an emphasis was placed on conveying what you, the administrator, need to know to keep your Internet Information and Proxy Servers healthy, happy, and operational—24 hours a day, 7 days a week. In addition to our own extensive, in-the-field experience, we queried many experienced Web and Proxy Server administrators and asked them a few questions:

- What do you do to keep your Web servers, and/or your Proxy Servers, up and running? What do you do to ensure that they continue to run as they are supposed to?

- What facts about the product, its use, and its integration with your specific environment did you learn the hard way?

- What have you done incorrectly (and correctly) during your installation and maintenance of these products?

- What would you like to share with other IIS and Proxy server administrators?

It is this information, together with our own experiences, that we used to assemble this book. We focused primarily on IIS, Proxy Server, and their integrated product; and on the operation issues involved with those products. Due to space and time constraints, there were issues we had to avoid or only partially cover. We avoided client-related issues, except when necessary. Both components of this book are server products, and writing about clients seemed inappropriate.

We have also avoided the topics of Windows Server 2000 (Window NT 5), Internet Information Server 5, and the next release of Microsoft Proxy Server, except when absolutely necessary. We hope that the life expectancy of this book will survive until both of these products are released and stable, but they are probably not relevant to you now. If there is one thing that both of us have grown to hate after years in the technology field, it is going to a conference (or buying a book) that spends 75% of its time talking about how great things will be in the future. We have problems to solve right *now*, and we are sure you do, too!

Throughout this book, you will find IIS@Work, Proxy@Work, and 24seven Case Study sidebars. The @Work sidebars contain specific situations and problems that we have encountered in the field while deploying these products. We felt it important to use some special mechanism to emphasize how other companies are approaching problems. The case studies at the end of each chapter are often longer than the @Work sidebars and deal with more general problems and solutions that some companies have faced. (The actual names of the companies have been changed.)

Who Should Buy This Book?

It is important to note that although *IIS 4 and Proxy Server 2 24seven* is aimed at the more experienced system administrator, it is just as beneficial to the novice. If this seems like a contradiction, it's not. This book does not go into great detail on basic concepts, such as networking or Windows NT security, because we assume you already have knowledge in those areas. For the established system administrator, this is a refreshing change in a computer book. For the novice, *IIS 4 and Proxy Server 2 24seven* makes an excellent how-to supplement to conceptual beginner books.

Our focus throughout this book is on deployment. Everything that we discuss is done with an eye towards how you are likely to use the products, as well as their helper products and services, within your organization. We don't spend a lot of time on theory or on information that is likely to have little or no benefit in the field. Instead, we focus on the use of the products, the pitfalls to watch out for, and the special tips and tricks that you can use to make the products fit your particular needs.

Anyone who has deployed; is about to deploy; or is considering deploying IIS 4, Proxy Server 2, or any one of their many supporting technologies, will benefit from this book—even if it sits on your shelf, only to be pulled down when some odd problem arises that even a seasoned administrator doesn't expect.

If you are studying for the MCSE exams, this book will be helpful, but should not be considered an exam study guide. If that is what you are seeking, purchase a copy of *MCSE: Internet Information Server 4 Study Guide* by Matthew Strebe and Charles Perkins (Sybex, 1998) and/or *MCSE: Proxy Server 2 Study Guide*, by Eric Rozell and Todd Lammle (Sybex, 1998).

Assumptions

This book is based on IIS 4 and Proxy Server 2. However, many of the topics we discuss also have relevance for earlier and future versions of either product. Based on the betas of Windows 2000 and IIS 5, much of the information in this book will apply to these products, as well. Because this book is dedicated to one version of each of the two products, you will often find that using this information with earlier versions may be confusing or that certain functionality is not supported. Certain actions and capabilities of the newer versions of these products are also not discussed here, primarily because we know that you need solutions now—not next year, or the year after, and not solutions that take a week to implement, but solutions that are effective today.

In the text, we assume that the operating system, as well as the services that we discuss, are installed on the C:\ drive—the default installation location. You can install the products in differing locations and simply change our references whenever appropriate for your system.

We have also assumed throughout this book that you are an Intel processor user. We did this intentionally so that we did not waste time and space providing two separate paths to software. If you are a Compaq Alpha user, you are probably used to substituting the \I386 path for a \ALPHA path so that you can find the software you are looking for.

How This Book Is Organized

Although IIS and Proxy compliment each other quite nicely, they are two distinctly separate programs. Since this book covers these two different topics, it seemed fitting to break the book into two sections (with an appendix at the end). Each section is broken into chapters that cover a specific topic in detail, with the goal of making it easier to find an answer when you need one.

Part One—IIS 4

This section covers all the day-to-day details that will make your job easier. You will explore topics, such as planning and implementing IIS installations and tuning your server for performance. You will also learn the basics of IIS architecture. If you know how something is built, it makes it a easier to fix when something goes wrong. Finally, you will look at many of the add-on products that are useful in IIS installations.

In Chapter 1, we introduce the IIS architecture and consider some of its basics. We also discuss the add-on products that you can take advantage of, or that are built into, IIS. The chapter introduces the product and its supporting services, pointing you in the necessary directions for the rest of the book. Chapter 2 gets down to business, with an in-depth discussion of the installation of IIS 4, including service account discussions, fault tolerance, clustering issues, and more.

In Chapter 3, we discuss the central service of IIS, the Web Server service, including configuration, load distribution, content control discussions, and more. Chapter 4 discusses File Transfer Protocol (FTP) publishing, including virtual directory maps, load distribution, distributed access, and other common FTP deployment and management issues.

In Chapter 5, we cover advanced configuration and management of IIS services, including concepts such as Bandwidth Throttling, command-line administration, content ratings, and other rigorous topics.

Chapter 6 moves away from the basic services that come with IIS and on to one of the more advanced services that you can install with the Option Pack, the SMTP service. It addresses issues related to POP3 routing and configuring the service's transport rules. It also provides you with the code for an active server page (ASP) that lets you check the contents of the SMTP server without a POP3 interface. Chapter 7 considers another related protocol that comes with IIS, the NNTP service, including methods that you can use for groupware and discussion group design. There is also an extensive discussion of the limitations of the IIS-packaged NNTP service and the pitfalls to watch out for.

In Chapter 8, we consider some of the remaining IIS add-ons, including a brief discussion of their installation and use. These services, including Microsoft Transaction Server

(MTS) and Microsoft Message Queue Server (MSMQ), are complex, stand-alone components that integrate with IIS 4. We also cover basic troubleshooting.

Chapter 9 discusses the use of Microsoft's Index Server, a powerful tool for information management inside of an organization and for the presentation of an organization's Web site. Chapter 10 discusses security considerations for IIS, including the integration of IIS security and NT security. We also discuss how to configure IP Address and Domain Name restrictions.

Chapter 11 covers the use, configuration, and benefits of Microsoft's Certificate Server product, which offers a way of providing highly secure control over who can access information on your Internet servers.

While most Microsoft BackOffice products are easy to install, such installations are not always going to be optimal for your site—particularly as your site grows and changes. In Chapter 12, we talk about monitoring and optimization techniques to use to make sure that you are getting the maximum performance from your IIS installation. In Chapter 13, we look at common problems, troubleshooting techniques, and issues that you may encounter with different IIS installations, including TCP/IP and DNS problems and troubleshooting techniques.

Part Two—Proxy Server 2

In this section, you will find valuable information on Microsoft Proxy Server 2. You will learn about Proxy Server's architecture, installation, configuration, and integration into your existing network environment. The first chapter in Part Two (Chapter 14) discusses the architecture of Proxy Server 2, including some discussion of its new features and of the different types of proxies that you can run within your organization.

Chapter 15 is a discussion of the issues that you must evaluate before you install Proxy Server, including how to control access and how to handle load balancing across distributed installations. We also discuss the specifics of installing and configuring the Proxy Server product.

In Chapter 16, we discuss resource access management and consider the issues involved in granting access to the Internet through Proxy Server and cache configuration. In Chapter 17, we look at how to set clients up to work with the Proxy Server installation, from special configuration issues to the management of RAS over Proxy Server.

As with IIS, the default installation of Proxy Server will not always be the most appropriate for your environment. Managing the installation and ensuring that it performs at the highest possible level is the subject of Chapter 18, where we delve into how to monitor and optimize Proxy Server. Chapter 19 looks at the common issues involved in installations and discusses the troubleshooting steps that you will take to resolve these issues.

Appendix

The Appendix covers the Microsoft Internet Information Server Resource Kit. The IIS Resource Kit is a supplement to the IIS documentation that you may already have. This appendix contains a description of each chapter in the Resource Kit, as well as a description of what you will find on the Resource Kit CD.

More to Come

We hope that the material in this book answers some of those nagging questions that you have about IIS 4 and Proxy Server 2 and that it helps to prevent a few problems in the future. Most importantly, we hope that it helps get you out of the office by 5:00 P.M.!

Part 1

IIS 4

Topics Covered:

- Explaining IIS architecture
- Planning and implementing IIS
- Publishing your Web and FTP site
- IIS Mail and News service
- Adding functionality to IIS
- Understanding IIS security
- Monitoring and optimizing IIS
- Understanding troubleshooting methods

IIS Architecture

Internet Information Server (IIS) is a scalable enterprise network tool for publishing FTP and Web content. The use of IIS is expanding with the widespread growth and popularity of both Internet and intranet sites.

When working with server platforms and the services that run on top of them, the first step in learning anything new is to establish a basic foundation. With IIS, understanding the underlying architecture is the foundation that will prepare you for more complex administrative tasks. You will use your knowledge of the IIS architecture for everything from troubleshooting to configuring advanced IIS installations.

In this chapter, you will learn the basics of Microsoft's IIS 4 architecture. Knowing how IIS is constructed will help you to not only understand how IIS works but also to troubleshoot problems later. It is also a necessary part of appreciating how the various components of Microsoft's Internet and intranet solutions integrate with each other. In fact, a solid understanding of the architecture of IIS will serve you well not only in working with Proxy server but also in working with other add-on services that Microsoft and other third-party vendors provide to extend the functionality of the Windows NT server platform.

Microsoft calls IIS a *core product* because IIS is designed to work with a variety of related components of the Windows NT platform, such as NT's built-in security. In addition to NT's security, IIS communicates and integrates with the Microsoft Management Console (MMC), Microsoft Message Queue (MSMQ), Microsoft Transaction Server (MTS), and a host of other services. Each component in this family of products is treated as an object of the underlying operating system. Microsoft's entire approach to creating networking services is *modular*, and IIS is one of the modules that you will use often.

What do we mean by modular? Before Microsoft introduced the Windows operating system, PC operating systems used *monolithic code*. Monolithic code refers to the fact that each and every program that runs on the operating system—no matter how large or small—is entirely self-contained within a single executable. Although several programs print to your printer, each one has to duplicate the code to facilitate that connection; and without including that code within the executable for the program, the program cannot support printing. Moreover, there must be a series of codes embedded within the program—or the documents that the program handles—for the program to be able to print anything.

Microsoft changed all that in Windows, using a type of file known as Dynamic Link Libraries (DLL). DLLs contain common application code. Now many applications can use a common DLL to print. In today's model, no application needs to contain code to support printing, per se; it simply needs to know how to reference the DLL, which in turn handles the printing activities. This modular approach has helped to streamline application development; it has also made it easier to use the same program with multiple printers or other devices. To this day, Microsoft still uses DLLs in their operating systems.

Microsoft used another modular design idea in the Windows NT operating system. In Windows 3.*x* and DOS, any program that had to continually interact with the operating system was implemented as a Terminate and Stay Resident (TSR) application. In NT, Microsoft introduced "Services." Most of the functions of an NT Server are implemented as services. Some of the most common services include the server service, the workstation service, and the browser service. As you add to your NT Server environment new components whose designs require that they always run when the server is operating, these will most likely be Windows NT Services. IIS and its related components are Windows NT Services. The following is a list of some of the Windows NT Services that you will be exposed to in this book:

- Internet Information Server (IIS)
- Microsoft Management Console (MMC)
- Microsoft Transaction Server (MTS)
- Data Access Components
- Index Server
- Certificate Server
- Site Server Express
- Microsoft Message Queue (MSMQ)

Although the name Internet Information Server seems to imply that it is a full server product, actually, it is a service that runs on top of Windows NT Server. Because IIS is a service, it can take advantage of NT's modular design and interact with other services and components of NT. For example, IIS uses the Windows NT Directory Database, which is the central repository of all user accounts, group accounts, and NT machine accounts. Because IIS can use the Directory Database, there is no need for duplicate IIS user account information.

In addition to services, it is important to understand how protocols work when you consider the Internet, or for that matter, any time you are communicating between two computers (or in the Windows environment, between two network applications). *Protocols* specify what rules communication between two computers, or two applications running on a single computer, will adhere to. You can think of a protocol as a set of guidelines for a conversation—if you are speaking English, and the other party is speaking Chinese, communication will be difficult. Protocols ensure that both parties involved in a communication exchange are speaking in the same language. In the next section, we will discuss the TCP/IP protocol suite—a set of protocols that govern communications across the Internet.

IIS Architecture and TCP/IP

IIS relies heavily on the Transmission Control Protocol/Internet Protocol (TCP/IP). TCP/IP is an industry standard suite of protocols. This means that TCP/IP is not a single networking protocol, but actually several protocols that are typically considered to be combined into a single package. TCP/IP contains multiple protocols because each protocol handles specific types of data transfer or error reporting. Understanding the basics of TCP/IP can help you to troubleshoot networking problems. (For more information on troubleshooting, see Chapter 13.) Knowing TCP/IP basics is also essential to understanding how IIS works.

Before we get into a discussion of how IIS and TCP/IP work together, you must understand the TCP/IP core protocols. There are several core protocols. Each one is designed for a certain type of network communication. Each one of the core protocols is listed here, along with brief descriptions of their use.

> **ARP**   ARP is one of the first steps in establishing a connection to a remote host. The Address Resolution Protocol (ARP) finds a computer's hardware address from a known IP address.

> **TCP**   Transmission Control Protocol (TCP) is one of the two transport protocols that actually carry data. When you request a Web document, it is TCP that carries that data.

IP   Internet Protocol (IP) is used for addressing, routing, and forwarding network packets. When you specify a Web site you want to reach, it is IP that routes that request.

ICMP   When a destination cannot be reached, it is the Internet Control Message Protocol (ICMP) that responds with a Destination Host Unreachable message. This is an error- and status-reporting protocol.

IGMP   Internet Group Management Protocol (IGMP) is a new protocol to the TCP/IP suite. Its primary responsibility is group registration. When you start your computer, IGMP announces your presence to routers.

UDP   User Datagram Protocol (UDP) is the other transport protocol within the TCP/IP suite. When an Internet client machine starts, if it is a Dynamic Host Configuration Protocol (DHCP) client, it will request an IP address from DHCP servers in your network. This request is sent over UDP.

FTP   File Transfer Protocol (FTP) is a TCP/IP core protocol, as well as an application. You can use FTP to transfer files to and from TCP/IP hosts.

HTTP   HyperText Transfer Protocol (HTTP) is not one of the TCP/IP core protocols, but we included it here because of its relevance to IIS. HTTP is the protocol that you use to request Web documents.

Now that you have a basic idea of what the TCP/IP core protocols are, let's examine the process of requesting and receiving a Web site document. Here's how it works:

1. At the client machine running the Web browser, enter a Uniform Resource Locator (URL) and press Enter.

2. The client computer sends the request to a configured Domain Name System (DNS) server.

3. The DNS server either checks its own records, or queries another DNS server until it finds a record for the requested URL.

4. The DNS server responds to the original URL resolution request with the IP address of the site.

5. The client checks to see if it can connect to the Web site in the local network. If it cannot, it uses ARP to locate the hardware address of the router that forwards the network traffic.

6. After finding the hardware address of the router, the client sends an HTTP GET request to the Web site. (The document that it requests can vary depending on user input or the configuration of the Internet server.)

7. The Internet server checks to see if the requesting user has the proper permissions to access the file. If so, the server sends back the requested document. Each component of the Web site, such as graphics and frames, has to be accessed by individual HTTP GET requests and file session establishments.

This is the basic process of how a Web browser connects to a Web server. The major steps of this process are repeated for every communication between the client and the server. The use of ARP and DNS occurs whenever the client requests a resource from outside the domain it is currently communicating with. Therefore, once the client establishes communications with the Web server, it will not repeat the process of locating a Web server again until the client requests a different Web server.

There are many possible responses that the server can send back to the client after the connection is made. While IIS supports several different types of communication protocols, including the File Transfer Protocol (FTP) and the HyperText Transport Protocol (HTTP), we will concern ourselves only with HTTP or Web communications in the following section.

When returning documents through HTTP, IIS can respond to client requests in one of three ways:

- It can return a static file.
- It can launch a Common Gateway Interface (CGI) script.
- It can launch an Internet Server Application Programming Interface (ISAPI) extension.

Let's take a look at how IIS responds to client requests using each of these methods:

Static Files   Static files reside on the hard disk of the IIS and respond to the client request. The actual client request is sent as a HyperText Transfer Protocol (HTTP) GET request using the Transmission Control Protocol (TCP) port 80. When the server receives the request, it checks to see if the user has the appropriate permissions to access the requested file. IIS does not change the file's contents in any way. This is a simple request and response.

CGI Scripts   Common Gateway Interface (CGI) applications are simply script files that execute on the server-side of the IIS process. When a client requests a file with an executable extension, IIS will launch that executable; but it is the CGI script, or scripts, within the executable that returns the results to the requesting client machine. The results are returned as an HTML document. You can use CGI scripts to perform simple database queries, create user counters, or create other dynamic HTML documents.

ISAPI Extensions   When an Internet client requests a file with a DLL extension, IIS checks to see if the code from the DLL already exists in memory. If it does not, IIS loads the DLL. If it does already exist in memory, IIS uses the existing code. The advantages of using ISAPI over CGI are mainly that ISAPI will have improved performance because of its close integration with the Windows NT environment. Since CGI scripts must run in a separate process from IIS, this takes up system resources. On the other hand, the fact that ISAPI applications run in the same memory space as IIS means that poorly written ISAPI code could crash your IIS server. It's a trade-off, but most Web developers are now using ISAPI for the enhanced performance and industry-wide support.

Two files not listed here are ASP and IDC. ASP files are Microsoft Active Server Pages, and IDC files are Internet Database Connector files. We didn't list them because IIS handles them differently. Actually, IIS executes them using ISAPI extensions and something called a *script map*.

NOTE   You will always use an HTX (HTML template) file with an IDC file. Though HTML templates files are somewhat beyond the scope of this discussion, they are an important supporting technology when using Internet Database Connectors.

A script map is a list of file extensions and associated ISAPI extensions. When a client requests a file with an ASP or IDC extension, IIS checks the script map for an associated ISAPI extension. The ISAPI application then reads the data file and returns the results to IIS, who forwards them to the requesting client.

Before IIS can execute files (CGI, ISAPI otherwise) serve up Web pages, or provide access to file downloads, it must be configured correctly. To ensure that everything processes correctly across all of these IIS-provided services, you have to maintain the configuration of the service. IIS maintains all configuration within the IIS Metabase.

Understanding the IIS Metabase

Back in the days of MS-DOS, all configuration information was stored in the Autoexec .bat and Config.sys files. When Microsoft introduced the Windows operating system, they also introduced a new concept: INI files. INI files contain all the various aspects of your system's configuration. Microsoft continued the use of INI files until the release of Windows NT. In NT, all system configuration information is stored in the Registry. The NT Registry contains information such as your hard disk configurations, your security policies, as well as your screen colors. Without the Registry, your system will not function.

In IIS 4, all configuration information is stored in something very similar to NT's Registry, which is called the IIS Metabase.

The NT Registry has a tree structure. This tree structure is known as the Registry's *hierarchy*. The tree structure is a common metaphor in computer programming because of its usefulness in storing ordered sequences of information that go from the most general to the most specific. The IIS 4 Metabase is no different from the Registry in that it also has a hierarchy. The Metabase is similar to the NT Registry not only in having a hierarchy but also in having both binary and textual data contained in it. The IIS Metabase is stored in a file named METABASE.BIN, which NT places in the %SystemRoot%\system32\inetsrv directory by default. You can change the location, but there generally isn't a real benefit to doing so.

To edit the IIS Metabase, you will use a tool similar to the Registry Editor. This tool is part of the Microsoft Internet Information Server Resource Kit. The program is called the Metabase Editor. You can load it by running METAEDIT.EXE. The Metabase Editor has an intuitive graphical user interface, as shown in Figure 1.1.

Figure 1.1   Metabase Editor graphical interface

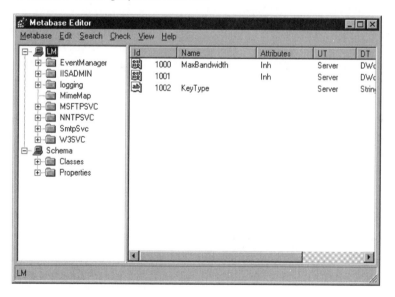

The Metabase is a huge subject to which we could devote an entire book; however, we won't go into any greater detail in this book because as an administrator, you don't have to mess with the actual Metabase much. Just like the Windows NT Registry, you will perform most changes to the Metabase using dialog boxes found in the administrative interface. For IIS 2 and 3, Microsoft provided two administrative interfaces—a proprietary interface and a Web-based interface. With the release of IIS 4, the administrative interface for IIS is now in the MMC (Microsoft Management Console).

IIS Support Services

IIS by itself is an effective platform for serving HTML files to Web browsers. But Microsoft has created a core of applications that increase the functionality of IIS 4 by facilitating its security and ease of use. The following are the supportive services that add power to IIS 4:

Microsoft Management Console (MMC)   All IIS settings can be controlled through this application. It has a two-pane set up, similar to the desktop Explorer, which displays the hierarchical structure of your network on the left (the scope pane) and the contents of the currently selected folder on the right (the results pane). The MMC's flexible ability to manage services, some of which may not even be available yet, comes from its use of Snap-ins that can be individually loaded on or unloaded from the MMC.

Microsoft Transaction Server (MTS)   A system integration package that provides the ability to execute multiple operations as a single operation. It does this by ensuring that all parts of an operation succeed or else the entire operation fails. This transaction support is critical to financial activities that occur over the Internet. For example, imagine that you use the Internet to take money out of one account and deposit it into another. If the system crashes after the money is subtracted from one account but before it is added to the other account, you lose your money. MTS ensures that the entire action fails if any one part of it fails so that you won't lose your money.

Microsoft Index Server   Provides search engine functionality for Web sites. Index Server scans all of the Web pages on a server, and other documents that have a scanning filter, and creates an index that contains every word that is found. When a user does a search, all pages that contain the search phrase are returned in a Web document. The user can click the hyperlink to view the documents that were found.

Certificate Server   Microsoft requires a certificate from a certificate authority in order to use Secure Socket Layer, a protocol used to secure data exchanges between Web browsers and Web servers. Certificate Server allows you to act as your own certificate authority when generating SSL keys, the digital files used to encrypt data.

Active Server Pages (ASP)   Conducting business over the Internet is fundamentally based on accessing the information in databases. ASP supports IIS's ability to connect to databases by generating Web pages dynamically as they are needed.

Microsoft Management Console (MMC)

In Windows NT 4.*x* and previous iterations, each administrative task had its own user interface. For example, you might be familiar with User Manager for Domains and know how to create and administer user and group accounts, but this does not mean that you will be able to figure out how to use Server Manager. To alleviate the confusion over having multiple administrative interfaces, Microsoft created the Microsoft Management Console (MMC). The MMC was earmarked to release in the next version of NT, now named Windows 2000. However, Microsoft released the MMC, as well as other Windows 2000 components, early in the Windows NT 4 Option Pack.

The MMC is a central interface that hosts administrative programs called *Snap-ins*. There are Snap-ins for everything from user account administration to configuring Windows NT's security policy. When you install IIS, the MMC Snap-in Internet Service Manager is installed to your system so that you can add it to your MMC configuration. You will use MMC Snap-ins to manage most of the other IIS-related components. You will see various screens from the MMC throughout this book. In fact, one of the other MMC Snap-ins is the Microsoft Transaction Server management console, which the next section introduces.

Microsoft Transaction Server (MTS)

In most modern-day, complex Web environments, the primary purpose of the site is to provide real-time access to a back-end data environment. If your site provides a simple display of data, you can often perform the needed administrative functions by using only HTML pages and active content in the form of Active Server Pages or CGI scripts. However, if you need to perform complex interactions (such as handling customer orders, inventory, or accounts payable), your site needs to perform more complex processing.

IIS@Work: Microsoft Transaction Server

To understand how Transaction Server works in conjunction with IIS, you must first understand the process of a transaction. A transaction is a process with multiple steps. Each step must be completed and checked off before the next step can begin. If any one step cannot be completed, all steps are rolled back (changed to their original state).

IIS@Work: Microsoft Transaction Server *(continued)*

For example, imagine that you have a company that sells refrigerator magnets. Your company might implement Transaction Server in the following way: A customer visits the company Web site, fills out an order entry form, and clicks a button to send the order. Next, your system checks the inventory database to see if the magnets that your customer requested are available. Assuming that they are in stock, the system removes the requested order items from standing stock.

The system then checks to see when the next shipment date to your customer's geographical location will be. If it is within the time frame that your client specified, the system puts the order into the shipping schedule. Next, the system checks the client's account standing. If the client is in good standing, the customer is billed, and the order transaction is complete. However, if the client's account is not in good standing, your system can roll back all the information as if the transaction never took place.

Microsoft Transaction Server is definitely an integral part of Web commerce. You will not work directly with MTS in this book—it is more often a discussion for developers than for administrators. However, it is important to know of its existence because it will likely be deployed in your enterprise.

From an application developer's standpoint, the work involved in writing a network application is considerably more involved than writing a single-user application. (About 40% of the job is related solely to networking issues and not to the program itself.) With MTS, developers can write applications for a single user, and MTS will automatically scale it and manage it for network use. This allows developers to concentrate on the particulars of an application, not on networking issues. In particular, it removes the need for developers to ensure that their components can scale effectively for large installations; it provides powerful fault tolerance and protection features; and it simplifies other complex development tasks.

Microsoft Index Server

Microsoft Index Server is a complete indexing tool for your Web site. Imagine that you have a large Web commerce site and you want your customers to be able to easily find the product that they are looking for. You can use Index Server to create a small (site-only) search engine. With Microsoft Index Server, you can index the properties and all the text from each one of the documents contained within your Web site. Internet users can use a simple Web query form to send queries to the query engine. The query engine searches for the specified information and returns the results to the requesting user in the form of an HTML document. You will learn more about Microsoft Index Server in Chapter 9, "Index Server."

Certificate Server

Since more and more companies are using electronic commerce as a means to do business, the need for secure, reliable data transfer is crucial. The Microsoft Certificate Server is a server application that provides the management of digital certificates, including their issuance, renewal, and revocation. These digital certificates let Internet users send personal information across the wire without having to worry about someone capturing the data. Now you can be confident that your credit card number will not fall into the wrong hands while making online transactions.

The purpose of the Certificate Server is only to provide a reliable means of identification. Certificate Server uses digital certificates for transmissions by utilizing Microsoft's Secure Sockets Layer (SSL), or other underlying security protocols, to facilitate secure connections. It is actually the security protocol, such as SSL, that facilitates the secure transfer of data. You will learn more about Microsoft Certificate Server in Chapter 11, "Certificate Server."

Active Server Pages

Active Server Pages is a method of creating dynamic HTML documents. A dynamic document is one in which the contained data can change each time you load the document in your Web browser. Active Server Pages accomplishes this by using server-side scripting that is embedded within the HTML document. This means that the script runs on the server-side of the process, not the client-side. Your client browser does not need to understand the scripting language in order for it to run.

In order to use Active Server Pages, you have to have a database containing data; and you rely on other related Microsoft services, such as MS Data Access Components.

MS Data Access Components

The functionality of most Web sites would be greatly diminished if they could not access databases. Most Web sites access some sort of database, whether it is an inventory, personnel records, or some other data source. Historically, many Web data sources were read-only; however, in the last year or so, full Web front ends for databases have become much more common. Without databases, Web sites would just be electronic advertisements.

To facilitate Web-to-database connectivity and to simplify what was previously a very complex data access model, Microsoft created MS Data Access Components (MSDAC).

Data Access Components comprise several different sets of technologies, most notably, ActiveX Data Objects (ADO) and the underlying OLE DB consumers and providers. Prior to the Data Access Components, to provide Web access to your databases, you had to use an Open Database Connectivity (ODBC) driver and a Data Source Name (DSN) for each database you wanted to access. Your Web application connected to the DSN—a wrapper for the database's ODBC driver—and used that connection to access the data stored within the tables that made up the database. If there were several databases that you had to access from a single Web site, you would need multiple DSNs and multiple ODBC drivers (depending on what types of database you were referencing, such as SQL Server or Oracle). Needless to say, such an arrangement could get quite slow and bulky very quickly.

The ODBC model is built specifically for accessing relational and ISAM databases; but recent changes in the way that we work with data stores have led many to conclude that any place that stores data should be accessible using database management techniques. ODBC is not capable of such access methods, while the Data Access Components are. You can still use the DSN to connect to data stores from the various MSDAC technologies, but it is neither necessary nor particularly beneficial to do so.

When using MSDAC in the most useful manner, things are typically quite different. You no longer need to specify a DSN or have an ODBC driver. Instead, MSDAC performs a series of steps for every database connection—a series of steps that are pretty straightforward. Because MSDAC is such a powerful tool and because it is extremely likely that you will use it in solutions within your organization, it is useful to understand the principles of how it works.

First, the client application (typically by using ActiveX Data Objects, though applications written in C++ can use COM interfaces directly) makes a call to the OLE DB client stub, also known as a consumer because it consumes data. The OLE DB client stub acts as an interface for the OLE DB Providers. (When you install a database application, it will install an OLE DB provider for that application.) The OLE DB providers take the place of the old ODBC drivers and the DSNs by providing low-level access to the database, as shown in Figure 1.2.

Figure 1.2   The Microsoft MS Data Access Components process

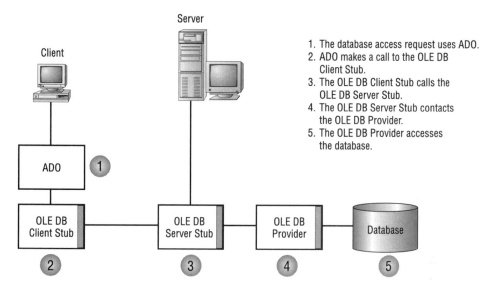

1. The database access request uses ADO.
2. ADO makes a call to the OLE DB Client Stub.
3. The OLE DB Client Stub calls the OLE DB Server Stub.
4. The OLE DB Server Stub contacts the OLE DB Provider.
5. The OLE DB Provider accesses the database.

The application no longer needs to have substantial information about the underlying database solution because the OLE DB provider handles that on the application's behalf. Additionally, and on more of a theoretical level, MSDAC uses COM components and interfaces to implement its functionality. This is a model that Microsoft has also applied to most technologies that you will use to manage complex Internet sites and services. The COM-based model simplifies the management and extension of server services, making it easier for you to implement and customize such services in your environment.

The MS Data Access Components streamline the linking of Web sites to databases. However, older data sources (for example, dBase III data sources) may not have OLE DB providers. In this case, the MSDAC model shown in Figure 1.2 would be modified slightly with the OLE DB provider calling through to the ODBC driver for that data source.

It seems that traveling through all of these stubs and providers would be slower, not faster. In fact, there are two main benefits to MSDAC: First, you can use the same code to access any data store from an SQL Server database, to an Oracle database, to an Active Directory tree. Second, because the OLE DB connections use the principles and techniques of Microsoft's Component Object Model (COM), the communications are actually significantly faster than they would be when using an ODBC driver.

The Microsoft Message Queue

Microsoft Message Queue (MSMQ) is a store and forwarding application that utilizes message queues. Within the context of MSMQ, the term *message* refers to the data stored in the queue. There are two types of queues that MSMQ uses: the store-queue and the forward-queue. You use MSMQ in large network environments. For example, if you have a large company that has branches and inventory across the US, you could use MSMQ to provide a framework to facilitate distributed network application processes between branches. MSMQ provides the following features:

- MSMQ Explorer Management Console
- Full COM support
- Simple Application Programming Interface
- Transaction support
- Message routing support
- Reliable message delivery
- One-Time, in-order message delivery
- Directory service–based architecture
- MTS integration
- Clustering support
- IIS Active Server Page support
- Windows NT security log integration
- Built-in message encryption

NOTE   Since the focus of this book is the system administrator and MSMQ is an application developer's tool, we will not go into any greater detail on MSMQ in this book. For detailed information on MSMQ, please refer to the Microsoft Web site at www.microsoft.com.

Site Server Express

Once you have created and published your Web content, you will want to know how your site is performing. Microsoft Site Server is a tool for just that purpose. Microsoft's Site Server Express 2 is included in the Windows NT 4 Option Pack. Site Server Express 2 contains a subset of the features found in the full Site Server version.

You can use Site Server Express to create a map of your Web site. You can use that site map to help you determine if links should be streamlined to facilitate better connections within your site. You can also use Site Server Express to see how many users are accessing a particular document within your site or to create bandwidth usage reports. All of these functions are quite useful in administering your Web site. When you use Site Server Express to create reports, the results are generated in the form of an HTML document that you can see with any Web browser. For more information on Site Server Express, see Chapter 8, "IIS Add-On Services."

IIS 4

PART 1

Internet Connection Services

The Internet Connection Services are a set of four remote access services. Microsoft designed the Internet Connection Services with Internet Service Providers (ISP) in mind. These services allow remote users to connect to the Internet through your Windows NT Server (running the Internet Connection Services). The four services are as follows:

The Microsoft Connection Manager   This provides support for the Point-to-Point-Tunneling Protocol (PPTP), as well as other remote access functions.

The Connection Manager Administration Kit   This is a group of wizards used to establish connection profiles.

Internet Authentication Services   This provides remote user authentication.

Connection Point Services   This provides centralized administration of phone books, client configurations, and data compression.

Using Active Server Pages

To better understand how you can use Active Server Pages on your Web site, let's take a look at a company that we will call OnlineAuction.com. OnlineAuction.com is an Internet auction house that specializes in selling cars for salvage yards.

The Problem

Salvage yard owners can rarely leave their businesses without fear of lost revenue. However, salvage yards must buy new inventory to fill their clients' needs. This requires someone to attend an automotive auction to purchase wrecked vehicles. Whoever attends must be knowledgeable in the salvage industry. The auction attendee should know car values and know what vehicles have the most desired parts. This usually means that the owner must attend or risk spending money on unneeded stock by sending an inexperienced buyer.

The Solution

OnlineAuction.com was created so that owners wouldn't have to leave their business in order to buy stock.

Here's How It Works

The participating salvage yard needs a computer with an Internet connection in order to access OnlineAuction.com. The auction house, not the salvage yard, pays to be on OnlineAuction.com. The salvage yard can access OnlineAuction.com and see when the next auction will take place. The salvage yard must have an account with the auction house in order to place any bids. Since these auctions are not open to the general public, the user must have a login ID. After the user logs in, they may enter the auction.

Since the auction house sells many items, the salvage yard can query the auction house inventory to see if there is anything of interest. These query pages have drop-down lists that contain general categories of auction items, for example: Airplanes, Boats, Cars, and Trucks. Because the auction house does not always have all of these categories of items for sale, this list needs to be able to change dynamically with the inventory, and it can do so by using Active Server Pages.

When the user accesses the auction item query page, the server-side process runs a query of the database to determine what categories exist. These items comprise the auction's drop-down item list.

Without Active Server Pages, the auction's drop-down list would only be able to contain predefined categories, instead of being able to provide the most current list of items that are available for auction.

2

Planning and Implementing IIS

Preparing and installing IIS can be an intimidating task, even for the most experienced administrator. A methodical approach and careful attention to procedure will result in the desired outcome of a properly functioning application. Throughout this chapter, you will learn about everything involved in a successful IIS installation, from planning your IIS installation and the pre-installation information you should know, to configuring IIS after your installation is complete.

Before you install any network software, you should always plan your installation. You have probably heard this before, but it really is true. There are many professional network engineers who install software without planning it properly, and later wonder what went wrong. When you don't plan your installation, the results are very unpredictable. You may get lucky and set up your installation properly, but do you really want to take that chance?

Although most books recommend planning your network application installation, they seldom offer examples of what that planning entails. Planning is much more than just writing down the steps that you intend to perform (although that's a start). You must also allow for future growth and good resource allocation. Try to think about what tools you have at your disposal and how you can best use them. Also, consider various installation plans and pick the one that best suits your needs. Another part of planning your installation is selecting the right server.

In order to guide you through an effective installation, this chapter will cover the following topics:

- Planning your installation
- Selecting a Windows NT server
- Complying with hardware requirements
- Understanding permissions
- Using IP addresses
- Subnetting
- Understanding the Domain Name System (DNS)
- Rolling out your installation
- Configuring your server
- Implementing fault tolerance

Selecting the Right NT Server

When installing any Microsoft BackOffice product, you want to consider what type of NT Servers you have to work with. The type of server that you perform your installation on can affect how well your network applications work.

You can install Windows NT Server 4 as one of three types of servers. Each one has a unique function within your network environment. Understanding what each type of installation does will help you to know which server is best for you. Let's examine the three Windows NT Server 4 installations:

Primary Domain Controller (PDC)   A PDC is the Windows NT Server that maintains the only active copy of the Directory Database. The Directory Database is the central repository of all user, group, and machine accounts within your NT domain.

Backup Domain Controller (BDC)   A BDC is a Windows NT Server that can process network logon requests. This means that when a user attempts to logon, a BDC can validate that request. BDCs maintain a read-only copy of the Directory Database from the PDC.

Server Only   An NT machine that you install as a Server Only will not process logon requests. These servers are only for running network applications, such as IIS. By not processing logon requests, important system resources are freed up for application processing.

You can install IIS on any of these Windows NT Server types. However, you will want to consider the other network services that you already have running on each server in your network. For example, if you have the Dynamic Host Configuration Protocol (DHCP) server service, Windows Internet Name Service (WINS), and Domain Name System (DNS) services running on one of your network servers, you may not want to install IIS on this machine. Of course, this is all relative to the power of the server machine that you want to install IIS on, and the expected use of your Internet site. For example, if you are creating a Web presence that incorporates heavy database use and a large number of expected hits each day, you will want to consider using a Windows NT Server that is installed as a Server Only. Of course, you must be able to justify the additional cost of a stand-alone server just for IIS.

Although using a Server Only installation provides a very robust IIS solution, it is not always necessary. Many network administrators find that they have a Windows NT Server Domain Controller in their network that can easily handle the load of their Internet presence. There are no steadfast rules as to how to choose which server to install IIS on; you will have to trust your own judgement. Just make sure that the computer you select meets the minimum hardware requirements.

I recommend always using a stand-alone server for any client-server applications because your server will not be busy processing other services, such as user logons. I will some-times opt to use a Domain Controller when the company does not have the resources available to use a stand-alone server.

Minimum and Recommended Hardware

Picking the right type of Windows NT Server to install IIS on is only part of what you must do in order to make sure your server will perform. You must also select a machine that meets the minimum hardware requirements not only for NT but also for IIS.

The following is a list of the minimum and recommended hardware requirements:

Processor   Microsoft recommends that you use a Pentium 90-MHz processor or higher. At the minimum, you must have at least a 486 66-MHz processor. Remember, the faster your processor, the better your overall performance will be.

Memory   You can almost never have too much memory. Microsoft recommends 128MB or higher. At the minimum, you must have 32MB.

Hard disk   The amount of free disk space that you will require depends on how big your Web and FTP sites are, as well as the size of your other related applica-tions, such as a SQL database. At the minimum, you must have 30MB of disk space free to install IIS.

ı make sure that your server meets the minimum hardware requirements, you are
nstall IIS. During the IIS installation, you will be asked to specify an IIS account.

IIS@Work: An Ideal Scenario

The type of server you need greatly depends on two things: the amount of money
you have to spend on your server and the workload you are expecting your server to
handle. For example, in South America there are several off-shore casinos that operate on the Internet. These casinos run complex Java Script front ends that link to SQL
databases. The amount of users that these servers must support at any one time is
staggering.

I recently got a chance to see one of these servers up-close. It was a dual Pentium 450
with 528 megabytes of RAM and several 10-gigabyte hard drives. This server is able
to simultaneously process thousands of sports bets, as well as other online transactions. This is one situation where a powerful server is money well spent.

While the dual Pentium with an enormous amount of RAM is perfect for an operation
like an online casino, your ideal server may be a single Pentium 200 with 128 megabytes of RAM.

Understanding the IIS Service Account

Windows NT Server will not allow any unauthorized access to resources. This means that
NT must validate every client resource access request by checking the user's logon against
a list of resource permissions. A user accessing a resource through the Internet is no different. All of the files that comprise your Web site are still resources contained and managed by your Windows NT Server. This means that a user cannot access these files
without proper permissions.

NOTE A series of steps must take place prior to a user bringing up a home page
of a Web site. Because we will be discussing the client process in detail in Chapter
13, "Troubleshooting IIS," we will skip to the part of the process where the client
actually requests an HTML document.

When an Internet user wants to access a Web site (whether that site is part of an intranet
or the Internet), NT must process the user's request. It is no different than when a local
network user requests access to a database or permissions to print a document. NT must

make sure that the user's logon ID has the appropriate permissions to access the document with the level of privileges the user is requesting. For example, if you were to enter in your Web browser a URL that you want to go to (`www.sybex.com`), your user account must have permissions to access that site. How does your user account have access permissions on a Windows NT Server that you have never been to before? This is where the IIS service account comes in.

It would be ridiculous to think that every IIS administrator worldwide has to create a logon for each Internet user who will access the site. In that case, Microsoft would have to create millions of accounts for all the users who access their site daily. Instead of creating individual accounts for each user who will access the site, there is a single IIS administrative account that takes the place of individual accounts.

When you install IIS, it automatically creates an IIS service account. By default, this account is named *IUSR_ServerName*, where *ServerName* is the name of your server. When the IIS installation creates this account, it automatically gives this account membership to the Domain Users and Guest groups. IIS also sets the account properties so that the user cannot change the password and so that the password never expires. You don't want the user to be able to change the password because many people will share this account. You don't want the account's password to expire because this is the account that your Internet user requires in order to access your IIS server. If you have your NT policies configured so that passwords expire every so often, having the service account's password set to Password Never Expires is crucial.

TIP   If you do not have the IIS service account's properties configured so that the password never expires, you will have to remember to manually change the password at the expiration interval, otherwise your IIS server will not work for anonymous users.

Before we begin discussing installation, let's brush up on basic TCP/IP issues.

Basic IP Addressing

TCP/IP is a configurable protocol, and all clients that utilize it must be configured as follows:

1. All clients require a unique IP address. An IP address is comprised of a network ID and a host ID. The network ID identifies the TCP/IP network that a user is on, and the host ID identifies the individual host. For example, all users in the same TCP/IP network will have the same network ID as part of their IP address, and they will have a different host ID.

2. All clients require a subnet mask, which is used to distinguish the network portion of an IP address from the host portion, in order to determine if a destination is local or remote.

3. If connecting in a WAN, a default gateway is required. A default gateway is, in essence, the IP address of the router that TCP/IP clients will use to send all packets destined for other networks. A default gateway is not required in a LAN environment.

IIS relies on the networking protocol suite TCP/IP. The IP portion of the TCP/IP protocol suite is the part of the protocol suite that handles routing and addressing. Just as you address an envelope with your name, street address, city, state, and postal code, an IP address also has several parts to it. IP addresses are broken into four sections. Each section in the IP address is called an octet. Each octet can contain any number between 1 and 255. Since there are four sections containing 255 possible combinations each, the total number of combinations is four billion, two hundred ninety-four million, nine hundred sixty-seven thousand, two hundred ninety-six (4,294,967,296). Although there appear to be plenty of IP addresses to go around, we are actually running out of them. At the time that this book was written, there were already plans to create an addressing scheme that will accommodate growth into the foreseeable future.

Whether an organization or an individual, everyone who intends to host a site on the Internet requires an IP address, which they must apply for. Who you get your address from depends on how many addresses you require.

IP Address Classes

IP address ranges are broken into groups, called classes, so they can be more easily identified. The three classes of IP address are as follows:

Class A   There are only 126 Class A addresses in the world. The first octet of a Class A address will always start with a decimal value in the range of 1 to 126. Each Class A address has 16,777,216 IP addresses.

Class B   There are 16,384 Class B addresses, each one containing 65,536 IP addresses. The first octet in a Class B address will always begin with a decimal value in the range 128 through 191.

Class C   There are 2,097,152 Class C addresses, each one containing 255 IP addresses. The first octet in a Class C address will always begin with a decimal value in the range 192 through 223.

> **NOTE**   Although there are two more classes of IP addresses, they are reserved for diagnostic, or future, use. Since knowing about Class D and E addresses will not help you with IIS, we will not discuss them. For an in-depth discussion on TCP/IP, see Gary Govanus' *TCP/IP 24seven* (Sybex, 1999).

In a Class A address, the first octet denotes the network portion of the address. For example: in the address 12.24.231.10, the first octet (12) is the part of the address that is unique. No other network can use 12 in the first octet. The rest of the address (24.231.10) is the actual host ID. This is the unique address of the computer (or TCP/IP device) within the network 12. Although there can be other 24.231.10 addresses in the world, none can start with the IP address 12.

In a Class B address, the first two octets contain the network portion of the IP address. For example, in the IP address 131.107.2.200, the first two octets (131.107) denote the unique network ID. The rest of the address (2.200) is the specific host ID within the 131.107 network.

In a Class C address, the first three octets are unique. For example, in the address 207.49.189.14, the first three octets (207.49.189) denote the network address. The rest of the address (14) is the network host ID.

Subnetting

Now we're going to throw a wrench in the machine. The "wrench" is called *subnetting*, which is the process of taking any of the IP address classes and breaking them down even further. This is similar to how a city breaks up postal codes in certain areas to better serve their customers. By taking a single IP address range and breaking it into several smaller address ranges, you can create multiple network sites within your organization. Because subnetting is quite important, this section provides a quick overview so that you can better administer your IIS.

Every TCP/IP host must have a *subnet mask*, which is a decimal value that TCP/IP uses to distinguish the network portion of the IP address from the host portion. A subnet mask appears just like an IP address. It is a 32-bit number that we usually see in decimal form as four distinct sections of numbers, such as 100.102.10.12. To understand a subnet mask, you must translate the IP address and the subnet mask into binary form.

Ones and Zeros

Computer systems only understand two things: ones and zeros. Using just ones and zeros, your computer does mathematical equations, generates graphics, and creates sounds. Because humans don't speak in ones and zeros, we need an interface that makes more sense. This is where our operating systems come in. MS-DOS is nothing more than an interpreter for us to use instead of using ones and zeros. Each zero or one in a value is called a bit. When you hear someone say, "That is an 8-bit number," they are referring to the fact that the number has a total of eight ones and zeros in it. Combinations of ones and zeros make up a given value in decimal form. For example, the binary value 11111111 is equal to 255 in decimal. That is one 8-bit number. Combinations of 8-bit numbers are usually expressed in decimal because we can more easily understand them in this form. The exception is when dealing with subnetting. Although we express our subnet masks in decimal format, it is far easier to learn how they work in binary.

The IP address 207.189.49.10 looks like 11001111 10111101 00110001 00001010 in binary.

Here's how it works: Each bit in the IP address has a corresponding decimal value. The values are 128, 64, 32, 16, 8, 4, 2, and 1. Each one of these bits can be turned on or off depending on the bit value: 1 or 0. Any bit that is set to 1 is turned on, any bit that is set to 0 is turned off. So if you set the binary bit values of an 8-bit number to 10000000, you are only turning on the first bit (128). This means that the binary value 10000000 is 128 in decimal.

Let's try one more. If you set the binary bits in an 8-bit number to 10010000, you are turning on the first bit (128) and the fourth bit (16). This means that the decimal value is 128 plus 16, or 144.

Pulling It All Together

Now let's see how everything comes together using subnetting. A subnet mask masks a portion of the IP address so that IP can determine if a destination is in the same subnet, or whether the information must be passed through a router. As you learned earlier, subnet masks are usually expressed in decimal form. So a typical subnet mask would be 255.255.255.0. This particular subnet mask masks the first three octets or 24 bits. As long as the first three octets of any destination IP address are the same as the sending host, the destination is considered local (in the same subnet). The process that TCP/IP uses to determine if the local host and the destination host are in the same subnet is called

ANDing out. ANDing works by comparing the IP address of the local host (in binary) with the subnet mask (in binary). Each individual bit of the IP address is compared to the corresponding bit of the subnet mask. Any combination of 1 and 1 make a 1 value in the ANDed out total, while any other combination makes 0. Consider the following example. If you take the IP address 207.49.189.10 and the subnet mask 255.255.255.0 and convert them to binary, you get the following:

```
207.49.189.10 = 11001111 00110001 10111101 00001010

255.255.255.0 = 11111111 11111111 11111111 00000000

ANDed Value = 11001111 00110001 10111101 00000000
```

The first bit (128) in the first octet is 1 in both the IP address and the subnet mask. This means that the ANDed value is 1. As you can see, the third bit (32) in the first octet is set to 0 in the IP address, and 1 in the subnet mask. This means that the ANDed value is 0. If you continue this process, you end up with the final ANDed out value previously shown.

After TCP/IP ANDs out the IP address of your local computer, the process is repeated, using the same subnet mask for the destination host as before. The following is an example of the ANDing out of a destination IP address:

```
207.49.190.11 = 11001111 00110001 10111110 00001011

255.255.255.0 = 11111111 11111111 11111111 00000000

ANDed Value = 11001111 00110001 10111110 00000000
```

After the IP addresses of both the destination and source computers are ANDed out, TCP/IP compares the two ANDed values. If they are identical, the destination is considered local (on the same network). If the values are different by even one bit, the destination host is considered remote, and the connection must be made through a router. In the previous example, you will notice that the ANDed values are not the same. The last two bits in the third octet are different. This destination is in another network.

Understanding Internet Host and Domain Names

Although you can connect to Internet sites using the IP address, it would be quite cumbersome to have to remember all the IP addresses for every site you want to go to. This is why host and domain names were created.

You may have seen host and domain names, such as www.microsoft.com. The host name portion is the www part. The domain name is the rest, microsoft.com. The name *www* really has very little meaning. It is nothing more than the name of the computer in the remote domain that you want to connect to. A lot of people believe that you must type *www* at the beginning of a Web address in order to connect to the site. In reality, www could just as easily be *server*, or any other name. The rest of the name, microsoft.com, has a bit more meaning. There is a hierarchy to Internet names. In the example microsoft.com, *microsoft* is the company name, and *com* is the top level domain name. It means that this site is a commercial site (for profit). There are several top-level domain names. The following is a list of the current top-level domains:

Com   These are commercial sites.

Gov   All Government sites use .gov extensions.

Mil   US Military sites use .mil extensions on their domain names.

Org   These are non-profit organizations.

Net   These are network service providers.

Edu   Educational institutions use .edu extensions on their domain names.

Num   You will very rarely see a .num extension on a domain name. These are only used for phone numbers.

Arpa   Arpa is only used for reverse lookup zones.

XX   These are two letter country codes that follow a domain name.

NOTE   Although several other top-level domain names are about to be put into use, at the time that this book was written, they were not yet widely used.

In order to use a domain name on the Internet, you must first register that name with the Internet community. To register a domain name, you must contact Internic, the Internet Network Information Center. You can contact Internic on the Web at www.internic.net.

NOTE   Traditionally, all domain names were registered by Internic. Now Internic has a new Web site for domain name registrations: www.networksolutions.com.

When you contact Internic to register a domain name, you must specify the name and IP address of a server that can resolve your domain's host names to IP addresses, as well as other registration information. You are responsible for maintaining your own name servers.

Even though you can use host names to connect to an Internet site, in actuality, your computer really only uses IP addresses. Therefore, the process of using the host and domain names is really one of translation, in that your computer must find an unknown IP address from a known host and domain name. Originally, these translations were performed by connecting to a central repository of host and domain names that mapped names to IP addresses. This central repository was located at Stanford Research Institutes Network Information Center (SRI-NIC).

A problem arose from the centralized approach to name resolution. SRI-NIC was soon overrun with name change requests. For this reason, the Domain Name System (DNS) was created. DNS is a distributed database of host and domain names that are resolved to IP addresses. Tens of thousands of DNS servers are currently online. Many of these DNS servers are responsible for only a handful of name resolutions; while others manage hundreds, or even thousands, of host name resolutions.

Further Understanding DNS

In a Microsoft networking environment, host name resolution can be performed by various means. You can resolve host names using the HOSTS file on your local computer. As a last resort, you can resolve host names through Microsoft's NetBIOS name resolution methods. The most widely accepted method of host name resolution is the Domain Name System (DNS). In a Microsoft network, DNS is implemented as a service on a Windows NT Server.

When a client computer (called a resolver) queries a DNS server for a name resolution, the DNS server will check to see if it has a domain record (zone) for the requested name. An example of a zone record name is microsoft.com. If the DNS server has a zone record for the requested domain, it will look for a host name record that matches the DNS query. For example, www. If the host record is located, the DNS server will send the IP address for the requested host back to the resolver. If the host or zone records do not exist on the DNS server, the DNS server can send the query to another DNS server, and the process is repeated.

Eventually, a DNS server in the chain can send an *iterative query*, which is a query that is sent to the root-level domain name servers. At the root-level domain name servers, the query is not for a particular host name, but rather for the top-level domain name (.com). The top-level domain name servers will point the requesting DNS server to a name server for the top-level domain. At the top-level domain name server, the requesting DNS server will query for the full domain name, such as microsoft.com. At this point, the top-level domain name server will send a query reply to the original DNS server with the IP address of a DNS server that should have a microsoft.com zone record. The original DNS server will then query the name server specified by the top-level name server for microsoft.com. The microsoft.com name server will then send a query reply to the original requesting DNS server. The last step in this process is for the DNS server that you originally contacted to send your computer the query results with the IP address of the host that you want to connect to.

TIP   For information on troubleshooting DNS problems for your IIS machine, please see Chapter 13, "Troubleshooting IIS."

Rolling Out Your IIS Installation

Once you have *planned* your IIS installation, you are ready to *roll out* your IIS installation. A rollout is the actual installation and availability of your new software. You could just install IIS, push it into production, and hope for the best. However, it is much better to have a rollout plan. Some of the best rollouts are accomplished by performing an installation in an isolated segment of your network. An isolated segment means that the cabling that you are connecting your IIS server with and the client machine that you are testing your installation from are not connected to the same network that the rest of your company is. This makes the site unavailable to the general public until you have tested the software in a variety of situations.

IIS is a little different from most software applications because after you install it, it cannot do very much. First, you have to manually publish your Web content. After the Web content is published, you need to test it to ensure that it is working as it should. Don't make the IIS server available until you have fully tested your Web content. Try each link within your site to ensure that they are all working properly. Also, make sure that any applications you install within your site function properly. Proper testing at this early stage will eliminate problems later.

Installing IIS

You install IIS as part of the Windows NT 4 Option Pack. The installation instructions for IIS in this chapter are actually the Option Pack installation instructions. We will only briefly go over any non-IIS–related steps in the installation.

To install IIS from the Microsoft Windows NT Server 4 Option Pack CD-ROM, insert the CD-ROM disk into your computer's CD-ROM drive. Windows NT Server 4 will automatically open your Web browser and load the Welcome page. To complete the installation, perform the following steps:

1. In the Welcome page, click the Install link. Your Web browser will advance to the Installation page. (You must have both the Windows NT Server Service Pack 3 and Internet Explorer 4.01 installed to continue.)

2. Click the Install Windows NT 4 Option Pack link. NT will display the File Download dialog box.

3. Click the "Run this program from its current location" radio button, then click OK. NT will open the Windows NT Server 4 Option Pack Installation program.

4. In the Windows NT Server 4 Option Pack Installation Wizard, click Next. The Installation Wizard will advance to the End User License Agreement screen.

5. Click Accept. The Installation Wizard will advance to the Installation Type screen.

6. Select the type of installation you want to perform. Your choices are Minimum, Typical, and Custom. If you choose Minimum or Typical, the Installation Wizard will advance to the IIS 4 installation. (Since you will learn about other related services later in this book, we will perform the Custom installation). Click Next. The Installation Wizard will advance to the Components screen.

7. Select the individual components that you want to install. Click Next. The next screen that the Installation Wizard will display depends on what options you selected in the Components screen. We will assume that you selected the most common components. Next, you will see the Internet Information Server Files Location screen.

8. Select the location where you want the Installation Wizard to place your IIS files. Click Next. The Installation Wizard will advance to the Transaction Server screen.

9. Select the location where you want the Installation Wizard to install your Transaction Server files. Click Next. The Installation Wizard will advance to the Transaction Server Administrative Account screen.

10. Select whether you want to use the system account or an NT domain account. Click Next. The Installation Wizard will advance to the Index Server screen.

11. Select the location where you want to install the Index Server files. Click Next. The Installation Wizard will advance to the SMTP Service screen.

12. Select the location where you want the Installation Wizard to install the SMTP mail queue. Click Next. The Installation Wizard will advance to the Microsoft Message Queue (MSMQ) screen.

13. Select your MSMQ Role. (For information on MSMQ Roles and other MSMQ-related topics, see Chapter 8, "IIS Add-ons.") Click Next. The Installation Wizard will advance to the MSMQ Enterprise Information screen.

14. Specify the enterprise name and the site you want to create. Click Next. The Installation Wizard will advance to the MSMQ Installation Location screen.

15. Select the location where you want the Installation Wizard to place your MSMQ administration and SDK files. Click Next. The Installation Wizard will advance to the Microsoft Certificate Server screen.

16. Specify the location of the database and log files. Click Next. The Installation Wizard will advance to the Certificate Server Setup screen.

17. Specify your organization information. Click Next. The Installation Wizard will advance to the Installation Status screen. At this point, the Installation Wizard will copy files to your hard disk. After the Installation Wizard copies the files to your hard disk, it will display the Finish screen. Click Finish.

IIS and the Windows NT Server 4 Option Pack are now installed on your server. You are ready to perform basic server configuration and to publish your Web content.

Basic Server Configuration

Basic server configuration, like other aspects of network administration, can either be performed immediately after installation or later. Although you can perform IIS system administration from the HTML-based Administration Pages, they are not as widely used as the Microsoft Management Console (MMC).

Although there are many administrative configuration options within IIS, this section will explore some of the most common ones found in the server properties. You will use the "WWW Service Master Properties for Server" dialog box to make most of your configuration changes. You must be within the MMC to access this dialog box. To open the MMC and access the "WWW Service Master Properties for Server" dialog box, perform the following steps:

1. Click the Start menu. Go to Programs ➢Windows NT 4 Option Pack➢Internet Information Server➢Internet Service Manager. NT will open the MMC.

2. Expand the Internet Information Server group. The MMC will display the IIS server.

3. Right-click the IIS server. The MMC will display a quick menu. Select Properties. The MMC will display the Server Properties dialog box.

4. Click the Edit button. The MMC will display the "WWW Service Master Properties for Server" dialog box.

You will see several tabs in the "WWW Service Master Properties for Server" dialog box. The following is a description of the tabs and their purposes:

Web Site   This tab has configuration information, such as the maximum number of simultaneous connections the server will handle, and configuration of logging.

Operators   You can use the Operators tab to assign operators permission to existing NT domain accounts.

Performance   The Performance tab is useful in tuning your IIS server for performance. Using a slide-bar, you can adjust the number of users it supports. You can also adjust Bandwidth Throttling.

ISAPI Filters   These are DLLs that IIS uses to process information requests. The ISAPI Filters tab is a listing of the ISAPI Filters (DLLs) installed on your IIS server.

Home Directory   You can use this tab to specify the setting for your home directory, such as whether the directory exists on the local server or on a remote server. You can configure settings, such as access permissions.

Document   When an Internet user requests access to a Web server without specifying a particular document, such as `www.microsoft.com`, the server responds with a default document. This is usually your site's home page. You can use the Documents tab to set the default document value.

Directory Security   You can use the Directory Security tab to set the security permissions that allow access to your IIS. You can configure Secure Socket Layer (SSL) communication, enable or disable anonymous access, and deny access to your site based on an IP address or Internet Domain Name.

HTTP Headers   One of the new features of IIS 4 is the ability to configure content ratings and content expirations. You can use the HTTP Headers tab to configure these options.

Custom Errors   When trying to access an Internet site, you may have received an error message that says, "Document does not exist." In this tab, you can create your own custom responses to user requests.

IIS 3 Admin   You can use the IIS 3 Admin tab to configure a particular Web site to be compatible with older IIS 3 Administrative Tools.

In Chapter 5, "Advanced Configuration and Administration," you will learn more about the "WWW Service Properties for Server" options and what they do. The configuration options are mentioned here in case you want to configure any of them immediately after installing IIS 4. For example, if you want to administer IIS from within an IIS 3 server installation, you have to set the IIS 3 Admin compatibility option. You will learn how to configure this option in Chapter 5.

Understanding IIS Fault Tolerance

Fault tolerance refers to a server's ability to recover from a disastrous event, such as a hard disk failure. When considering what kind of server fault tolerance solutions you want to provide, think about how important your server's information is. For example, your Web presence may generate millions of dollars worth of sales. A disastrous event could cause the loss of a substantial amount of money. Even though you will probably have a tape backup of your data, the time it takes to restore that data could be very costly. Fault tolerant solutions allow your server to continue to work during the disastrous event.

Protecting the information on your hard disks is the major concern when considering fault tolerance. Hard disk failure accounts for the majority of lost information and lost time. This is actually a very easy problem to solve; like most computer solutions, the answer is to throw money at the problem. One of the best solutions for hard disk fault tolerance is a *RAID array*. RAID, Redundant Array of Independent Disks, is a combination of three or more hard disks and a special controller card. Your computer sees these disks as one disk drive. Data that your system writes to the disk array will be written across all disks in the array, along with other information for disaster recovery. If any one of the disk drives fails, the remaining disks take the lost disk's place. This is only a temporary fix until you replace the lost disk, but at least you can continue to operate.

Another disk fault tolerant solution is to create a *mirror set* (RAID 1), which is similar to a RAID array because it uses multiple disks to facilitate disaster recovery. However, in this case, it uses only two (and no more) disks. In a mirror set, the data is written to both disks at the same time. If one of the disks fails, the other has a complete copy of the information and can continue to work. The down side to a mirror set is that you lose half of the disk space you are paying for, and you do not get the same performance that you would from a RAID array. Either solution will be expensive, but you have to ask yourself, "Is it worth it?"

NOTE The RAID advisory board (www.raid-advisory.com) maintains a complete listing of all disk fault tolerant strategies.

Clustering Your IIS Server

Another form of fault tolerance is *clustering*. Clustering is where two computers share the network application workload. Network users will actually connect to a virtual server. Figure 2.1 shows the cluster virtual server.

Figure 2.1   Microsoft clustering

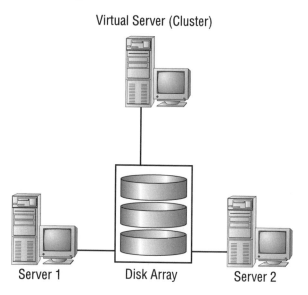

Virtual Server (Cluster)

Server 1   Disk Array   Server 2

Unlike other methods of fault tolerance, clustering allows you to bring your server down without affecting your users. When a server that is part of a cluster is brought down, the other server in the cluster takes over. The amount of time it takes for the backup cluster server to take over depends on the cluster configuration. There are three common types of Microsoft cluster configurations:

Active/Active   In this configuration, one server takes over for a failed server. The failover times (the amount of time it takes for the second server to take over) range from 15 to 150 seconds. This could be unacceptable if your Web presence is essential. This configuration is designed for clusters where the two servers have different software on them, with each one handling a separate network load.

Active/Standby   In this configuration, one server is designated as a standby server. If the primary (active) server fails, the standby becomes active. The failover times are approximately the same as the active/active failover times.

Fault-Tolerant   When you cannot afford to be down, this is your solution. In a fault-tolerant configuration, both servers process requests simultaneously. When one server fails, the other takes over immediately. Your failover times are generally less than 1 second.

An MS Cluster Server is implemented by having a disk array separate from either server in the cluster. Both servers share the disk array. In this way, each server has access to the other server's data.

NOTE At the time this book was written, Microsoft was working on releasing a clustering package that would allow up to 32 servers to participate in the cluster. This new software is called Windows NT Load Balancing Service (WLBS). For more information on Microsoft clustering, please see the Microsoft Web site at www.microsoft.com.

Installation Name Changes Can Cause Odd Results

Installation of IIS 4 using the Windows NT Option Pack CD-ROM is a simple and straightforward process—so simple, in fact, that administrators often forget that problems can occur. We recently encountered a problem with an IIS that stumped us for nearly an hour and had stumped the on-site administrator for several days. Solving the problem was relatively simple; but realizing what the problem was required good troubleshooting technique.

The Problem

The company installed a machine with Windows NT 4 and IIS 2, left the machine for some time, and then installed the Option Pack. In that time, several different administrators and assistants touched the machine, each performing miscellaneous installations on it in order to prepare it as a Web server. Once the Option Pack installation was complete and the Web site was installed, users within the same domain as the machine were able to access the site without any problems; but whenever users outside the domain tried to access the site, they received either a Windows NT Challenge/Response dialog box or a simple authentication dialog box (depending on their browser). Entering a valid domain user account allowed the user to log in without any problems; but because the machine was destined to be an Internet Web server, it needed to allow access to the site without any login. The local administrator was unable to deduce the problem.

The Solution

After some careful checking and troubleshooting, we realized that the machine had originally been set up with one computer name. But the name was later changed; therefore, the *IUSR_computername* account no longer matched the actual computer name. This caused the problems with the local login. A simple trip to the User Manager solved the problem. We simply added a new account with the correct user name to the machine's local domain and disabled the old account. We then changed the entries in the IIS Properties dialog box.

Summing It Up

While IIS installations are very straightforward, they do not always allow for unexpected changes. When you encounter a problem with an IIS installation, you should carefully perform the appropriate troubleshooting tasks to address the problem. In this case, solving the problem required several different types of troubleshooting tasks—from checking the actual performance of the browser, to analyzing the IIS properties for the Web site, to looking at the Network dialog box and the User Manager. Taking things one step at a time allowed us to solve the problem quickly and efficiently, and to get the Web site up and running.

24seven CASE STUDY

3

Publishing Your Web Site

After you have installed and configured your IIS server, you will have to manually publish any Web or FTP sites that you want network users to access. Publishing means making one or more documents available through IIS. The process of publishing is quite easy. In this chapter, we will discuss the various aspects of publishing your Web content, including publishing single and multiple sites, as well as the tools you will use to perform these tasks. You will also learn two ways to publish your Web content: the MMC and the Web Publishing Wizard.

Getting Started

To begin, you must first have the documents to publish. Publishing a Web site is not the same as publishing an FTP site. FTP sites are non-graphical sites, so you can simply publish a directory, and the FTP server service does the rest. (We will discuss FTP in Chapter 4, "Publishing Your FTP Site.") However, if you are publishing a Web site, you must have graphical documents to publish. There are a variety of types of Web documents that you can publish using IIS. The most common are HyperText Markup Language (HTML) documents.

As the IIS system administrator, you will probably not have very much to do with the actual design of the site, but it's always a good idea to know the basics.

Understanding HTML Basics

HTML is an industry standard scripting language for Internet and intranet use. When an Internet user accesses a Web site, typically, they are requesting a default document (the site's home page). When the Web server receives this request, it will read the default documents script and generate the Web output. The end user will see colors, graphics, and text. The following is an example of HTML script:

```
<html>

<head>

<title>Welcome to In Alameda - http://www.in-alameda.com</title>

<meta name="DESCRIPTION" content="News, movie reviews, and commentary
from the island of Alameda, California. The site post news monthly
and updates its site within 36 hours when major events occur on the
island. It also provides a column on Oakland, California, called
Oakland Surf">

<meta name="KEYWORDS" content="news, Alameda, Oakland, California">

</head>

<body BGCOLOR="#000000" LINK="#ff0000" VLINK="#ff0000">

<p><center><img SRC="declogo.gif" WIDTH="400" HEIGHT="100"
NATURALSIZEFLAG="0"

ALIGN="BOTTOM"></center></p><hr>

<blockquote>

<p><b><font COLOR="#ffffff"><center>This is a sample HTML document
for the IIS/Proxy Server book to show how HTML code tags transform
text into graphic documents when the text is viewed on a Web
browser.</center></b></p>

<HR>

</blockquote>

<center><a href="index.html"><img src="home.gif" width=149 height=41
border=0 alt="Go to In Alameda's Home Page"></a></center>

</body>

</html>
```

To the non-programmer, HTML might look like gibberish. However, it is not difficult to learn. Each area of the HTML document has a distinct purpose. Tags separate the sections of the document. The tags represent the different styles of the document, such as colors, font types, and alignment. Each tag is encased between two brackets, like this: < >. Most tags require a start and an end tag. The only difference between a start and an end tag is the forward slash (/) preceding the text in the end tag. When your Web browser reads the HTML document, it will build the Web page that you see on your screen. Figure 3.1 shows what the previous HTML script looks like to the end user.

Figure 3.1   Sample Web page

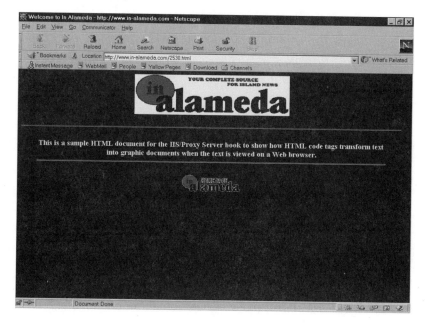

This was a simple script, meant to show you basic HTML. As you can see, the script takes on a whole new look when you view it through a Web browser. If you are interested in expanding your HTML knowledge, the Web is full of useful sites devoted to HTML.

NOTE   You could spend days searching through HTML sites, but here are a few that I have used: http://builder.cnet.com/Authoring/html/, http://werbach.com/barebones/barebone_table.html, and http://www.geocities.com/SunsetStrip/Alley/5616/.

As an IIS system administrator, you should be familiar with the following file types and their uses:

HTML   These are simple, scripted text files. The majority of the files that you publish will be HTML documents. HTML documents are usually comprised of home pages and related links.

ASP   Active Server Pages are server-side script files used to create custom Web applications. The advantage to ASP files is that IIS converts the VBScript contained in them into plain HTML script on the client-side. This allows you to create custom Web solutions without worrying about browser compatibility.

IDQ   Internet Data Query files are scripted queries that you call from an HTML document that contains form fields.

HTX   HTX files are used in conjunction with IDQ files. When a user opens an HTML document containing calls to an IDQ file, the query results are displayed to the user within an HTX document that is pre-configured with the query result format.

Publishing Your Web Site Using the MMC

A Web site is just a directory on your server that IIS allows Internet users to access. When Internet users navigate around your Web site, they are viewing the contents of a directory on your server. (There are exceptions. For example, when you have configured IIS to use Virtual Directories on other servers.) For IIS to let Internet users into your site, you must publish it. The process of publishing your site means pointing IIS to the right directory, thereby making it accessible to users. You can accomplish this by using the Web Publishing Wizard or by using the MMC.

The MMC is a new graphical tool that you can add to Windows NT 4. Before using the Web Publishing Wizard or the MMC to publish your Web site, you will want to have the directory structure already in place.

NOTE   In the next release of Windows NT (a.k.a. Windows 2000) the MMC will be the standard interface for performing system administration.

To use the MMC to publish your Web content, perform the following steps:

1. Click the Start menu. Go to Programs ➤ Windows NT 4 Option Pack ➤ Internet Information Server ➤ Internet Service Manager. NT will open the MMC.

> **TIP**   Here's a neat trick you can do with snap-ins in the MMC to save them to a file. Select Save As from the file menu and save the ISM snap-in on the desktop as a file called iis.msc. This way, you can get to the MMC right off of the desktop instead of having to do the Start ➢ Programs ➢ NT Option Pack ➢ Internet Information Server ➢ Internet Service Manager routine every time you want to get to the MMC.

2. Expand the Internet Information Server group. The MMC will display your IIS server.

3. Expand the IIS server. The MMC will display your IIS server options.

4. Right-click the server name. The MMC will display a quick menu.

5. Select New group ➢ Site. IIS will display the New Web Site Wizard.

6. In the New Web Site Wizard dialog box, enter a description for your Web site. Click Next. The New Web Site Wizard will advance to the next screen.

7. Click the "Select the IP Address to use for this Web Site" drop-down list and select the IP address you want to use. You can also set the TCP port number you want to use in this dialog box. Click Next. The New Web Site Wizard will advance to the next screen.

8. Enter the path to the directory that contains your Web content in the "Enter the path for your home directory" field. If you want to allow all Internet users access to your site, make sure that the "Allow anonymous access to this web site" check box is marked. Click Next. The New Web Site Wizard will advance to the next screen.

9. Select the access permissions that you want to allow for your Web site. You must allow Execute and Write permissions if you are planning on using a hit counter. Click Finish. The New Web Site Wizard will publish the directory.

When you have completed these steps, Internet users will be able to access your Web site using the IP address that you assigned during publication.

> **NOTE**   To access your site using the host and domain name (e.g., www.organization.com), you must create a record on the DNS server that your domain is registered to use. You will learn more about using host and domain names later in this chapter.

Publishing Your Web Site Using the Web Publishing Wizard

Although you can publish your Internet sites from either the MMC or the Web Publishing Wizard, there are differences in these two utilities. The major difference between using the MMC and the Web Publishing Wizard is that you can use the Wizard from a client to publish to a remote IIS.

Many ISPs allow their users to create and manage personal Web sites. Users who want to take advantage of this service must have some way of uploading their Web content to the ISP's servers. In the past, the ISP would create FTP sites for each customer and set permissions so that each customer could upload and delete their own files. The problem with this type of configuration is that your customers must be proficient in using an FTP client. FTP clients are generally command-line utilities that require some foreknowledge to be successful in using them. You cannot call the average FTP client software "intuitive."

But users can easily manage their Web content with the Web Publishing Wizard. The Web Publishing Wizard is a standard Microsoft Wizard application that takes the user by the hand and leads them through the publication process.

To publish a Web site using the Wizard, perform the following steps:

1. Click the Start menu. Go to Programs ➤ Microsoft Web Publishing ➤ Web Publishing Wizard. NT will start the Web Publishing Wizard.

2. Click the Next button to begin the publication process. The Web Publishing Wizard will advance to the next screen.

3. Select the location of the local files that you want to publish. If you want to publish the entire directory's contents, make sure that the Include Subfolders check box is marked. Click Next. The Web Publishing Wizard will advance to the next screen.

4. In this screen, specify a description of your site in the Descriptive Name field. Click Next. The Web Publishing Wizard will advance to the next screen.

5. This screen allows you to specify the location where you want to publish your files. (This is how you can send files to a remote server, such as an ISP.) Click Next. The Web Publishing Wizard will contact the remote site.

6. The remote site will request user authentication. Enter your user credentials in the Enter Network Password dialog box. Click OK. The remote site will validate your user name and password. If your credentials are verified, you will be allowed to continue. At this point, the Web Publishing Wizard will go to the final screen.

7. Click Finish. The Web Publishing Wizard will publish your Web site.

NOTE The Web Publishing Wizard may require you to input configuration information if you are publishing to a remote server.

Configuring Your Home Directory

When you publish a Web or FTP site, you must specify a home directory. The home directory is where IIS will direct user requests that do not specify a particular file. For example, if you enter in your Web browser a URL that you want to access, such as www.sybex.com, you are only specifying a computer and a domain; you are not specifying a file for IIS to retrieve. When a user does not specify a particular file to download, IIS returns the default document of the home directory to their browser.

You can specify a home directory through the MMC. When you publish a site, IIS automatically configures the home directory location. The only time you have to configure it manually is when you decide to change the home directory location.

Changing Your Home Directory

Reasons for changing your home directory location vary. You may want to create a new directory structure for each site you manage. To change the home directory location, perform the following steps:

1. Click the Start menu. Go to Programs ➤ Windows NT 4 Option Pack ➤ Internet Information Server ➤ Internet Service Manager. NT will open the MMC.

2. Expand the Internet Information Server group. The MMC will display your IIS server.

3. In the Internet Information Server group, right-click the site you want to configure a home directory for. The MMC will display a quick menu.

4. Click Properties. The MMC will display the Site Properties dialog box.

5. Click the Home Directory tab. The Site Properties dialog box will change to the Home Directory screen.

6. Click the Browse button. The MMC will display the Browse For Folder dialog box.

7. Select the home directory location for your site. Click OK. The MMC will return you to the Home Directory screen.

8. Click OK.

Now that you have changed your home directory location, all user requests will be routed to the new directory location. IIS treats this directory as a single site, unless you specify that IIS should use other directories within your site structure. When IIS points users' requests to directories outside your home directory, these directories are called virtual directories.

Understanding and Configuring Virtual Directories

As we have just discussed, you must specify a home directory for each Internet site you create. The home directory is a default location where IIS directs user requests that do not specify a particular file. When you create your home directory, by default, IIS makes the entire directory structure accessible to the network. This means that the root of your site, as well as all subdirectories, are included in your site structure and are accessible by the network. Typically, Internet sites are maintained within a single directory structure, so this poses no problems. However, there are times when you may want to use directories in locations other than the actual site directory, or you may want to use ones that are on completely different computers. Virtual directories provide this service.

IIS treats a virtual directory as if it is a subdirectory of your home directory. To the network user, there is no difference between a virtual directory and any other directory that is part of your site. An administrator must specify the location of the virtual directories, which can exist on your local server or on a remote server. However, virtual directories are usually on remote servers. When a user requests a virtual directory location from an IIS server, IIS acts as a proxy by contacting the remote computer and retrieving the files that the user requested.

Creating a Virtual Directory

To create a virtual directory, perform the following steps:

1. In the MMC, expand IIS. The MMC will show the configuration options for IIS.
2. Right-click the Web site that you want to add a virtual directory to. The MMC will display a quick menu.
3. Select New ➤ Virtual Directory. The MMC will display the New Virtual Directory Wizard.
4. Go to the "Alias to be used to access virtual directory" field. Enter a name for Internet users to specify the new directory with. Click Next. The New Virtual Directory Wizard will advance to the next screen.

5. In the next dialog box, enter the physical location of the directory. This can be on another computer in the network. If the virtual directory is local, specify a path (C:\myvirtualdirectory). If it is remote, specify a UNC (\\servername\ sharename). Click Next. The New Virtual Directory Wizard will advance to the next screen, which displays access permissions.

6. Check the appropriate permissions for your site. Click Finish. The New Virtual Directory Wizard will make the virtual directory available.

The virtual directory you created can now be accessed by users by specifying the Web site URL with a front slash (/), and the ALIAS name you specified when creating it. For example, if you have a Web site called www.sybex.com and you want to create a virtual directory called Funstuff, specify the alias name *Funstuff* when creating the virtual directory. The URL that users will specify to access this virtual directory would be www.sybex .com/Funstuff. If desired, this URL could be pointed to by using hyperlinks in the www.sybex.com Web site. In this manner, the Web site load can be distributed across multiple servers.

Distributing the Web Site Load across Multiple IIS Servers

You must identify the type of load your IIS server will support. Deciding whether your site supports a heavy or light load is very subjective. Microsoft's corporate Web site receives over one million hits per day, while other Web sites may only get a few users per day. If you determine that users will access your site frequently, you may want to configure your site structure so that multiple IIS servers handle the load.

When considering distributing your IIS load, you should also use common sense. For example, don't set up multiple dual-Pentium servers to handle the load of your Web site that contains last year's family vacation. While Microsoft does not define what heavy and light server loads are, you can use your own judgement to decide what you truly need. Most administrators who decide to use virtual directories to distribute their load are managing large corporate entities that get thousands of user hits per hour.

As you have learned, IIS can use virtual directories to create a distributed directory structure that is transparent to Internet users. You may decide to do this because the resources you want to publish happen to exist on other servers. But, when properly planned, this makes a great way of distributing the load of user requests across multiple servers so that no one server must handle all of the user requests. However, using virtual directories to distribute the IIS load will only work if the individual components of your site are accessed evenly. For example, if the majority of your site access is directed toward one particular resource, such as technical support, you must partition that resource into sections that you can distribute across servers, as Figure 3.2 shows.

Figure 3.2   Distributing load through virtual directories

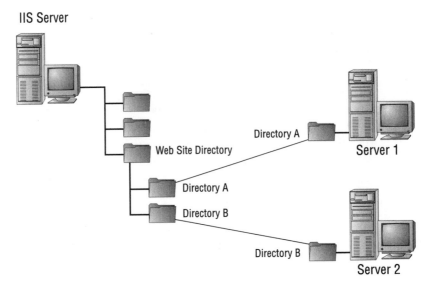

While distributing your Web content across multiple servers and configuring virtual directories to help distribute the load works in many cases, there are some instances where it would not be beneficial at all. Consider your Web content. If 75% of the user requests your server receives are for a particular resource, such as your technical support home page, using virtual directories will not help. The IIS server will simply be directing the majority of network traffic to one location. In these types of situations, you may need to do something different, such as round-robin DNS entries.

Typically, a DNS server will have only one entry for a particular host, but not in the case of round-robin DNS entries. As the DNS administrator, you would create multiple entries for a single host, but you would point each entry to a different IP address. Consider the following example where multiple entries are created for the same site using different IP addresses.

www.companyx.com	131.107.2.10
www.companyx.com	207.49.189.12
www.companyx.com	10.134.14.200

When a client computer requests DNS resolution for a host name, it will only use the first name returned. However, the DNS server will change the order of the DNS entries for the next client request so that, one-by-one, each of these entries will be used. All you have to do is copy your Web site to the multiple IIS servers that are listed on your DNS server.

The only real drawback to this approach is that, although you are distributing the load from an initial contact basis, DNS does not have any way of knowing which servers are being used the most. For example, several users could be downloading large files across the Net while DNS is still sending more users to this location based on the simple round-robin DNS method. DNS has advantages and disadvantages, but it is still better than nothing if you need to distribute your load.

Distributing Web sites across multiple IIS servers can help reduce the load on any one server. However, there are times when you may want to do the opposite. Instead of distributing a single site across multiple servers, you may want to put several sites on a single server.

Configuring Multiple Web Sites

The majority of Web administrators will manage single-site servers, which is an IIS server that publishes just one site. A single IIS server can accommodate several Web and FTP sites at once. Although IIS can manage multiple sites, it cannot do it alone. In order to configure multiple sites on a single IIS server, you must do one of three things: specify multiple IP addresses on your Windows NT Server, use different port numbers for each site, or use host header names.

Using a unique IP address is the preferred method because it is easy to implement and is widely supported. Using unique port numbers will require each Web client to manually specify the port number for a given site. This is non-standard and will make it more difficult for users to hit your site. The last method is using host header names. Host header names will only work on Web browsers that support host headers. Although this is now a standard, you may experience problems with older client browsers.

Creating Multiple IP Addresses

The preferred method for using a single IIS server to host multiple sites is to have unique IP addresses for each site. Let's examine how to configure these addresses.

ISPs and IPPs

Just as ISPs provide access to the Internet, there are companies that will manage and publish your Web sites. An Internet Presence Provider (IPP) is a company that specializes in publishing sites for various companies and individuals. IPPs provide a service similar to what ISPs provide. Quite often, ISPs are also IPPs, providing both access to the Internet and Web presence for clients.

Although the lines that separate ISPs from IPPs are somewhat fuzzy, you can use this simple rule to distinguish the difference: ISPs allow users to access the Internet and provide access back to your Web server. IPPs host Web and FTP sites on their equipment, which means that you do not need to own a computer to have a site on the Internet.

To configure multiple IP addresses on your Windows NT Server, perform the following steps:

1. Right-click the Network Neighborhood icon on your desktop. NT will display a quick menu.
2. Select Properties. NT will open the Network dialog box.
3. Click the Protocols tab. Select the TCP/IP protocol and click the Properties button. NT will open the Microsoft TCP/IP Properties dialog box.
4. Click the Advanced button. NT will open the Advanced IP Addressing dialog box.
5. In the IP Addressing section of the screen, click the Add button. NT will open the IP Address dialog box.
6. Enter the new IP address that you want to bind to your network adapter. Click Add. NT will return you to the Advanced IP Addressing dialog box.
7. Click OK. NT will return you to the Microsoft TCP/IP Properties dialog box.
8. Click OK. NT will return you the Network dialog box.
9. Click OK. NT will bind the new IP address to the network adapter card and prompt you to restart your machine.

Configuring IP Addresses

After you have bound multiple IP addresses to your Windows NT Server, you must configure your individual sites before you can use them. When an Internet user requests access to a particular site, they will do it with either an IP address or with a host and domain name. However, when an Internet client specifies an Internet site, an IP address must be referenced. For example, if a client enters a host and domain name in a Web browser, the host and domain name will be resolved to an IP address before any communication between the two hosts can be established. It is these IP addresses that IIS uses to distinguish individual site directories.

To configure an IP address for a site, perform the following steps:

1. In the MMC, select the site you want to assign an IP address to. Right-click the site. The MMC will display a quick menu.

2. Select Properties. The MMC will display the Site Properties dialog box.

3. Select the Web Site tab (FTP Site tab if applicable). Click the IP Address drop-down list and select the IP address you want to configure for this site. Click OK. The MMC will point all requests for this IP address to the selected site.

Configuring Content Control

There are four Content Control options within IIS. These options are not similar to each other. In fact, the only thing that the Content Control options have in common is that they are found on the same screen within the Web Site Properties dialog box. Though unrelated, the Content Control options are on the same screen because they are simple check boxes that do not intuitively go anywhere else within the IIS structure.

Understanding the Content Control Options

The four Content Control options are Log Access, Index This Directory, Directory Browsing Allowed, and FrontPage Web. As the IIS administrator, you will configure these options on a per-server basis. Let's examine the function of each of these options.

Log Access   You use the Log access option to turn on tracking of user access. When an Internet user requests access to this site, IIS will record these requests in the log file. You can turn this option on for a whole site, a single directory, or for just one file.

Index This Directory   Index Server is a support add-on for IIS. With Index Server, you can create an index of every document within your site. You can allow users to query your site using search words and to locate a particular document within your site structure. The Index This Directory check box turns on the ability for Index Server to index your site. When this check box is not marked, Index server will bypass the location when indexing.

Directory Browsing Allowed   When Internet users request access to a particular site without specifying a file, they will receive the default document. However, when IIS does not have a default document to return, one of two things happens: IIS either returns an error page, or it returns an HTML-generated document that lists all the files in the directory structure. If you mark the Directory Browsing Allowed check box, you are turning on the ability for users to view your directory structure. You will want to exercise caution when using this option because you may not want users to view all the files in your directory.

FrontPage Web   FrontPage is a Microsoft Web development tool. The advantage of using FrontPage over other Web development platforms is that FrontPage has a graphical user interface and is fairly intuitive. When you use FrontPage to develop sites, you cannot just publish the sites using IIS. You must install IIS FrontPage Server Extensions on your IIS server. The FrontPage Server Extensions allow IIS to read the FrontPage content. When you use the FrontPage Web check box within the Web Site Properties dialog box, you are letting IIS know that this site contains FrontPage code.

NOTE   You will learn more about FrontPage Server Extensions in Chapter 8, "IIS Add-Ons."

Using the Content Control Options

To use the Content Control options, perform the following steps:

1. In the MMC, right-click the Web site that you want to configure Content Control options for. The MMC will display a quick menu.

2. Select the Properties options. The MMC will open the Web Site Properties dialog box.

3. Click the Home Directory tab. The MMC will display the Home Directory screen.

4. Select the Content Control options that you want to turn on. Click OK. MMC will set the options that you checked and will close the Web Site Properties dialog box.

Changing Your HTTP Port

There are two transport protocols within the TCP/IP protocol suite: TCP and UDP. Each of these protocols provides unique services for network communication. TCP is connection-oriented, sessions must be established between two hosts before any data can be transmitted; while UDP is connectionless, requiring no sessions. UDP simply sends out packets and does not expect any response back from the receiving machine. When a UDP packet is sent, it is the responsibility of the application that sent the frame to determine if the packet arrived in satisfactory condition. When an application sends a packet over TCP, TCP will ensure that all packets arrive to the destination machine undamaged.

Although there are some differences between the way that TCP and UDP manage packets sent over them, there is one major similarity: Each protocol uses ports as end points to communicate. You can think of TCP and UDP ports as channels on a television. Although you may know that a program you want to watch is out there, this is not enough. In order to find the program, you must also know what channel it is on.

In TCP/IP communication, the port number is similar to the television channel. When an Internet client computer requests access to a TCP/IP host, the client must also know what port number to use. For example, a client requesting access to a Web site will use TCP port 80 by default. There are many predefined port numbers, called *well-known port numbers*. Some of the most common well-known port numbers are listed here:

TCP 80   HTTP

TCP 21   FTP (File Transfer Protocol)

TCP 23   Telnet (Terminal Emulation)

TCP 25   SMTP (Simple Mail Transfer Protocol)

TCP 53   DNS (Domain Name System will use either TCP or UDP.)

UDP 53   DNS

UDP 67   Bootp Server (Bootstrap Protocol Server)

UDP 68   Bootp Client

UDP 161   SNMP (Simple Network Management Protocol)

Although you can configure the port numbers that your IIS server will use, keep in mind that users must know and specify this number in order to access your site. While changing the port numbers will help to keep out unwanted users, it is a fairly low level of security. If you want to secure your IIS server with a higher level of security, see Chapter 10, "IIS 4 Security Configuration."

If you decide that you want to change the port number of your Web service, perform the following steps:

1. In MMC, select the site whose port number you want to change. Right-click the site. The MMC will display a quick menu.

2. Select Properties. The MMC will display the Site Properties dialog box.

3. Select the Web Site tab (FTP Site tab if applicable). In the TCP Port field, enter the new port number that you want Internet users to specify. Click OK. The MMC will require Internet users to specify the new port number in order to access this site.

Putting It All Together

Quite recently, I spent a weekend publishing a Web site for a small computer manufacturer. This company sells PCs in a major US city and internationally on the Internet. There were several key factors in rolling out this site:

- Installing IIS 4
- Ensuring proper DNS entries
- Testing the Web content
- Testing credit card transactions
- Making the site accessible to the Internet

This company, we'll call them X Computers, wanted an e-commerce solution. The site had to provide information on services and new computer systems, and had to be able to accept credit cards.

I began the rollout on a Saturday morning around eight. The first step was installing IIS. The installation was fairly uneventful and included the following:

- IIS 4
- Index Server
- The third-party program Cold Fusion.

After the server products were installed, I copied existing Web content to a directory on the Windows NT Server that contained IIS. Using the MMC, I published the Web content by specifying a virtual server IP address. This company also hosts other Web sites, so using a virtual server IP address allows X Computers to house multiple Web sites on a single Windows NT Server.

The developer who created this company's Web site used the third-party application Cold Fusion to gain access to their SQL Server database. Cold Fusion uses a hybrid file type that is a mixture of HTML, Transact SQL, and some proprietary script. When Internet users access X Computer's Web site, they will be able to query the SQL database for specifics on computer systems.

After installing everything, I tested the site by using a local computer in a segmented network. There were some minor bugs in the Cold Fusion scripts; but once we got those ironed out, everything else worked fine.

Next, I had to test the credit card transaction process. To test the IIS server's ability to handle credit card transactions, we had to be on the Internet. I removed the server from the segmented network and gave it a real IP address. After running some tests, we felt comfortable making the site accessible to the general public.

The next step was to create a DNS entry for this server. X Computers uses their own DNS server to provide name resolution for not only their site but also for others. I created a DNS host record for the server. Next, I needed to see if I could access this site from outside the local network. For this task, I enlisted some help. I called a friend and had him log on to his ISP and see if he could reach the site. After successful access from more than one ISP, I gave the server a clean bill of health.

4

Publishing Your FTP Site

In this chapter, we will discuss the key topics involved in administering your FTP sites, such as FTP site publication, security, and virtual directories. FTP is an Internet standard protocol for transferring data from one TCP/IP host to another. Before you decide whether or not to set up FTP on your IIS server, you need to know more about what FTP is. To understand FTP and any of the other Internet protocols and related services, you should know how new ideas become Internet standards.

Internet Standards

All Internet standards are published in documents called Requests for Comments (RFC). Before an RFC is an Internet standard, it must be carefully examined by experts to ensure that it is a good idea. The process by which RFCs become Internet standards is quite interesting. A board of people vote on every proposed idea. The group that votes on standards is the Internet Architecture Board (IAB). While the IAB votes on standards, there are actually two groups that control the future of the Internet: IAB and the Internet Society (ISOC).

The ISOC is an organization devoted to furthering Internet use. The ISOC encourages the development of the Internet. You could think of the ISOC as the public relations department for the Internet, although you are not likely to see any ISOC commercials. ISOC works at a higher level—with telephone companies and large organizations.

While ISOC encourages Internet use, the IAB acts as the technical advisors for the Internet. When a new Internet standard is proposed, the IAB members examine the idea and look for its flaws and strengths. After a review, the IAB decide by consensus whether or not to adopt the idea as a new Internet standard.

First, someone must come up with a new idea for how to do things on the Internet. That person proposes the idea (as an RFC) to IAB. Each IAB member puts in his or her recommendations and votes on whether the proposal should become a standard. This whole process could take days, weeks, or even months to turn an idea into a new standard.

When the IAB is done reviewing an RFC, the board issues one of the following standard classifications: Required, Recommended, Elective, Limited Use, or Not Recommended. Depending on which standard classification the IAB issues, the original idea will be implemented or not.

File Transfer Protocol

The File Transfer Protocol specification is currently listed in RFC 959. The File Transfer Protocol (FTP) was created in 1973 for the following reasons:

- To promote sharing of files (computer programs and/or data)
- To encourage indirect or implicit (via programs) use of remote computers
- To shield a user from variations in file storage systems among hosts
- To transfer data reliably and efficiently

Though it can be used directly by a user at a terminal, FTP is designed to be used by programs. In short, FTP is a bi-directional data transfer protocol that allows you to copy files to and from remote hosts, regardless of the file system in place on either host.

To function, FTP requires two applications: the FTP client software and the FTP server software. NT has shipped with an FTP server service for some time. However, you will probably want to use the version that ships with IIS as you will likely manage a Web presence as well. As far as the FTP client goes, there are many to choose from. While you can use most Web browsers (such as Internet Explorer) as FTP clients, most do not support both file upload and file download. NT does provide a full-bodied FTP client. However, it is a command-line program, and you must be familiar with FTP commands in order to use it. The following is a list of the FTP commands used for your NT FTP client software:

!   Escape to the shell

?   Print local help information

append   Append to a file

ascii   Set ascii transfer type

bell   Beep when command completed

binary   Set binary transfer type

bye   Terminate FTP session and exist

cd   Change remote working directory

close   Terminate FTP session

delete   Delete remote file

debug   Toggle debugging mode

dir   List contents of remote directory

disconnect   Terminate FTP session

get   Receive file

glob   Toggle metacharacter expansion of local filenames

hash   Toggle printing # for each buffer transferred

help   Print local help file information

lcd   Change local working directory

literal   Send arbitrary FTP command

ls   List contents of remote directory

mdelete   Delete multiple files

mdir   List contents of multiple remote directories

mget   Get multiple files

mkdir   Make directory on the remote computer

mls   List contents of multiple remote directories

mput   Send multiple files

open   Connect to remote TFPT

prompt   Force interactive prompting on multiple commands

put   Send one file

pwd   Print working directory on remote computer

quit   Terminate FTP session and exit

quote   Send arbitrary FTP command

recv   Receive file

remotehelp   Get help from remote server

rename   Rename file

rmdir   Remove directory on remote

send   Send one file

status   Show current status

trace   Toggle packet tracing

type   Set file transfer type

user   Send user information

verbose   Toggle verbose mode

Being familiar with the FTP client commands can be useful if you ever have to troubleshoot problems on your FTP server. For example, to copy a file to your local computer that is on a remote server named *server* in the sybex.com domain, you would use the following syntax from the NT command prompt:

```
ftp
open server.sybex.com
get filename
```

As you have learned, for FTP file transfer to take place, there must be a client and a server. An FTP server is a service that provides clients with network access to a directory structure. The directory structure may be an actual single directory on the server, or it may be a series of virtual directories that appear as one tree structure but actually exist on more than one server.

In NT, an FTP server can be an individual service you install, or it can be part of the IIS package. We will examine the FTP server service within IIS.

Installing the FTP Service

When you installed IIS, you were given the choice of installing other related services, such as the FTP server service. If you did not choose to install the FTP server service at that time, you must install it prior to publishing any FTP sites.

To install the FTP server service, reinstall the Windows NT 4 Option Pack and select the FTP Server service.

Creating a New Site

After you have installed the FTP server service, you can publish your FTP site. Unlike publishing Web sites, you don't have to create special documents that your FTP server will use. FTP is a simple file transfer utility, so all you have to do is specify the directory you want users to access. When users navigate within your FTP site, they are simply viewing the contents of the directory that you specified as an FTP site.

As you learned in Chapter 3, you can use the MMC to publish your site whether it is a Web or FTP site. Before using the MMC to publish your FTP site, you will want to have the directory structure already in place.

To use the MMC to publish your FTP site, perform the following steps:

1. From the Start menu, go to Programs ➤ Windows NT 4 Option Pack ➤ Internet Information Server ➤ Internet Service Manager. NT will open the MMC.

2. Expand the Internet Information Server group. The MMC will display your IIS server.

3. Expand the IIS server. The MMC will display your IIS server options.

4. Right-click the server name. The MMC will display a quick menu.

5. Select New ➤ FTP Site. IIS will display the New FTP Site Wizard.

6. In the New FTP Site Wizard dialog box, enter a description for your FTP site. Click Next. The New FTP Site Wizard will advance to the next screen.

7. Click the "Select the IP Address to use for this FTP Site" drop-down list and select the IP address you want to use. (In this dialog box, you can also change the default TCP port number from 21 to the one you want to use.) Click Next. The New FTP Site Wizard will advance to the next screen.

8. In the "Enter the path for your home directory" field, enter the path to the directory that contains your FTP content. Also, make sure that the "Allow anonymous access to this FTP site" check box is marked. Click Next. The New FTP Site Wizard will advance to the next screen.

9. Select the access permissions you want to allow for your FTP site. Your choices are Read or Write. Read permission allows users to download files, while write permission allows users to upload files. Click Finish. The New FTP Site Wizard will publish the directory. If your site is stopped, right-click and select start.

As soon as you have completed the New FTP Site Wizard, Internet users will be able to access your FTP site by the IP address that you assigned during publication. To access your site using the host and domain name, you must create a record on the DNS server that your domain is registered to use.

You have learned how to publish your FTP site using a single directory, but there are instances where you may want to publish FTP directories on other servers as part of one FTP directory structure. This is when knowing how to create FTP virtual directories comes in handy.

> **TIP** IIS automatically creates three sites: Administration, Default Web, and Default FTP. You can copy your site content to these directories and use them instead of publishing new ones. These sites also make excellent test sites for trying out new administration tasks.

Creating an FTP Virtual Directory

FTP virtual directories are very similar to the Web virtual directories you created in Chapter 3. Remember that virtual directories are simply extensions of the home directory location of any site. Virtual directories can be on remote servers or on the same server as the home directory location. The difference between Web and FTP virtual directories is that Web virtual directories are viewed as graphical content, while FTP virtual directories are seen as extensions of a tree structure.

To create an FTP virtual directory, perform the following steps:

1. Go to the MMC and expand IIS. The MMC will show the configuration options for IIS.

2. Right-click the FTP that you want to add a virtual directory to. The MMC will display a quick menu.

3. Select New ➤ Virtual Directory. The MMC will display the New Virtual Directory Wizard dialog box.

4. In the "Alias to be used to access virtual directory" field, enter an alias name that Internet users will specify this directory with. Click Next. The New Virtual Directory Wizard will advance to the next screen.

5. In the next dialog box, enter the physical location of the directory. (This can be on another computer in the network.) For a local virtual directory, enter a path (for example, c:\ ). For a remote virtual directory, enter a UNC name (for example, \\computername\sharename). Click Next. The New Virtual Directory Wizard will advance to the next screen, which displays access permissions.

6. Check the appropriate permissions for your site. Click Finish. The New Virtual Directory Wizard will make the virtual directory available.

Just like with Web virtual directories, you may choose to distribute your FTP load by placing frequently used directories on separate servers and then specifying each of these locations as a virtual directory for FTP access.

Configuring FTP Properties

After you have published your FTP site and configured your virtual directories, you may want to configure additional options for your site. The types of options that you can configure range from setting general security to configuring how many users can access your site at any one time.

To access the FTP Site Properties dialog box, perform the following steps:

1. Click the Start menu and go to Programs ➢ Windows NT 4 Option Pack ➢ Microsoft Internet Information Server ➢ Internet Service Manager. NT will open the MMC.

2. Expand your IIS service. The MMC will display the IIS components.

3. Right-click your FTP site. The MMC will display a quick menu.

4. Select Properties. The MMC will display the FTP Site Properties dialog box.

5. Select the tab and options that you want to configure for this site.

In the FTP Site Properties dialog box, there are five tabs that you can use to configure various options for your FTP site. The five tabs are as follows:

- FTP Site
- Security Accounts
- Messages
- Home Directory
- Directory Security

Each tab contains grouped FTP site configuration options.

FTP Site

On the FTP Site tab, you can control options, such as the number of simultaneous users that can access your site. There are six fields that you can configure within the FTP Site tab. Each one is described here:

Description   You can type a brief description of your FTP site in this field. You will use this description to identify your site.

IP Address   You can assign a particular IP address to this FTP site. You will need to do this if you are hosting multiple FTP sites on a single IIS server because FTP sites cannot use host header names.

TCP Port   A client must specify a particular TCP port number to transfer data between two TCP/IP hosts. If a client does not explicitly specify a port, the client software will use the default port. As the administrator, you can change the default port to any other number between 1 and 65,536.

NOTE   Port numbers 1 through 1,023 are already used by well-known programs, so you may want to assign a number higher than 1,023. However, I have seen administrators use some of the well-known port numbers on their sites without problems, as long as the assigned services are not running on that server.

Connection   You can use this section of the FTP Site tab to control the number of users who can access your site simultaneously and to configure the connection time-out value. There are two radio buttons and two fields. The radio buttons are Unlimited and Limited To. If you specify Unlimited, your site will pose no limitations on the number of users who can access it at any one time. If you specify Limited To, you must specify the number of users that can access your site simultaneously. (The default is 100,000.) The other option in this section of the screen is the time-out value. The time-out value controls how long the FTP service will wait for an inactive user to communicate any information before the FTP service will disconnect that user.

Enable Logging   This section controls whether or not logging is turned on and what format the log is saved as. It contains a check box to turn on logging and a drop-down list to choose the log format. We will discuss more about IIS logging in Chapter 12, "IIS Monitoring and Optimization."

Security Accounts

The Security Accounts tab contains the FTP administrative account information and allows you to configure the anonymous account that the FTP client will use if you allow anonymous logon. There are two sections to this tab: Allow Anonymous Connections and FTP Site Operators. Each one is described here:

Allow Anonymous Connections   This check box turns your site's anonymous connection option on or off. If the Allow Anonymous Connections option is turned on, you must specify a default user account for the FTP client to use to access your site's data. By default, the IUSR_*servername* account is used. Another option in this section is the Allow Only Anonymous Connections check box. This option will prevent users from logging in with their own user account and password, since only the anonymous account is used. Keeping user accounts from being transmitted across the network in this manner can provide a measure of security.

FTP Site Operators   In this section, you can configure NT Domain accounts that you want to give administrative privileges to on your FTP site. The Operators field lists the current administrators of this site. To add a new administrator, click the Add button and select the NT Domain account that you want to add.

Messages

An FTP feedback message contains information that allows you to interact with your users in a virtual setting, such as a greeting message when a user logs on. Remember that most FTP clients are non-graphical, so users will not see anything on their screens when they connect, unless you configure a greeting message. There are three types of feedback messages that you can configure within the screen: Welcome, Exit, and Maximum Connections.

A Welcome message is what your FTP clients see when they access your FTP site. It is important to clearly describe the contents of your site here because visitors often use this information to decide if your site will be of value to them.

The Exit message is the last thing your FTP clients see when leaving your site. This is your chance to thank users for visiting your site or to advertise another site.

One of the most important messages you can configure is the Maximum Connections message. This message is displayed to users when the maximum connections limit has been reached. As the administrator, you can configure the number of connections that your FTP site will accept. While it may seem that you would not want to limit the number of connections, it is a good idea to do so because you only have a limited amount of network bandwidth, but the server will continue to process user requests even if each user is experiencing slow performance. It is better for a user to see a message indicating that the site is busy than to connect and have very slow performance.

The Maximum Connections message is an important public relations tool for your FTP site. If a user tries to access your site and cannot do so because of excess connections, the user may become frustrated and may not return. The Maximum Connections message gives you an opportunity to ask your users to be patient and to try again later. It's a nice way to achieve good virtual public relations.

Home Directory

A home directory is the location where your IIS server will send client requests that do not specify a particular directory. On this tab, you can configure the home directory location, as well as some basic directory access permissions, and the file listing style.

This screen has one field and several radio buttons and check boxes, which are broken into two sections: FTP Site Directory and Directory Listing Style.

FTP Site Directory Contains the path to your FTP site's home directory and three check boxes. The three check boxes are home directory permissions. The options are Read, Write, and Log Access. Read access to download files, Select Write access to upload files, and Select Log access to track users by IP address when logging is enabled (just like with the WWW service).

Home Directory Contains the Directory Listing Style section. This section has two radio buttons: UNIX and MS-DOS. UNIX and DOS computers list their directories in a slightly different manner. If you have a preference for your directory listing style, you may select the radio button for the style that you want clients to see. The UNIX style listing will display more detailed information, while the MS-DOS style may be more familiar to your users (depending on their experience).

Directory Security

By default, all clients will be able to access your FTP site. In most cases, having access for all clients is the correct configuration. However, there are situations in which you want to limit the access to your site to a select group of computers.

The Directory Security tab contains two radio buttons that toggle the security mode. The two radio buttons are ("By default, all computers will be...") Granted Access or Denied Access. Depending on which option you select, the "Except those listed below" field takes on a different meaning. If you select "By default, all computers will be Granted Access," computers listed in the "Except those listed below" field will be denied access. If you choose the "By default, all computers will be Denied Access," computers listed in the "Except those listed below" field will be granted access.

If you decide to implement security on a per-machine basis, you will want to consider which option will best work for you.

Changing Your FTP Port

There are two transport protocols within the TCP/IP protocol suite: TCP and UDP. Each of these protocols provides unique services for network communication. You also learned about ports. A port is essentially an end destination for network communications. When a client connects to a remote host for Web or FTP service, the client must specify a port to connect to. For either service, the client will use the TCP transport protocol. The difference is in the port that the client will specify to get to the end destination. For Web service, the client will attempt to connect to TCP port 80 by default. For FTP service, the client will attempt to connect to TCP port 21 by default.

Just like with your Web service, you can configure the port numbers that your IIS server will use. Remember that if you change them, anyone accessing your site must know the port number to use. While it is usually not a good idea to change these numbers because it causes confusion on the user's part, some administrators will opt to do this to enhance security. If you decide to change the port number, remember that all users must know and specify the port number to access the site.

To change the port number of your FTP service, perform the following steps:

1. Go to the MMC and select the FTP site whose port number you want to change. Right-click the site. The MMC will display a quick menu.

2. Select Properties. The MMC will display the Site Properties dialog box.

3. Select the FTP Site tab. In the TCP Port field, enter the new port number that you want Internet users to enter. Click OK. The MMC will require Internet users to specify the new port number to access your site.

Is FTP Still Out There?

In the last few years, FTP sites have been disappearing from sight. There used to be thousands of sites; now they are being replaced with Web sites. One key factor in the growth of HTTP sites is that they are graphical and entertaining, while FTP sites are non-graphical and a bit boring. So, why use FTP at all? Even in today's "entertain me" society, there is still room, and need, for FTP sites.

FTP sites have traditionally been file download sites for drivers, patches, and service packs. Now, administrators will choose a Web interface over FTP just because more people understand how Web sites work and find them more pleasant to look at. However, FTP is still going strong; it's just in an invisible market. Consider the following example:

We just set up an FTP site for a group of companies that share the same graphic designer. These companies are a mix of Internet operations with diverse product lines and business practices. They all maintain their own IIS systems and databases. In fact, the only thing that these companies have in common is the graphic designer who creates the artwork for their Web sites.

In most cases, in order to have someone access your company Web site and make changes to graphics, you need to grant that remote user a higher level of access than your general Internet users. This poses security risks. To eliminate this security concern, these companies decided (at the artist's recommendation) that they would all share the cost of an additional server. The idea being that each company would create a virtual directory pointing toward a physical directory on the new server. The new server was a Windows NT Server, Server Only machine with IIS installed and the FTP service started.

The Problem

We ran into a problem with FTP on a Server Only NT Server. FTP could not use any NT Domain accounts. In fact, the only account it would accept was the default Anonymous User account.

The Solution

This was easily fixed by changing the Anonymous User's account password so that only the graphic designer could access the FTP site remotely.

Summing It Up

By sharing one FTP server and by using virtual directories to point to the graphic directories on the FTP server, the graphic designer could access all the artwork for each company without having higher level access to anything else on the sites.

24*seven* **CASE STUDY**

5

Advance Configuration and Administration

One of the truly amazing aspects of IIS 4 is how well it scales to suit your environment. You can have a single Web site or several Web and FTP sites on one server and still manage them with ease. In this chapter, we will discuss some of the configuration options that you can use to set up your IIS environment the way you want, including the following:

A single IP address for multiple Web sites   This option frees you from having to bind multiple IP addresses to your server.

Custom HTTP headers   You can include HTTP headers in documents that you send to clients with custom configuration options that the client can use for varying purposes.

Content expirations   This option allows you to control how long a client will cache documents for.

Custom errors   You can manage the specific error messages that users will see when the server cannot process a request.

Content ratings   You can set rating levels on your Web content so that clients can determine if they want to view site information.

Bandwidth Throttling   This feature lets you control how much bandwidth any particular site on your server can have.

Remote administration   You can use the HTML-based IIS administration for remote management.

Default document   Configuring a default document lets you control what document a remote user will get when no document is specified.

IIS 3 compatibility   This feature lets you configure a IIS 3 site so that you can manage it from the MMC.

Configuring Multiple Sites Using a Single IP Address

As IP addresses become harder to get, there is growing concern that they may run out. Typically, each site on your IIS server must have its own IP address. This is no longer the case. HTTP 1.1 supports an added tag within a site to facilitate multisite hosting over a single IP address. You can now use a single IP address to host several sites, leaving addresses available for other use.

While this can help you efficiently manage your IP addresses, much like anything else in computers (and life), there are always advantages and disadvantages. Though you can use HTTP 1.1 to host multiple sites on a single IP address, not every browser will be able to view your sites. This does not mean that the majority of Internet users will not be able to access your site, but those users with older browsers will not be able to. Browsers that currently support HTTP 1.1 are Microsoft Internet Explorer 4 and Netscape 3.

Adding a Host Header Name

Hosting multiple Web sites using a single IP address can only be accomplished by adding a host header name to your Web site. Remember, not all browsers support the use of host headers, so configuring this option may mean that your site is not accessible to your full customer base.

To give your site an HTTP host header name, perform the following steps:

1. Open the MMC and expand your IIS server. Right-click the site that you want to configure an HTTP host header name for. The MMC will display a quick menu.

2. Select Properties. The IIS Service Manager will display the Web Site Properties dialog box.

3. Click the Web Site tab. Next, click the Advanced button of this tab. The IIS Service Manager will display the Advanced Multiple Web Site Configuration dialog box.

4. Click the Add button in the "Multiple identities for this Web Site" section of the screen. The IIS Service Manager will display the Advanced Web Site Identification dialog box.

IIS 4

5. Click the drop-down list of IP addresses and select the IP address that you want to use for this site. In the Host Header Name field, enter the name you want to use for this site. (Optionally, you can select a specific TCP port number to use.) Click OK. The IIS Service Manager will close the Advanced Web Site Identification dialog box and return you to the Advanced Multiple Web Site Configuration dialog box.

6. Click OK. The IIS Service Manager will return you to the Web Site Properties dialog box.

7. Click OK. The IIS Service Manager will close the Web Site Properties dialog box and return you to the MMC.

NOTE Once you have configured your host header names, you must create DNS entries for each of the header names as if they were regular hosts.

Although you have learned how to configure a host header name so that a single IP address can host multiple sites, since not all Web browsers support this feature, how do you ensure that all Internet clients will be able to access your site? You can use something called a *cookie*. Cookies are objects attached to Web client browser software that store information, such as the last time a site was accessed or the last time a file was downloaded. You can use cookies to create a virtual host header. In order to do this, an administrator must perform registry editing and use a .asp file in the scripts directory. This is not an everyday administrative task, but for detailed information on using cookies, please refer to the Microsoft Internet Information Server Resource Kit or any number of Internet sites devoted to writing cookies.

Host name headers are not the only types of HTTP headers that you can use on your Web sites. You can also configure special headers for other functions.

Configuring Custom HTTP Headers

There are many other HTTP headers that you can configure for your site. For example, you can use the Cache-Control: max-age = value to configure how long a Proxy Server will cache pages from your site. The setting is in seconds; and you can use it to configure your site, directory, or even a single page within your site.

Some of the other HTTP headers that you can configure are listed here:

Cookies Cookies are objects that client browser software can use to store general information. This information could be a unique identification number that will distinguish the host from other hosts that are accessing a particular site.

From   You can use the From header to send the e-mail address of the requesting user back to you.

Accept   This header contains a semicolon-separated list of representation schemes (document content) that will be accepted in response to a user's request.

User-Agent   This header is for statistical purposes and the tracing of protocol violations. It identifies the software of the requesting client. To use the User-Agent header, the first white space delimited word in the document must be the software product name, with an optional slash and version designator.

These are just some of the HTTP headers that you can configure. For details on HTTP headers, you can use any of the search engines on the Internet and search for *HTTP Headers*. Depending on the search engine that you use, a greater or lesser number of HTTP headers will be returned.

To configure HTTP headers, perform the following steps:

1. Open the MMC and expand your IIS server. Right-click the site that you want to configure an HTTP header for. The MMC will display a quick menu.

2. Select Properties. The MMC will open the Web Site Properties dialog box.

3. Click the HTTP Headers tab. Next, click the Add button in the Custom HTTP Headers section of this tab. The IIS Service Manager will open the Add/Edit Custom HTTP Headers dialog box.

4. In the Add/Edit Custom HTTP Headers dialog box, enter a name value in the Custom Header Name field. In the Custom Header Value field, enter a value for the header (for example, `max-age=1800`). Click OK. The IIS Service Manager will close the Add/Edit Custom HTTP Header dialog box and return you to the Web Site Properties dialog box.

5. Click OK. The IIS Service Manager will close the Web Site Properties dialog box and return you to the MMC.

Now that you have configured custom HTTP headers, including the `Cache-Control:` `max-age` = value, which controls how long a Proxy Server will cache the page, you may also want to control how long an individual browser will cache a page. This is controlled through the Content Expiration setting in the Web Site Properties dialog box.

Configuring Content Expirations

By using HTTP custom headers, you can control how long Proxy Servers will cache the pages from your site. This is fine if your Web clients are accessing your site through Proxy Servers. However, you may want to control how long an individual client will cache your

Web content regardless of Proxy Servers. You can manage the time a client will cache information from your site by setting the content expiration from within your Site Properties dialog box.

After you enable content expiration, you must choose a content expiration method. The content expiration methods control when your content actually expires on the client computer. There are three choices:

Expire Immediately   If you choose to set your content expiration so that it expires immediately, Web clients will not cache your site content at all. This option is useful if you have HTML pages that change often and you want your clients to always have the most up-to-date information.

Expire After   This content expiration option is the most widely used. This option allows clients to cache site content, but sets a predetermined limit (minutes, hours, or days) on how long the content is cached before the client must reload the data from the server. Having your Web clients cache information makes the connections from their end appear faster; and by being able to set a time limit on how long the client will cache the information, you get the best of both worlds—performance and content accuracy.

Expire On   The Expire On option is useful if you have information that will not be valid after a certain date. You can use Expire On to control how long Web clients will cache your site content. You do this by setting a date on your content. When this date is reached, clients must reload the site content from the server.

To configure the content expiration for your site, perform the following steps:

1. Open the MMC and expand your IIS server. Right-click the site that you want to configure the content expiration for. The MMC will display a quick menu. Select the Properties option.

2. The MMC will open the Web Site Properties dialog box.

3. Click the HTTP Headers tab. Next, click the Enable Content Expiration check box. The IIS Service Manager will highlight the Content Expiration section of the screen.

4. At this point, you must choose the expiration method you will use. Your choices are Expire Immediately, Expire After, or Expire On. Select the radio button for your expiration method and click OK. The IIS Service Manager will close the Web Site Properties dialog box and return you to the MMC.

Content expirations are another way of fine-tuning your IIS server so that it will best serve your users.

Creating Custom Errors

Web error messages are typically responses to user requests for documents that are not available, but can be responses to any number of general errors. One of the most typical responses is the HTTP/1.1 404 Object Not Found message. This message is not very descriptive. Using custom error messages, you can create custom responses that are far more descriptive and useful.

The first step in implementing custom error messages is to create the HTML document that you want to display. The following example will help you in creating your own custom error message:

```
<html><head><title> File Not Found </title>

<meta name="robots" content="noindex">

<META HTTP-EQUIV="Content-Type" CONTENT="text/html;
 charset=iso-8859-1></head>


<body>

<h2>Error</h2>

<p><strong> Document not found </strong></p>

<p>The Document you requested is not available or no longer exists on
this server. Check the URL and try again. </P>

</body></html>
```

This HTML text generates an error page that looks like Figure 5.1; although, the text in Figure 5.1 is different from that in this example.

Let's examine how to configure IIS to display a custom error message page in response to a file that is not found.

To configure IIS to use a custom error page, perform the following steps:

1. Open the MMC and expand your IIS server. Right-click the site that you want to configure the custom error message for. The MMC will display a quick menu.

2. Select Properties. The MMC will open the Web Site Properties dialog box.

3. Select the Custom Errors tab. Next, select the specific error that you want to use the custom error page for (for example, error 404). With the error highlighted, click the Edit Properties button. The IIS Service Manager will display the Error Mapping Properties dialog box.

Figure 5.1   Custom error page

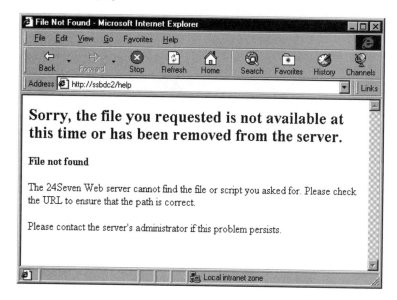

4. From the Error Mapping Properties drop-down list, select one of the options: File, Default, or URL. Assuming that you are using a custom error HTML document, select the File option. In the File field, enter the location of the HTML document that you want to use. Click OK. The IIS Service Manager will close the Error Mapping Properties dialog box and return you to the Web Site Properties dialog box.

5. Click OK. The IIS Service Manager will close the Web Site Properties dialog box and return you to the MMC.

Custom error messages can help your users better understand what the error messages that they get actually mean.

Configuring Content Ratings

One very exciting new feature of IIS 4 is the ability to configure content ratings. Content ratings are very similar to the rating system that motion pictures use. While the motion picture association uses letters to designate their ratings, IIS uses categories and numbers to represent the rating level of Internet content. For example, a Web site may have a Violence rating of 3.

There are four rating categories: Violence, Sex, Nudity, and Language. Each one uses a sliding-scale rating system. The categories and their levels are listed here:

Violence 0 = No violence; 1 = Fighting; 2 = Killing; 3 = Killing with blood and gore; and 4 = Wanton and gratuitous violence.

Sex 0 = None; 1 = Passionate kissing; 2 = Clothed sexual touching; 3 = Non-explicit sexual touching; and 4 = Explicit sexual activity.

Nudity 0 = None; 1 = Revealing attire; 2 = Partial nudity; 3 = Frontal nudity; and 4 = Provocative frontal nudity.

Language 0 = Inoffensive slang; 1 = Mild expletives; 2 = Moderate expletives; 3 = Obscene gestures; and 4 = Explicit or crude language.

To configure the rating system on your Web site, perform the following steps:

1. Open the MMC and expand your IIS server. Right-click the site that you want to configure content ratings for. The IIS Service Manager will display a quick menu.

2. Select Properties. The IIS Service Manager will open the Web Site Properties dialog box.

3. Click the HTTP Headers tab. Next, click the Edit Ratings button. The IIS Service Manager will open the Content Ratings dialog box.

4. Select the Ratings tab. The IIS Service Manager will display the Ratings screen.

5. Click the "Enable Ratings for this resource" check box. The IIS Service Manager will highlight the Category and Optional Information fields, as well as the Rating slidebar.

6. From the Category field, select the category that you wish to configure for this site, such as Violence, Sex, or Nudity. After you select the category, use the Rating slidebar to adjust the rating level from 0 to 4. You may also enter an optional name of the person responsible for this rating in the Optional Information field.

7. Repeat step 6 for each category that you want to configure. When you have finished configuring your ratings, click OK. The IIS Service Manager will close the Content Ratings dialog box and return you to the Web Site Properties dialog box.

8. Click OK. The IIS Service Manager will close the Web Site Properties dialog box and return you to the MMC.

The ratings that you have just configured are simply HTTP headers, like the ones you learned about earlier in this chapter. When a client requests access to a site that has the content ratings configured, the client will receive the rating headers first. The client will then determine if the currently logged on user can access this site. Most new browsers support content ratings.

Configuring Bandwidth Throttling

One of the challenges that many Internet service providers face is the control of network bandwidth. The term *network bandwidth* refers to the amount of data that can pass through a given network architecture. To better understand network bandwidth, consider the following analogy: A garden hose provides a means to transport water from one location (the spigot) to another location (wherever you are watering). A fire hose provides the same type of service. The difference lies in the amount of water that each hose can supply. The larger the hose, the more water that can pass through it. In reality, there are other factors that can affect the amount of water that you get out of a hose, such as water pressure.

It is much the same in computer networks. Except that instead of water, data must be transported. The network cable, network cards, and hubs control the flow. The amount of data that can pass through your network is called *bandwidth*.

Bandwidth is one of the most serious concerns for any network administrator. Every time a user logs on to your network, it takes up some of your available bandwidth. Multiply that by the number of users you have and the other network requests for service that take up bandwidth, and you may have a slow network. In regards to IIS, this means that if you host more than one site, you may have an unbalanced site bandwidth issue. One of the sites you host may be receiving hundreds, or even thousands, of hits per day and may be consuming the majority of your available bandwidth. In IIS 4, the administrator can control this.

Bandwidth Throttling is the ability to control the amount of bandwidth that a particular site can use. Configuring this option allows the administrator to manage multiple sites so that network users can access all of them.

To configure Bandwidth Throttling, perform the following steps:

1. Open the MMC and expand your IIS server. Right-click the site that you want to configure Bandwidth Throttling for. The MMC will display a quick menu.
2. Select Properties. The MMC will open the Web Site Properties dialog box.
3. Click the Performance tab. Next, click the Enable Bandwidth Throttling check box. The MMC will highlight the Maximum Network Use field.
4. Enter the amount of network bandwidth that you want to allow this site in Kilobits/Sec.
5. Click OK. The MMC will close the Web Site Properties dialog box and return you to the main MMC screen.

Using Remote HTML-Based Administration

So far, you have used only the MMC to perform all IIS administration. While the MMC is the administrative tool of choice, you cannot use it for every situation. You can only use the MMC when you are administering a local server. There may be times that you are not geographically close to the servers that you must administer. This is when HTML-based administration comes in handy.

HTML-based administration is a Web site that you can use to perform most of the administrative tasks for your IIS server. Figure 5.2 shows the HTML-based administrative site as it looks in a browser.

Figure 5.2   HTML-based administration page

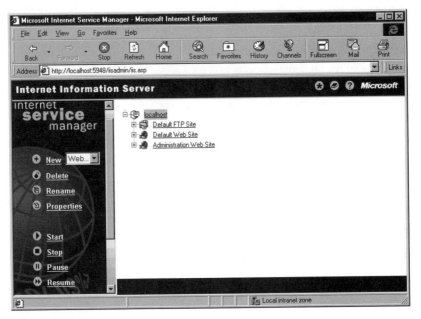

When you install IIS, it automatically installs the Administration Web Site. You will not be able to use the site until you configure your security settings because, by default, the Administration Web Site is configured to allow access to only one IP address: the address 127.0.0.1. This address is a reserved IP address that is used for diagnostic (loop-back) functions. 127.0.0.1 calls the internal TCP/IP protocol stack. This means that you can only use the Administration Web Site from the local machine.

To configure the Administration Web Site so that you can access your IIS server from anywhere, perform the following steps:

1. Open the MMC and expand your IIS server. Right-click the Administration Web Site. The MMC will display a quick menu.

2. Select Properties. The MMC will open the Web Site Properties dialog box.

3. Click the Directory Security tab. Next, click the Edit button in the "IP Address and Domain Name Restrictions" section. The IIS Service Manager will display the "IP Address and Domain Name Restrictions" dialog box.

4. Click the Granted Access radio button. Click OK. The IIS Service Manager will close the "IP Address and Domain Name Restrictions" dialog box and return you to the Web Site Properties dialog box.

WARNING   Since this is a remote administration tool, it can be dangerous if it falls into the wrong hands. Depending on your situation, you may want to configure the security of the remote administration site by denying access to all computers except the one or two computers that you know you will be using for remote administration.

---

5. Click OK. The IIS Service Manager will close the Web Site Properties dialog box and return you to the MMC.

Let's examine the types of administrative tasks that you can perform from the Administration Web Site.

Almost anything that you can do from the IIS Service Manager of the MMC can be done from the Administration Web Site. For example, you can create new sites, manage existing sites, read log files, and even stop and restart your IIS server services. The Administration Web Site's home page is broken into two sections: a left and a right pane. On the left pane, you will see the following options:

New   This link opens a dialog box that asks you to input a name for your new site. You can follow the simple on-screen instructions to publish a new site.

Delete   To use this option, you must first select the site or directory you want to delete from the right pane of the screen. Click the Delete link, and IIS removes the site or directory from your inventory.

Rename   You can rename a site or directory by clicking this link and specifying the new name.

Properties   To configure any of the advanced properties of a site, directory, or page, click this link after selecting the object that you want to configure from the right pane.

In the right pane of the Administration Web Site's home page, you will see your Web sites and their directory structures. You can expand sections of the tree hierarchy to view the contents that you want to manage.

The Administration Web Site is your best administrative tool for remotely managing your Web sites.

Setting the Default Document

Sometimes users request exact HTML documents; but more often than not, users simply specify a host and domain name (such as www.company.com) in their browsers. When a user specifies a host and domain, but no particular file, IIS returns the default document from the home directory (the root of your site). The default document in IIS is called default.htm; but you can change this to any filename that you want. If you do decide to change your default document name, be sure to reference this name in all of the HTML documents of your Web content.

To configure your default document, perform the following steps:

1. Open the MMC and expand your IIS server. Right-click the site that you want to configure the default document for. The MMC will display a quick menu.

2. Select Properties. The MMC will open the Web Site Properties dialog box.

3. Select the Documents tab. Next, click the Add button. The IIS Service Manager will display the Add Default Document dialog box.

4. Enter the name for the default document that you want to use. Click OK. The IIS Service Manager will close the Add Default Document dialog box and return you to the Web Site Properties dialog box.

5. Click OK. The IIS Service Manager will close the Web Site Properties dialog box and return you to the MMC.

There is more to configuring default documents. In IIS 4, you can configure several default documents. Here's how it works:

When a client computer requests access to your Web site without specifying a particular file, IIS will look in the site properties and see if a default document is specified. If there is more than one document listed, IIS will look in the home directory for the one at the top of the list. In this way, you can control the search order for default documents. To configure the search order, click the up or down arrows in the Default Document field of the Documents tab in the Web Site Properties dialog box.

Setting IIS 3 Compatibility

Although it is not very common, you may find mixed environments where you have older versions of IIS in the same network with IIS 4. Since the MMC is a fairly new tool, older versions of IIS did not use it. They did, however, have an IIS administrative Service Manager similar to the one in the MMC. Administrators used this tool to perform all system maintenance, just as you use the MMC in IIS 4.

In mixed environments, you can administer your IIS Web site from the older version's administrative interface. However, you can use this feature on only one of the Web sites on your IIS 4 server.

To configure the default Web site for IIS 3 compatibility, perform the following steps:

1. Open the MMC and expand the IIS group. Right-click the IIS server that you want to configure IIS 3 compatibility for. The MMC will display a quick menu.

2. Select Properties. The IIS Service Manager will display the Server Properties dialog box.

3. Click Edit. The IIS Service Manager will open the "WWW Service Master Properties for Server" dialog box.

4. Select the IIS 3 Admin tab. Click the drop-down list of Web sites and select your default site. Click OK. The IIS Server Manager will close this dialog box and return you to the Server Properties dialog box.

5. Click OK. The IIS Service Manager will close the Server Properties dialog box and return you to the MMC.

Bandwidth Throttling—Is It for You?

One of the most important configuration options is Bandwidth Throttling. Not every site administrator will have to consider using Bandwidth Throttling. It's only real benefit will be for administrators who host multiple sites.

When you have only one site to administer, there is no need to control how much bandwidth that site gets. However, when there are multiple sites present, you may have problems with one site overpowering the others. This was exactly the case for a friend of mine who owns an ISP.

The Problem

My friend, we'll call him Bob, owns a small ISP that services a few hundred customers. He also hosts approximately ten Web sites on his IIS server. Of the Web sites that Bob hosts, one is very active. The others are small, less trafficked sites. The active site eats up most of Bob's bandwidth. On more than one occasion, the other sites have complained.

The Solution

Bob called me in to help solve his bandwidth issues. I used Performance Monitor, the standard NT performance monitoring utility. I used the Network Segment Object, the %Network Utilization Counter, the Web Service Object, and the Measured Async I/O Bandwidth Usage Counter. I was able to determine the total amount of bandwidth used and the total amount of bandwidth that each site used. I quickly realized that the really active site was, at times, taking up 100% of the available bandwidth. While the best solution here would be to upgrade the existing network links to faster speed links, this was not financially feasible for Bob. Since Bob had only promised the owners of the active site a limited amount of bandwidth to begin with, the quick and easy solution was to enable Bandwidth Throttling.

Summing It Up

After enabling Bandwidth Throttling, we used the Performance Monitor utility to measure the results. This time, we observed a noticeable difference in how the other sites responded when accessed. Problem solved.

IIS Mail Support

Of all the services that the Internet and the accompanying TCP/IP protocol suite provide, electronic mail (e-mail) is arguably the best known and most widely used. Over the past few years, e-mail has become the key communication system for any company that wants a powerful collaborative environment—both internally and externally—with vendors, customers, and other groups. IIS provides an industry-standard e-mail solution using the Simple Mail Transport Protocol (SMTP). With IIS and SMTP, you can easily design processes to transmit and deliver mail. In this chapter, we will look at how to configure your e-mail system using SMTP, as well as some other considerations of the issues involved in the implementation of SMTP, such as IIS' lack of support for the sister POP3 protocol.

The Internet Mail System

Internet mail is a relatively straightforward process (having corollaries in the mail services provided by most countries) in which the sender addresses a message, whose structure is specified by the SMTP protocol, to another user or users (the recipients) at a specific address. Common examples of mail addresses show how the address is constructed. Typically, it is a user name, followed by an @ symbol, followed by a domain name. For example, our e-mail addresses are `shanes@cybersol.net` and `markl@cybersol.net`.

Once the message is sent, the recipient uses an e-mail program to read the message. While the two ends of the process are simple (and are made even simpler with modern day mail clients), the transmission process itself is rather complex. The implementation of the transmission process is handled by SMTP.

Sending E-Mail

The mail delivery process starts when a client program—such as Microsoft Outlook, Outlook Express, or Lotus Notes—sends a message to an SMTP server. For the purposes of this discussion, a client knows only one server; so all messages originating on the local client, regardless of their final destination, go to the same server. This SMTP server (often referred to as the local SMTP server) is responsible for figuring out what to do with the message, which is an ASCII file with a bunch of special text headers. These headers have the same function as the address information that is normally found on the front of an envelope.

If the destination domain of the e-mail message is a local domain for the server (for example, the e-mail is sent to mark1@cybersol.net, and the SMTP server is smtp.cybersol.net), the ASCII message is stored on that server. Otherwise, the message is forwarded to another server, called the destination server.

All SMTP servers on a network can communicate with one another using the same language; in the case of e-mail, that language is the SMTP protocol. The transmitting server also makes use of the Domain Name System (DNS) protocols to lookup the address that it should forward the message to.

The POP3 Component and Its Role in E-Mail Delivery

The SMTP server sends the e-mail to another domain where the message is received by the destination server. However, this server does not use SMTP; it uses the Post Office Protocol (POP). POP is a protocol that lets a user's client program retrieve an e-mail sent with SMTP.

> **NOTE** POP servers are typically referenced with a version number. The most common version of POP in use on the Internet today is version 3, so you will often see POP servers referred to as POP3 servers.

A server that provides the POP3 service waits for connections from clients. When a client connects to the POP3 server, the client must identify itself to the server by using a username and password. The POP3 server validates the user based on these incoming credentials. Once the POP3 server successfully validates the user, it distributes to the client program any e-mails that are addressed to the users that the POP3 server is currently storing. These e-mails are stored in the SMTP message storage on the server. In other words, a POP3 server is also an SMTP server. Typically, the SMTP storage has a different directory for each mail user on the system. These directories are the server-side equivalent to a user's inbox. The directory structure makes it easy for POP3 to quickly and efficiently retrieve all messages from the SMTP storage for the validated users.

Two server processes are involved in the sending and retrieval of e-mail—SMTP and POP3. SMTP sends e-mail and uses port 25 while POP3 retrieves e-mail, distributes it to the client(s), and uses port 110. Figure 6.1 shows the transmission process when using SMTP and POP3.

Figure 6.1   The roles of SMTP and POP3 in the e-mail delivery process

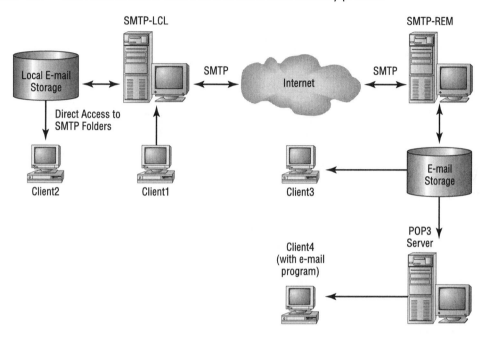

> **NOTE** It is possible to write an application that reads mail messages directly from the SMTP storage on the receiving server and lets users view them as text files—which, after all, is what they are. However, as a rule of thumb, managing e-mails in this manner is much more cumbersome than using the POP3 protocol to retrieve them from the server storage.

As you can see in Figure 6.1, regardless of an e-mail's final destination—whether it is within the local domain or outside of it—the transmitting client always sends all outgoing mail to its SMTP server, SMTP-LCL. Client1 and SMTP-LCL communicate using SMTP, as do SMTP-LCL and the remote SMTP server SMTP-REM. If the mail sent by Client1 is destined for a domain directly serviced by SMTP-LCL, the SMTP server will deposit the e-mail into the directory on the server that corresponds to the client's mailbox. The client can retrieve the e-mail from the server in one of two ways:

- The client can directly access the mail message by reading it from the file storage location where the files reside. To use this option, the client must have access rights to the file system, and the client must be using some type of program that can read the ASCII files directly.

- The client can connect to a POP3 server (either on the SMTP-LCL machine or on another machine in the same domain that has been configured to pull messages from the storage on the SMTP machine). This POP3 server, which has access to the file system on the SMTP machine, retrieves the files from the SMTP storage and distributes the files to the user's local mailbox.

On the other hand, if mail sent by Client1 is addressed to a domain that is serviced by another SMTP server (in the figure, it is SMTP-REM), the local SMTP server (SMTP-LCL) establishes a network connection (using our old friend TCP/IP) to the appropriate remote server (SMTP-REM) and transfers the mail using SMTP.

WARNING   It is important to recognize that after the SMTP server deposits mail to the mailbox on the file system, it does not care what happens to the message—SMTP's part of the process has been accomplished and is complete. In fact, there is no formal connection between SMTP (the transmission protocol) and POP3 (the delivery protocol). Effective mail management requires the creation of a connection between the two.

IIS Mail Solutions with Collaborative Data Objects

Before you run out and install the SMTP and POP3 services onto your Web server, be aware of one problem: IIS provides SMTP services but not POP3 services. In fact, the SMTP service that IIS provides is actually a scaled-down version of the SMTP services provided by Microsoft's Site Server product or by a high-volume product such as Microsoft Commercial Internet System (MCIS), which supports mailboxes and the transfer of messages from the users' mailboxes on the SMTP server to their client applications.

The IIS SMTP service provides only mail delivery functionality; it is not intended to aid in the receipt of mail by clients. With only one directory for all incoming messages, IIS SMTP does not sort messages in any way or provide the directory mapping that we discussed earlier in the context of SMTP servers. IIS SMTP performs two basic tasks: It either forwards mail to other SMTP servers (if the mail is addressed to a remote domain), or it stores any messages destined for itself in a single, global directory (which can be found at `\Mailroot\Drop` by default).

How it is that SMTP can sort through all the potential text files (e-mails) that might find their way into the Drop directory and identify which files are destined for a particular e-mail recipient? Microsoft has provided the Collaboration Data Objects for Windows NT Server, often called the CDO for NTS library. The CDO/NTS exposes certain messaging objects that you (or developers in your organization) can use in an Active Server Pages script, a Microsoft Visual Basic application, or a Microsoft Visual C++ application to access and manipulate e-mail for a particular user. In this way, Microsoft provides you with the means to write your own mail clients for IIS SMTP. The CDO/NTS library is very complete. In fact, you can use a very simple Active Server Pages (ASP) script to perform the necessary processing to provide a particular user with access to the local messages stored on the SMTP server for that user.

In the next section, we take a brief look at an ASP script written by a programmer friend of ours that allows us use the CDO/NTS library to retrieve e-mail messages.

Using an ASP Script to Return E-Mails from the IIS SMTP Service

The following code shows how you can use ASP (with server = side VBScript) to provide users with e-mail information from the IIS SMTP server.

```
<!--
Using the CDO for NTS Library to Read E-mail
for a Specific User from an Active Server Page
Other solutions are similar.
-->
<%@ LANGUAGE = "VBScript" %>
<%
If (Request.ServerVariables ("REQUEST_METHOD") = "POST") Then
    UserName = Request.Form("Name")
    Email = Request.Form("email")
Else
    ' Assume it is GET
    UserName = Request.QueryString("Name")
    Email = Request.QueryString("email")
End If


If (Address = "") OR (UserName = "") then
```

```
        Response.Write "You have to supply UserName and email <BR>"
        Response.End
    End If


    Set objServConnect = Server.CreateObject ("CDONTS.Session")
    objServConnect.LogonSMTP UserName, Address
    Set objInbox = objServConnect.GetDefaultFolder(1)


    If objInbox Is Nothing Then
        Set collMessages = Nothing
        Response.Write "Can't get folder. <br>"
        objServConnect.Logoff
        Response.End
    End If


    Set collMessages = objInbox.Messages


    If (collMessages.Count = 0) Then
        Response.Write  "<center> User <b>"  & UserName & "</b>" & _
            " (email:  <b>" & Address & "</b>) does not have messages"
        Response.End
        objServConnect.Logoff
    End If


    Response.Write  "<center> User <b>"  & UserName & "</b>" & _
        " (email:  <b>" & Address & "</b>) has <b>"& _
        collMessages.Count & "</b> message(s) </center> <p>"


    Response.Write "<TABLE BORDER=1 WIDTH=100% >"
    Response.Write "<TR> <TD WIDTH=10% > <i>ID</i></TD>" & _
        "<TD WIDTH=15% > <i>From</i></TD>" & _
```

```
        "<TD WIDTH=15% > <i>Subject</i> </TD> " & _
        "<TD WIDTH=60% > <i>Message Text</i></TD> </TR>"


    For eMessages = 1 To collMessages.Count
        Set objMessage = collMessages.Item(eMessages)
        Response.Write "<TR> <TD WIDTH=10% >" & eMessages & "</TD>" & _
            "<TD WIDTH=15% >" & objMessage.Sender.Name & "</TD>" & _
            "<TD WIDTH=15% >" & objMessage.Subject & "</TD>" & _
            "<TD WIDTH=60% >" & objMessage.Text & "</TD> </TR>"
    Next


    Response.Write "</TABLE>"
%>
```

Let's take a quick look at some of the most important things happening in this code. The first important line

```
    Set objServConnect = Server.CreateObject ("CDONTS.Session")
```

creates the SMTP session. The line after it

```
    objServConnect.LogonSMTP UserName, Address
```

performs the necessary login process for the user to access the SMTP server. The script uses the LogonSMTP method to perform the login.

The next line

```
    Set objInbox = objServConnect.GetDefaultFolder(1)
```

uses the GetDefaultFolder method to set the Inbox as the default folder. This step ensures that the script will have access to the contents of the folder. However, the IIS SMTP service does not use a folder named Inbox, but instead uses the Drop folder.

Even though IIS SMTP stores all the messages for the entire domain within the Drop folder, the CDO/NTS objects let us obtain only those items that are destined for our authenticated user, whose user ID and password were verified during the login process. After retrieving all of the existing messages for the user, the code builds a table and places the messages within individual rows in the table.

The script accepts two parameters: name and e-mail. You can specify values for these parameters by passing them directly within the URL, as shown here:

```
http://klsserver/scripts/
CDOread.asp?name=Mark&email=mark@klsserver
```

Alternatively, you could build an HTML form that lets the user enter the information into a pair of text fields, processes the login request, and returns the appropriate information. The code in the `CDOread.asp` file as written can handle either the POST or GET HTTP method, so either means of putting the data up is acceptable.

> **NOTE** Even though Microsoft does not provide a POP3 service with IIS, it is a relatively simple process for one of your developers to write a POP3 server or modify an existing service. An obvious example would be for the developer to modify the POP3 service sample provided with the Win32 SDK to use CDO/NTS and simulate full POP3 functionality.

Installing the SMTP Service

Before we consider the issues surrounding the installation and configuration of the SMTP service, it is important to recognize the environment in which this installation occurs. For example, our shared network has very few machines (8) connected across a LAN. We use a Fully Qualified Domain Name (FQDN) structure, which means that e-mail sent to the SMTP server on our local net is addressed to `mark@klsserver`. If we used domain names, the e-mail would instead have to be addressed to `mark@klsserver.klsent.com` or `mark@klsent.com`.

You can install the SMTP service by selecting either the Typical or Custom installation from the Windows NT Option Pack. If you choose a Custom setup, the first dialog box displayed by the setup program lets you select the components to install on your server. In this dialog box, select Internet Information Server and click the Show Subcomponents button to open the Internet Information Server dialog box. This displays the IIS subcomponents, including the SMTP service, as shown in Figure 6.2.

> **NOTE** We used the NT 4 Option Pack CD-ROM to perform the installation and configuration described in this chapter.

Once you make your component selections and continue with the product's installation, the setup program displays a dialog box that prompts you for a mail root location. The directory `c:\inetpub\mailroot` is the default location. When the installation of the

Figure 6.2   The SMTP Service is one of the IIS subcomponents.

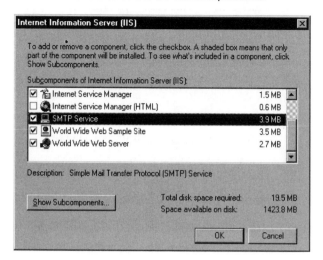

SMTP service and the option pack is complete, the setup program will have installed the following directories into the \inetpub\mailroot directory (or whatever you chose to name it):

\Badmail   This directory stores undeliverable (outbound) messages.

\Drop   This directory stores all the mail for a specific SMTP domain. Each file in this directory represents the ASCII text for a single mail message. It is important to recognize that the filenames within this directory do not correspond to user-names and that you will not be able to determine from looking at the filenames who a particular message is destined for. This is the directory that CDO/NTS looks into when you use it to retrieve messages for a single user (as in the script that you saw previously).

\Pickup   As soon as a mail message is placed into this directory, the SMTP ser-vice will grab the message and either deliver it directly to the \Drop directory or send it off to the SMTP server for the destination domain (after reconciling the domain name using DNS services). As soon as the message is placed into the \Pickup directory by any means—even by manually copying it—the SMTP ser-vice will attempt to deliver the message. Your applications can create an SMTP-compliant text file and drop it into the \Pickup directory if they wish to take advantage of SMTP services without being constructed as a full SMTP client.

NOTE As a rule, if you want to place messages directly into the Pickup directory, you should create them elsewhere first (in a Temp directory or something similar) and copy them into the Pickup directory when they are finished. Otherwise, the SMTP service will attempt to transmit the message while it is being edited, and will waste processor cycles continuing to make the attempt until the file is closed and can actually be transmitted.

\Queue   If IIS can't deliver a message immediately because of a network problem or other issues, the message is queued up in this directory. The SMTP service will hold onto the message for a configurable length of time and try to retransmit it.

\Route, \SortTemp, and \Mailbox   IIS SMTP uses these directories to sort and rearrange outgoing messages to make their delivery more efficient. If several messages need to be sent to the same remote host, IIS SMTP will try to send them all by using a single connection instead of by transmitting each one individually, which would require multiple reconnection cycles.

Constructing a Mail Message

You can easily package your own mail messages and drop them into the \Pickup directory using a text editor, such as Notepad. While full compliance with the SMTP protocol specification requires the generation of some odd header information, you can still create SMTP mail files directly. In such a case, the mail file must look similar to the following:

x-sender: markl@klsent.com

x-receiver: shanes@cybersol.net

From: markl@klsent.com

To: shanes@cybersol.net

Subject: Sample SMTP Message

This is the body of the message, which must follow an empty line that indicates the end of the header text and the beginning of the message body.

Using this simple technique, you can easily create SMTP messages and drop them into the Pickup directory for forwarding by the SMTP service.

Checking the Status of the SMTP Service

After the SMTP service is installed, you can use several different methods to determine whether it is currently running. One method used by experienced administrators is to go to the Control Panel or the Server Manager and open the Services applet. The SMTP Service's status will be listed in the Services dialog box.

You can also get a list of running services by invoking the `Net Start` command at a command prompt. Finally, you can get information about the status of the SMTP service within the IIS plug-in for the Microsoft Management Console (MMC).

Using Telnet to Communicate with the SMTP Service

You can also use Telnet to establish a connection with the SMTP port of the server. You can easily do this by invoking the telnet program, as shown here:

```
telnet localhost smtp
```

It is not recommended that you use Telnet to connect with the SMTP port unless you are familiar with the Telnet protocol because keeping the SMTP port open across telnet exposes a significant security risk for your network. Telnetting into the SMTP server can provide you with direct access to the server from a remote location—whether for administrative purposes or simply to access the messages in their constituent directories—but leaving that port accessible is a bad idea. Historically, some of the most useful and common hacker exploits of NT have involved an entrance through a Telnet connection to the SMTP port.

Starting the SMTP Service Manager

After the service is installed, you can make changes to the SMTP configuration from the IIS plug-in to the MMC or from the HTML-based administration pages, depending on your configuration. If you use the HTML-based administration pages, you can access those pages either by selecting SMTP Service Manager (HTML) from the SMTP Service group or by navigating your browser to `http://localhost/mail/smtp/admin/`. Even though the MMC window looks a bit different than the browser-based management window, both windows provide similar functionality to the user.

Throughout this book, we will use the MMC for administration tasks because it is the preferred tool. However, you can use the HTML-based administration pages to perform almost all of these tasks.

Configuring the Default Domain Properties

One of the best places to begin configuring SMTP properties is the setting for the default domain properties. Conceptually, the domain is the lowest unit of the server organization. The domains that SMTP operates with are identical to the DNS domains discussed in Chapter 2. Moreover, if a computer does not participate in the Domain Name System, the domain name for e-mailing purposes is the computer name. IIS uses the default computer name for the TCP/IP protocol properties in the Network Control Panel applet as the default domain name.

To list the properties of a specific domain, click the Domains entry in the left pane of the MMC. The right pane will show all of the configured SMTP domains. Next, right-click the desired domain in the right pane and choose Properties from the pop-up menu to open the Properties dialog box. Figure 6.3 shows the properties for the klannt NT Server domain.

Figure 6.3   The domain properties for the klannt NT Server domain

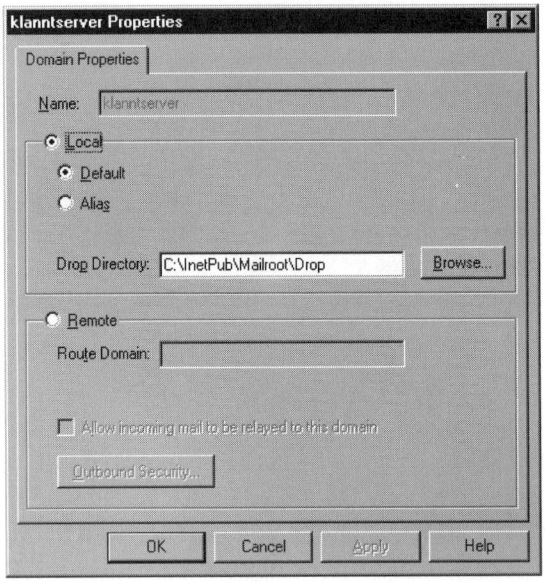

Every machine must have at least one default local domain, so you cannot use the Alias or Remote radio buttons for the default domain. However, you can change the default \Drop directory for the domain. You can also create additional domains for the SMTP service.

Using the SMTP Server Service to Process Mail

After you run the installation program, the SMTP service will already be set up to serve the default domain without any special configuration. Users specifying the server as the SMTP server in their domain can send mail directly to the server. Users who name the SMTP server as their SMTP server can also mail to anyone else who is using the same server. However, if you configure your favorite e-mail program to use the new SMTP server (for example, Outlook Express), when you try to send e-mail to anyone outside of the domain, you will receive the error message shown in Figure 6.4 (from an Outlook dialog box).

Figure 6.4 The "unable to relay" error message

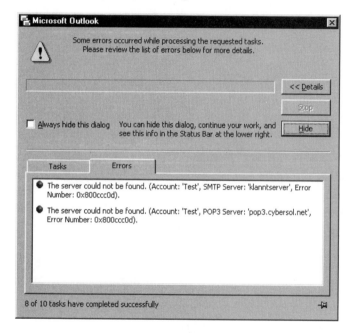

This error message is a bit convoluted and probably has more information than is absolutely necessary; but the point of the whole thing is that, for some reason, the SMTP server was unable to send the message out to the target SMTP server (a process called relaying). The problem occurs because the SMTP server, at least at this point, has no idea where the target domain (cybersol.net in the case of Figure 6.4) is located. The server needs to look up the MX record for cybersol.net by using a DNS server, and to relay the e-mail message to the SMTP server responsible for receiving incoming e-mail for that domain.

By default, the SMTP server service will not relay e-mail to any domain not configured in the SMTP site. This default setting prevents unrestricted transmittal of unauthorized messages, which is a more significant problem than you might imagine. In fact, the cable modem service that we use to access the Internet recently had to reconfigure its SMTP settings because they did not initially block relaying, and the system was flooded for five straight days by a company sending marketing spam out to the better part of the entire Internet!

The way around this particular restriction is to either create a remote domain or to change the settings in the Relay Restrictions dialog box, which is opened from the Directory Security Property page of the SMTP site.

You can go to the Relay Restrictions dialog box and choose the Allowed To Relay option, which will allow the relaying to continue. If you do this, the message will successfully leave your e-mail client and seem to have been transmitted. However, if you open the Queue directory, you will find that the message still exists in that directory, and that another file—an RTR file—has also been created by the SMTP service. Closer examination will reveal that the system is still unable to transmit e-mail to an outside server because it still does not know how to reconcile the provided domain name (cybersol.net) to an actual IP address.

At this point, it is important to note that if you have IIS installed on the NT system and you are connected to the Internet, it is likely that your NT networking setups include references to one or more DNS computers. More specifically, and as discussed in Chapter 2, if you have a local NT Server that is running the DNS service, it includes entries, at a minimum, for the nine root domain servers used to perform Internet domain name resolution in the United States. These are in the cache.dns file. Should such a situation exist, SMTP will transmit the file successfully without any further problems, presuming that the target address is valid.

Configuring the SMTP Site

You will need to manage site properties when setting up your SMTP site. To begin working on these properties, right-click the Default SMTP Site entry and choose Properties from the resulting pop-up menu. This opens the Default SMTP Site Properties dialog box. You can configure the properties for the Default SMTP site within this dialog box.

Setting Site Properties for the Default Site

The first page of the Default SMTP Site Properties dialog box includes information about ports to use, site description, IP address, and so on. By default, the SMTP server will use port 25 for all addresses assigned to the machine. You can change this default port by clicking the Advanced button. This opens the Advanced Multiple SMTP Site

Configuration dialog box, where you can configure the site to listen on different ports and on different IP addresses. You might do this in the event of a machine with multiple IP addresses, such as a multi-homed Web server. But this isn't the best idea because the SMTP protocol of other computers on the Internet always assume that your server uses port 25 as the location of the SMTP service. Figure 6.5 shows the Default SMTP Site Properties dialog box.

Figure 6.5   The Default SMTP Site Properties dialog box on the first page

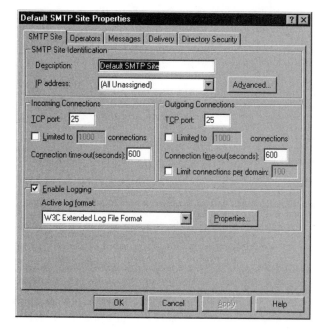

If you want your server to work correctly, you will want to carefully manage the connection properties. The more powerful the server, the more connections it can handle. Similarly, less powerful servers may not be able to handle more than 1,000 connections. The SMTP Property page lets you specify inbound and outbound connections, as well as timeout values for disconnecting idle transmission sessions.

The SMTP Site Property page also lets you set the standard logging operations that are an important part of every service installed with IIS. As with WWW, FTP, and NNTP (which you will learn about in Chapter 7), the mail server can generate logs in different formats with different log rotation frequencies.

Setting Up Security Accounts for the SMTP Site

By default, anyone who is a member of the Administrators group can administer the SMTP server. Additionally, if you have Administrator rights, you can grant permissions for other users or groups who can administer the server from the Operators tab.

Setting Message Properties for the SMTP Site

You can configure generalized information about messages from the Messages tab of the Properties dialog box. For example, to prevent the server from accepting huge amounts of data from clients, you might want to limit the size of messages being sent to the server by indicating limits in the Maximum Message Size and Maximum Session Size dialog boxes. The Maximum Message Size parameter specifies a limit on the message size that the SMTP service will accept. If a message is larger than this limit, it will not be accepted.

Some mail applications may attempt to avoid this limitation by sending files that exceed the limit in smaller blocks, essentially creating a series of e-mail messages. If all the messages being forwarded in a single session—that is, in the series of e-mail messages— exceed the limit that you specify in the Maximum Session Size, the SMTP server will cut off the client's connection and will either transmit all of the information already received or will discard it all.

> **WARNING**   As you might expect, the Maximum Session Size parameter must be larger than the Maximum Message Size parameter.

The limits that you set on message and session size will apply not only to clients directly connecting to this server but also to other servers trying to relay messages to the server. These SMTP servers might be transmitting several messages over a single connection, so the amount of transferred data can easily exceed the Maximum Session Size if you set it to be too small. Therefore, you should choose this size carefully—2, 5, even 10MB files are common in today's Internet. It is best to minimize the negative impact that the settings have on your users, so try to think about your intended use before setting this option.

After a disconnect, remote servers will try to resend the message. When the connection is closed by your SMTP server because the Maximum Session Size is exceeded, the remote server will immediately try to reconnect and resend the messages. This process is repeated by the servers until the messages are successfully transmitted or until some other third parameter, such as a maximum number of retries, is reached.

The number of messages per connection is another performance-related parameter whose value you can set on the Messages Property page. If there are many messages to send, it could be worthwhile to make your server establish several connections. This enables multiple messages to be sent simultaneously, instead of individually, in sequence, over a single connection. This message limitation will apply only to outgoing connections from the server (relays).

> **TIP** To gain some decision-making information for determining a proper number of messages per connection, you should use the Windows NT Performance Monitor. Look at the Messages Sent per Second Counter of the SMTP Server Object in the Performance Monitor. The limit that you set should be less than the maximum values that Performance Monitor displays.

You can also limit the maximum number of recipients for a single message from this page. This is useful for ensuring that no one is using your bandwidth for large block e-mails. The Internet standard specifies that if a message is sent to more than 100 users, the originator should receive a non-delivery report (NDR). However, IIS SMTP actually creates additional connections and sends the additional addressees down the new connections.

Setting Mail Delivery Properties for the Site

As you might expect, the Delivery property page lets you specify delivery-specific properties. As you saw earlier in this chapter, when a message can't be delivered after the first try, it goes back to the Queue directory. The server will try to resend the message the number of times specified on the Delivery Property page and will wait the amount of time specified on the same page between redelivery attempts. Whenever the maximum number of attempts has been reached, an NDR is sent to the originator, and the message is removed from the Queue directory.

Before a message is eventually delivered to its destination, it is entirely possible (even likely) that it will be routed through many different domains and, as such, will be handled by many different servers. Each server that the message encounters as it transits domains is treated as a single hop. The number of hops can be determined by looking in the Received fields in the message header. Each server handling the message adds its own Received header to the e-mail message. As soon as the number of hops exceeds the preset limit that is specified on the Delivery page, an NDR is generated.

Understanding and Using a Masquerade Domain   By default, the SMTP server will stamp its default domain name on e-mail message headers. However, you may want to avoid this and display another domain name in the header. Changing the domain makes the message look as though it was sent from someplace other than its originator—a feature that is both good and bad, depending on the situation. To change the domain stamp, you must enter a custom value in the Masquerade Stamp setting.

Using masquerade domains makes sense when you have a large number of domains within your organization that are distributed widely but you want all e-mail from users within the organization to appear to outside parties as if it came from the same location.

Setting the Fully Qualified Domain Name   The Delivery Property page also lets you set your machine's fully-qualified domain name. By default, this name is automatically taken from the information in the DNS configuration tab or from the TCP/IP properties in the Network Control Panel applet.

Fully-qualified domain names are important to ensure that delivery works correctly. If, for some reason, your system supports TCP/IP and the Domain Name system, but you want your fully-qualified name to be different than the domain name, you can set this here. Unfortunately, we can't provide you with any good examples of when you would do this—in fact, it is uniformly bad policy and has the potential to cause serious confusion within your organization, making your administration task that much more difficult.

Specifying a Reverse Lookup

It is possible to prevent mail spoofing (a technique where individuals fake return addresses and even SMTP domain information). When the Perform Reverse DNS Lookup On Incoming Messages option is selected, the server will verify (by doing a reverse DNS lookup) that the IP address for the domain inserted in the From header matches the original IP address in the header. When the lookup is successful, the domain name is inserted in the Received field. When the lookup is unsuccessful, only the IP address is shown. This security feature, however, will substantially slow down the performance of a busy server.

Setting Outbound Message Security

The SMTP server can use various security schemes and techniques for its outbound connections. The capability of varying your security measures increases the computer's level of security (that is, resistance to attack) when sending e-mail. There are two options for security: You can make a selection for the entire site or one for each domain that the server is configured for. SMTP can either use clear text authentication (similar to basic authentication for the Web server) or Windows NT Challenge/Response authentication.

> **NOTE**   It is important to recognize that only Microsoft client programs, such as Internet Explorer or Microsoft Outlook, can take advantage of the Windows NT Challenge/Response security model.

You can also implement Transport Layer Security (TLS) encryption. TLS is the outbound connection that is equivalent to Secure Sockets Layer (SSL) encryption. To take advantage of TLS support, both machines (the SMTP server and the relay target) must have a secure key pair installed that match each other. You will learn more about SSL and its associated Microsoft technology, Microsoft Certificate Server, in later chapters.

Setting Security Options for Inbound Connections to the SMTP Site

On the Directory Security tab of the Default SMTP Site Properties dialog box, you can configure server security for inbound connections. This page is the corollary to the outbound Connection Security tab discussed in the previous section.

The options on this page are also very similar to the options of other services you have configured, such as WWW and FTP. In addition to authentication schemes used for inbound connections and the ability to set data encryption parameters using TLS and IP address restrictions, the mail server also includes the relay restriction, which you learned about earlier in this chapter.

By default, the mail server does not permit mail relays for any connections, unless an incoming connection has been successfully authenticated.

Using a Smart Host with SMTP

You can solve some of the problems detailed in earlier sections of this chapter by using a powerful feature of the IIS SMTP service called a *smart host*. A smart host is a machine that processes all outgoing messages bound for remote domains rather than sending the messages directly to the domain. A smart host can act as a mail gateway for the company because it is connected to both the Internet and intranet simultaneously. Therefore, it can easily resolve different types of domains and transmit successfully to each of them.

The smart host will also run the SMTP service and has simultaneous connections to the internal LAN and to the Internet. All you have to do is configure the local SMTP service so that it passes messages for all remote domains to the local smart host, essentially using the smart host as a mail gateway. When the smart host is configured correctly, all outgoing messages to unknown domains are sent to it for processing.

If you do use a smart host, you might have a situation in which it makes sense to route most domains through a smart host, but you have other domains whose servers you can access via more efficient routes. In such a case, you have to create new entries for the domains that you know about and indicate a routing domain for each newly created domain. E-mail for those domains will be routed through the routing domain instead of through the smart host.

Creating Remote and Routing Domains

The MMC lets you create a new domain for the default SMTP site through the New Domain Wizard. To display this wizard, right-click the Default SMTP Site in the MMC, choose New, and then select Domain. The wizard will ask you for two pieces of information: the domain type (local or remote) and the domain name.

You can also establish remote domains as routing domains by manipulating the Remote Domain Properties option. The option can be accessed by right-clicking the remote domain in the MMC and selecting the Properties option from the pop-up menu. A *routing domain* lets you specify a route to an intermediate domain that may be more efficient than going to the smart host. You will generally use routing domains only for those domains that you *do not* want to transmit to through the smart host.

SMTP in the Enterprise

While SMTP services are important and useful, many enterprises find the need for a more complete e-mail solution, such as Microsoft Exchange Server or Microsoft Site Server, which both provide extended SMTP support, as well as POP3 support. However, for many smaller enterprises, SMTP support (particularly when coupled with an ASP solution like the one shown earlier in this chapter) can be very useful. Moreover, some smaller companies find that an outbound-only e-mail solution is an effective marketing tool, which also protects against undesired flow of personal e-mail into the enterprise. Using SMTP Services in this manner can be very useful.

Recently, we used SMTP services effectively in another manner. A company where we deployed an Internet solution wanted to generate auto-responder e-mails to their clients without going through their primary mail server. Their Web server was outside their network firewall, over which they had blocked some types of transmissions. They were already tunneling through a conduit to write information to a database and didn't want to do it again for mail services.

The Problem

The challenge was setting up their Web server and associated mail services so that the server would support outbound mail only. We also had to make sure that no additional tunneling through the firewall was required. Finally, we had to ensure that our solution did not clog their existing mail services by using the necessary levels of transmissions to support an unknown number of Internet responders.

The Solution

We enabled SMTP services on the Web server and added some additional tables to the database and an update query to the site itself so that the customer would have a permanent record of every e-mail sent out by the auto-responder.

Summing It Up

Deploying SMTP services on the Web server allowed us to avoid firewall issues, reduce traffic inside the network, and avoid clogging the enterprise's main server. Furthermore, by configuring the SMTP server correctly, we did not have to create support for incoming mail. Additionally, by disabling relaying, we were able to ensure that no one else could access the SMTP server in order to send their own mail.

24seven **CASE STUDY**

7

Working with IIS News Services

IIS is a complete Internet tool with support, in the form of Windows NT Services, for a wide variety of Internet protocols and standards. The Network News Transfer Protocol (NNTP) and the news server that IIS includes, which you can use to implement the NNTP protocol in your network, are an integral part of IIS. News servers provide an intuitive and widely used means of creating a simple collaborative environment. This environment (and its underlying protocol) let you create bulletin boards and similar areas where people can engage in online discussions.

NNTP Services

Microsoft's NNTP Service—like other services, such as the SMTP Service—is powerful and robust enough to support thousands of users. In a news server implementation, the service is robust enough to support thousands of *concurrent* users accessing the news feed simultaneously.

> **NOTE** The Microsoft News Server is also commonly referred to as the NNTP Service.

The NNTP Service over IIS is implemented in accordance with the Internet Standard Network News Transfer Protocol. NNTP not only lets users access bulletin boards and read and post articles, it also enables IIS to communicate with other news servers on the Internet in order to supply a *news feed*. Basically, a news feed refers to the ability of multiple news servers to exchange news articles with each other (such articles are often referred to as messages, or, in end-user jargon, as *posts*).

Internet News Delivery Systems

Before the introduction of the World Wide Web, one of the things that made the Internet popular—and still does for many people—was the way it enabled a virtually unlimited number of users to exchange news and other public information. One way to exchange this information is to use mailing lists, another way is to use a news system. In the following few sections, we will explore both potentialities, along with their advantages and disadvantages.

Internet Mailing Lists

A *mailing list* contains the e-mail addresses of all of the list's subscribers—that is, everyone who wants to receive all the information posted to the list. An e-mail message sent to the mailing list is sent to each member of the list. The latest mailing list software maintains the list of subscribers automatically. The mailing list member reads the post to the mailing list inside of their e-mail client, just like a regular e-mail message.

A subscriber can simply send e-mail to the mailing list using a special keyword that is specified by the list manager (such as *delete* or *subscribe*) in the message text to remove or add their e-mail address to the list. However, even if a mailing list system is fully automated, it can have serious drawbacks. A great deal of overhead is required to update and maintain an accurate list of e-mail addresses for members. The system administrator (whether computer or human) needs to closely manage address changes. Also, resending each e-mail message to all subscribers could easily generate huge amounts of network traffic. A better solution is to use some method of centralized storage and distribution.

USENET News

Many of today's news servers take advantage of the USENET Internet news system, which offers the benefits of centralized news storage and easy distribution. The cornerstone of this system is a single news server that contains the entire news repository. Clients connect to the news server and view a list of news article headers, which are similar to e-mail headers. If the client wants to read a particular article, they can download the entire article from the server.

Clearly, the USENET mail system has significant advantages over the mailing list structure. For example, clients with limited disk space can select only the messages they want to read from the list of articles stored on the server. The entire overhead of news processing now rests on a single news server computer. Centralized news storage necessitates the introduction of a specific protocol to describe commands used by a client to post new articles, enumerate a server's newsgroups, and perform other tasks that are not required with the Internet mailing list system. NNTP is the protocol used by news clients and servers. This protocol is just complex enough to accomplish news-related tasks, but it doesn't have to worry about establishing reliable client-server connections and other lower-level tasks. Like HTTP, NNTP rides on top of TCP, which takes care of the mundane tasks of establishing connections, verifying data delivery, and so on. The news server runs a specific background process that awaits client connections on the news port (by default, port 119) and services them when they arrive. IIS implements the news server using the NNTP Service.

News Distribution

News clients, such as Outlook Express or Netscape Messenger, use NNTP to connect to a centralized host to read and post news articles. As you'll recall from earlier discussions, the Internet consists essentially of many interconnected LANs.

For example, the LAN maintained by the University of Nevada, Las Vegas, is connected to the LAN maintained by the University of California, Los Angeles. The USENET architecture specifies that each LAN can have only one centralized news "host." (We refer to it in quotes here for the simple reason that, in most cases, the LAN will have multiple hosts, which perform the role of backups, or "slaves," to provide redundancy—but the network can recognize only a single news host as the primary.) For the purposes of this discussion, let's assume that we are working with two centralized news servers, `news.unlv.edu` and `news.ucla.edu`. Because of the way the USENET feeds work, a graduate student's question that is posted on a public newsgroup on the `news.ucla.edu` news feed will eventually make it into the same public newsgroup that is displayed on a Ph.D. candidate's computer that is accessing `news.unlv.edu`.

Understanding the way in which a news article posted on a single centralized host gets to another host, which is possibly located on the other side of the world, is at the core of understanding NNTP and the power of USENET. Individual news servers are interconnected with each other; however, there are so many news servers on the Internet that they can't possibly be interconnected with all of the other news servers that exist. Aside from being an ongoing management nightmare (because you have to continue adding news servers each time a new one comes online), such an arrangement would be prohibitively slow.

Instead, each news server connects to a certain number of other news servers, including common, shared servers that are often referred to as *intermediate hosts*. These intermediate hosts have connections to a large number of other news servers and propagate the information to the servers. In this way, the message will still make it from one server to the other even if the two servers never connect to each other directly.

The manner that NNTP uses to feed news from one machine to the next is also very important. Because a server can be connected to more than one peer, sending the entire news database from one server to another doesn't make any sense. For example, if Server A receives news messages in the `alt.rec.collecting.stamps.discuss` group from Server B, Server A has to discard all of this content when it receives it again from Server C. This wastes the bandwidth that is used to transmit and receive the entire network database on both ends. Needless to say, if you multiply this model by the thousands—the number of NNTP servers in existence on the Internet—you can see what an incredible waste of transmission space, computer power, and processing time this would be.

Instead, NNTP uses a more sensible alternative, rather than this flooding scheme. The receiving host obtains a list of new articles from the sending host and then decides which articles it needs to receive. Usually, the system administrator can configure the news server to receive certain groups only from certain hosts.

You can create a simple model of the Internet NNTP news feed that looks similar to Figure 7.1. Clients connected to `news.unlv.edu` post messages to the news server. The news server sends the posts to an intermediate server, such as `news.uunet.net`. The intermediate server sends the posts to the `news.ucla.edu` news server, thereby creating a virtual connection between the two clients.

> **NOTE**   It is important to understand that, as with mail services, the support for NNTP over IIS is limited. Other servers can connect to the IIS machine and receive news; however, the IIS machine cannot receive news articles from other servers. In fact, the only way to build newsgroups on IIS NNTP is from client submissions. If you want full newsgroup support, you should purchase the Microsoft Commercial Internet System (MCIS), Microsoft Site Server, or a comparable product.

NNTP Over IIS

Now that you better understand the ways in which the Internet implements NNTP, let's take a look at some of the specifics of NNTP over IIS.

An Internet news system is organized in the form of thousands of articles on a wide variety of topics. To provide order for the thousands of articles, messages are combined by topic into *newsgroups*. An individual news server, such as an IIS implementation with

Figure 7.1   The simple model for NNTP transmissions over the Internet

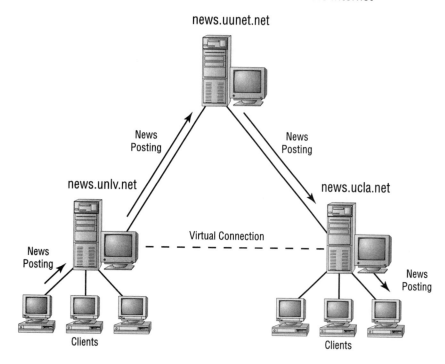

NNTP, is the list of newsgroups and the database of news articles residing on the server. As soon as a newsgroup is created, the user can connect to the news server and start posting messages. The NNTP Service keeps track of when posted articles were created and when they should be deleted, and it uses expiration policies to enforce an article's lifetime. By creating more than one expiration policy, you can establish different rules for different newsgroups.

For example, on the `klsent` IIS server, we created a few newsgroups for internal use only, including the `klsent.book.chapters` and `klsent.book.graphics` newsgroups. Using newsgroups in this manner lets us make notes to each other without needing a two-way communication method, such as a phone line.

As part of the setup for each news server, you specify how long to save each article in the newsgroup, using expiration policies. As the administrator, you can set service rules to govern the length of time that the server will retain the message. Once the news server expires an article, it deletes it from the server. Setting reasonable lifetimes prevents the news server from becoming clogged with old articles that no longer have meaning.

An NNTP server is often valuable within a corporate intranet—particularly if you don't use a groupware product, such as Exchange Server or Lotus Notes. Such a server can become an excellent centralized location for posting important corporate or department information. Many companies use internal newsgroups for posting human resources bulletins, providing upcoming corporate event information to users, and even for creating use groups for project management purposes. If your corporate LAN/WAN is extensive—that is, if you have multiple networks in multiple physical locations—use of news servers can easily support distributed discussions and reduce telephone and other communications costs, such as faxes. Additionally, newsgroups are often a better solution than simple e-mail because they provide a centralized message store and a history of postings to the newsgroup itself.

Installing the NNTP Service

The first step in implementing the NNTP Service on your IIS machine is to install it. To install NNTP from the NT Option Pack CD-ROM, follow these steps:

1. Choose the Custom option because the NNTP Service is not installed by either the Minimal or the Typical installation selection.

NOTE If you initially installed IIS with either the Minimal or Typical selection, or if you did a custom install without including NNTP, you can add NNTP by choosing the Add/Remove Components option within the Service Pack Setup program.

2. Select IIS from the Components list.

3. Click the Show Subcomponents button.

4. In the Internet Information Service dialog box, select the Internet NNTP Service option from the list.

5. Click the Show Subcomponents button again to display the Internet NNTP Service dialog box. Notice that the dialog box displays two components: the service and the service documentation. Make sure you install both; you will most likely find that you need the service documentation in the future.

6. After selecting both components, click OK on all the dialog boxes to continue the installation.

Directory Structure Selections for the NNTP Service

The NNTP Service installer creates two separate directory trees that will be used by the NNTP Service. The first, \InetPub\News, contains all of the HTML-based administration files, scripts, and other necessary management files for the NNTP Service. The second, \InetPub\nntpfile, will contain all the information pertaining to the news database(s) that you will administer from the NNTP Service. As soon as you complete the NNTP Service installation, new files are created directly under `\InetPub\nntpfile`. These files are used exclusively by the NNTP Service to perform tasks, such as maintaining an internal *hash table* for news articles and indexing files with auxiliary article information.

A hash table is a special data structure that is used to organize large amounts of data (such as a news database) when different data items (such as individual articles) must be quickly accessed. Each data item has an identifier (such as an article ID) that is used to locate the entire item (such as the text of the article). The news server uses the hash table to convert an identifier or a key that is meaningful to the user to a value which the service uses to compute the location of the corresponding element in the table-like structure. The files contain enough information to enable the server to rebuild a corrupted news database (not that this database is likely to become corrupted).

Usually, the administrator does not need to directly access directories or files in `\InetPub\ nntpfile`. One directory that deserves special attention, however, is the `\InetPub\nntpfile\root`. The NNTP setup program automatically creates several groups in this directory during installation: `control.cancel`, `control.newsgroup`, `control .rmgroup`, and `microsoft.public.ins`. Every news server will create unique directory structures, depending on the newsgroups on the server; but each of them will be built automatically within the root directory.

Managing the NNTP Service

Once the NNTP Service is installed, you will need to configure it to suit your needs. However, compared to the Web server or even the FTP server, the NNTP Service is not highly customizable—most of its performance is dictated by NNTP. The most important of the minimal configuration options provided by the NNTP Service is the creation of newsgroups. Therefore, we will primarily focus on creation of newsgroups in this section.

As with any component of IIS, the NNTP Service can be managed using more than one tool. With the news server snap-in, the MMC enables you to manage the news server on your local computer, as well as any other news server installed on the same local area network, or within the same domain, or in a trusted domain. Using the HTML-based administration tools, you can manage news servers over the Internet; you don't need any special software other than a Web browser. The HTML-based administration pages are accessible from your Start menu or by navigating to `http:///computername/news/admin`.

NOTE By default, the Web server denies access to this URL by all IP addresses other than the loopback 127.0.0.1 (that is, the loopback from the browser on the local machine). If you intend to manage your news server using a Web browser, go to the Default Web Site in the MMC, locate the News virtual directory, and display the Directory Security page of the News Properties window. The list of acceptable IP addresses will appear.

To access the administration pages from the Start menu, follow these steps:

1. Go to Start ➢ Programs.
2. Select Windows NT 4 Option Pack ➢ Microsoft Internet Information Server ➢ Microsoft NNTP Service.
3. You will see the NNTP Service Manager (HTML) entry here.

Whether you are using the MMC or the HTML-based administration pages, keep in mind that only authorized users can manage the NNTP Service. You'll learn how to modify the list of users in the "Security Accounts" section, later in this chapter.

As you've seen in previous chapters, management tasks can be accomplished using either the MMC or the HTML-based administration pages. For simplicity's sake, the discussions in this chapter will focus on using the MMC to perform all management tasks. Unlike the more complex Web Publishing Service, the NNTP Service operates a limited set of logical objects: news site, newsgroup, expiration policy, and current session. The NNTP Service can support only a single site on the physical machine (unlike the WWW and FTP servers, which allow you to have multiple sites on the same machine). To support multiple news sites, you will need Microsoft Site Server or MCIS.

When you navigate to NNTP, the MMC will display the Default NNTP Site, expiration policies, directories, and current session objects. A list of newsgroups maintained by the NNTP Service isn't visible within the MMC, but you can access the newsgroup list by displaying the Default NNTP Site Properties dialog box.

Understanding and Managing Properties for the Default NNTP Site

All the configuration settings for the NNTP Service are accessible and manageable from the Default NNTP Site Properties dialog box, shown in Figure 7.2. To open this window, right-click the Default NNTP Site in the MMC and select the Properties option from the resulting pop-up menu.

Figure 7.2   The Default NNTP Site Properties dialog box

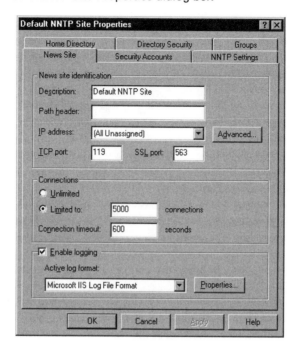

In the following sections, we will consider each of the tabs on the Default NNTP Site Properties dialog box individually. We will begin with the News Site tab, since that is the default selection.

Administering from the News Site Tab   The News Site page of the Default NNTP Site Properties window lets you change the news site identification information, connections, and logging properties. The Description entered here will be displayed in the MMC next to the news server icon. The Path Header describes how a news article is identified as it passes from server to server. Individual news articles are formatted much like an e-mail message—headers are followed by a message body. The message headers identify exactly how the news article appeared on the server, along with other useful information that is specified by the protocol.

News servers intercommunicate in order to propagate news articles among themselves. Every time a message hops from one server to the next in its path, that news server's name is added to the path header. For example, in the case of our `klsent` server, the default entry for the path header would be something like `news.klsent.com`. You can change the default entry from the News Site tab. However, this is generally only done if you are transmitting spam from your news server, or if you want to alias the news server for your internal network.

By default, the NNTP Service uses TCP port 119 for unencrypted (plain-text) transmissions. If you are using SSL, those transmissions occur through port 563. These ports are known to all news clients, thereby allowing users to connect to the servers without knowing in-depth configuration information. The MMC will let you change the default ports; but without a good reason—perhaps a security consideration—you generally will not do so. Doing so requires you to reconfigure your clients appropriately so that the clients know what port to look on for news information.

Similar to the Web and FTP services, you can run the NNTP Service on a machine with more than one network card or with more than one IP address assigned to the same card. The default IP Address setting (All Unassigned) accepts connections destined to all configured IP addresses. You can change this setting by simply choosing another option from the list box. Clicking the Advanced button displays the Advanced Multiple News Site Configuration dialog box, which gives you access to other powerful features. Using this dialog box, the administrator can specify pairs of IP addresses and ports—allowing you to control access to the news server based on the IP address the client is connecting with.

The Connections area of the News Site tab lets you specify the number of connections the NNTP Service will accept. You can either allow an unlimited number of connections or specify an upper limit on the number of concurrent connections.

The Connections Timeout option specifies a time limit after which inactive clients will be disconnected. By default, this value is 600 seconds. The server will automatically disconnect clients after 10 minutes of inaction on their part.

Like any component of IIS, the NNTP Service can generate extensive activity logs. These log files contain detailed information about connecting clients, issued commands, and the completion status of commands. The NNTP Service supports the same variety of log settings and formats as the Web and FTP servers do, and most of the same logs as the SMTP server. The first step in generating log information is to select the Enable Logging check box on the News Site page. The second step is to log permissions on individual directories that the news contents are stored in. To do this, you need to learn how to set directory properties, which is discussed in the next section of this chapter.

NOTE   Logging information is an important part of any administrator's duty list for effective management. In later chapters, we will talk about some of the benefits of logging and will consider some of the security issues that logging can help you to address.

Using the Home Directory Tab   Similar to the services you have looked at previously, the NNTP Service has a root directory and virtual directories. However, the function of these directories in the NNTP Service is somewhat different. The NNTP Service uses the root directory and virtual directories to store the messages that compose the newsgroups. The directory structure under the NNTP root directory mimics the newsgroups that the news server hosts. The name of a specific newsgroup can be obtained by traversing the directory tree. For example, the newsgroup `klsent.iisproxy.chapters` could be found three layers down in the tree, under the `\klsent\iisproxy\chapters` directory tree. By default, the NNTP Service creates an initial, or home, directory in the `\InetPub\nntpfile\root` directory. It is possible, however, to spread directories representing newsgroups across multiple hard drives, multiple directories, or even multiple computers. (In which case, the directory hierarchy would have to appear somewhere other than under `\InetPub\nntpfile\root`.) You might do this in the event there is insufficient hard drive space in the default location; you might also do it for other reasons specific to your environment. You will accomplish this task by creating a virtual directory.

To create a virtual directory, right-click the Default NNTP site icon in the MMC and choose Virtual Directory from the New menu. IIS will prompt you for two important pieces of information: the newsgroups that should be hosted in this virtual directory and the physical location of the directory itself. To see a list of virtual directories associated with a site, click the Directories folder in the MMC window.

You can locate both the home and virtual directories on the local machine or on another computer within your network. The properties for the home directory are controlled through the home directory page of the Default NNTP Site Properties window. The properties for virtual directories, however, are controlled through the Virtual Directory page of the Properties window for the virtual directory in question. You can access this page by right-clicking the virtual directory inside the MMC and choosing the Properties option from the resulting pop-up menu. Figure 7.3 shows this page.

The directory path for the virtual directory is specified in the Local Path edit box. If you check the A Share Located On Another Computer option, the browse button will become a Connect As button, and the Local Path box will change to a Network Directory box. The Network Directory path is specified by using its Uniform Naming Convention location (for example, `\\`*computername*`\`*share*) and valid user credential, which you must enter in the Network Directory Security Credentials dialog box. This dialog box is displayed when you click the Connect As button.

Figure 7.3   The Virtual Directory tab for the properties of virtual directories

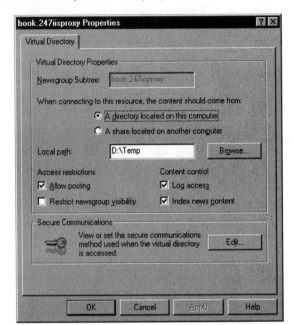

The Access Restrictions and Content Control check boxes affect the user's ability to post articles in the specified directory (actually in all newsgroups hosted under the specified directory). Restricting the newsgroup visibility causes news clients to not show newsgroups when the client does not supply a user name and password and when the server does not support anonymous connections. When logging is enabled (which you learned how to do in the previous section), checking the Log Access check box forces the server to create a log entry for each client connection. If you are using Index Server (which you will learn about in Chapter 9), checking the Index News Content box will result in Index Server indexing all existing messages, making them searchable through the Web front end.

Under normal circumstances, NNTP is not a secure protocol—client and server exchange all information in unencrypted format, over the network. Such an arrangement may cause problems, particularly where the newsgroup contains sensitive information. In such an environment, you can click the Edit button in the Secure Communications area of the page to enforce secured connections, even to the extent of enforcing 128-bit secured connections.

Using the Directory Security Tab   The Directory Security page's name is not the most indicative of its purpose. This page actually lets you configure security parameters for the *entire* news site, not just the component directories of the site. The Directory Security page displays only two buttons—one which controls access and authentication methods, and one which controls restrictions on client connections.

By default, connecting clients don't have to provide a user name or password to connect to the NNTP server. Such a security structure works just fine for a public news site where anybody is welcome to connect and read the news. However, if a NNTP server is intended to be used only for private newsgroups, you will often want to require the user to enter his or her name and password. The NNTP Service is capable not only of restricting anonymous access but also of supporting different *authentication schemes*—methods that the client and the server negotiate and agree upon to transfer credentials from the client to the server. Clicking the Edit button in the Password Authentication Method area allows the administrator to disable anonymous access to the server. If anonymous access is disabled, one of the authentication schemes must be enabled.

Like the Web server, the NNTP Service supports three types of authentication: basic authentication (in which the user name and password are transferred as clear text), the NT LAN Manager (NTLM) authentication scheme (in which the actual user ID and password never traverses the physical network, only an encrypted version of each, and which we have also referred to as the NT Challenge/Response scheme), and client certificate-based authentication (in which the client is uniquely identified to the server over an encrypted connection by a *digital certificate*, a mathematical verification of identity). Unlike the Web server, NNTP does not let client and server negotiate schemes on the fly. If the server does not accept anonymous connections and is configured to accept basic authentication credentials, the news client must be configured to pass in the basic authentication information, or the login validation will fail.

Implementing access control to your NNTP server that is based on a user's credentials is a powerful security feature. Like the other components of IIS, the NNTP Service can restrict access based on the client's IP address or domain name. To set these restrictions, click the Edit button in the IP Address and Domain Name Restrictions area. The corresponding dialog box is essentially the same as the ones displayed by the Web and FTP Services and has the same function. In other words, if a user is trying to log in from a blocked domain, his or her possession of a valid password and user name does not matter because the blocking information is evaluated first.

Using the NNTP Settings Page   The NNTP Settings page is where the general server parameters are set. If posting is allowed (Allow Client Posting is checked), the news administrator can limit the size of a single article by using the Limit Post Size option. The administrator can also limit the total size of all posted articles across an established connection by using the Limit Connection Size option. (Both options are similar to their counterparts in the SMTP Service.) When setting these limits, don't forget to take file attachments into account. Many messages, particularly those on news servers, will include executable or other binary attachments (such as pictures). Attachments are encoded, so every character in a binary file could feasibly be represented by a printable character and can be included in the text of the news message. Attaching files can result in substantial increases in a message's size.

There are two places in the Default NNTP Site Properties dialog box where you can choose the Allow Post option—on the Home Directory or Virtual Directory page and on the NNTP Settings page. You can also control posting from the Properties windows of individual newsgroups. Configuring posting capability in three locations enables precise news server control. The Allow Post option on the NNTP Settings page has the broadest effect. The Allow Posting option on the Visual and Home Directory pages affects only newsgroups hosted along the specified path. The Properties window of the individual newsgroup affects only that newsgroup. Such a high level of granularity provides you with a very high level of control, as well.

News servers transfer news messages from one server to another. In a public newsgroup, this presumably takes place until the messages make it to every news server in the world. The NNTP Service over IIS is capable of providing a news feed to other servers, but it will not accept content from them. (This is a limitation of the service as it is packaged with IIS.) The Allow Servers To Pull News Articles From This Server check box controls the NNTP Service's ability to provide a news feed. Disabling it will result in no messages being transferred to other news servers.

When news servers exchange their contents, they can also send each other news articles that have special control headers or a CMSG string in their subject line. Such news articles can also be posted directly by a news client. These messages are called control messages and usually reside in a special newsgroup hierarchy on the server, such as `control` `.cancel` and `control.addgroup`. Control messages are used to ask the server to perform some administration task, such as creating newsgroups, deleting existing groups, or deleting certain messages. Control messages are transferred just like any other message; the message's author (client or manager) does not need to have any administration rights to your server. In a way, anyone who knows NNTP well can create control messages and force the server to manipulate groups and messages. This ability is not generally desirable for enterprise servers or any server that maintains secure groups, so you may want to uncheck the Allow Control Messages check box. Doing so will disable the server's ability to be managed by such messages.

If posting is allowed for specific newsgroups, a client can post any message it wants to (limited only by the size of the message). Again, this might not be the appropriate setting for all groups on your server. For example, suppose you have a newsgroup on your server, called `klsent.webdevelopment.companyone`, that is specifically related to a development project, which you could easily conclude was a Web front-end development project for the company named *companyone*. Before anyone posts a message, you may want to have the message reviewed by someone to ensure that it relates to the project in question. This task can be accomplished by making the newsgroup a *moderated newsgroup*. Articles posted to a moderated newsgroup don't show up on the server automatically. Instead, the news server forwards them to an e-mail address that you specify. The e-mail recipient—in this case, perhaps a project manager—reviews each message and decides whether to post it or delete it. This process ensures that only approved content is actually displayed on the newsgroup.

The SMTP Server for Moderated Groups option on the NNTP Settings page configures the mail server used by the NNTP Service to connect and send e-mail notifications regarding new postings. The Default Moderator Domain option specifies the domain to which the e-mail should be forwarded. In the event that the news server cannot deliver the notification of the new message successfully, it will generate an e-mail specifying the error and forward it to the news server administrator's e-mail account.

TIP   By default, e-mail from a news server does not contain any information in the From header. For non-delivery reports to be correctly sent to the e-mail administrator, you need to instruct the server to add a From header. To do so, you must perform a registry hack. Create a `MailFromHeader` key of type `DWORD` in the `HKEY_LOCAL_MACHINE\SYSTEM\CurrentControlSet\ Services\NNtpSvc \Parameters` tree, and set its value to 1.

Using the Groups Tab   Maintaining current newsgroups and creating new groups is the NNTP Service's primary purpose. You can administer group information from the Groups tab of the Default NNTP Site Properties dialog box. This page lets the administrator create a new group, adjust the properties of an existing group, or delete a group entirely from the server. In the Groups tab, click the Edit button to change the properties of a current newsgroup or click the Create New Newsgroup button to add a newsgroup to the server. Clicking either of these buttons will display the Newsgroup Properties dialog box, as shown in Figure 7.4.

Figure 7.4   The Newsgroup Properties dialog box

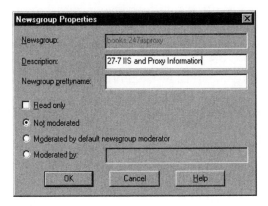

As you can see in Figure 7.4, newsgroups are identified to the server by both a name and a description. Some news browsing software also provides the group's nickname (or *prettyname*), so you will probably want to enter a simple name for the group in that field. The nickname can even contain foreign language characters (in Unicode). You can also create newsgroups that are read-only, meaning that clients won't be able to post messages to the group.

The Newsgroup Properties dialog box is the third place in NNTP Service administration where you can specify posting permission. If the server is moderated, the server needs to know where to send the new posting e-mail notifications. If the Moderated By Default Newsgroup Moderator option is selected, the server will automatically create an e-mail address in the following form:

`group@default_domain`

Group is the name of the current newsgroup, and *default_domain* is the moderator's domain, as specified on the NNTP Settings page (discussed in the previous section). If for some reason you want a single person to administer all groups on the server, you can enter the address of that individual in the Moderated By edit box.

NOTE   There is no place in this dialog box to specify the physical location of the newsgroup. The news server will decide on its own where to host newsgroups, based on its virtual directories or its default home directory location.

In the event that you have decided to support control messages on your server, newsgroup moderation comes in very handy in managing such messages. By default, the server has three control groups where control messages can be posted: `control.cancel`, `control.newgroup`, and `control.rmgroup`. By changing the properties of these groups and making them moderated, you can examine control messages before they affect the server. If a control message is approved, you can let it through; otherwise, you can delete the message. Making control groups moderated is, generally, a better solution than simply banning control messages—if for no other reason than because it helps you identify who might be trying to control your server without your approval.

Managing Site Administrators from the Security Accounts Page   By default, only members of the Administrators group are permitted to make changes to the NNTP Site properties. However, from the Security Accounts page, you can specify a list of users and/ or groups allowed to administer the SMTP Service. Note that these security settings will also apply to HTML-based administration.

Like the Web Publishing Service, the NNTP Service runs as the local System account and impersonates the anonymous user for all non-authenticated incoming connections. The server accesses news articles in the context of the IUSR_*servername* user—the default anonymous Internet user for the system. To avoid confusing the passwords, check the Enable Automatic Password Synchronization check box. IIS remembers the password entered in the service manager for IUSR_*servername* and the actual password in the user database for the IUSR_*servername* account.

Now that we have navigated the entirety of the Default NNTP Site Properties dialog box, let's move on to consider some of the other important issues with NNTP site administration. In the next section, you will learn more about expiration policies and their management.

Considering Expiration Policies

Expiration policies contain the rules that define the lifetimes of news articles—that is, how long they remain on your server before deletion. To view existing expiration policies, click the Expiration Policies icon in the MMC. To create a new expiration policy, rightclick the Default NNTP Site in the MMC and choose the pop-up menu's New option, Expiration Policy sub-option. The resulting wizard will require the following information for each new expiration policy that you create:

- The policy name.
- The newsgroups affected: all groups or selected groups only. If the policy will apply to selected groups only, the names of those groups must be entered. The wildcard character (*) can be used to denote *any*.
- Expiration conditions, including the total size of the newsgroup, the age of the article, or both.

A list of current expiration policies can be viewed in the MMC from the sub-tree under the Default NNTP Site. The expiration functions of the NNTP Service are controlled by two registry entries in the `HKEY_LOCAL_MACHINE\SYSTEM\CurrentControlSet\Services\NNtpSvc\Parameters` tree:

NewsCrawlerTime   The type is `REG_DWORD`. The default value is 30 minutes, which defines how often the server should search for expired articles as specified by the expiration policies.

NumExpireThreads   The type is `REG_DWORD`. The default value is 4, which specifies how many threads are used by the server to search for expired messages each time `NewsCrawlerTime` expires.

Viewing Currently Connected Users

Monitoring different aspects of server performance is an important administrative task that is performed on a regular basis. Several tools are available to the NNTP Site administrator that show past and present server status. Performance counters, available from the Windows NT Performance Monitor utility and the NNTP Service logs, can each provide a large amount of information about the server and its performance.

The MMC can also display a list of currently connected users. To view this list, click Current Sessions in the tree below the Default NNTP Site Object. If the server allows anonymous connections, the user name field will display a computer icon rather than an actual user name.

Corruption Recovery with NNTP

The NNTP Service is capable of hosting gigabytes of news (presuming that you have the hard drive space necessary to store all that information). News articles are stored in relatively small text files. To help speed performance, the news server uses auxiliary files to help organize potentially thousands of independent files in a searchable data structure. Even when messages are accidentally moved or deleted, the index and hash files still contain references to them and their original physical location. Moving groups to different directories without rebuilding the index file can cause the server to "forget" that it still has articles and not just empty newsgroups. To recover from such a situation, the NNTP Service provides a Rebuild option. To rebuild a server, you must first stop the NNTP Service. Once you have stopped the service, you can rebuild the newsgroups by right-clicking the site and choosing Rebuild Server from the Task options in the pop-up menu.

The dialog box provides three rebuild options:

Standard   The Standard option is the fastest. It rebuilds only the hash table file (GROUP.LST).

Medium   The Medium option rebuilds files that the server perceives to be faulty.

Thorough   The Thorough option rebuilds all files. It is the most time-consuming option.

Once a server is rebuilt, you can restart the NNTP Site from the MMC.

We have considered all the major components of an IIS Server installation—Web services, FTP services, SMTP Services, and NNTP Services. In the next chapter, we will consider some of the common add-on services that you will use with IIS, after which we will move on to a discussion of Index Server in Chapter 9.

24_seven_ **CASE STUDY**

Newsgroups as an Inexpensive Groupware Alternative

As outside consultants, we encounter a wide variety of corporate problems that must often be solved in unique ways. In general, our task is twofold: Find a solution to the problem that addresses and fulfills the majority of the company's goals, and find the most inexpensive way to deploy that solution on their behalf.

One of the most common situations we encounter is the small enterprise that believes it will find real value in some kind of groupware product, but cannot justify the substantial expense of a Lotus Notes- or Microsoft Exchange-based solution. We are often asked to provide alternative suggestions in such cases. Many times, we are even asked about the cost to develop a custom alternative.

Luckily, with the power of IIS and its supporting technologies in our court, we have been able to deploy semi-custom solutions at a minimal cost to the client and with minimal development time on our part for many of these situations. Our solution: to use NNTP with custom newsgroups, allowing for the posting and tracking of threads, conversations, progress reports, and more.

In a recent environment, the client wanted us to deploy secured newsgroups that would be simple and easy for individuals inside the department and up the project management chain to access, while ensur-

ing that the newsgroups could not be accessed by anyone who is not in the appropriate department.

The Problem

Creating a secured newsgroup situation where certain newsgroups were accessible by certain users; some users would have access to them all, but most users would only have access to some subset of the newsgroups maintained on the server.

The Solution

The solution was relatively simple. First, we removed support for anonymous logins from the newsgroups in question. Second, we moved each set of departmental newsgroups onto their own NNTP server, we created Windows NT groups corresponding to the servers, and we added users to the groups appropriate for their membership individually.

Summing It Up

Solving groupWare and information management issues is always a complex task; however, using all the tools at hand can often provide you with a useful and inexpensive solution to a problem. In the case of NNTP Services, you can use an interface familiar to most users (typically, their mail client) and a bulletin-board-style method of information sharing in order to simplify deployment and to keep costs low.

IIS Add-On Services

IIS is more than just an application to let you deliver HTML pages to remote clients and create FTP sites. It is also a full range of tools that help you to analyze the contents and performance of a server and monitor, to detect hits on the server, and even to create usage reports. In this chapter, you will learn about five add-on features to IIS and how you can use them to simplify management, to ensure sufficient scalability, and to make your site more user-friendly. While some of these services are relatively straightforward—such as the FrontPage Extensions—others are complex, powerful services that may form crucial segments in your overall enterprise solution. Effective use of these additional services can greatly simplify the design, maintenance, and administration of complex, multi-part Web sites, as well as the local technology necessary to support such implementations.

Considering Some Common Add-On Services

IIS also includes components that enable Web servers to accept uploaded files from a client using HTTP. Without the use of this pre-built component, you would need to write ASP scripts or ISAPI DLLs for the server to accept such files. Two major IIS components provide this extra functionality (among other features): Site Server Express, a scaled-down version of Microsoft's Site Server commercial product; and the FrontPage 98 Server Extensions, soon to be replaced (in many environments) with the FrontPage 2000 Server Extensions.

Site security is an increasingly important topic—particularly communications security, which guarantees the end-user a fully secure Internet connection. The most common technique for providing such a connection is through transmission encryption. The most common protocol for transmission encryption over the Internet is the Secure Sockets Layer (SSL).

You will often find, particularly in site deployments containing complex processing activities, that it is advantageous to use a mechanism that can store all of the information associated with a given task and ensure that the task will complete itself at some point in the future. Microsoft Message Queue Server (MSMQ) provides just such a service.

Although all of these add-on features relate to each other at some level, we will consider each of them separately for simplicity.

Understanding Microsoft's Site Server Product

Microsoft's Site Server Express is a product that ships with the Option Pack. However, you can purchase the full version of the product, called Site Server, from Microsoft. It is worthwhile to understand some of the differences between the two as you read the section on the Site Server Express product.

The full version of Microsoft Site Server creates several reports in addition to the summary report that is available in Site Server Express. Site Server also provides a full-featured version of Content Analyzer. With this version of the Content Analyzer, you can export a tree view of the site to an HTML file by choosing Export from the File menu in the Content Analyzer window. (This option is disabled in the Express version.) Doing this allows you to create an interactive HTML-based table of contents to a site in a single step.

Site Server Express can only generate and save the summary HTML report, but the full version can generate many different reports. With the full version of Site Server, it is possible for you to create reports that show all incoming and outgoing links, different media types (Java applets, .AVI files, and so on), broken links, and many other types of information. With Site Server Express, you can perform a variety of different searches on your site by choosing the Quick Search option from the Tools menu in the Content Analyzer window. You can perform searches and print out the results with Site Server Express; but if you want to export results to HTML, you must use the full version of Site Server. If you aren't satisfied with the predefined reports, the full version of the Content Analyzer allows you to create a custom search and export it to an HTML file.

Understanding Microsoft's Site Server Product *(continued)*

By choosing Display Options from the View menu, you can display as much or as little detail as you want. For example, you can filter the site by the various object types, such as HTML files, images, and so on. Publishing the report results will create a single file that contains only the information that you select from the possible filters. This file is automatically stored in a compressed form for easy e-mailing or copying to a diskette. However, this feature is not available in Site Server Express. In Express, the Publish item on the File menu is permanently disabled. The Site Server Express summary report does, however, provide a link to the top of the browser window that explains how you can upgrade to the complete version of Site Server.

Understanding the Site Server Express Product

Site Server Express incorporates report and analysis tools, as well as the Microsoft Posting Acceptor component. These tools will help you manage content and analyze usage on your server. This section takes a look at each of the tools and components of Site Server Express and their usage.

When you install Site Server Express, choose the Custom installation option. Next, choose Site Server Express from the list of items that appears in the Microsoft Windows NT 4 Option Pack Setup window. Click Show Subcomponents to display the Site Server Express window. The first two subcomponents support analysis features and the second two relate to publishing and file upload features.

Site Server Express creates only a summary usage report. Site Server Express does not create all the reports available in the full version of Site Server. The summary report in Site Server Express provides a link at the top of the browser window that explains how you can upgrade to the complete version of Site Server.

The Content Analyzer

The Content Analyzer is a tool available in Site Server Express that lets a Web Site developer represent a site visually. This tool is available to you only if you select the Analysis–Content subcomponent when installing Site Server Express. The cornerstone of Content Analyzer is the *WebMap*, which visually represents the entire Web site. In the WebMap, all hyperlinks to other pages are clearly shown to ease site management and repair (of a broken link, for example).

When you start the Content Analyzer, you must first connect to a valid URL. You do this by choosing New from the file menu, and then choosing Map from URL in the submenu in the Content Analyzer window. This example uses the virtual directory that contains the HTML-based help for the Windows NT Option Pack. The URL for this site is `http://localhost/IISHelp`. After the connection is established, the Content Analyzer starts exploring the Web site. It examines each file, image, and any other resource included in the site to create the WebMap. Depending on the number of files on the site, this process can take a long time. (On our machine, it took more than five minutes to explore the IIS Help file.) If you find yourself waiting too long to explore an unexpectedly intricate site, you can stop the Content Analyzer at any time by clicking Cancel in the Creating Map dialog box.

After the Content Analyzer has completed the exploration stage, it saves all the site's data in a special file. By default, this file is named *domain*`.WMP` and is located on your hard disk at `\Program Files\Content Analyzer Express\Reports`. The Content Analyzer can also save a summary report to an HTML document. The Content Analyzer generates HTML statistics of the selected site, which are stored in the *domain*`_SUMMARY.HTML` file in the same directory as the WMP file. The HTML report contains the link to the WMP file, named `WebMap For LocalHost`. (This is true only when connected to a local machine, in which case the domain name is *localhost*. However, if you instead connect to a machine named *www.microsoft.com*, the machine will create a file named `MICROSOFT_SUMMARY.HTML`.)

The Content Analyzer provides two distinct views of the site: a tree view on the left and a cyberbolic view on the right. The tree view is hierarchical. The home page is shown as the root, and the individual pages and other resources are represented as the leaves. The cyberbolic view accentuates the Web-like structure of the site. All links between objects, such as Web pages, are shown graphically in different colors. By default, black represents the main route—a main hyperlink from one page to another. Because there can be more than one way to move from one page to another, pages accessible by alternative routes are shown in green. Blue indicates an object residing on a different server—that is, an external link. Red indicates that the resource is unavailable—that is, a broken link.

NOTE To view the alternate routes, you must select the Show Alternate Routes option in the Display Options dialog box. You can access this from the View menu.

You can "surf" using either the tree view or the cyberbolic view and explore the set of interconnected documents in as much depth as you want.

You should now have an idea of what the Content Analyzer for Site Server Express can do. If you want the functionality provided by many of the grayed-out menu items, you can acquire and install the full version of Site Server.

> **NOTE**   If you haven't caught on by now, Site Server Express is intended to show you many of the features of Site Server. If your Internet site requires many of those Site Server features, you are likely well-served purchasing the full-version product.

IIS 4

PART 1

Usage Import and Report Writer

The Usage Import and Report Writer tools are aimed at a common objective: to generate a significant volume of statistical information about IIS, especially about the Web Publishing Service and the FTP Service. These tools are available to you only if you select the Analysis-Usage subcomponent when installing Microsoft Site Server Express.

The purpose of these tools is actually quite simple: Every time the WWW Service or the FTP Service processes a request, it creates a new entry in the log files for the server. The Usage Import application takes logs generated by IIS and converts them to a relational database—a Microsoft Access file. This .MDB file provides an efficient place to store and manipulate the logged data. Report Writer is a fancy front end for this database. Report Writer takes parameters either directly from the user or from predefined templates and uses them to query the database created with the Usage Import tool. The Site Server Express version of Report Writer does not allow you to create reports from scratch, although it does provide about two dozen report templates from which you can choose. Since the data is stored within an Access database, you can use the Access or Visual Basic IDEs to open the database and create your own reports directly against the data. Figure 8.1 shows the relationship between the IIS log files, the Usage Import tool, and the Report Writer.

When you install the tools, the installation program will create a default MSUSAGE.MDB database that initially does not contain information from your IIS logs. Once you run the Usage Import tool, the database will be populated with all the real data that the tool found within the logs.

> **TIP**   The original version (that is, without any data) of MSUSAGE.MDB can be found in its compressed form, template.zip, in the UA Express directory of your Program Files tree.

Figure 8.1   The relationship between the Usage Import tool, the Report Writer, and the IIS log files written by the WWW and FTP Services

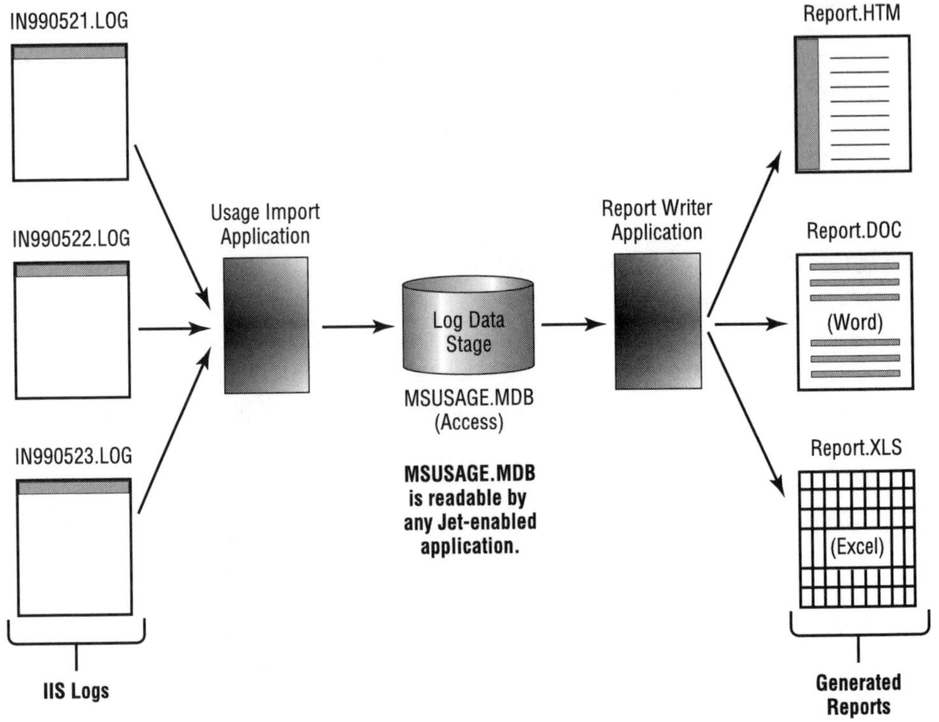

The Publishing Subcomponents

The last two subcomponents that you can install with Site Server Express are the Posting Acceptor and the Web Publishing Wizard. These tools do not deal with server statistics or usage analysis. Instead, the Posting Acceptor enables IIS to accept files posted to the server with the Web Publishing Wizard (on the client machines) or from other client applications.

For example, suppose an ISP lets users place their own Web pages onto the Internet by hosting those pages on the user's behalf. When users develop their own pages at home, they need to be able to transfer those pages from their home computer to the server at the ISP. The ISP could use FTP to provide this service; but many endusers probably are not familiar with the FTP protocol and may find it confusing.

A simpler solution for publishing pages exists and is supported by the Posting Acceptor subcomponent. The way it works is that the user encapsulates the data they want to upload within HTTP packets and sends it off to the server using the HTTP POST command, which the browser handles for the user automatically. After the data reaches the server, the server's responsibility is to save the data into a file (in the appropriate location). You could use a Perl script, an ISAPI DLL, or a CGI application to parse the data in the header and write it into separate files, as is appropriate. However, this solution is rather complex and, for that matter, clunky. It is simpler and more efficient to use the Posting Acceptor.

The Posting Acceptor is an ISAPI DLL that not only processes files transferred by the client, but also accepts several different kinds of transmissions, including standard HTTP-based transmissions and the Microsoft WebPost APIs. The WebPost APIs allow programmers to create client applications that perform file transferring actions between client and host computers. The Web Publishing Wizard installed with IIS and Personal Web Services, as well as the Microsoft File Upload Control, all make use of these APIs; so there is no need for you to write any code in order to use them. If you want your applications to have the ability to publish pages to the Web server, they can use the Web Publishing Wizard.

The FrontPage Server Extensions

When we first considered the usefulness of the Posting Acceptor in the previous section, we considered the example of a user who has the ability to develop but not host their own Web content. Instead, the user publishes the Web content to a directory on their ISP's server. This allows the content to be viewed on the Internet. We looked briefly at the Posting Acceptor, which is good for uploading small numbers of files and non-complex HTML (or HTML add-on) programs.

However, in today's marketplace, many users are able to use an application (such as Microsoft FrontPage) to create complex, active pages with powerful graphics and additional functionality built in. Developing such a site and transferring it to a Web server is not as simple as simply posting the pages.

While there are a great many tools to aid in Web Site development, we will consider FrontPage 98 (and 2000) and Visual InterDev 6 because they both bear heavily on our discussion of Server Extensions. Both products make it easier to upload your content once you have created it, but at a cost—the Web server must have the Front Page Server Extensions installed for your code to publish and run properly.

FrontPage Server Extensions are included with the Typical or Custom installation of the Microsoft Windows NT Option Pack. After FrontPage Server Extensions are installed and configured, the developer can use Visual InterDev or FrontPage Explorer to connect remotely to a server to design and deploy new sites and individual pages.

> **NOTE** It is worth recognizing that Microsoft has ported the FrontPage Server Extensions to a number of platforms and products, including the Alpha version of NT and Apache's Web server. Go to the Microsoft FrontPage Web site at www.microsoft.com/frontpage to find installation programs for the Server Extensions for other computers, operating systems, or Windows NT Servers running non-IIS server products.

FrontPage is a tool that simplifies Web site development. It features WYSIWYG editing capabilities, wizards to simplify development, and all of the other nice features that you have come to expect from Microsoft development tools. Moreover, the FrontPage Explorer lets you show entire Web sites in different views. For example, you can display the site as a set of directories or as a graphic with a Web-like structure.

FrontPage is a useful tool, but much of its power comes from its ability to manipulate built-in objects on the server. These built-in objects are installed as part of the FrontPage Server Extensions. The FrontPage Server Extensions are a set of CGI scripts that interact with the FrontPage frontend. FrontPage uses CGI scripts because of their ability to execute on multiple servers, as discussed in the earlier note.

The FrontPage Editor is a graphic HTML editor that simplifies the development of ASP, HTML, and even Internet Database Connector (IDC) files; and is also capable of inserting *FrontPage Components* onto a Web page. A FrontPage Component could be a simple hit counter or a much more complex, scheduled image that is displayed on the page on a specified schedule. All of the component's functionality is implemented at the FrontPage Server Extensions, which are administered by the FrontPage Server Administrator.

The FrontPage Server Administrator

The FrontPage Server Administrator is installed with IIS, or whenever you install the Server Extensions on a non-IIS machine. The server components do not require the entire FrontPage application—only the server-side scripts are needed. Server components are also used by other applications, such as Visual InterDev. The FrontPage Server Administrator application, shown in Figure 8.2, is located in the Internet Information Server group of the Windows NT Option Pack.

The FrontPage Server Administrator is fairly straightforward. If a Web server hosts more than one site, each site must have the server extensions installed. To install FrontPage Server Extensions, click the Install button and choose the correct server type. The dialog box shown in Figure 8.3 will appear.

Figure 8.2   The FrontPage Server Administrator application

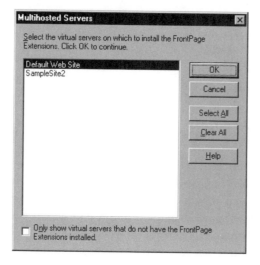

Figure 8.3   The Multihosted Servers dialog box

As you can see, this example installation of IIS includes two Web sites: a default Web site (the KLSENT Web site) and a test location, named SampleSite2. Clicking OK at this point will install FrontPage Extensions onto the Default Web site because it is the only Web site selected in the dialog box. The Upgrade and Uninstall options in the FrontPage Server Administrator dialog box are self-explanatory.

The FrontPage Server Extensions consist of many different CGI scripts. After you install the Server Extensions, you will likely notice some funny-looking directories (most of them start with an underscore) in your site's home directory. These directories are created by the FrontPage Server Extensions installation program and should not be modified or deleted. If some of the directories or files get deleted by mistake, you can use the Check and Fix option from the Administrator as your means of correcting the problem. There is no need to reinstall the entire set of Server Extensions from the CD-ROM. Instead, Check and Fix will review all of the Server Extensions and fix any problems that it locates.

If you want to disable authoring ability for a specific site, even when FrontPage Server Extensions are installed, you can do so by clicking the Authoring button. If authoring is disabled, FrontPage will not be able to connect to the specified site; instead, it will display an error message alerting the user to the fact that authoring has been disabled for the site in question.

Even when authoring is enabled, only designated users can edit the site. Clicking the Security button displays the Administrator Name and Password dialog box. The name of the account that you enter into the dialog box will be entered into the list of people who can edit this site.

To tighten security restrictions on a given server even further, you can enter an IP address or use the wildcard character [*] to specify a range of addresses from which authoring is allowed. The IP Address dialog box is accessed by clicking the Advanced button in the Security dialog box.

Using SSL for Secure Communications

Data transmitted using the HTTP protocol (the client-server protocol used to transmit information on the Web) is very easy to read because it is transmitted in a clear-text format. If you have a network analyzer, such as Microsoft's Network Monitor, you can see and interpret every HTTP request and response that a user makes. For most Web browsing, the capability to see what someone else is transmitting over the Web isn't a big deal because most Internet servers contain public information. However, sensitive, private data can be at risk because the data can be monitored and is not secure.

You can perform sensitive operations with a greatly reduced concern about a lack of privacy by establishing a secure underlying connection in which all of the data passing between any two machines is *encrypted*. The Secure Sockets Layer (SSL) and the Private

Communication Technology (PCT) protocols allow for a very secure link between two machines, such as between your server and client machines. This link not only keeps the data privileged, it also allows the two machines to authenticate each other.

Understanding Basic Principles of Encryption

Suppose you want to send a confidential message to your cousin over the Internet, and you do not want anyone who might intercept the message to be able to read it. To protect the message, you will *encrypt* or *encipher* it. You encrypt the message by changing the letters within the message in a complicated manner, rendering the message unreadable to anyone except your cousin.

You supply your cousin with a cryptographic key that your cousin will use to unscramble the message and make it legible. In a conventional *single-key* cryptosystem, you share the cryptographic key with your cousin *before* you use it to encrypt the message. (You may send it in another e-mail, mail him a copy, and so on.) For example, a simple single-key cryptosystem might shift each letter in the message forward three letters in the alphabet, with the SPACE character immediately following the letter Z (so the letter X would show up as a space in the cyphertext). For instance, the word DOG becomes GRJ. Figure 8.4 shows a one-line document encrypted with the single-key cryptosystem.

Figure 8.4   A line of text encrypted with a simple cryptosystem

> **NOTE**   Obviously, this is an extremely simple cryptosystem, about as secure as a cereal box decoder ring. Any cryptosystem you use—whether single key or public key—will, by nature, be substantially more complex.

Your cousin will get the message and shift all the letters back three letters in the alphabet to decrypt it, which would convert GRJ back to DOG. Figure 8.5 shows the key for the single-key encryption system used in Figure 8.4.

Figure 8.5   The decryption key for the simple cryptosystem

The Limitations of Conventional Single-Key Cryptosystems

In conventional single-key cryptosystems, both the transmitter and the receiver use a *single key* (the same key) for both encryption and decryption. Thus, the transmitter and receiver must initially exchange a key through secure channels so that both parties have the key available before they can send or receive encrypted messages over unsecure channels. Figure 8.6 shows a typical exchange using a single-key cryptosystem.

Figure 8.6   A line of text encrypted with a simple cryptosystem

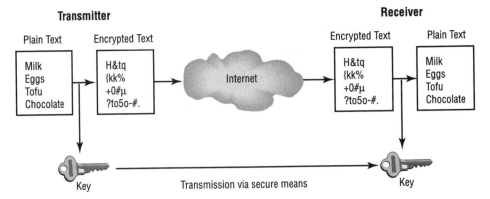

The primary flaw when you use single-key cryptosystems on the Internet is that they require that both parties know the key before each transmission. In addition, because you want only the recipient to have the ability to decrypt your transmissions, you must create different single keys for each individual, group, or business to which you transmit. Clearly, you will have to maintain an inconveniently large number of single keys. Also, if you use a secure channel for exchanging the key itself, you could simply transmit the data along the same secure channel (which defeats the purpose). However, most people do not have access to a secure channel and, therefore, must transmit the data along an unsecure channel. Modern-day cryptographic transmissions use a new type of cryptography, called a *public-key cryptosystem,* to avoid the issues that surround maintaining single-key cryptosystems.

Understanding Public-Key Cryptosystems

A *public-key cryptosystem* requires two related, complementary keys. You can freely distribute one key, the public key, to your friends, your business associates, and even to your competitors. You will maintain the second key, the *private key*, in a secure location (on your computer) and never release it to anyone. The private key unlocks the encryption that the public key creates, as shown in Figure 8.7.

Figure 8.7   The basic model of the public-key cryptosystem

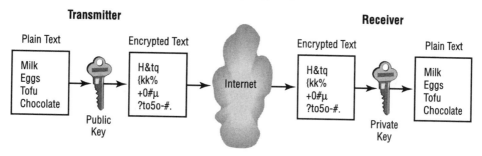

With a public-key cryptosystem, your cousin can publish their public key anywhere on the Internet or send it to you within an unencrypted e-mail. You can encrypt a message using your cousin's public key. After you have encrypted the message, only your cousin can decrypt it with their private key—even you, the sender (and encrypter), cannot decrypt the message. When your cousin wants to send a message back to you, your cousin will encrypt that message using *your* private key. Then, only you can decrypt your cousin's message with your private key.

The public-key protocol effectively eliminates the need for the secure channels that conventional single-key cryptosystems require. Two groups of individuals—Rivest, Shamir, and Adleman; and Diffie and Hellman—designed the fundamental algorithms governing cryptography within a public-key cryptosystem. You will learn more about the Rivest, Shamir, and Adleman (RSA) implementation in later sections in this chapter because it is one of the underlying protocols that you will use to implement SSL on your server.

Understanding Digital Signatures

Public-key encryption programs make extensive use of message authentication. *Message authentication* is a method that message recipients can use to verify a message's origin and validity. The message authentication process is relatively straightforward. The sender must use the sender's secret key to encrypt a unique value corresponding to the message's contents, thereby *signing* the message. The secret key creates a *digital signature* on the message that the recipient (or anyone else for that matter) can check by using the sender's public key to decrypt the digital signature.

With the process of digital signing, the message recipient can prove that the sender is indeed the true originator of the message. Because only the private-key holder can create a digital signature decryptable by the public-key, the digital signature guarantees the identity of the message sender. Moreover, because a digital signature processes the file and creates a unique number representative of the file's contents, date, time, and so on, the digital signature, when verified, proves that no one has modified the file during or after the transmission.

Understanding the Digital Signature's Construction

Signing programs generate the digital signature value through a two-step process. The receiving program uses a similar process to verify the signature. First, the signing program passes the assigned function through a mathematical function called a *hash*. The hash function creates a unique value from the bytes that compose the file. Moreover, the hash function computes the value in such a way that you cannot derive the file from the hash value.

After creating the hash value, the signing program encrypts the hash value using the file signer's (the user's) private key. Finally, the signing program writes a signed version of the file, which usually includes information about the signing program and indicators of where a signed file begins and ends.

To verify the signature, the file's receiver first runs software to decrypt the signature's hash value using the sender's public key. After the software program decrypts the hash value, it stores the hash value in a temporary location.

The receiver's software program parses the file through the same hash that the sender originally used to create the hash value. Next, the receiver's software program checks the computed hash value against the decrypted hash value. If the values are the same, the receiver's software program informs the user that the signature is accurate and that the message is authentic.

Understanding the Rivest, Shamir, and Adleman (RSA) Algorithm

It is important for you to understand that even though you will most frequently use public-key cryptography to encrypt textual messages, the computer accomplishes public-key cryptography by applying a set of mathematical actions to the data. Programmers collectively refer to the set of mathematical operations as an *encryption algorithm*. One of the most successful and important algorithms in public-key cryptographic systems is the *RSA Algorithm*. Earlier versions of *Pretty Good Privacy* (one of the most well-known encryption programs), as well as many other types of modern-day encrypted transmissions and encryption programs, use the RSA Algorithm.

TIP   Digital signatures are not the same as electronic signatures. Digital signatures help to clearly identify message creators and senders. In an electronic message, a digital signature carries the same weight that a hand-written signature does in printed correspondence. However, unlike handwritten signatures, digital signatures are virtually impossible to forge. Digital signatures are dynamic—each is unique to the message it signs. The data in the message and the private key that the sender uses to encrypt the message are both mathematical components in the signature's construction. Electronic signatures, on the other hand, are simply a copy of a handwritten signature (such as on a fax or on the package-signing keyboards that UPS uses).

When you consider encryption, you must differentiate between an algorithm, which is a mathematical construct, and a program like the underlying code for the Secure Sockets Layer (SSL), which applies the algorithm to accomplish a task. In other words, an algorithm is like a hammer: without a hand (a program such as SSL) to swing the hammer, the hammer is useless.

Three mathematicians at the Massachusetts Institute of Technology (MIT) created the RSA Algorithm. (One of them, Ronald Rivest, has a homepage at `http://theory.lcs` `.mit.edu/~rivest`.) The RSA Algorithm randomly generates a very large prime number (the public key). The algorithm uses the public key to derive another very large prime number (the private key) through some relatively complex mathematical functions. A later section in this chapter explains the mathematics in detail. Users employ the keys to encrypt documents that two or more individuals send between themselves and to decrypt documents after addressees receive them.

The four foundation properties for the RSA Algorithm (as Rivest, Shamir, and Adleman have defined them) are as follows:

1. Deciphering a message's enciphered form yields the original message. Conceptually, you could write that equation, as shown here:

    `D(E(M))=M`

    In this equation, *D* represents the deciphering action, *E* represents the enciphering action, and *M* represents the actual message.

2. *E* and *D* are relatively easy to compute.

3. Publicly revealing *E* does not reveal any mathematically easy way to compute *D*. Therefore, only the user holding the value *D* can decrypt a message encrypted with *E*.

4. Deciphering a message *M* and then enciphering the message results in *M*. In other words, the converse of the previously shown function holds true, as shown here:

```
E(D(M))=M
```

As Rivest, Shamir, and Adleman point out, if someone transmitting data uses a procedure that satisfies Property 3, another user trying to decipher the message would have to try all the possible keys until the would-be decipherer found a key that fulfills the requirement E(M)=D. This evaluation is relatively simple when the encrypting numbers are 10 or even 20 digits in length. However, historic RSA encryption schemes use up to a 512-bit number (a number that has 154 digits in a decimal representation) for both the public key (E) and the private key (D). In addition, both numbers are very large prime numbers. To process those numbers takes incredible computing power—in fact, to date, no one has been able to break a 512-bit key using a brute-force attack (that is, trying all possible keys until the program finds a match). Modern-day systems use 4,096-bit numbers or larger.

A function that satisfies Properties 1 through 3 in the RSA Algorithm list is a *trap-door one-way function* because you can easily compute the function in one direction but not in the other. The function is called *trap-door* because you can easily compute the inverse functions after you know certain private (trap-door) information.

Understanding Hash Values Better

A hash function is a mathematical function that creates a unique value from the bytes that compose a given input—a string, a file, or some other type of binary data. Moreover, a hash function computes the value such that you cannot derive the original information from the hash function.

You can consider a hash value as a unique number that represents the incoming data stream's exact contents. Each time you pass the same stream of data (for example, a file) through the hash, the hash will always return the same hash value.

Going One Step Further with Certificates

Using encryption and hashes to create digital signatures is a powerful technique and one with significant benefits and uses on the Internet. However, digital signatures by themselves still lack one thing—a guarantee that the digital signature in question (or, for that matter, the public key in question) actually belongs to the company or individual that you believe it belongs to. To address this problem, you need to add *digital certificates* and *certificate authorities* to the equation.

A digital certificate is a standardized document that includes a user's public key and is digitally signed by a certificate authority to prove its validity. A certificate authority is a central authority that verifies the identity of the owner of a public key and digitally signs the certificate used to distribute the key.

Getting into the Secure Sockets Layer

So far in this section, we have considered encryption methods and schemes; we have examined digital signatures, certificates, and certificate authorities; and we have considered the usefulness of hash functions in the construction of this identifying information. The Secure Sockets Layer (SSL) puts all of these concepts together to create a standard means for establishing a secure channel of communication over several different protocols. SSL provides an authenticated and encrypted link through which any sort of TCP socket communication can take place. We can use SSL to provide a secure conduit for HTTP requests and responses so that sensitive information, such as credit card numbers and other financial data, can be transmitted securely across the Web.

There are two basic stages in an SSL communication: the handshake stage and the data transfer stage. In the handshake stage, the secure connection is set up; algorithms are agreed upon; keys are exchanged; and the endpoints are authenticated. Once all these steps are complete, data transfer begins. During the ongoing data transfer process, information is passed to SSL; it is encrypted, transmitted, and decrypted; and then is handed off to a higher-level entity, such as a Web server or client browser. The medium of communication is seamless to the higher-level application that is using SSL, as though encryption weren't being conducted at all. In fact, if it weren't for the little locking symbol in the corner of your browser, you would never know when you were communicating across a secured link.

SSL requires that a communication channel be established between the client and the server. For example, with HTTP, SSL uses a TCP socket on port 443, rather than on HTTP's standard port 80. Once the TCP connection is established, the SSL handshake process begins.

Once the SSL connection enters the data transfer stage, data sent to the secure connection is broken up into messages that are both encrypted using the session key and digitally signed. The receiving end receives the encrypted messages and verifies the digital signatures before attempting to decrypt the data. Having data messages signed in addition to being encrypted further secures the validity of the data source and the integrity of the data.

Private Communication Technology

The Private Communication Technology (PCT) protocol, which is very similar to SSL, was developed by Microsoft to address a number of issues with SSL 2 and 3. Here are some advantages of PCT over SSL:

- It reduces the number of packet transfers during the handshake stage.

- It provides an even more flexible means for algorithm negotiation.

- It allows for higher levels of message-signing security during the data transfer stage.

- It patches up a rather obscure security hole that could potentially occur when client-certificate authentication uses less secure (shorter bit-length) keys.

When communicating over a secure link between Internet Explorer and IIS, the PCT protocol will be used by default, rather than the SSL protocol.

Setting Up IIS for Secure Web Communication

Now that you understand the concept of secure Web communication, let's take a look at the details of setting up IIS so that you can take advantage of its security options. First, you must install one or more certificates onto the server so that secure communications can be enabled. Then you must select configuration options for the secure communications.

Key Manager Before an SSL or PCT link can be established to a server, the server must have a certificate installed so that authentication and session key exchange can occur properly. Certificates are purchased from a certificate authority or can be generated using Microsoft Certificate Server (which you will learn about in Chapter 11). You must run Key Manager to properly install a certificate on IIS. You can start the Key Manager in one of three ways:

1. Activate the IIS plug-in in the MMC and click the hand-holding key icon on the toolbar.

2. Click the Key Manager button on the IIS plug-in's Directory Security Property page.

3. Run the `keyring.exe` program located in the `c:\winnt\system32\inetsrv` directory.

On the left side of the Key Manager window, there is a hierarchical view of the Web machine and all of the services for which you can install certificates. (In this book, we focus on installing certificates for the Web service, but secure communications can be used for a number of different services.) Once you add a key to the server, you can highlight the key to display the details of its certificate in the right-hand pane of the Key Manager. Details will include the key's current functional status, the validity period details for that particular certificate, the key length, and the various components that make up the X.500 Distinguished Name for the server.

You can double-click a key's icon to invoke the Server Bindings dialog box. On a multi-hosted server, the Server Bindings determine which keys will be used for which Web sites. If, on a single machine, you have multiple virtual sites requiring secure communications, you will require multiple keys on that machine—one for each site needing secure communications. If you have multiple Web sites that use the same IP address and ports, these sites must *all* use the same key.

WARNING   Binding multiple host names to the same IP address and port will be problematic with certificates because only the host name that matches the Common Name in the certificate will actually work.

Creating a New Key

To begin creating a new key, choose the `Create New Key Wizard` command from the Key menu in Key Manager. The wizard will guide you through the process of creating a new key. The first step is to create a request for a new key. You will have to send the new key request to a certificate authority in one of two ways—either by having the wizard create a certificate request file that stores the information in a text file, or by having the wizard automatically send the request to an online authority. The second option will only be available to you if Certificate Server is installed on your server.

The New Key Wizard prompts you for a key name, a password to be used for verification purposes when you receive your certificate from the authority, the key length, and the X.500 Distinguished Name fields that identify your server. If you want your secure connections to work (always an important consideration), the Common Name must match the host name that your clients will be entering on their browsers. Once you have entered all of this information, you will either need to submit the request file to a certificate authority (following whatever procedures the authority enforces), or your request will be automatically processed online if you selected the Online option in the wizard.

Should you choose to submit the request file manually, you will receive your certificate from a certificate authority in the form of a file for your Web server. After receiving this file, use Key Manager to install the certificate. In the left-hand pane of Key Manager, select the disabled key that corresponds to the request that you made and choose Install

Key Certificate from the Key menu. You will be prompted for the filename and password you specified when you generated the request. At this point, your key should be installed, and you can now specify any bindings for that key that you want to use.

Key Manager also lets you back up and restore server keys using the Export and Import options on the Key menu. Backing up your keys is a good idea because server key certificates can be relatively expensive. If you inadvertently delete a key from within Key Manager and don't have a backup, you will have to request a new key certificate from your certificate authority.

SSL Configuration Options You Can Manage from the MMC

As you might expect, IIS has a high level of flexibility in the configuration of SSL options. At the highest level, the Web Site Property page allows you to determine what port will be used for SSL communications for a particular site. At the home directory, virtual directory, directory, and file levels, you can configure a fine granularity of security detail. For example, you can specify whether a specific resource will use SSL and exactly how you want to configure SSL for that resource's use.

The Secure Communications dialog box, which you access by clicking the Edit Secure Communication button on the Directory Security Property page, displays several options that you can configure. For each resource on a particular machine, the Secure Communications dialog box offers the entire range of options for requiring, allowing, or denying the use of SSL and client certificates. At the top of the dialog box, there is a button that returns you to Key Manager and a second button that you can use to manipulate encryption settings.

> **WARNING**   The Encryption Settings option will let you specify that the key length for the symmetric encryption portion of SSL must be 128 bits, allowing you to restrict secure connections to only the highest level of encryption. However, this option is only functional on Windows NT Servers with built-in 128-bit security capabilities. As a result of U.S. export restrictions, these servers can only be purchased in the U.S. and Canada.

Microsoft Transaction Server (MTS)

While the IIS product has historically been oriented toward outside access—via the Internet or the Web—the growth in corporate frontends deployed as intranets and extranets, together with the expanded support for data in the enterprise, has resulted in the need for many services that apply both to external and internal application development. One such service is Microsoft Transaction Server (MTS), a server product designed to help simplify the creation of multi-tier, multi-user environments.

In the multi-tier model, applications are broken up into three types of components—user services (frontends, such as through the Web); business services, which implement the application's logic; and data services, which maintain the business' actual data—typically on SQL Server or some other highly scalable relational database product.

The application infrastructure in a multi-user environment is composed of the services that enable many users to access the application and underlying data at the same time, while the services maintain the integrity of the data and processes that keep the business in working order. The application infrastructure includes services that manage resources, such as threads and database connections, security, and transactions.

While the multi-tier model has been available for some time, developers were forced to spend a large portion of development time creating the application infrastructure under which these applications ran.

MTS eases the transition from single-user to multi-user development by providing the application infrastructure for building scalable, robust enterprise applications. MTS is a component-based transaction processing system for building, deploying, and administering server applications. MTS is part of the Windows NT 4 Option Pack.

MTS Concurrency Model

When a distributed application provides services to multiple users, it can receive many simultaneous calls from clients. Also, it can have its business logic running in more than one process on more than one computer. The synchronization issues involved with managing multiple threads on multiple computers are very complex to program. Using a simple concurrency model to develop distributed applications enables you to focus on writing the business logic for your application rather than the synchronization code.

MTS provides this simple concurrency model through *activities*. An activity is the path of execution that occurs from the time a client creates an MTS object until the client releases that object. During the activity, the client makes calls to the MTS object. To service those calls, the MTS object may create additional MTS objects that are part of the same activity. The activity ensures that all MTS objects created on behalf of the original client do not run in parallel. You can think of an activity as a single logical thread of execution. Using activities enables you to write your MTS components from the point of view of a single user.

Resource Management

As an application scales to a larger number of clients, objects in the application must share resources, such as network connections, database connections, memory, and disk space. Therefore, these applications must use them only when necessary. Effective resource management improves scalability. Two MTS resource managers are *Just-in-Time Activation* and *Connection Pooling*, which are explained next.

Just-in-Time Activation   MTS helps conserve server memory by keeping an instance of an object alive only when a client is calling the object. This practice is known as Just-in-Time Activation. It allows the server to handle more clients than is possible when the object remains active. When a client calls a method on an object, MTS activates the object by creating it and allowing the client call to proceed. When the call returns and the object is finished with its work, MTS deactivates the object by removing it from memory. Later, when the client calls the object again, MTS reactivates the object. You can take advantage of Just-in-Time Activation by building a component to indicate to MTS when its work is complete.

Connection Pooling   MTS also allows the use of resource dispensers, which can pool resources for more efficient use. For example, the ODBC 32 Driver Manager is an ODBC resource dispenser. When an ODBC database connection is released, the ODBC resource dispenser returns the connection to a pool, rather than releasing it immediately. If another MTS object requests the same connection, the connection will be assigned from the pool, saving unnecessary network trips to recreate the connection.

Security

Because more than one client can use an application, a method of authentication and authorization must be used to ensure that only authorized users access business logic.

MTS provides security by allowing you to define *roles*. A role defines which users (Windows NT user accounts and groups) are allowed to invoke interfaces on a class. You map each role to specific classes or interfaces on those classes. Then you add Windows NT users and groups to their appropriate roles. MTS ensures that those NT users and groups can only access the classes and interfaces to which their roles are mapped. Developers don't have to write any special code in their components to handle this processing; rather, it's automatically provided by MTS.

All-or-Nothing Work Management

Work done in a distributed multi-user application can involve changes to database tables and even non-database entities, such as message queues. Often more than one object in an activity is initiating changes. Because the work in any single object can fail, the application must be able to handle situations where some objects fail, but others succeed. Work cannot be left in an inconsistent state where some of the work is done, but other parts are not.

MTS transactions provide an all-or-nothing model of managing work. Either all the objects succeed, and all the work is committed; or one or more of the objects fail, and none of the work is committed. Based on the outcome, any database tables or files affected by the work are either all changed or not changed at all. They are not left in an inconsistent state.

The programming required to manage transactions across multiple databases and non-database entities is very difficult to implement in an application, which has caused administrators the world over nightmares for years. MTS provides this transaction management service as part of its application infrastructure. MTS automatically creates transactions for components when they are activated. MTS also automatically handles cleanup and rollback of a failed transaction. When you use MTS, you don't have to write any transactional code in your components.

The MTS environment consists of components and packages, as described in the following sections.

Components   An MTS application provides business services to clients. MTS applications are implemented as a collection of COM DLLs, with each DLL implementing different business services in the application. The components are registered for use in the MTS run-time environment. Such components are often referred to as MTS components, and objects created from them are often called MTS objects.

A client accesses the application by creating objects from the components and calling methods in those objects. Those objects may create additional objects to complete the client's request.

To use a component with MTS, it must be a COM DLL. Components that are implemented as executable (`.exe`) files cannot run in the MTS run-time environment. Other requirements, such as self-registration and type library support, are met automatically when you create the component with Visual Basic. (Though they may not be when you create the component with other languages, such as Visual C++.)

Packages   Each component that runs under MTS must belong to a *package*. A package contains a group of related component classes and their associated type libraries. You create a package and add components to it by using the MTS Explorer. You can then deploy and administer the components in the package as a group.

Packages define security boundaries for your application. MTS does not check security when one component calls another inside the same package. However, MTS does check security when a method is called from outside the package. Therefore, when you decide which packages to place your components in, you must deploy them to match the security needs of your application.

Packages also define fault isolation boundaries for the application. Unless otherwise specified, the components in a package all run in the same server process. If one component fails, it causes all the components in the process to fail. It does not cause components in other packages to fail because those components are running in separate processes. This is an additional factor to consider when determining which packages to put your components in.

Resource Managers

A resource manager is a system service that manages durable data. Resource managers ensure that data is not lost or corrupted in the event of a system failure. Examples of resource managers include the following:

- Databases, such as Microsoft SQL Server 6.5/7 and Oracle versions 7.3.3 and 8
- Durable message queues, such as Microsoft Message Queue Server
- Transactional file systems

MTS automatically works with resource managers on your component's behalf. For example, if your component uses a transaction that performs database updates on a Microsoft SQL Server database, MTS automatically creates and manages the transaction in the SQL Server database. Your developers don't have to write any transactional code in their components. MTS handles everything of substance on their behalf.

> **NOTE** MTS supports resource managers that implement either the OLE Transactions protocol or the X/Open XA protocol. The MTS Software Development Kit (SDK) provides a toolkit for developing resource managers.

Resource Dispensers

A resource dispenser is a service that manages non-durable, shared-state data on behalf of the components within a process. Resource dispensers are similar to resource managers, but resource dispensers do not guarantee durability. They are useful for managing shared state data that does not need the overhead of being protected from a system failure. MTS provides two resource dispensers:

- ODBC resource dispenser
- Shared Property Manager

The MTS SDK provides a toolkit for developing resource dispensers.

ODBC Resource Dispenser   The ODBC resource dispenser manages pools of database connections for MTS components that use the standard ODBC interfaces. The resource dispenser automatically reclaims and reuses database connections. This reduces the memory and network connections that the database connections consume on the MTS server and increases scalability. The ODBC 32 Driver Manager is the ODBC resource dispenser. The Driver Manager DLL is installed with MTS.

Shared Property Manager   The Shared Property Manager provides synchronized access to application-defined, process-wide properties (or variables). You can use it for a variety of tasks, such as maintaining a Web page hit counter, caching static data, or providing smart caching to avoid database hotspots.

Microsoft Distributed Transaction Coordinator

The Microsoft Distributed Transaction Coordinator (DTC) is a system service that coordinates transactions that span multiple resource managers. Work can be committed as one transaction even if the transaction spans multiple resource managers on separate computers.

NOTE The DTC was first released as part of Microsoft SQL Server 6.5 and is included in MTS. The DTC ensures that transactional work is either all committed, or that none is committed.

As you learned in the previous section, transactions and transaction management are important parts of MTS. A *transaction* is a collection of changes to data. When a transaction occurs, either all of the changes are made (committed) or none of them are made (rolled back). MTS can automatically enlist objects and their associated resources into transactions and can manage those transactions to ensure that changes to data are made correctly.

As shown in Figure 8.8, three business objects work together to transfer money from one account to another. The Debit object debits an account and the Credit object credits an account. The Transfer object calls the Debit and Credit objects to transfer money between accounts. Both the Debit and the Credit objects must complete their work in order for a transaction to succeed. If either object fails to complete its task, the transaction is not successful. Any work that was done is rolled back in order to maintain the integrity of the accounts.

Figure 8.8   A simple MTS model of business objects

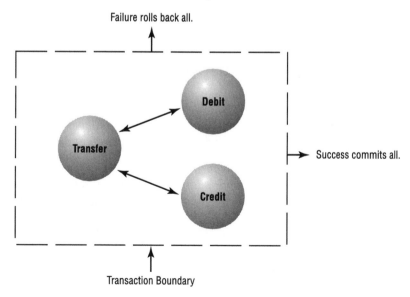

NOTE When you install MTS from the NT Option Pack, you can install sample files that show (to some extent) how MTS works. The CD-ROM includes an MTS example of bank transactions that evidences logic similar to that shown in Figure 8.8.

ACID Properties

A transaction changes a set of data from one state to another. For a transaction to work correctly, it must have the following properties, commonly known as the ACID (Atomicity, Consistency, Isolation, and Durability) properties:

Atomicity Atomicity ensures that all changes from all of the objects involved in the transaction are committed as one unit. Either all changes are committed, or all changes are rolled back to their original state. There is no other possible outcome. For example, if the Debit object fails during a transfer of money, the Credit object is not allowed to succeed because this would cause an incorrect balance in the account. All objects either succeed or fail as one unit.

Consistency Consistency ensures that durable data matches the state expected by the business rules that modified the data. For example, after the Transfer object successfully transfers money from one account to another, the accounts must truly have new balances.

Isolation Isolation ensures that concurrent transactions are unaware of each other's partial and uncommitted results. Work that is completed by concurrent transactions can be thought of as occurring in a serial manner. Otherwise, they might create inconsistencies in the system state. For example, consider two transfers that happen at the same time. The first transfer debits the account leaving it with an empty balance. The second transfer sees the empty balance, flags the account as having insufficient funds, and then fails gracefully. Meanwhile, the first transfer also fails, for other reasons, and rolls back to restore the account to its original balance. When the changes are not isolated from each other, the two transfers resulted in an incorrect flag on the customer's account. Isolation helps ensure that these kinds of unexpected results do not occur.

Durability Durability ensures that committed updates to managed resources (such as database records) survive communication, process, and server system failures. Transactional logging enables you to recover the durable state after failures.

All of these properties ensure that a transaction does not create problematic changes to data between the time the transaction begins and the time the transaction commits. Also, these properties make cleanup and error handling much easier when updating databases and other resources.

Two-Phase Commit

When transactions are processed on more than one server, a two-phase commit ensures that the transactions are processed and completed on either all of the servers or on none of the servers. There are two phases to this process: prepare and commit. You can use the analogy of a business contract to illustrate the two-phase commit process.

In the prepare phase, each party involved in the contract commits by reading and agreeing to sign the contract. In the commit phase, each party signs the contract. The contract is not official until both parties have made a commitment. If one party does not commit, the contract is invalid. MTS coordinates and supports the two-phase commit process, making sure that all objects of the transaction can commit and that the transaction commits correctly.

The MTS Explorer runs as an MMC snap-in. It is the administrative tool that you use to manage components and packages. Using the MTS Explorer, you can perform tasks, such as:

- Create a package.
- Add and delete components from a package.
- Set package properties, such as security, identity, and activation.
- Set component class properties, such as transaction and security.
- Distribute packages.
- Install and maintain packages.
- Monitor transactions.

MTS lets you control and manage distributed applications in your enterprise. MTS components can be accessed from both local applications and from external applications, including outside access from the Web. MTS integrates well with several other services that run over NT, one of which is the Microsoft Message Queue Server.

Microsoft Message Queue Server

As your Web sites get more complex and as database transactions become a part of your Web site's everyday access process, you will find that your server is waiting for a complex task to finish that may take minutes or hours, or may be unreliable over a dial-up networking link. In such situations, you will want to use a mechanism capable of storing all of the information associated with a task and ensuring that the task is, in fact, completed at some point in the future. This is Microsoft Message Queue Server's (MSMQ) job.

Understanding Basic Message Queue Concepts

You can think of messages on computers as being similar to an e-mail, except that the message gets delivered to parts of the operating system rather than to mail servers around the world. The concept of MSMQ is similar to the e-mail metaphor. When you send e-mail to a remote domain, your machine is generally not involved in the final delivery of the message. Your machine communicates solely with your local mail server, which is responsible for getting the message to the appropriate person at the appropriate domain. As far as you are concerned, once you hit send, the message is successfully sent from your client program to your network's e-mail server.

Once your server has received your message, it basically guarantees that it will deliver your mail. If links between your mail server and the destination fail, the mail server holds onto the mail and keeps trying to deliver until it is successful. If, for some reason, a major failure occurs and the mail cannot be delivered (for example, a bad address), the mail server generates an error message describing the problem and the failure and returns the e-mail to the sender's inbox. Essentially, MSMQ Services perform the same role as the mail server does for your e-mail.

To understand MSMQ's role better, consider this example. Suppose that you own a computer manufacturer. You need to be able to simultaneously update a customer information database, an orders database, and an inventory database. Everything would work smoothly if you could build, box, label, apply postage, and ship a customer's new computer to them *while they waited on the phone*. However, this is probably an unrealistic goal—most customers hate to hold for five minutes, let alone for five days while the transaction goes from start to finish. Instead, what you need to do is store all the information required to ship the computer, let the customer know that the computer has been ordered, and use some mechanism that guarantees that the computer does ultimately ship.

Once the information has all been successfully stored within this mechanism, you can conclude the call with the customer and begin the process of building and shipping the computer. The mechanism that performs the actual shipment of the computers pulls shipment requests from the front of the queue and processes them at its own pace. In this model, each shipment request is considered a single message.

MSMQ provides a number of features that aid in the creation of these message queues. First, MSMQ is designed to span an enterprise of interconnected servers. A queue can exist on one server, but in order for a message to be placed into that queue, it might have to be sent through one or more intermediate servers until it arrives at the destination computer (the one with the queue). In this sense, MSMQ works like a mail server. This mail-server quality of routing messages across a network is what provides MSMQ with its redundancy and fault tolerance. A message can be easily replicated between MSMQ servers. If any machines or network connections fail, a new route can be found to the destination server through a different series of intermediate servers.

MSMQ also provides a means for prioritizing each message so that urgent messages are sent to their destination faster than standard messages. Furthermore, MSMQ takes advantage of the Windows NT Security Model so that messages can be digitally signed to guarantee the identity of the sender, or encrypted to protect the message data. MSMQ can integrate its messaging schemes with other messaging software so that you can take advantage of e-mail delivering schemes to forward messages between MSMQ Servers.

Considering the Various MSMQ Server Roles

Before we consider exactly how you will deploy queues, let's take a look at how you can deploy MSMQ Servers across your network, and the different roles that the MSMQ Servers takes in different situations. There are five main role types that an MSMQ Server can fall into, as described here:

Primary Enterprise Controller (PEC)   This is the main MSMQ Server for the entire organization. There should only be one PEC, and it must be installed before any other site controllers can be created.

Primary Site Controller (PSC)   This is the main MSMQ Server for each site. (The PEC also serves as the PSC for the site it happens to be in.) Each site controller is in charge of storing the hard data for any queues that exists at its site, as well as handling client receipt and delivery of messages at the site.

Backup Site Controller (BSC)   Stores a read-only copy of the PSC's database and also serves as a backup in case the PSC goes down. The BSC also helps to balance the load demand on the PSC by being able to service many kinds of client requests.

Routing server   This is any MSMQ Server that is not a PEC, PSC, or BSC. Routing servers provide intermediate message forwarding capabilities but do not keep a copy of the PSC's database. All MSMQ Servers are routing servers, even if they perform other duties, as well.

Connector server   This is an MSMQ Server that communicates with another messaging scheme using additional software. For example, you might have a connector server for linking MSMQ with Microsoft Exchange e-mail Servers.

The current version of MSMQ requires Microsoft SQL Server to be installed in order to provide a consistent means for the MSMQ servers to communicate with one another. The data that MSMQ stores in the SQL Server database is called the *MSMQ Information Store* and contains information about the enterprise topology, the sites and locations of various MSMQ Servers, and configuration information for queries stored on the network. When a new MSMQ Server is installed or a change takes place on a server, such as the creation of a new queue, this information is replicated between all the MSMQ servers in the enterprise using messages passed to the servers that tell them to update their SQL databases. The queues themselves—that is, the messages stored in the queues themselves—are stored in memory-mapped files that MSMQ accesses directly.

Understanding the Types of Message Queues

The message queues that applications can take advantage of are divided into two general categories: public queues and private queues. *Public queue* information is replicated throughout the enterprise using the MSMQ Information Store and can be searched for and queried by applications. *Private queues,* on the other hand, do not have their information replicated by the Information Store. Therefore, if an application intends to use a private queue, it must have some outside knowledge of the queue. By default, private queues are not shown in the MSMQ Explorer unless you explicitly enable their display for each server.

In addition to the standard private and public queues that applications send messages to, MSMQ provides a number of other types of queues that serve secondary roles but have features that enhance the direct use of private and public queries, as detailed in the following list:

Journal queues   MSMQ uses journal queues to keep backup copies of messages that are being sent or received. MSMQ supports two types of journaling: source journaling and target journaling. Source journaling creates a copy of the message when it is first sent; therefore, it is up to the application sending the message to specify whether it will use source journaling. Each machine has a queue named *journal*, which is not associated with a specific public queue, where the machine stores source journal copies.

Target-journaled messages, on the other hand, are copies made of messages when they are received by the queueing machine. Target-journaled messages are also kept in journal queues, but they are maintained on the normal queue on each machine. When a message is received from a standard queue, a copy is placed in the queue's corresponding journal queue. Unlike source journaling, target journaling is enabled for an entire queue rather than for each individual message. The extra copies created by journaling are important because they help ensure the robustness of the queued messages in the event of data loss or system failure.

Dead letter queues   MSMQ uses these queues to store messages that were not delivered. A message can end up in a dead letter queue for any number of reasons. The most common examples include addressing to a non-existent target queue or an execution timeout. Each server maintains its own dead letter queue.

Transaction queues   Message receipt by these queues can be part of a transaction. MSMQ can act as a resource manager for transactions, which means that it will automatically work in a two-phase commitment scenario within an MTS transaction. For MSMQ, a transactional task is complete when a client's local MSMQ Server successfully receives a sent message, but this does not mean that the transaction has actually reached its destination queue. However, because MSMQ guarantees delivery of a message once it is received, successful receipt of the message by the local MSMQ Server is sufficient to complete a transaction.

To mark a message as part of a transaction, you simply add a flag to a standard message. Transaction queues can only hold transaction messages, and non-transaction queues cannot receive transaction messages. Non-transaction messages sent to a transaction queue will fail and will be subsequently placed within the dead letter queue on the server. Transaction messages that are sent to a non-transaction queue will fail, as well; but these are placed in the transaction dead letter queue. The transaction dead letter queue for an MSMQ Server is named *Xact Dead Letter* and contains any failed transaction messages.

Administration queues   An application can specify such a queue when it sends a message. The specified administration queue will receive an acknowledgement indicating whether the message was successfully retrieved. If the message was not, a reason for the error is attached to the message. When an application sets up an administration queue, it can specify what kinds of acknowledgements it wants sent to that queue. For example, an application might not be interested in having positive acknowledgements sent because it automatically assumes that the message was sent successfully; rather, it might only be interested in negative acknowledgements.

Report queues   These queues receive report messages that detail the path that a message made as it was propagated to its destination queue. Report queues can be useful tools for MSMQ managers who want to monitor the flow of messages across their enterprise.

System queues   These queues are private queues that MSMQ uses to communicate information across the enterprise.

Now that you have a feel for the types of MSMQ Servers that exist and the type of queues that you can create, let's examine exactly how to set up MSMQ and evaluate the various configuration options at your disposal.

Installing MSMQ

MSMQ is available for installation from the Windows NT Option Pack. MSMQ is only available for installation using the Custom Installation option for the setup program. You must install the core services; you can optionally install the Software Development Kit, the MSMQ Explorer, and the help documentation for MSMQ.

After you choose to install MSMQ, you must specify the server role that this particular installation of MSMQ falls into. If you don't have any other MSMQ Servers in your enterprise, the MSMQ installation must be a PEC. Any other selection requires that you specify the name of the PEC so that MSMQ can locate it. If you choose to install a PEC, you are prompted for the name of your enterprise, as well as the name of your site, because the PEC also acts as a PSC.

WARNING   You must have Microsoft SQL Server 6.5/7 installed on the local machine before you can make it a PEC, a PSC, or a BSC.

To install a PSC, you need the name of a PEC. To install a BSC, you need the name of a PSC. To install a routing server, an independent client, or the MSMQ RAS connectivity service, you will need the name of either a PSC or a BSC. Any role besides the PEC gives your machine the option of communicating over a secure link with its parent machine; but recognize that for this to work, the pre-existing server *must* have secure communications installed and enabled.

After you have specified your machine's MSMQ role and specified its parent server (if necessary), the setup program prompts you for the directory in which you want to install MSMQ. By default, this directory is `c:\program files\msmq`, but you can choose any directory you want. For PEC, PSC, or BSC systems, you need to specify the location of the SQL Server database directory and size of the database for your MSMQ Server. The MSMQ database only holds MQIS information, so it doesn't need to be particularly large, unless you have an involved enterprise installation with many servers.

If you have multiple network cards or protocols installed, the setup program asks you to specify your connected networks in the MSMQ Connected Networks dialog box. In most situations, all your MSMQ clients and Servers can connect to one another directly, so you will need a single connected network. This is the case with most corporate intranet deployments. If you have MSMQ Servers or clients that are not able to communicate directly with one another but must route messages across disjointed networks, at least one MSMQ Server on the network needs to have both connected networks configured so that it can route messages between the networks.

If you are installing a new PSC, you are effectively adding a new site to your MSMQ configuration. One of the pieces of information that you need to provide when adding additional sites is the cost of your new site's links to the other existing sites. *Link costs* are numerical values that you assign to each site to represent how hard it is to reach a specified site from your site.

Your MSMQ Servers use your link cost values to determine the most efficient way to route messages between sites. Routes with a smaller accumulative link cost are used before routes with a larger accumulative link cost. If the most efficient route fails, the routes with higher costs are used as backups. Depending on the speed of your connections, you may want to set all the link costs to a value of one to provide MSMQ with the most communication options for each message.

Managing MSMQ

You can manage MSMQ using a MMC snap-in, called the MSMQ Explorer. The MSMQ Explorer shows the MSMQ hierarchy in the left pane. At the top of the tree is the name of the enterprise. The Sites, Connected Networks, and the EC (referred to as the Enterprise Server) folders are beneath the tree. Let's take a look at the Enterprise Properties dialog box and the three tabs it contains.

The General page   The General page lists global options for the entire enterprise. For instance, on the General page, you can change the default lifetime of a message in the enterprise. The lifetime is the amount of time that a message is stored in the message queues without being read before it is moved to the dead letter queue. You can set this option on a per-message basis, as well, which is often useful. If you do not specify this option, the default value set on the General page takes precedence.

The MQIS Defaults page   This page lets you set when updates of the Information Store can be sent from any site controllers in the enterprise. You can set these values for specific sites; but by setting them at the enterprise level, you are also setting the defaults for any new sites created. You can set two timer intervals here: one for communications within the site (to back up the site controllers) and one for Information Store communications to other sites (in particular, to the PEC). By default, internal-intrasite communication is set to 2 seconds, and external-intersite communication is set to 10 seconds.

The Security page   The last page in the Enterprise Properties window is the Security tab. All of the various objects that make up an MSMQ installation are individually securable. The Security page lets you configure the security descriptor for a particular object—the Enterprise object. The Security page should look familiar because the same structure is used to set security descriptor information on any number of objects, including file security on an NTFS partition. Here, the Security page is used to set security on the MSMQ Enterprise object.

MSMQ Server in a WAN Environment

As the Internet becomes more important in everyday business, the benefit of a server product (such as MSMQ) in a WAN environment becomes clearer. MSMQ's ability to handle information processing for vastly distributed networks is a clear benefit to the far-flung organization.

Recently, we did some work with an organization that had operations in the Caribbean and central information processing locations in Central America and Florida. Their concern was making sure that data entering their Caribbean location through a local frontend was being processed and handled appropriately at their central information processing locations. There were local instances of SQL Server at all the locations, but data was being real-time processed through an intermediate COM component as it was passed up to the central Information Stores.

The Problem

The challenge was to ensure that every transaction, modification, deletion, or addition to the local databases in the Caribbean was passed to the centralized storage

database. Furthermore, we needed to design error handling such that if the transaction did not get delivered because of a network failure or other problem, we would receive notice.

The Solution

Using MSMQ, we placed the PEC at the Florida location, and placed PSCs at each of the other locations. We designed queues to handle the transfer of all the data between the locations. We also designed supporting queues to handle system messaging and so forth.

Summing It Up

This was a complex problem, which was made more complex by the inconsistent nature of communications over satellites. It required some serious system design work. This situation is one that each of us will see more often in the future. However, effective use of the MSMQ Server and the appropriate distribution throughout the organization allowed us to make a simple and elegant solution rather than having to create an exceedingly complex one.

9

Index Server

Microsoft Index Server 2 is a content-indexing utility that is packaged with the Windows NT Server 4 Option Pack. You can use Index Server to provide your Web clients with a quick and easy way to scan your site contents to find a particular file or general subject matter.

As the IIS administrator, you will use Index Server to maintain an index of information on your Web server and to manage searches of that information. One of the main advantages of Index Server 2 is that you can configure it to scan and maintain indexes for all files on your virtual directory, as well as to filter and index files, such as Microsoft Word documents and Microsoft PowerPoint presentations, with no additional administration. You can think of Index Server as a simple search engine for your site.

Before you can use Index Server to perform searches, you must configure the content you want indexed. In this chapter, we will discuss how to install and configure Index Server on your site so that you can perform text and property queries to find information quickly.

Installing Index Server

When you install IIS 4, it will not automatically install Index Server 2. Even after you do install Index Server, it will not (by default) index any of your site's content. You must manually create a *corpus*. A corpus is the body of documents that you want Index Server to index. Then you must create the queries that users will use to find information on your site.

If you did not install Index Server when you installed IIS, you must make sure that you have sufficient system resources to run Index Server. Index Server will require between 3 and 12 megabytes of hard disk space for the Index Server program files (depending on the languages you install) and a varying amount of system memory to perform indexing. The following list describes the minimum and recommended memory requirements for Index Server, based on the number of documents you plan to index:

Less than 100,000   32MB

100,000 – 250,000   32MB (64–128 recommended)

250,000 – 500,000   64MB (128–256 recommended)

More than 500,000   128MB (256+ recommended)

In addition to the memory requirements, you must also consider your free disk space. Microsoft recommends having enough free disk space to equal at least 40% of the corpus. This is to allow proper space for indexing. Remember, this is a minimum requirement; for the best performance and reliability, you should have well beyond 40% of your corpus available.

Index Server supports multiple languages, so you can perform queries on international sites. In addition to the disk-space requirement for your corpus, you should also have enough disk space to install all the languages you intend to index. The following is a list of the languages that Index Server supports:

- Dutch
- French
- German
- Italian
- Japanese
- Swedish
- US English
- UK English
- Simplified Chinese

TIP You can install additional languages during your Index Server installation by selecting Optional Components from the setup wizard.

To install Index Server, perform the following steps:

1. Insert your Windows NT 4 Option Pack CD-ROM into your CD-drive. The Windows NT Server 4 Option Pack Installation Wizard will begin.

2. In the Microsoft Windows NT 4 Option Pack Setup screen, click the Next button to continue. The wizard will display the Add/Remove All screen.

3. Click the Add/Remove button. The wizard will display the Select Components screen.

4. Check the Microsoft Index Server check box. Click the Next button. The wizard will copy the Index Server 2 files to your system. When this is finished, it will display the Final screen.

5. Click Finish. Index Server is now installed on your system.

Let's examine some of the Index Server terms that you must know as an administrator. Knowing these terms will help you to understand any supplemental text you read in the future. The following list describes terms and their meanings:

Corpus   This is the collection of documents that you are indexing.

Catalog   A catalog is a group of files that contain Index Server information about the corpus, as well as the index itself. This is the highest level unit within the Index Server hierarchy. Each catalog is a completely self-contained entity. Index Server queries cannot span multiple catalogs. You will usually create a separate catalog for each Web site hosted on your server.

Scope   A scope is the entire area that will be included in an index. An administrator creates the scope of the corpus to include all documents that must be indexed.

Indexes   An index is a list of words and properties found in the documents that you configure to be indexed. To the user, these word lists and properties are transparent. The user will perform a search on a given word or type of document and Index Server will search through the indexes looking for a match. When a match is found, Index Server will return only the document names that matched the search criteria.

Content filter   Index Server will index files other than HTML. Because some applications store documents in a proprietary format, the content filter provides a way of reading these documents so that the words can be indexed.

Word Breakers   Content filters send streams of text. Since different languages separate words in different ways, the Word Breakers provide a way of separating words for each language that you create indexes for.

Normalizer   When the Word Breakers send words, they do not change the case of the letters or their punctuation. The normalizer cleans up the words by getting rid of capital letters and all punctuation. Additionally, the normalizer will remove *noise words*. Noise words are common words that you will have no need to index, such as *and, or,* and *but.* These words would only add unnecessary clutter to your indexes.

Creating an Index

Index Server runs completely independent of the IIS 4 service. In fact, even if you stop the IIS service, Index Server will continue to index the site content that you have configured it to. Creating an index requires three steps: scanning, filtering, and indexing.

Scanning

Scanning determines all the data that needs to be indexed on all of the virtual directories. The directories can include those found on Novell NetWare servers (if you have configured virtual directories to point to them). While you could very easily include every directory on your server in the index, this would not be wise. You would only cause Index Server to create indexes of information that your users will probably never need. In this section, we will discuss selecting directories to index. In the next section, "Administering Index Server," you will learn how to exclude directories from being indexed.

There are three types of scans: full, incremental, and manual. The following list describes each scan and its function:

Full scans   Occur the first time a directory is added to the list of indexed servers. In a full scan, all documents are added to a list of items to be filtered. This type of scan requires the most time and processor usage.

Incremental scans   Check for changed files and add them to a list of items to be indexed. They are performed when the Index Server is started or when a file is changed.

Manual scans   Are performed by the administrator from the MMC.

When you have made significant changes to your site, you may want to force a scan immediately so that users will be able to query for the new information right away.

To manually scan a directory, perform the following steps:

1. From the MMC, go to Index Server ➤ Web ➤ Directories. The MMC will display the scope of directories in the right pane.

2. In the right pane of the MMC, right-click the directory you want to scan. The MMC will display a Quick menu.

3. Select Rescan. Index Server will display the Full Rescan? dialog box. The two options within this dialog box are Yes and No. The Yes option performs a full rescan of the directory. The No option performs an incremental scan of the directory.

Filtering

After you have performed your scan, you can filter the scan results. Filtering is the process of taking the list of items to be filtered, temporarily converting these files to text with the use of the filter DLLs, and creating a word list. There are three files used in filtering. They are as follows:

- Filter
- Word Breaker
- Noise Word Data

The filter DLLs act as a converter so that the Index Server can read specific application files. For example, in order to have Index Server index the contents of a Microsoft Word file, you would need to have a MS Word filter DLL loaded so that Index Server knows how to read the file. Index Server comes with the following filter DLLs:

- HTML 3 (backward compatible)
- Microsoft Word
- Microsoft Excel
- Microsoft PowerPoint
- Test files
- Binary files

When the filtering process comes across files with unknown extensions, one of two filters will be run on it. Depending on the FilterFilesWithUnkownExtensions registry setting (either 0 or 1), the file could have either the null or the default filter applied to it, as follows:

Null Filter   Registry setting of 0, which returns the file properties only (name, size, date)

Default Filter   Registry setting of 1, which returns the file properties and the ASCII contents of the file

During scanning, Index Server could very easily come across files that are in use. When this occurs, the file is skipped and tried again later. This will continue to happen until the number of filter attempts is equal to the FilterRetries registry setting. If errors occur during filtering, they are stored in the Application Log in the Windows NT Event Viewer.

During the filtering process, Index Server must separate streams of text into individual words. The word-breaker DLLs provide this service. Word-breaker DLLs are language dependent, so each language you install will have a different word-breaker DLL.

The last step that occurs in filtering is the separation of common words from the complete list of words found. This is done to decrease the size of the finished index. Common words such as *and*, *I*, *or*, *a* are stored in a file located in the `%systemroot%\system32` directory. This file is named `noise.dat`. The `noise.dat` file can be edited with any text editor, such as notepad, so that you can include additional words that you want to remove from your index searches.

You can change the name and location of the Noise word file by editing the registry and specifying a new location. The Noise word registry location is `HKEY_LOCAL_MACHINE \SYSTEM\CurrentControlSet\Control\ContentIndex\Language\<language>\NoiseFile`.

Index Server uses a child process called the *CiDaemon*. In Unix environments, a daemon is synonymous with a service. It is a background process that you cannot see. The CiDaemon is responsible for performing filtering.

Indexing

After Index Server filters the documents in your scope, the word lists are used to create a shadow index. A shadow index is like a temporary holding area. Index Server uses shadow indexes as a means of caching data that will later be merged with the Master Index. Because you could potentially have a large scope with many thousands of words to index, it could take a considerable amount of time to merge all of the words into the Master Index. This is where the shadow index comes in. Index Server writes the word list into the shadow index and moves the data to the Master Index incrementally.

At times, Index Server will merge two or more shadow indexes into one shadow index. This is called a shadow merge. A shadow merge will free up hard disk space and RAM because duplicate entries will be removed.

Another type of merge is the *annealing merge*. Annealing merges are similar to shadow merges in that they combine shadow indexes. In an annealing merge, there can be more than one shadow index left. Annealing merges result in better query time because they reduce the number of indexes that are searched.

The last type of merge is a master merge, the result of which is one master index. Master indexes are highly compressed records of all the words that occurred in the indexed items since the last master began. You will learn when master merges occur and how to control them in the next section, "Administering Index Server."

Administering Index Server

In this section, you will learn how to add and remove virtual directories to the list of servers to be indexed, how to force merges, how and when to force a scan of your virtual directories, and how to secure your Index Server.

There are two ways to administer Microsoft Index Server. The first is through the MMC. The other method is through an HTML-based form. From the MMC interface, you can do any of the following:

- Start or stop the Index Server Service.
- Change Index Server Properties.
- Change Catalog properties.
- Add or remove catalogs and directories.
- Force a scan on a directory.

Microsoft is deeply committed to the MMC. All future releases of Microsoft Server products will be controlled through the MMC. Figure 9.1 shows the Index Server snap-in in the MMC.

Figure 9.1   Index Server MMC snap-in interface

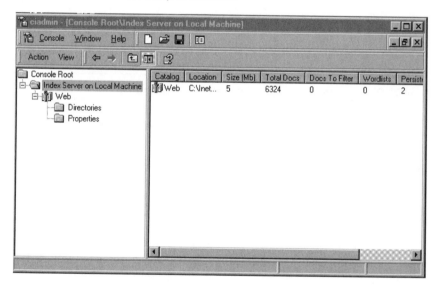

The other interface that you can use to administer an Index Server is the HTML-based Web page interface. The HTML-based administrative Web page can be found in the %systemroot%\system32\inetsrv\iisadmin\isadmin directory of the local host and is named admin.htm. From the Administrator page, you can view statistics about your Index Server. Some of the statistics that you can view are as follows:

- # Active queries
- # Cached queries

- # Pending queries
- # Rejected queries
- # Persistent indexes
- # Wordlists
- # Unique keys
- # Documents filtered
- # Documents pending
- # Documents change
- # Directories to be scanned
- # Running queries
- % Hits
- % Misses
- Total queries
- Queries per minute

> **NOTE**   As an Index Server administrator, you should always consider system security. Index Server will not allow users to search for Web pages that they don't have access to. This means that if a user searches for all documents containing the word *stereo* but does not have access to documents containing the word *stereo*, the search will result in zero found items.

Adding Directories

Index Server will automatically include all directories and their subdirectories in the index. You can manually add additional directories that you want included in your searches to this list by performing the following steps:

1. Go to Start ➢ Programs ➢ Windows NT 4 Option Pack ➢ Microsoft Index Server ➢ Index Server Manager. Windows NT will open the MMC and display the Index Server on Local Machine node.

2. Click the + symbol to expand the Local Machine node. The MMC will display the Web object. Click the + symbol on the Web object to expand the Directories and Properties objects.

3. On the Directories object, right-click to display the Quick menu. Select New ➢ Directory. The MMC will display the Add Directory dialog box.

4. In the Add Directory dialog box, select the path to the directory you want to add and click OK.

The documents contained in the directory you selected will now be included in your index.

Performing Queries

In this section, we will examine the types of queries that Index Server can perform, as well as a quick and easy way to create index search pages.

A query is a search performed on your Index Server. It is important to know the types of queries Index Server can run and how to perform them. The Index Server can use the following query operator types:

Free-Text   Free-text is the first type of query a user can search for data with. In a free-text query, nouns are extracted from the phrase entered, and the indexed documents are searched for that noun. To specify a free-text query, a user places a dollar sign ($) before their query. A user can also check the option box (if it is available) on the Web site they are searching to perform a free-text search.

Vector Space   This type of query performs searches for words based on set values that the user assigns. This query can also display results by order of the assigned values. To specify the value of a word or phrase, the numerical value is placed in brackets next to it. For example, if you want to search for the phrase "*Sybex books,*" but you want to also view the pages that have the word *24seven*, your search would be entered like this:

```
"Sybex books"[200], 24Seven[300]
```

These values are completely arbitrary. The person performing the query simply makes them up. The larger the value, the more weight that word or phrase has in the search.

Property Value   This type of search is called a property value query. You can search for exact values or relational values. To search for an exact value, place a pound symbol (#) before the item in question. To search for a relational value, place an at symbol (@) before the property and value you are searching for. For example, to search for all files that are larger than 1M, you would enter

```
@size > 1000000
```

Operators help you to refine your searches. The first and most widely known types of operators are Boolean operators, but you can also use Wildcard or Proximity operators.

Boolean operators   This type of search uses the words *AND*, *OR*, and *NOT* to limit the query results. If you want to search for a phrase that contains a Boolean operator, place quotation marks around the phrase. For example, in order to search for peanut butter and jelly, you would type **"peanut butter and jelly"** as your query. If you type **peanut butter AND jelly**, this search returns all documents containing any of these words.

Wildcard operators   To use this type of operator, use an asterisk (*) to search for all words that contain the preceding or proceeding letters. You can also use a double-asterisk to search for different forms of a specific word (run** = ran, running).

Proximity operators   Placing the word *NEAR* in between two words in your query will return documents where the two words are closest together at the top of your result page. All words that are more then 50 words apart are given the same value on the result page.

Creating a Query

In order for users to perform queries, you must create or specify a Web document that they can use to perform those queries with. The Microsoft Internet Information Server Resource Kit comes with many administrative tools that you can use to administer your IIS server, as well as the related services, such as Index Server. One of these tools is the Index Server Query Wizard. The Index Server Query Wizard is an easy-to-use, graphical tool that can create query pages.

The Index Server Query Wizard prompts you for some basic information. Based on your input, the Query Wizard creates three files. The three files are search.htm, search.idq, and search.htx. Each one of these files provides a specific function. The following list describes each file and its purpose:

Search.htm   This is the document that you will publish to allow your users to perform queries. Search.htm is a simple HTML document that contains form fields that call to an .idq file.

Search.idq   The Internet Data Query file contains the actual query language that Index Server will use to perform the query.

Search.htx   After the .idq file queries the Index Server, the results are generated in the .htx file and displayed to the user.

Because the Index Server Query Wizard is part of the Microsoft Internet Information Resource Kit, you must install the Resource Kit and install the Index Server Query Wizard separately. To install the Index Server Query Wizard, perform the following steps:

1. Go to Start ➢ Programs ➢ Internet Information Server Resource Kit ➢ Utility ➢ FrontPage IDQ Wizard ➢ Install the IDQ Wizard. NT will start the IDQ Installation Wizard.

2. In the Welcome screen of the Installation Wizard, click OK. The Wizard will advance to the File Location screen.

3. Select the installation directory and click the Install button. The Installation Wizard will copy the necessary files to your system. The installation is now complete.

After installing the Index Server Query Wizard, you can start the Wizard from the FrontPage Editor by selecting File menu, New; or you can simply double-click any existing .idq file on your system.

Due to the complexity of the dialog box layout and the importance of creating index search queries, we will examine each step in the Index Server Query Wizard.

The first screen in the wizard is a Welcome screen. The second screen contains the file creation options (see Figure 9.2). This screen has three file creation fields. Each one is necessary to create your query. As you know, the .htm file will be the document that you publish. Your users will see this page when performing their queries. The .idq file is the actual query language file. This file contains the search strings. The final field on this screen is the .htx field. This file is where the output of the query will be displayed.

Figure 9.2   Index Server Query Wizard File Creation page

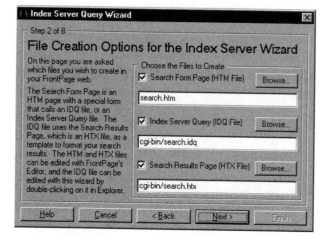

The next screen is Search and Query Page Options. Here, you configure whether users can define variable values when performing queries. You also point to the result output file and the query file that you specified in the previous screen. Figure 9.3 shows the variable options.

Figure 9.3 Index Server Query Wizard Search and Query Page Options

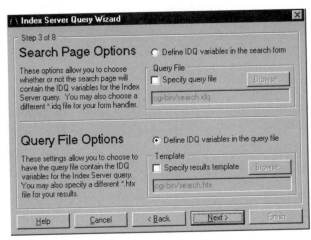

The next screen is the Search Options for Index Server Queries screen – page 1. Within this screen, you specify query depth and sort order. The query depth is a way of controlling how much information the query results will contain. The query sort order controls how the query results are displayed to the user, in either ascending or descending order. Figure 9.4 shows the Search Option screen.

Figure 9.4 Index Server Query Wizard Search options – page 1

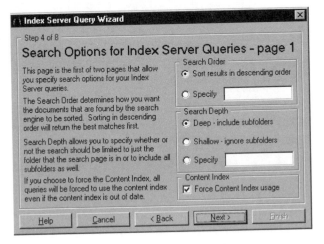

The next screen is a continuation of the previous screen. In Search Options for Index Server Queries – page 2, you can specify how many rows of data the search will return, as well as how many records will be displayed on each page. You can also configure the starting directory for the query and a specific catalog to use, as Figure 9.5 shows.

Figure 9.5   Index Server Query Wizard Search Options – page 2

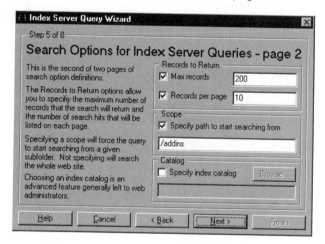

Step 6 in the Index Server Query Wizard is the Search Results Page Template Options. This page controls what specific information users will see when performing their queries. Each item is a check box, as Figure 9.6 shows.

Figure 9.6   Index Server Query Wizard Search Results Page Template Options

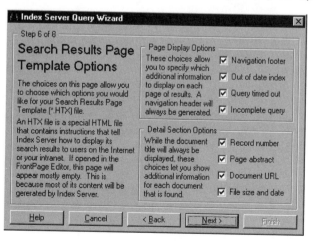

Step 7 in this process is the HTML Page, Text, and Link Color Options screen. This screen controls the colors displayed on your users' query results, as Figure 9.7 shows.

Figure 9.7 Index Server Query Wizard HTML Page, Text, and Link Color options

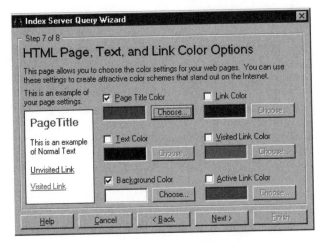

The final step allows you to edit the .htm and .htx files. You will only do this if you are customizing your output further than what the Wizard allows. Figure 9.8 shows The Index Server Query Wizard is finished screen.

Figure 9.8 The Index Server Query Wizard is finished.

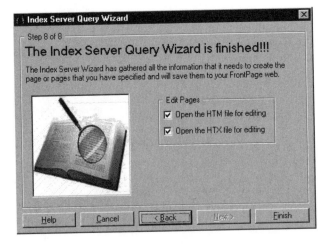

After using the Index Server Query Wizard, you simply publish the `.htm` file that it creates within your Web content. When users access this page, they will be able to perform queries.

Tuning Index Server

As the system administrator, you may have to make changes to the system to tune it for the best performance. To enhance performance of Index Server, you will need to change things, such as when it should merge the indexes and what to do with unknown file types. Most Index Server configurations are made in the registry under the `HKEY_LOCAL_ MACHINE\\System\CurrentControlSet\Control\ContentIndex` key.

To change when shadow merges occur, you can configure the MaxWordList and MinSize-MergeWordList registry settings. Shadow merges will occur when the number of word lists is greater than the value of the MaxWordList setting. They will also occur when the total size of all word lists is greater than the MinSizeMergeWordList registry value.

You can also control when annealing merges occur by configuring the MaxIdealIndexes registry entry. Annealing merges will occur when the total combined amount of shadow and master indexes is greater then the MaxIdealIndexes registry value. They can also occur as a function of time passed and the MinMergeIdleTime and MaxMergeInterval registry entries.

Another administrative task is controlling when master merges occur. You can control this by configuring the MaxFreshCount, MinDiskFreeForceMerge, MaxShadowFree-ForceMerge, and MaxShadowIndexSize registry values. Master merges will occur when the amount of changed indexed items in the current master index is larger than the Max-FreshCount registry setting. They will also occur when the total size of all the shadow indexes is greater than the MaxShadowIndexSize registry setting. The registry can also start a master merge when the disk space (MinDiskFreeForceMerge registry value) is low and is occupied by a specified amount of the shadow index, as set by the MaxShadow-FreeForceMerge registry value.

Index Server and Tight Security

You don't have to have Index Server in your network environment in order to use IIS. In fact, many administrators don't use Index Server at all. However, in the right network, it is invaluable. Take, for example, a government contractor that I worked with, which serves as a good example of where and how you might use Index Server in your network.

This government contractor's site contains hundreds of documents containing thousands of lines of text. Having to search through each document to look for a particular one could take a considerable amount of time. Security being a concern for this organization, they decided to use Microsoft IIS and Index Server for their Internet server and indexing needs.

This contractor has some unique requirements as far as IIS and Index Server are concerned. For starters, the IIS computer sits outside of the firewall that keeps Internet users off their internal network and away from sensitive information. In this type of environment, security is the main concern. Before this site went public, the NTFS permissions for every document were carefully examined to determine if there was any way that unauthorized users could gain access. After the permissions were examined, Index Server was installed. Through this whole process, the server was in a segmented network so that if anything went wrong, no unauthorized access could be gained. After Index Server was installed, the scope was defined, and the index was created.

The next step in the process was to create custom query pages for Internet users. A team of Web developers created several custom query solutions. Each was examined, and the best was chosen and implemented.

IIS 4 Security Configuration

When you choose to install IIS and publish Web content to the Internet, you are potentially making it accessible to every person in the world. In order to keep the information on your IIS server protected from unauthorized access, it is import to know how security works with IIS 4 and Windows NT. In this chapter, you will learn various aspects of how to configure security for your IIS system, including NTFS file permissions, the IUSR_*computername*, and limiting access by IP address.

Understanding the Windows NT and IIS Connection

When IIS was first released, many public comments were made by industry professionals about its apparent lack of security. In fact, IIS didn't have much internal security, but this was not a program flaw. Microsoft designed IIS to use the existing security of Windows NT Server. Since you can only run IIS on Windows NT Servers, this seemed reasonable. In later releases, Microsoft added security features to enhance the existing level of security found in Windows NT Server.

When securing your Internet Information Server, you must always keep in mind the fact that your IIS Web security is only as good as the security on your NT installation.

The user accounts and directory permissions you use to secure your LAN are the same whether users are connecting through a local workstation or over the Internet. NT does not allow any unauthorized access to resources. This means that every user must have a valid user account and password before being allowed to read even a simple text file. However, multiple users can share a single user account and password for access to your Web site. When you install IIS on your NT Server, the IIS Installation Wizard automatically creates an NT user account called IUSR_*computername*. This account is the one that IIS will use for all anonymous connections.

IIS@Work: Internet Access

When you browse the Internet, most sites allow you to access their various pages without having to give a username and password. Since Windows NT Server will not allow any unauthorized access to system resources, you might wonder how this is possible. Here's how it works: When the user connects to an IIS server, the user's computer sends an HTTP GET request to the server using the TCP protocol from the TCP/IP protocol suite. This TCP request is sent using TCP port 80. TCP port 80 is the HTTP service. IIS will accept this request and process it through the system using the IUSR_*computername* account as the account name that requested this resource. For Windows NT Server, the account was verified and authorized.

While the IUSR_*computername* account provides a way for anonymous users to access files on your Windows NT Server without having individual accounts, it is not always the desired approach. Some administrators will want to secure a limited number of files, while others will want to secure an entire site. Whichever way you decide to go, you will be using Windows NT Server security.

In this book, we break NT security into four sections:

- Users and groups
- Passwords
- Auditing
- File security

Let's examine each of these sections and their effect on your overall security.

Users and Groups

In order to understand how you can secure IIS, you must be familiar with Windows NT Server's security model.

Domains and Workgroups

The first step in securing NT is managing user and group accounts. A user account is the username and password that network users will log on with. A group is a collection of valid user accounts.

Windows NT breaks up groups into two classes: Global and Local. Global groups are groups that contain users from the Windows NT Domain that the Global group was created in. A Local group, in contrast, can contain any user or Global group account from any Windows NT Domain.

You should create Global groups to contain user accounts and Local groups to assign access permissions to resources. To grant users access to a resource, you should make the Global group that the user is a member of a member of the Local group that has the permissions to the resource.

Windows NT uses the concept of Domains and Workgroups as a way of dividing network resources. You can group all computers and users into a Windows NT Domain. A Workgroup is not that different. A Workgroup is also defined as a grouping of computers and users. They differ in the way they manage security.

A Windows NT Workgroup can contain Windows NT Workstations and/or Windows NT Server Stand-Alone Servers. The major drawback to a Windows NT Workgroup is that each computer must maintain its own accounts database. NT uses an accounts database to store all user account information, such as username and password. Because each computer in the Workgroup has its own accounts database, duplicate user account information exists on every computer. If a user changes their password, it must be changed on all computers in the Workgroup. This creates a lot of administrative overhead. The optimal Windows NT Workgroup would have no more than 10 users in it.

A Windows NT Server Domain is different in that all user account information is stored on a central computer called a Windows NT Primary Domain Controller (PDC). Because of the centrally located user accounts database, each user must have only one logon account.

You can structure IIS as part of either a Windows NT Server Domain or by placing it on a Windows NT Server Stand-Alone Server in a Workgroup. Because Internet users will only access your site through IIS, you only require a single user account. However, if you want to provide secure Web access, or just change access to certain pages within your site, you will have to create and manage multiple user accounts.

IIS 4

PART 1

NOTE   A Windows NT Server Stand-Alone Server is a computer that you have installed Windows NT Server on that does not participate in domain security—meaning it does not use user accounts from a Windows NT Server Domain.

Securing User Accounts

There are many people in the world who love to access someone else's data, sometimes for no other reason than to prove that they can. You must always be on your toes and take precautions to secure your site from these intruders. One of the first steps in securing your server is renaming the Windows NT Server default Administrator account.

Renaming the Administrator account is essential in locking down a Windows NT Server for a couple of reasons. First, *Administrator* is usually the first username that hackers try to break in with. By renaming the Administrator account, you will have more time to react when you notice unauthorized access attempts. The other reason that you will want to rename this account is that it is the only account in NT that cannot be locked out. An account lockout occurs when someone tries to log on to the system with a valid username but with an invalid password. You can configure your NT system to lock the user account so that even if the person eventually gets the password right, it will not matter because the account is locked. Since the Windows NT Server Administrator account cannot be locked, a hacker can spend all night on that account and eventually get in.

To rename the Administrator account, perform the following steps:

1. Click the Start menu. Go to Programs ➢ Administrative Tools ➢ User Manager for Domains. NT will start User Manager for Domains.

2. Click the Administrator user account. From the User menu, select Rename. User Manager for Domains will display the Rename dialog box.

3. Type the new administrative account name and click OK. The administrative account name is now changed.

Another thing you will want to consider is the user accounts that you grant administrator privileges to. By reducing the number of users who are a part of the administrator group, you will reduce the possibility that someone will guess an account name with administrative privileges and try to break into it.

Even if you have secured your administrative accounts fairly well, you will still want to be conscious of your lower-level user accounts. Especially when the data accessible in your network is extremely sensitive. You may want to assign usernames that are extremely difficult to guess. By assigning difficult usernames, it will take much longer for someone to find an account that they could use to break into your network. The downfall of using difficult usernames is that you may have difficulty remembering them yourself. This could be an acceptable trade-off in some situations.

The final thing an administrator can do to secure NT with usernames is to enable account lockouts. Windows NT Server will not, by default, lock out user accounts. You must configure the Account Lockout properties. You can configure Account Lockout properties from the Account Policy dialog box of User Manager for Domains, as shown in Figure 10.1.

Figure 10.1   Account Policy dialog box

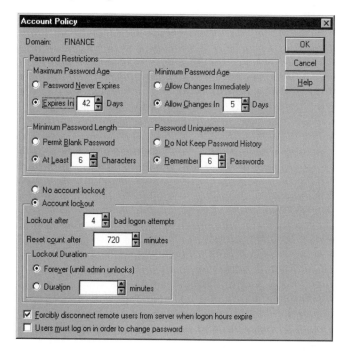

In the Account Policy dialog box, you can configure the following items:

Account Lockout   Use this field to specify how many attempts a user can make before the system will lock them out.

Reset Counter After   This feature is used so that if a user accidentally enters the wrong password, the system will reset the counter so that it does not keep climbing and lock out the user in the future.

Lockout Duration   You can control how long the user will be locked out. Your choices are Forever or a specific duration. This is handy if there are no local administrators, and it could take some time before an administrator can unlock an account. In environments where security is a major concern, this will always be set to Forever.

Forcibly Disconnect Remote Users This feature is great for kicking users off at a specific time. However, this is not very practical in an IIS environment because most administrators want their Web site up 24 hours a day. If you configure the system to forcibly disconnect users after certain hours, your site could be inaccessible to Internet users, as well.

Passwords

In the User Policy dialog box, you can also specify password restrictions. Password restrictions allow you to specify the following items:

Maximum Password Age You will use this feature to control how often a user must change their password.

Minimum Password Age This feature allows you to force a user to keep a password for a specified length of time.

Minimum Password Length You can use this feature to configure how many characters a user's password must be.

Password Uniqueness This feature will remember old user passwords so that they cannot reuse them.

The purpose behind requiring users to change their passwords at set intervals is so that, in the event that someone was able to acquire a user's password, they will only be able to use that account for a limited time.

The next step in securing passwords is to make them more difficult to guess by requiring a minimum password length. By choosing passwords with lengths that are at least eight characters, users are more likely to choose passwords that are not single words but short phrases that are contracted. There are a number of password crackers (hacker utilities) that use dictionary lists to try to acquire user passwords. If passwords are not single words, most cracking programs, which rely on word lists, will not work. It's not fool proof, but it's a start.

TIP If security is a major issue on your network, you may choose to require passwords that contain letters, numbers, and symbols (such as $%^&*). The reason for requiring this is because of programs called brute force password crackers. Unlike crackers, which run from word or dictionary lists, brute force crackers work by trying every possible combination of letters, numbers, and symbols. Requiring users to use letters, numbers, and symbols in their passwords will increase the amount of time used to crack the password. In tests, these utilities have taken hours to crack just a few passwords.

Auditing

One of the best ways to ensure security of your LAN is to have as much information about the activity of your network as you can get. Windows NT Auditing provides this service. Auditing can keep a record of the success or failure of system events, such as:

- Logon and logoffs
- File and object access
- Use of user rights
- User and group management
- Security policy changes
- Restart, shutdown, and system events
- Process tracking

In addition to monitoring system events, you can also use auditing to track the following file and directory usage:

- Read
- Write
- Execute
- Delete
- Change permissions
- Take ownership

For security purposes, you will always want to monitor successful and failed logons and logoffs; file and object access; security policy changes; as well as file and directory, change of permissions, and take-ownership events. To enable the auditing of system events, perform the following steps:

1. Click the Start menu. Go to Programs ➢ Administrative Tools ➢ User Manager for Domains. NT will open User Manager for Domains.

2. Select Policies ➢ Audit. User Manager for Domains will display the Audit Policy dialog box.

3. Select the Audit These Events radio button. Next, select the individual items you want NT to audit. Click OK. User Manager for Domains will close the Audit Policy dialog box and return you to the User Manager for Domains main screen.

After you have configured the system's audit policy, most events will be audited automatically. However, some events must still be manually configured, such as file auditing.

You will configure file auditing on a file-by-file basis. Each file or directory that you want NT to audit must be configured individually. To configure file-level auditing, perform the following steps:

1. Using either Explorer or My Computer, locate the file that you want to configure auditing for and right-click it. NT will display a quick menu.

2. Select Properties. NT will display either the File Properties or Directory Properties dialog box.

3. Click the Security tab. Next, click the Audit button. NT will display the Directory Auditing (File Auditing if you are configuring a file) dialog box.

4. Click the Add button. NT will display the Add Users and Groups dialog box.

5. Select the users or groups whose access you want to audit. (Select the Everyone group to audit access of any user.) Click OK. NT will close the Add Users and Groups dialog box and return you to the Directory Auditing dialog box.

6. Close all remaining dialog boxes. You have now configured auditing for this file or directory.

File Security

File security is the last step in securing the NT side of IIS. In order to implement file security, you must have an NTFS partition on your server. Through NTFS security, you can choose which users have the ability to access files and their level of permissions. The following is a list of NTFS file and directory permissions:

- Read
- Write
- Execute
- Delete
- Change permission
- Take ownership
- Full control

When creating permissions for a directory, remember that the default permission within NT is for the Everyone group to have full control. To change the folder permissions, perform the following steps:

1. From either Explorer or My Computer, select the file or folder that you want to configure permissions for. Right-click the folder and select Properties. NT will display the Folder Properties dialog box (File Properties dialog box if you are changing file permissions).

2. Click the Security tab. In the Security tab, click the Permissions button. NT will display the Permissions dialog box.

3. You can add users, groups, or make changes to existing users and groups. If you want to add a user or group, click the Add button and select the user or group you want to add. To change an existing user or group permissions, select the user or group and then use the Type of Access drop-down list to select the level of access that you want to give the account.

4. Close all open dialog boxes.

The next step in securing your server is through IIS.

Security Implemented through IIS

While it is important to secure your server to the fullest with NT, there are certain security features that can only be implemented through IIS, such as IP address filtering. There are four ways to secure a Web site with IIS. They are as follows:

- IP access
- User authentication
- NTFS permissions
- Web permissions

The first way that you can secure your IIS Web site is through *IP access*. IP access is either allowing or denying a specific IP address access to your Web site. You can grant or deny access for a specific IP address, a complete subnet, or a domain (Internet domain, not NT). When granting or denying access for a domain name, it will take longer due to the name resolution process.

You can deny access to a specific IP address if you have been having problems with an unauthorized Internet user trying to access your Web site. To ensure that a user has no access to your Web site, you will want to deny their IP address, or even their entire subnet, access to your Web site. You can configure IP address restrictions from the MMC using the IIS snap-in.

Another feature of IP access is its ability to grant access to only a specific set of IP addresses. You will want to use this feature if there is sensitive material on your Web site. A way of securing your Web site with this feature is to allow only intranet access to your Web site. This technique, however, does not secure your Web site from internal hacks. To implement intranet-only access, you specify that all access is denied, then specify a limited range of access to just your organization.

> *TIP* If a user needs to access your Web site from home, using their own ISP (for example, a cable modem), you would also want to add this IP address to the list of IP addresses that are granted access.

To configure IP address restrictions, perform the following steps:

1. From the MMC, expand the IIS snap-in. The MMC will display the IIS hierarchy.

2. Select the site you want to configure an IP address restriction for. Right-click the site. The MMC will display a Quick menu.

3. Select Properties. The MMC will display the Site Properties dialog box.

4. Click the Directory Security tab. Next, click the Edit button in the IP Address and Domain Name Restrictions section. The MMC will display the IP Address and Domain Name Restrictions dialog box.

5. Select either the Granted Access or Denied Access radio button. If you select Granted Access, the IP addresses you specify will be granted access, and all others will be denied. If you choose Denied Access, all users will be able to access your site, except those who have the IP addresses you have specified. After selecting your access type, click the Add button to specify specific IP addresses. Click OK. The MMC will close the IP Address and Domain Name Restrictions dialog box.

6. Close all remaining dialog boxes.

> *TIP* If you want to restrict or permit a group of computers by IP address, you must specify the range of addresses using a starting IP address and subnet mask. For example, to specify all computers in the 207.49.189 subnet, you must enter 207.49.189.0 and the subnet mask 255.255.255.0.

The IP access you choose does not have to remain the same for the entire server. It is site specific (affecting the entire site) or directory specific (affecting only the specified directory). IP access is set to automatically grant the files and folders with the same permission as the directory whose IP access was originally set. If there are already existing IP access permissions located inside the directory most recently assigned IP access, you will be prompted to either overwrite with new permissions or to keep the existing permissions.

As you have already learned, the IUSR_*computername* account is specified during the setup of IIS. IIS setup automatically makes this user account part of the Guest and Everyone groups. Because of this, it grants permission to access every folder with the default NTFS permissions (Everyone Full Control). If desired, it is possible to change the username and permissions of the default user account. To change the name of the default user account from IUSR_*computername*, perform the following steps:

1. From the MMC, expand the IIS snap-in.
2. Right-click the server object. The MMC will display a Quick menu.
3. Select Properties. The MMC will display the Server Properties dialog box.
4. Click the Edit button. The MMC will display the WWW Master Properties for *Server* dialog box.
5. Click the Directory Security tab. In the Anonymous Access and Authentication Control section, click the Edit button. The MMC will display the Authentication Methods dialog box.
6. Click the Edit button. The MMC will display the Anonymous User Account dialog box.
7. Click the Browse button to see a list of system accounts. Choose the account that you want to use for anonymous access and click OK.
8. Close all remaining dialog boxes.

Allowing anonymous access to your Web site may, in fact, decrease the overall security risk to your network because user account passwords are not sent over the Internet. This is important because all Internet usernames and passwords are the same as the usernames and passwords that are used to log on to the regular NT system.

User Authentication

There are two types of authentication that you can implement when using IIS 4. The two types of authentication are as follows:

- Basic authentication
- Windows NT Challenge/Response

Basic authentication is the standard type of authentication specified by HTTP. While this form of authentication works for verifying users, it is not very secure. With basic authentication, usernames and passwords are sent as clear text. This makes it very easy for a person connected to either network (the network where the client is, or the network where the Web server is) to hack the system.

The other type of authentication supported by IIS is Windows NT Challenge/Response. With this type of authentication, unencrypted passwords are not sent over the network. This is much more secure than Basic authentication. The Challenge/Response form of authentication works with Internet Explorer versions 3 and higher.

When deciding which type of authentication you want to use, think about what types of Web browsers will be used by the those connecting to your IIS server. If they all will be using Microsoft Internet Explorer 3 or higher, you should definitely implement Windows NT Challenge/Response authentication. If the clients are going to be using browsers that may not all be IE 3 or higher, you will want to select both basic authentication and Windows NT Challenge/Response. In this way, clients will use Windows NT Challenge/Response whenever possible.

NTFS Permissions

The next step in securing your IIS machine is NTFS permissions. As you have learned in the previous section, NTFS permissions regulate who has what level of access to folders and files. The NTFS permissions that are present when you log on to an NT computer running IIS are the same permissions that are present across the Internet.

IIS@Work: Your Web and NTFS

As you learned earlier in this chapter, NTFS permissions affect how users gain access to documents. NTFS permissions are also an easy and effective way to create Web sites where certain documents are controlled. For example, let's say that you have a site where you want to sell cooking recipes. You would want everyone to have access to the home page, but you would only want people who paid to access the actual recipes pages. The best way to implement this is to use NTFS permissions so that the default permissions would apply to the home page, but the recipe pages would have a limited number of users accessing it.

The first step is to create a Windows NT Global group. Then you would create a Windows NT Local group and assign it permissions to the specific Web pages that contain the recipes. You would want to remove any existing permissions from the recipe pages so that only the Local group that you created has permissions. If an Internet user tries to access one of these pages, NT will prompt them for a username and password. Next, you would create individual user accounts for each Internet user who has paid for your service. You now have secure pages within your site.

Web Permissions

The next way to protect your Web sever is to implement Web permissions. Web permissions are unlike any other permission because they are generic and affect all users from any computer. The Web specific permissions are as follows:

- Read
- Write
- Execute

You should always have the Read permission turned on so that users can access your site. Although having the Write permission turned on along with the Execute permission can allow a user to upload a malicious file to your server, your site cannot run hit counters unless the Execute permission is enabled.

> ***NOTE*** Remember, NT and IIS security work hand in hand to provide one of the most secure Internet servers available.

Heavy Security Needs

24seven **CASE STUDY**

Last year, we worked with a large company to create a very secure Web environment. It was a unique situation with high-level security needs. We had to consider and eventually implement the enforcement of strong password security. Strong password security means that the users are forced to create complex passwords containing both uppercase and lowercase letters, as well as a numeric value. Because Windows NT Server does not provide this functionality itself, I used a Microsoft DLL file to add to the existing NT security.

In Windows NT Server Service Pack 2, Microsoft introduced a DLL file called passfilt.dll. Passfilt.dll forces users to create passwords with at least three of the following: one uppercase letter, one lowercase letter, one numeric value, or one special character. Additionally, passfilt.dll makes the user create a password that does not contain any part the username in it. It doesn't get any better than this. The only drawback here is that users must remember these complex passwords; but, at least in this case, security needs were more important than the convenience of the users.

Implementing passfilt.dll was not very hard at all. You can get detailed information on it from the Microsoft TechNet information library or from the Web at www.microsoft.com.

First, I installed the Windows NT 4 Service Pack 3. Next, I copied passfilt.dll to the %SYSTEMROOT%\SYSTEM32 folder. Finally, we used Regedt32.exe to add the value *Notification Packages*, of type REG_MULTI_SZ, to the Local Security Authority (LSA) key under HKEY_LOCAL_MACHINE\SYSTEM\CurrentControlSet\Control\LSA.

I double-clicked the Notification Packages key and added the value: PASSFILT. Then I clicked OK and exited the Registry.

After restarting the server, the new, strong password security was in place. Now Internet users, as well as internal users, had to create complex passwords. Boy, were those users upset!

11

Working with
Certificate Server

Secure Sockets Layer (SSL) is one of the IIS supporting technologies that you have learned about in previous chapters. As part of our discussion of SSL, we discussed the role that certificates play in the use of SSL across the Internet. Certificates can be issued from a variety of sources, but the most important consideration is verification of both the certificate and the issuing authority. In this chapter, we will discuss the use of Certificate Server within your environment as a means of providing necessary authentication services. We will consider how Certificate Server works, some basics about the architecture, and its installation and configuration.

Understanding the Use of Certificate Server

Microsoft Certificate Server provides a safe and easy means for you to become your own certificate authority and issue your own certificates. Being able to create certificates is not the only requirement for becoming a certificate authority. Verification of each user who requests a certificate is a process you perform before you hand the certificate over. You are also responsible for publishing a *Certificate Revocation List (CRL)*, which lists all of the certificates that are no longer valid for reasons other than the normal expiration of the certificate. Finally, it is critical for the certificate authority to guard the private key that it uses to create the digital signatures that are encapsulated within the certificates. If some individual is able to compromise the private key on the server, any certificate authentication, creation and verification performed from that point on is an untrusted (and untrustable) activity. Certificate Server helps you to perform authentification functions easily and with a consistent interface.

Certificate Server provides customizable services for issuing and managing certificates used in software security systems employing public-key cryptography, which is the basis for SSL. Certificate Server performs a central role in the management of software security systems to enable secure communications across the Internet, corporate intranets, and other non-secure networks.

Certificate Server receives requests for new certificates over transports, such as RPC or HTTP. It checks each request against custom or site-specific policies, sets optional properties for the certificate to be issued, and issues the certificate. Certificate Server also allows administrators to add elements to a Certificate Revocation List (CRL) and publish a signed CRL on a regular basis. Programmable interfaces are included for you to create support for additional transports, policies, and certificate properties and formats.

In general, Certificate Server generates certificates in standard X.509 format. Certificates in X.509 format are used in all commercial Public Key Infrastructure (PKI) products. PKI protocols, such as Secure Sockets Layer (SSL) and Secure/Multipurpose Internet Mail Extensions (S/MIME), use certificates in X.509 format.

How Certificate Server Works

The best way to understand how Certificate Server works and the steps that it takes in both the provision and the verification of the certificate is to closely examine Figure 11.1 and the discussion that follows it.

As you can see in the figure, the processing of the certificate request consists of five main steps, labeled 1–5 in the figure. In Step 1, the certificate request is submitted to the Certificate Server, along the *ICertRequest* COM interface. *ICertRequest* can be called from a number of places; however, the most common location is from an Active Server Page (ASP) or some other similar scripting host. The request itself must be either in the public-key cryptography standard (PKCS) #10 format (as specified in multiple Internet Request For Proposals [RFPs]) or in the format generated by the Key Manager utility (the executable named `keyring.exe`).

NOTE   The Key Manager utility is a graphical utility that is installed with the Windows NT 4 Option Pack, and includes facilities for generating public and private key pairs. It also installs server certificates for IIS.

Figure 11.1   How Certificate Server handles a certificate request

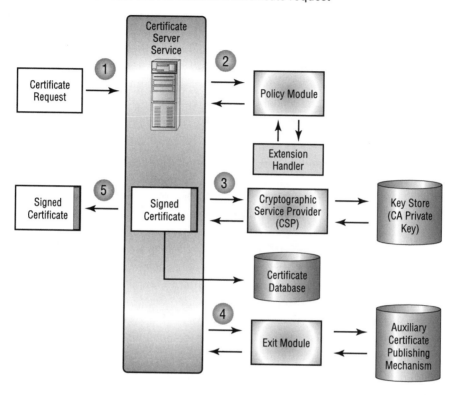

In Step 2, the Certificate Server runs the request using any installed policy modules. A *policy module* is a customizable object that implements the *ICertPolicy* COM interface. This particular object is responsible for implementing the policies that your certificate authority requires successful client adherence to before it can issue a certificate. For example, you might want to enforce that the designated organization for a specified X.500 Distinguished Name be your company name, or you might accept certificate requests only from people in a certain area code. You can even set the state of the request to Pending until further verification has been performed—for example, if you need to run a background check on the individual requesting the certificate or if you just want to have the request approved by a human security administrator instead of generating the certificate automatically.

In order to perform all of these tasks, the policy module examines any additional information that is packaged with the request. Certificate requests are capable of holding any proprietary information you want them to hold. For example, you might want to know an individual's phone number, address, social security number, and mother's maiden name. This information (for obvious reasons) isn't part of a standardized certificate request; however, you can customize Certificate Server to support the addition of such information by creating an *extension handler* whose job it is to interpret the added proprietary information. Your policy module can query the extension handler to interpret and access the extended information that it expects within the request. Using extension handlers, you can ensure that the server's decision about whether or not to grant a certificate isn't based strictly on the rather limited standard information in the request, but instead on both the standard information and the extended information you require for your environment.

Assuming the policy module approves the request, the actual building of the certificate takes place in Step 3. Certificate Server uses Microsoft's CryptoAPI, a cryptography application programming interface, to digitally sign the certificate. CryptoAPI interfaces on your behalf with any and all cryptographic service providers that you have installed on your system. In theory, your server might have several providers, each supplying a unique encryption service; but unless you have a very secure environment, you will most likely only have the Microsoft Base Cryptographic provider installed. Not only is a service provider responsible for performing the hashing and signing of the specified data, it is also responsible for the secure storage of public and private key pairs. Key pairs are stored in the provider's *key store*, which, in the case of the Microsoft Base Cryptographic Provider, is an encrypted database. In the case of a certificate authority, the cryptographic service provider uses the certificate authority's private signing key to create the digital signature. The cryptographic service provider signs the certificate request's date without Certificate Server even knowing what the certificate authority's private key is.

The result of Step 3 is a completed, signed certificate. Before the certificate is sent back to the requester, however, some tracking is necessary. Certificate Server logs all the information about the certificate it has just created, as well as information about the request that is in the certificate database. Without this information, you wouldn't be able to create a CRL if you needed to invalidate an individual's certificate.

In Step 4 of handling the certificate request, Certificate Server provides a means for exporting the certificate. The certificate is normally returned along the *ICertRequest* interface that the request came in on, but you might need to make your certificates readily accessible to other applications and components. Suppose you have an application that uses SSL and that will accept connections only from users with certificates on a predefined list, or perhaps you will use a collection of PKCS #7 certificate files to map client certificates to NT user accounts. In either case, you must be able to customize the way certificate information is published. You can do this by writing a custom Certificate Server *exit module*. An exit module is implemented as a COM server that exports the *ICertExit* interface and is registered with the server. After the potential exit modules have been called by the server, the certificate is returned to the entity that requested it, in Step 5.

Understanding the Certificate Server Architecture

As you have seen, Certificate Server is a development platform for building certificate authorities for enterprises or secure Internet applications. A configured and operational certificate authority will allow a site to issue, track, manage, and revoke certificates with minimal administration overhead and maximal security.

The Certificate Server consists of the server engine, the server database, and a set of modules and tools that work together to function as a certificate authority. External applications, modules, and administration tools use Component Object Model (COM) interfaces to interact with the server engine. Figure 11.2 shows the interfaces used by the server engine.

Figure 11.2   The components of the server engine and the COM interfaces they use

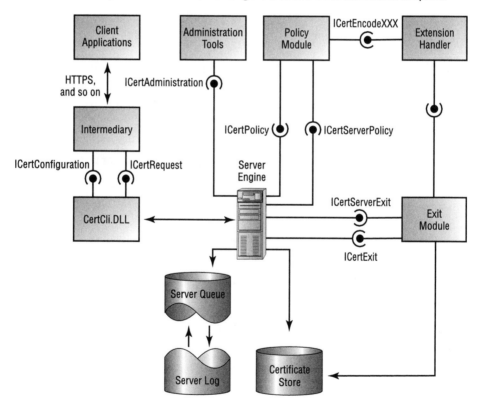

An operational certification system will typically have four major subsystems, as described in the following list:

Client   The client is the software that is used by the end user to generate a certificate request, send the request, and receive the finished certificate. A common client example would be Internet Explorer 5, or some other browser product. The client will typically interact with a custom interface maintained by the intermediary application.

Intermediary   The intermediary is a subsystem that consists of the intermediary application and the Certificate Server client interface (Certificate Server Web Client in the setup program). The intermediary application interacts directly with the client, receiving certificate requests and returning finished certificates. It communicates with the server engine through the Certificate Server client interface, which contains the *ICertConfig* and *ICertRequest* COM interfaces. An example of an intermediary application is IIS. The intermediary application can be implemented entirely through Active Server Pages.

Server   The server is the system that actually constructs the certificate. In addition to the server engine, two configurable components are included: the *policy module* and the *exit module*, both of which you learned about in the previous section. The policy module interacts with the server engine through the *ICertPolicy* and *ICertServerPolicy* COM interfaces. Exit modules (there can be more than one) interact with the server engine through the *ICertExit* and *ICertServerExit* interfaces.

Administrative client   The administrative client is the system that monitors and manages certificates and requests. The administrative client uses the *ICertAdmin* interface to communicate with the server engine.

Clearly, the Certificate Server product is designed with COM interfaces in mind—more so than some other servers because its very nature requires the presence of a programmatic interface. In general, Microsoft uses COM interfaces in all of its newer products to respond to such a need. Certificate Server is no exception.

While there are certain interfaces that you (or your development team) can manipulate to customize Certificate Server, you may not need to in some environments. However, Certificate Server will always need to access the CryptoAPI, so it is worthwhile to understand some specifics of how the CryptoAPI works.

Understanding the Windows Encryption API

As the popularity of the Internet grew, Microsoft was forced to integrate cryptographic support into its products. To provide users with the ability to manipulate encryption, Windows NT 4 Service Pack 3, Windows 95 OEM Service Release 2, and Microsoft's Internet Explorer 3.02 (and later) all include Microsoft's *CryptoAPI*. The CryptoAPI is a programming interface that you can use to add cryptographic functions to your programs. The CryptoAPI provides three basic sets of functions you will implement within your programs: certificate functions, simplified cryptographic functions, and base cryptographic functions. Figure 11.3 shows the model you will use to implement these functions.

Figure 11.3   The cryptographic model you will apply when you use Microsoft's CryptoAPI interface

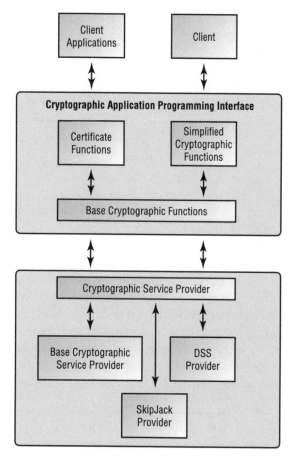

The simplified cryptographic functions include high-level functions for creating and using keys and for encrypting and decrypting information. The certificate functions provide the means to extract, store, and verify the digital signature certificates that transmitters may enclose with documents and to enumerate the certificates previously saved to a machine. At a lower level are the base cryptographic functions, which your programs should avoid calling to prevent conflicts resulting from Cryptographic Service Providers (CSP) that you have uninstalled, another program's required use of a particular CSP, and so on.

The CryptoAPI supports multiple cryptographic providers. For example, you might use Rivest, Shamir, and Adleman (RSA) encryption with some information; and you might digitally sign other information with the Digital Signature Standard (DSS). Table 11.1 lists the Cryptographic Service Providers (CSP).

Table 11.1 The Cryptographic Service Providers (CSP) that the CryptoAPI Supports

Cryptographic Provider	Encryption	Signature
PROV_RSA_FULL	RC2, RC4	RSA
PROV_RSA_SIG	n/a	RSA
PROV_DSS	n/a	DSS
PROV_FORTEZZA	SkipJack	DSS
PROV_SSL	RSA	RSA
PROV_MS_EXCHANGE	CAST	RSA

The CryptoAPI uses key databases to maintain password information. When you are creating an encrypted application, be sure to first create the necessary key databases. The best way to create an initial key database is to download all the samples from Microsoft's Developer Network, at http://msdn.microsoft.com/isapi/msdnlib.idc?theURL=/library/sdkdoc/crypto/aboutcrypto_19mh.htm. Among the samples at this site is a program named InitUser.exe, which creates the basic key databases you need to use the CryptoAPI. Alternatively, you can initialize the key databases yourself.

NOTE When you install Certificate Server, if the key databases have not been initialized already, the installation program will initialize them on your behalf.

Cryptographic Service Providers (CSPs)

A typical CSP is composed of a DLL and a signature file that the CryptoAPI uses to periodically verify the integrity and identity of the provider. Sometimes a CSP may implement some of its functionality in hardware in order to prevent tampering or to improve performance. Put another way, a CSP is a server able to perform a standard set of tasks invoked by the system through the CryptoAPI functions. An application should not assume that a CSP has capabilities exceeding the known standard. A CSP is just a removable plug-in module. The role played by a CSP makes it very similar to Windows drivers that implement print or graphic functions. Once you have registered the CSP, you may start using it without changing anything at the application level.

To ensure privacy, all the data a CSP manipulates (especially keys) is returned to the caller as opaque handles and remains inaccessible at the application level. Moreover, programs cannot affect the way the data is actually encoded. A program must limit itself to passing in the data and specifying the encryption type required. A provider can always return a type that explains what it can do and how. Different providers may use identical algorithms but must adopt different logic for padding and different key sizes.

Bundled with the CryptoAPI SDK is a default CSP called the Microsoft RSA Base Provider, implemented in `rsabase.dll`. It's a PROV_RSA_FULL type provider supporting the RSA public-key algorithm for both key exchange and signatures. (The key is 512 bits long.) The RSA Base Provider also uses RC2 and RC4 cipher algorithms for encryption with a 40-bit key. Applications should not rely on these lengths for a particular implementation, however, because CSPs can be swapped in without the application's knowledge.

Each CSP is associated with a database of key containers that stores all the private and public keys for the users accessing that computer. Each container has a unique name that is the key to the CryptoAPI programming world. Without this key database, all CryptoAPI functions will fail. The database typically has a default key container with the logon name of each user. However, a particular application may create a custom key container and key pairs during installation, assigning them the application's own name. Since the type of the provider affects the behavior of the cryptographic functions, two connected applications should use the same CSP, or at least CSPs with a common subset of functions. Figure 11.4 shows a simplified model of a key database.

Figure 11.4 A simplified model of the CryptoAPI key database generated by the Microsoft Base Cryptographic Provider

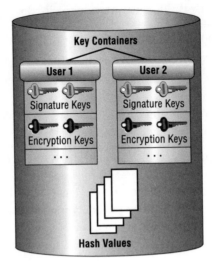

Key Database
(Single Provider)

The CryptoAPI Programming Model

Before adding public-key cryptography to real-world applications, you must become familiar with terms such as *context, session keys, exchange keys,* and *signature keys.*

A context represents an established session between CryptoAPI and the client application. To begin, you need to acquire a context. In doing so, you pass in the name of the key container you need and the name of the provider to which you want to connect. The handle you obtain must be used in all subsequent calls to the CryptoAPI routines.

A session key comes into play when it's time to encrypt or decrypt data. Session keys are volatile objects whose actual bytes never leave the CSP for reasons of privacy and security. The session key determines how a file is encrypted and must be inserted in a ciphered file to allow decryption. If you need to bring a session key out of the CSP for exchange or storage purposes, you will use *key blobs.* A key blob is a binary chunk of data and may be considered an encrypted and exportable version of the key itself. Blob stands for Binary Large Object.

The safekeeping mechanism is completed with exchange keys. They are pairs of keys (one public and one private) that take care of encrypting the session keys inside the key blobs and handling the digital signatures. A session key is created dynamically from the information stored in the user's key container. Once you have a session key, you are ready to make the calls that will scramble the bytes of the file.

Bear in mind that supporting cryptography in your applications doesn't require that you're familiar with the details of the RSA; Data Encryption Standard (DES); any other commonly used algorithm; or with subtle concepts, such as public and private keys.

Using the Cryptographic API's Basic Functions

When you want to use the CryptoAPI, you must apply the basic CryptoAPI functions within your programs, which will let you perform the three basic activity types previously discussed in this chapter. The CryptoAPI's designers divided its functions into four main areas: CSPs, keys, hash objects, and signatures. Within an encryption application, you will typically call the CryptAcquireContext function before any other function. This function lets you select or access a Cryptographic Service Provider. While the usage of the functions is complex, if you were writing a Visual Basic program (for example), you would declare the implementation of CryptAcquireContext, as shown here:

```
Declare Function CryptAcquireContext Lib "advapi32.dll" Alias _
    "CryptAcquireContextA" (phProv As Long, pszContainer As String, _
    pszProvider As String, ByVal dwProvType As Long, _
    ByVal dwFlags As Long) As Long
```

The CryptAcquireContext function returns a 32-bit Long value, which indicates to the remaining CryptoAPI functions that CryptAcquireContext established a working cryptography session. You may specify a particular Cryptographic Service Provider and key container through the pszContainer and pszProvider parameters.

After you have obtained a handle to the successful session, you can implement the functions shown in Table 11.2 to perform encryption activities within your programs.

Table 11.2   The CryptoAPI's Basic Functions

CryptoAPI Function	Description
CryptAcquireContext	Returns a handle to the key container in a Cryptographic Service Provider.
CryptCreateHash	Creates a hash object (a numeric interpretation of a value).
CryptDecrypt	Uses a decryption key to decrypt a buffer's contents.
CryptDeriveKey	Derives an encryption key from a hash object. Generally, you will hash a password or other specific string, create a hash object, and derive the key from that object.

Table 11.2   The CryptoAPI's Basic Functions *(continued)*

CryptoAPI Function	Description
CryptDestroyHash	Destroys a hash object created with CryptCreateHash.
CryptDestroyKey	Destroys a key, whether imported (with CryptImportKey) or created (with CryptDeriveKey).
CryptEncrypt	Uses an encryption key to encrypt a buffer's contents.
CryptExportKey	Returns a key blob from a key. A key blob is an encrypted copy of a key that you can transmit to a key's receiver. Generally, you will use a key blob to encrypt a single key and send it along with a single-key encrypted document.
CryptGenKey	Generates random keys to use with the Cryptographic Service Provider.
CryptGetHashParam	Retrieves data previously associated with a hash object.
CryptGetKeyParam	Retrieves data previously associated with a key.
CryptGetProvParam	Retrieves data previously associated with a Cryptographic Service Provider.
CryptGetUserKey	Returns the handle to a signature or previously defined key (as opposed to a key which you derive from a hash object).
CryptHashData	Hashes a data stream.
CryptImportKey	Extracts the key from a key blob.
CryptReleaseContext	Releases the handle to the key container.
CryptSetProvParam	Customizes a Cryptographic Service Provider's operations.
CryptSetProvider	Sets the default Cryptographic Service Provider.
CryptSignHash	Uses an encryption key to digitally sign a data stream. You will learn more about digital signatures in later sections of this chapter.
CryptVerifySignature	Verifies a hash object's digital signature.

Each function's description applies the CryptoAPI logically. For example, to export a key is a two-step process. The first step retrieves the user's public key from the Cryptographic Service Provider using `CryptGetUserKey`. After your program has retrieved the public-key handle, you can call `CryptExportKey` to get a key blob. You can then transmit the key blob to another user, who will use the `CryptImportKey` function to retrieve the key from the key blob.

Installing Certificate Server

When you install the Windows NT 4 Option Pack, Certificate Server is listed as an option in the Components list of the Setup dialog box. Selecting the Certificate Server option and clicking Show Subcomponents displays the Certificate Server dialog box.

You can install Certificate Server in its entirety, or you can disable some of the subcomponents. Since the subcomponents of Certificate Server are not particularly space consumptive (about 2Mb), we suggest that you install all of the subcomponents. The Certificate Server Certificate Authority provides the main functionality of Certificate Server, so you *must* install that component. If disk space is tight, you could skip the Certificate Server Documentation option, but you might be left a bit helpless later—so avoid doing so if you can. The Certificate Server Web Client option provides the capability to request certificates via Web browsers and is installed automatically when you choose the Certificate Server Certificate Authority. This capability is likely the main reason why you would choose to install Certificate Server, although certificates can be used for a number of other purposes, including e-mail encryption and signing, to name a common example.

As you have seen in previous chapters, most components contained within the Windows NT 4 Option Pack use predefined configuration settings, which result in a minimum of input from the user during installation. Certificate Server, however, is the exception to this rule. After you select the subcomponents of Certificate Server that you want to install and then continue with the installation process, the Microsoft Certificate Server Setup dialog box will appear, as shown in Figure 11.5.

The Configuration Data Storage Location settings define the location of various exposable components of Certificate Server, including the certificate authority's root certificate, which needs to be made publicly available to anyone using or verifying certificates generated by your server. The Database Location and Log Location options specify the location of the files that will hold the actual certificate information and the logs of the certificate requests. The format of the file is a Microsoft Access database, but it is not necessary to install Access for the installation to work correctly. The Database Location option specifies the location of the certificate database described in Figure 11.1.

If you click the Show Advanced Configuration check box and then click the Next button, the setup program will display an advanced Certificate Server configuration dialog box,

Figure 11.5   The Microsoft Certificate Server Setup dialog box

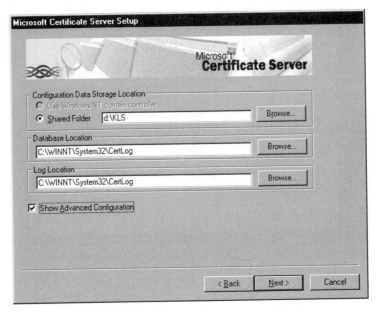

as shown in Figure 11.6. From this dialog box, you can configure a number of more specific options for your Certificate Server installation.

Figure 11.6   The Advanced Certificate Server Setup dialog box

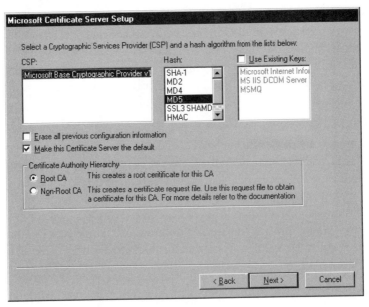

Although this dialog box seems to contain many options, there are actually only a few key concepts here. If you had multiple cryptographic service providers installed on your system, you could specify which one Certificate Server should use from this dialog box. However, as mentioned previously, you will generally use the Base Cryptographic Provider. (In fact, it is typically the only one installed on the server.) The Hash list lets you select the algorithm that the server will use to create and analyze the digital signatures your certificate authority will employ to validate certificates. As mentioned previously, CSPs are also responsible for storing the public/private key pairs that have been used for other applications. To use one of these pre-existing pairs, check the Use Existing Keys check box. The Erase All Previous Configuration Information check box lets you remove the configuration files for any previous versions of Certificate Server you might have installed on your machine.

> **WARNING**   Unless you have a specific reason for using an existing key pair and have absolute confidence that such a key pair is uncompromised, you should create a new key pair at the time you install Certificate Server. Doing so will guarantee that your certificates are completely trustworthy.

The Certificate Authority Hierarchy area contains two options: Root CA and Non-Root CA. Because the underlying operating system support for certificate hierarchies is not available in Windows NT 4, Certificate Server can be installed with the Root CA option only. This means that your certificate authority's own certificate will be signed by itself, rather than being signed by one of the publicly available certificate authorities.

The last step in the Certificate Server installation is to provide the information that will identify your certificate authority to the rest of the world. The options that the last Set up dialog box displays—CA Name, Organization, Organizational Unit, Locality, State, and Country—are all part of building the X.500 Distinguished Name that will uniquely identify your authority. At the bottom of this dialog box, the CA Description field provides a friendly description of the certificate authority that lets people know who you are and what your certificate authority is being used for.

We'll see the results of these configuration options in the next section when we go through the steps of requesting a client certificate for a Web browser.

Managing Certificate Server

To take advantage of the new certificate authority, go to the Certificate Server home page, which you can find at `http://localhost/certsrv`.

This home page provides you with links to the Certificate Administration Log Utility, the Certificate Administration Queue Utility, and the Certificate Enrollment Tools pages. It also provides a link to the Certificate Server Documentation, assuming you installed it. The Certificate Enrollment Tools page lists three options: Install Certificate Authority Certificates, Process A Certificate Request, and Request A Client Authentication Certificate.

Requesting a Client Authentication Certificate

When requesting certificates for client browsers, one of the most important fields of a certificate is the Subject field, which identifies the individual to whom the certificate is assigned. This Subject field contains an X.500 Distinguished Name in the following form:

```
C=US, O=KLS Enterprises, OU=Texts, CN=Craig Smith
```

For our browser to build a certificate request, it needs to let Certificate Server know the subject for the certificate. You can do this from the Certificate Enrollment Form page. To display this page, select the Request A Client Authentication Certificate option from the Certificate Enrollment Tools page.

The Advanced button at the bottom of the Certificate Enrollment Form page displays the Advanced Settings page, which lets you specify information such as the type of certificate you want. However, to accept the default settings and request the certificate, click the Submit Request button after completing the form. Internet Explorer will display another dialog box indicating that the browser is ready to download the certificate.

Installing the Certificate Authority Certificate

After you have installed your client authentication certificate, the browser will prompt you to install the certificate authority certificate. This certificate is required for your client to exchange the session key for the secure connection. Downloading the certificate authority certificate is a very simple process. Just click the Install Certificate Authority Certificates option from the Enrollment Tools page, which will display the Certificate Authority Certificate List page.

When you first install Certificate Server, you should see only a single option in this list: a certificate containing the information that you specified in the Certificate Server Setup dialog box. To install the certificate authority certificate, click the link. Select Open This File From Its Current Location and click OK to display the New Site Certificate dialog box. Click the View Certificate button to open the Properties dialog box, which displays a list of fields on the left and their values on the right.

The details for the Subject field are the same as the details for the Issuer field, which means that this certificate authority signed its own certificate. This type of certificate authority is known as a *root certificate authority*. When you click OK in the New Site Certificate dialog box, the browser will display the Root Certificate Store dialog box. This dialog box will ask if you want to add the certificate to the root store. It then displays information about the certificate. Here, you can also see confirmation that this is a self-issued certificate.

WARNING   Trusting root certificate authorities is, needless to say, a major security commitment. The root certificate authority has ultimate control over any certificate it issues. Before you specify yourself as a root certificate authority, you should be fully aware of the serious commitment you are making to confirm the identity of anyone you issue a certificate to.

Requesting a Server-Side Certificate

The other half of being able to establish secure connections is having a certificate for the server itself. The server-side certificate can be created automatically in Key Manager if Certificate Server is already running on your machine. Creating server certificates on an IIS machine that does not include a Certificate Server installation is a complex process, beyond the scope of what we are looking at here.

Administration of Certificate Server

Earlier in this chapter, we mentioned that all certificate requests and granted certificates were logged in the certificate database (a file in the Microsoft Access format). We also mentioned that you didn't need Access to install or manage the database. In fact, Certificate Server provides a Web interface from which you can see and administer existing certificates on the server. To get to the page, select the Certificate Administration Log Utility from the Certificate Server home page.

You can also look at each certificate individually. To do so, either click the Form View button or click a particular server's serial number. In Form view, each field of the certificate is shown. More importantly, Form view also provides a Revoke button that lets you revoke a certificate. Remember, certificates should be revoked when they are no longer valid. For instance, if an employee who had been previously issued a certificate left your company, you would revoke that certificate and add it to the CRL. The first step in doing this is to select the employee's certificate record in the database and click Revoke. The second step is to re-create the CRL by using the command-line utility CERTUTIL.EXE. To create a CRL, execute the following command from the console:

```
CERTUTIL -CRL
```

The dash at the end of the command tells CERTUTIL to put the list in the default location, which is the enrollment virtual root. This file is the PCKS #7 standardized CRL file available on your Web site. The CRL must be publicly available so that servers and clients can determine whether their certificates have been revoked.

The Requery button at the bottom of the Certificate Log Administration list will refresh the contents of the list. This capability might be important if you need to determine whether additional certificates have been created since you first generated the list or whether other administrators have revoked any certificates.

The other administration option available on the Certificate Server home page is the Certificate Administration Queue Utility. Selecting this option will display the Certificate Server Queue Administration page. This page is similar to the other administration page; the difference is that the queue page shows *all* certificate requests—even declined ones—together with their current status.

Command-Line Utilities

In addition to the Web interface, Certificate Server includes two command-line utilities that you can use to achieve greater functionality. For example, CERTUTIL.EXE lets you publish a CRL—a process that you cannot perform from the Web-based interface. You will also use CERTUTIL to deny or resubmit a pending request, to set certificate extension and attribute values, and to revoke certificates. The other command-line utility CERTREQ lets you submit certificate requests without using the Web interface. These utilities are very useful; however, with some inventive ASP scripting (as described briefly in the case study), you can take advantage of all of their capabilities from ASP pages.

Validating Salespeople in the Field

While Certificate Server is a very useful product, the danger inherent in certifying clients makes many companies opt for limited use of the product. However, in the context of making intranet information available to employees working outside the corporate network—for example, salespeople in the field—Certificate Server can be especially useful.

Recently, we worked with a company that was maintaining extensive database records in a SQL Server installation, including their entire sales, invoicing, inventory, and related databases. Their problem was that they had a staff of field salespeople who were outside the office most of the time. They wanted to grant access to the salespeople while also ensuring that people who were explicitly granted access were the only ones getting into the database information, that the users in the field could take advantage of the existing Active Server Pages interface to the data, and that—should a salesperson leave the company—they could easily remove individual rights without having to alert the entire sales force to a new password environment.

The Problem

While there are several ways to accomplish what they wanted, including using NT Challenge-Response authentication, they wanted to avoid having users use passwords over the Internet because of the risk of interception inherent in such transmissions. Moreover, they wanted the access grants to be "invisible" to both the salespeople and the clients they were meeting. Therefore, they needed to find a way to absolutely validate the user's identity and, at the same time, provide for easy, long-term management of user access.

The Solution

With Certificate Server, we were able to deploy certificates only to the salespeople. We were able to issue one certificate per person, each of which was installed on the representative's corporate-owned laptop. Easy revocation abilities let us handle the employee turnover, and mapping the certificate to an NT login let us control the access that the user had to the data stored on the SQL Server.

Summing It Up

Certificate Server provided us with a powerful, elegant, and highly secure way to ensure the identity of users. The addition of Certificate Server code stubs to the Web site required a minimal investment of time. We were able to begin dispensing certificates to users within only a few hours.

24seven **CASE STUDY**

12

IIS Monitoring and Optimization

While IIS will work just fine with a default installation and some minor configuration, you want to get the most out of it. The focus of this chapter is to help you configure IIS and Windows NT Server so that you can do just that. To do this, you need to know how to properly monitor IIS and NT, and how to tune your server for optimization.

Monitoring IIS

Because IIS is an add-on service for Windows NT, you can use some of the standard NT tools for performance tuning and optimization. One of the most useful NT tools is Performance Monitor. This utility allows you to capture and view system statistics. The most powerful functionality of Performance Monitor is its ability to export data to other data-processing applications, such as MS Excel and Access, so that you can create charts and measurement trend analysis databases.

The following terms will help you to better understand how to use Performance Monitor:

Object   An Object is a general category of performance data, such as Processor or Physical Disk.

Counter   A Counter is a specific item within a general category (Object), such as Processor: % of Processor Time.

Instance   An instance is an even more specific item within a Counter, such as Processor: % of Processor Time: Processors 0.

Scale   The scale is the unit of measurement that Performance Monitor uses to measure the data. The scale is configurable.

Performance Monitor comes with a default set of Objects and Counters. As you add services to your Windows NT Server, you do not have to manually add Objects and Counters. Applications and services that you install automatically add their own sets. While not all applications add Objects and Counters in NT, most of the major ones do. For example, when you install IIS, it adds the following Objects:

- Internet Information Services Global Information
- Web Service
- FTP Service
- Active Server Pages
- SMTP Server

You may see additional Objects, depending on what options you selected during your IIS installation. For example, you might see the NNTP Server Object. The key to effectively using Performance Monitor is knowing which Objects and Counters to use. Let's examine some of the most useful Objects and Counters for IIS system administrators.

Internet Information Services Global Object

The Internet Information Services Global Object contains Counters that are invaluable to an IIS administrator. It lets you analyze global characteristics of IIS, including the IIS cache, to determine if they are configured optimally.

The Internet Information Services Global Object contains two types of Counters: cache and bandwidth. The following is a list of its Counters, which category they fall into, and what information they offer:

Cache Flushes   A cache flush occurs when IIS detects a change in the contents of a published directory. It then flushes the cache and caches the directory again. This Counter measures how many cache flushes occur in the measured time frame.

Cache Hits   This Counter shows how efficient your IIS cache is. When a user requests a document, IIS attempts to get the data from the cache. A high number indicates that your cache is working well.

Cache Hits %   This Counter shows the percentage of total requests that are found in the IIS cache. You are looking for a high number relative to your site. Although the value is dependent upon your individual site, a value in the range of 80% to 90% is considered very good.

Cache Misses   This is the opposite value of Cache Hits. It tells you how efficiently your cache is working. You are looking for a low number here.

Cache File Handles   A file handle is an internal number generated by the operating system to identify a file. File handles change each time a file is accessed. IIS caches file handles so that user requests can be processed more quickly. This Counter shows information about how IIS is processing object requests. This is an informational Counter, so you are not looking for high or low values here.

Current Blocked Async I/O Requests   This is a bandwidth Counter. If Bandwidth Throttling is configured, IIS can deny a user's request for a specific site on your server. This Counter shows you if current user requests are being blocked by the IIS bandwidth-throttling setting.

Directory Listings   This is a cache Counter. Directory Listings are cached directories that IIS uses to respond to user requests for a directory list. This Counter is informational, so you are not looking for a particular value.

Measured Async I/O Bandwidth Usage   This is a bandwidth Counter. You can use this Counter to determine the total amount of network bandwidth that your server is using. This value is calculated over one minute. You want to see a value less than your current available network bandwidth.

Objects   This is a cache Counter. You can use this Counter to view the total number of cached objects within IIS, including directory listings and service objects.

Total Allowed Async I/O Requests   If you are restricting bandwidth using the IIS Bandwidth Throttling option, you can use this Counter to view how many user requests Bandwidth Throttling is allowing through the system. This is informational only. You are not looking for a specific high or low value.

Total Blocked Async I/O Requests   This Counter is very similar to the Current Blocked Async I/O Requests Counter. While that Counter shows the current amount of user requests that are being denied access due to Bandwidth Throttling, this Counter shows the total number of user requests that are being denied.

Total Rejected Async I/O Requests   This Counter shows the number of user requests that are denied access to the requested site and are not cached. When IIS blocks a user's request, it is cached so that when the bandwidth becomes available, the request can be processed. When a user request is rejected, the request is not cached.

Web Service Object

The Web Service Object, like the Internet Information Services Global Object, tracks information that is used to tune the performance of your server. The major difference between the two Objects is that the Web Service Object is specific to the HTTP service rather than to all IIS services.

You can use this Object to view specific data about a single Web site managed by IIS, or about all sites on the system. The Web Service Object Counters are as follows:

Anonymous Users/sec   Anonymous users are users who do not specify user account credentials when accessing a document through IIS. This Counter monitors the number of anonymous users that are accessing the system within a given time frame.

Bytes Received/sec   This Counter shows the number of bytes that IIS is receiving per second. Most of this traffic will be HTTP requests for data. The desired value is site dependent.

Bytes Sent/sec   This Counter shows the amount of data per second that IIS is sending in response to requests for data. The desired value is site dependent.

Bytes Total/sec   This is the sum of the Bytes Received/sec and the Bytes Sent/sec Counters. The desired value is site dependent.

CGI Requests/sec   Common Gateway Interface (CGI) is a scripting language for writing Web applets. This Counter is the number of CGI requests that IIS is processing per second. The desired value is site dependent.

Connection Attempts/sec   This Counter shows the number of connection requests that IIS is processing per second. The desired value is site dependent.

Current Anonymous Users   This Counter shows the current number of users who have connections to your server and have not specified NT user accounts.

Current Blocked I/O Requests   This Counter shows the requests that are currently blocked due to Bandwidth Throttling. Blocked requests are processed when the bandwidth becomes available.

Current CGI Requests   This Counter shows the current number of CGI requests that IIS is processing. The desired value is site dependent.

Current Connections   This is the sum of the anonymous and non-anonymous user connections. It is the total number of IIS users.

Current ISAPI Extension Requests   An Application Programming Interface (API) is an interface that applications use to communicate with the operating system. This Counter provides a way of standardizing code so that any vendor can write applications that will work within a given environment. ISAPI is the

Internet Service Application Programming Interface. It provides a way of creating custom Web applications that will run quickly on any browser. This Counter lets you view the current number of requests for ISAPI services that your system is processing. The desired value is site dependent.

Current NonAnonymous Users   Non-anonymous users are users who have provided valid NT user account credentials. This Counter shoes how many of these users are currently accessing your server.

Delete Requests/sec   An HTTP Delete request is used for removing a file from the system. This Counter lets you view the number of delete requests that the IIS Web service is processing. The desired value is site dependent.

Files Received/sec   This Counter shows the number of files that the IIS Web service is receiving per second. The desired value is site dependent.

Files Sent/sec   This Counter shows the number of files that the Web service is sending out per second. The desired value is site dependent.

Files/sec   This is the total number of file transactions, sent, and received per second. The desired value is site dependent.

Get Requests/sec   Internet clients use HTTP GET requests to download documents from your server. This Counter shows the number of HTTP GET requests that your server is currently processing per second. You use this Counter to gather information on your system. You are not necessarily seeking high or low values.

Head Requests/sec   HTML documents can contain a Head section. This section provides general information about a document to browsers. The Head Requests/sec Counter shows the number of HTTP requests using the HEAD method that your server is processing per second. The desired value is site dependent.

ISAPI Extension Requests/sec   This Counter shows the number of requests for ISAPI extensions that your server is managing per second. The desired value is site dependent.

Logon Attempts/sec   This Counter shows the number of logon attempts, either failed or successful, that your server is processing per second. The desired value is site dependent.

Maximum Anonymous Users   This Counter shows the highest number of simultaneous user connections that have used anonymous logons since your Web service began.

Maximum CGI Requests   This Counter shows the highest number of simultaneous CGI requests that your server has processed since the Web service began. The desired value is site dependent.

Maximum Connections   This Counter shows the highest number of simultaneous connections that your server has processed since the Web service began. This value shows combined instances of Web sites only.

Maximum ISAPI Extension Requests   This Counter shows the largest number of simultaneous ISAPI extension requests that your server has processed since the Web service began.

Maximum NonAnonymous Users   This is the highest number of concurrent connections by users who specified NT logon account information. This is measured since the Web service was started.

Measured Async I/O Bandwidth Usage   This Counter shows how much bandwidth your server is using. This is measured over a one-minute period.

Non-Anonymous Users/sec   This Counter shows the number of simultaneous user connections (using NT user account information) per second that the Web service is processing.

Not Found Errors/sec   When an Internet client requests a document that the IIS server cannot find, the user will receive an HTTP error message indicating that Error 404 File Not Found occurred. You can use the Not Found Errors/sec Counter to track the number of user requests that the server cannot satisfy because files cannot be found.

Other Request Methods/sec   The most common HTTP methods of requesting service are GET, PUT, POST, DELETE, TRACE, and HEAD. You can use this Counter to track request methods other than these.

Post Request Methods/sec   The most common use of the POST method is in HTML form fields. When a user requests that data be sent to the server, it is often sent using the POST method. This Counter allows you to view the number of POST requests that your server is processing per second.

Put Request Methods/sec   Internet users can send files to a server using the PUT method. This Counter shows the number of simultaneous user requests per second using the PUT method that your server is processing.

Total Allowed Async I/O Requests   This Counter shows the total amount of bandwidth (configured through Bandwidth Throttling) that your server has managed since your Web service began.

Total Anonymous Users   This Counter shows the total number of users using non-Windows NT logons that your server has processed since your Web service began.

Total Blocked Async I/O Requests   This Counter shows the number of I/O requests that your server temporarily blocked due to Bandwidth Throttling since your Web service began.

Total CGI Requests   This Counter shows the total number of CGI requests that your server has processed since your Web service began.

Total Connection Requests   This Counter shows the total number of connection requests, failed or successful, that your server has processed since your Web service began.

Total Delete Requests   When an Internet user wants to remove a file from an IIS server directory, the client's Web browser sends a request using the DELETE method. This Counter shows the total number of DELETE requests received since your Web service began.

Total Files Received   This Counter shows the number of files that the Web service has received since the service began.

Total Files Sent   This Counter indicates the number of files that the Web service has sent since the service began.

Total Files Transferred   This Counter is the sum of the Total Files Received and Total Files Sent Counters. It indicates the total number of files sent and received by your Web service since the service began.

Total Get Requests   In HTML, the GET request is used for retrieving files. This Counter shows the total number of GET requests that your server has processed since service startup.

Total Head Requests   Headers in HTML documents can contain data, such as how long a file should be cached in a client's browser. The browser may query the server to see if the headers contain information about updating the page. You can use the Total Head Requests Counter to view how many requests for header information your server has processed since service startup.

Total ISAPI Extension Requests   This Counter indicates the total number of ISAPI extension requests that your server has processed since service startup.

Total Logon Attempts   This Counter indicates the total number of user logon requests that your server has processed since service startup.

Total Method Requests   This Counter shows the total number of method requests that you server has processed since the Web service began.

Total Method Requests/sec   This Counter indicates the total number of method requests your server is processing per second.

Total Non-Anonymous Users   This Counter shows the total number of users using NT logons that your server has processed since your Web service began.

Total Not Found Errors This Counter shows the total number of document requests that IIS failed to service due to a File Not Found error. This Counter is also measured since the Web service was last started.

Total Other Request Methods This Counter shows the total number of request methods—other than PUT, GET, DELETE, TRACE, POST, and HEAD—that your server has received.

Total Post Request This Counter shows the total number of POST request methods that your server has processed since your Web service was started.

Total Put Requests This Counter shows the total number of PUT requests that your server has processed since your Web service began.

Total Rejected Async I/O Requests If you have configured Bandwidth Throttling, this Counter shows the total number of rejected I/O requests that your server has processed since your Web service began.

Total Trace Requests A TRACE request method is used for diagnostic purposes. This Counter shows the total number of TRACE requests that your server has processed since your Web service began.

Using the Windows NT Performance Monitor, you can monitor specific IIS Objects and Counters to help determine if your server is configured optimally. You also need to monitor your Windows NT Server to see if you can better configure it to operate with IIS.

Tuning Your Windows NT Server

Part of optimizing your server for IIS is configuring some of the Windows NT Server properties to enhance performance, as well as configuring the IIS-specific values. Just like IIS, in order to configure your Windows NT Server properly, you must establish its current level of performance. Your server may already be optimally configured. You won't know until you run Performance Monitor and see.

As we have already discussed, Performance Monitor uses Objects and Counters to track system performance. NT has its own set of Objects that you will want to use for tracking performance. To use the Performance Monitor Objects and Counters, you need to understand what system resources you are tracing. Windows NT system resources are broken into four categories: memory, processor, disk system, and network system. Each of these categories covers a group of potential resources. For example, the processor group covers multiple processors on a single system. Later in this chapter, we will discuss the Counters within Performance Monitor that are used to monitor these categories.

These are the core Objects in Performance Monitor:

Cache   This Object has many Counters that you can use to monitor an area of physical memory that holds recently used data.

LogicalDisk   The Counter in this Object monitors areas of disks (partitions).

Memory   This Object has Counters for viewing the system memory statistics.

Paging File   A page file is an area of disk space that the system uses to emulate physical memory. This Object has Counters for monitoring the system's page files.

PhysicalDisk   This Object has Counters for viewing the statistics of the physical disks on your NT computer.

Process   The Counters in this Object track the system load of programs running in NT.

Processor   This Object contains Counters for tracking the system processor and its load.

Redirector   A redirector is a client service. When a user types *F:* on their machine, there must be a way of directing the request to the network. This is the function of a redirector. You can use the Counters in this Object to monitor the systems redirectors.

System   This is a general Object that contains Counters on various system items.

Thread   A thread is the part of a process that communicates with the processor.

Now let's examine the four resource categories and which Objects and Counters to use to monitor their behavior.

Memory

Experience has taught me that adding physical memory to the system can solve most resource-related problems in NT. Knowing this, you should not blindly add physical memory without first testing to ensure that memory is indeed the problem. Performance Monitor has Objects and Counters that are used to determine if memory is an issue. The following list describes the Performance Monitor Objects and Counters that you should use to diagnose memory bottlenecks:

Memory: Pages/sec   Paging occurs when the system writes data to the page file and maps that area of disk to a physical memory address. The Memory Manager in Windows NT Executive Services manages this process. The average range for this Counter is between 0 and 20. You are looking for a low value indicating that NT is writing a low amount of data to the disk. If you find that excessive paging is occurring, add RAM.

Memory: Available Bytes Microsoft recommends having no less than 4MB of physical memory available. If this value drops below 4MB, you should consider adding RAM to your system.

Memory: Committed Bytes This Counter shows the amount of memory that applications have requested (in bytes). You should see a value that is less than the physical memory on your server; if not, add RAM.

Memory: Pool Non-paged Bytes The non-paged pool is memory that cannot be written to the disk. Processes that require non-paged pool memory are most often system processes but can be from applications, as well. This value should remain steady while applications are running. If this value increases while no new applications are open, you have an application with a memory leak. A memory leak occurs when an application requests memory and does not release the memory when it is closed. The next time the application is opened, it requests new memory. Sometimes you see a machine that runs out of memory. If you reboot the system, it works fine for awhile but eventually runs out of memory again.

Processor

Over the years, I've seen many system administrators add faster, or more, processors to their servers without verifying that they have a processor bottleneck in the first place. If you have the financial means, you can add the fastest processors on the market to your servers. But, for many companies, a processor upgrade is costly and unnecessary.

Just like with memory bottlenecks, you can use Performance Monitor's core Objects and Counters to diagnose processor problems. The key Objects and Counters to evaluate bottlenecks are as follows:

Processor: %Processor Time This Counter shows the total amount of processor time that your server's processor is spending on all system processing. This value should be below 75%. However, if you experience sustained processor usage above 75%, do further monitoring to rule out other causes of this bottleneck, such as low system memory causing excessive paging.

Processor: % Privileged Time Privileged processor time is the amount of time your system's processor spends on Kernal mode processes. Kernel mode processes call directly to the hardware. This value should also be below 75%.

Processor: % User Time User mode processes are the application subsystems and the applications that run in them. This value should be consistently below 75%.

Processor: Interrupts/sec This Counter shows how many processor interrupts are occurring per second in your system. The ideal value is dependent on your system hardware. If you see high, sustained rates of interrupts per second, you have to locate the hardware controller that is sending excessive interrupts and replace it.

System: Processor Queue Length   This Counter shows how many application processes are waiting to be processed. You should not have more than two waiting at any one time. If you find a high value here, you can offload applications, upgrade the system's processor, or add additional processors.

Server Work Queues: Queue Length   This Counter comes in handy if you already have multiple processors. While the System: Processor Queue Length Counter shows the total processor jobs waiting to be processed, the Server Work Queues: Queue Length Counter shows the number of jobs waiting to be processed by a particular processor. A sustained value of less than 2 is ideal. If you find high values, add faster processors.

Disk

This particular Object requires that you configure NT to allow Performance Monitor Disk Counters to work. Then, you can use Performance Monitor to monitor system activity as usual.

To enable disk performance Counters, perform the following steps:

1. Click the Start menu. Go to Programs ➤ Command prompt. NT will start the System Command prompt.

2. Type **Diskperf -y**. Exit the command prompt.

3. Restart your system. You can now use disk performance Counters within Performance Monitor.

NOTE   If you are using a disk array controller, you must type **Diskperf -ye** to enable the enhanced disk performance Counters that a disk array requires.

After you have enabled the disk performance Counters, you can use the following Objects and Counters to monitor the system's disk performance:

Disk: % Disk Time   This Counter shows the total amount of time that the disk is busy servicing read and write requests. You should see a sustained rate of less than 50%. If you see excessive disk usage, consider upgrading your disk system (controller cards, faster disks).

Disk: Disk Queue Length   When the system requests data to be read or written to the disk, the disk may have to queue the request until it can be processed. You want low values here. You should not see a sustained rate of more than 2 for this

Counter. If you find your disk is queuing more than two requests, consider upgrading your disk system.

Disk: Avg. Disk Bytes Transferred This Counter determines whether or not your disk system is running efficiently. When the system requests data to be read or written to the disk, it transfers as much data as it can at one time. This value is the average transfer rate. You want high values here. Check your disk documentation for the expected rate of transfer for your disk.

Disk: Disk Bytes/sec This Counter shows the amount of data (in bytes) that your disk is transferring per second. You want high values here. Check your disk documentation for your expected bytes per second transfer rate.

Network

You must consider the following when monitoring the network system:

Network Card This is the physical network adapter in your server. The type and speed of your adapter affects performance.

Protocols The protocols you choose affect your system's network performance. Try to choose a single protocol for your network. Binding multiple protocols adversely affects your server's performance.

Binding Bindings are the association of protocols with a network adapter card. Bindings are configured into an order. If you have multiple protocols bound to your server, the binding order affects which protocol the system uses first.

Cabling The type of network cable you choose also affects your overall performance. For example, to get the most out of 100-BaseT network cards, you should have Category-5 network cable.

Routers Routers are typically physical devices that separate networks. When a network packet gets sent to another network, it is the router that determines how the packet is sent. Buying a more expensive router usually means better performance.

Bridges A bridge is similar to a router in that it also connects networks. However, while a router routes network traffic to other networks, a bridge creates one network out of the original two. All network traffic goes to both networks.

Gateways Like a bridge or a router, a gateway is a central location where network traffic can pass through to another network. However, a gateway is commonly used for less frequent network traffic due to its high system overhead.

You can use the following Performance Monitor Objects to monitor network performance.

Network Interface: Bytes Total/sec   This Counter shows the amount of traffic that your network card is processing. You want high values here. Check your network card documentation for the recommended values for your specific card.

Network Interface: Bytes Sent/sec   This Counter shows the amount of network traffic sent from your server on this network card. You want high values here. Check your network card documentation for the recommended values for your specific card.

Server: Bytes Total/sec   This value indicates the total bytes per second that your server is processing, including all network cards. You want a high value.

Server: Logons/sec   This value indicates the number of logon requests that your server is processing per second.

Server: Logon Total   This value indicates the total number of logons that your server has processed since the server was started.

Network Segment: % Network Use   This Counter shows the total network bandwidth that your server is consuming. You want a low value here. This value should be less than 30% of your network bandwidth. If you find that your server is consuming more than 30% on a regular basis, consider segmenting your network in order to better streamline performance.

IIS Logging

Log files provide a way to track what's going on with your IIS system. IIS can create log files in ASCII text format, or it can send log data directly to any ODBC-compliant database. IIS supports the following four log file formats:

- Microsoft IIS Log file format
- NCSA Common file format
- W3C Extended Log file format
- ODBC logging

You can determine what format a log file is by the first two characters in the filename. The MS IIS Log files have *in* for the first two characters. The NCSA log files have *nc* for the first two characters. W3C Extended log files have *ex* as the first two characters. ODBC log files have two characters that are based on the file's size.

IIS will collect information from the following services: WWW, FTP, NNTP, and SMTP. After you turn logging on for a specific service, you can control which sites and virtual directories IIS will log. You must configure logging for each service independently through the service's Properties dialog box.

ASCII Log Files

The Microsoft IIS, NCSA, and W3C file formats are all ASCII formats. The difference lies in what logging options you can control and what application you can use to view the results. MS IIS and NCSA will not allow you to control any aspect of what you want logged. If you are not using a database and the ODBC logging format, you should use the W3C Extended log file format. It logs more information than the NCSA or MS IIS log file formats.

Microsoft included the NCSA log file format (even though it does not log as much information as the other log file formats) because it is an industry standard. If you have a log file analysis utility that supports NCSA standards, you can use it to view your log files. However, Site Server Express is included with IIS 5 and it makes a very good log file analysis utility to view the other file formats.

Viewing IIS Log Files with Site Server Express

In Chapter 8, we discussed how to create a site map using Site Server Express 2. Another useful function of Site Server Express is its log analysis capabilities.

Using the Usage Import program in Site Server Express, you can import any of the supported IIS log file types. Once one of these logs is imported, you can use Site Server Express Report Writer to analyze its contents. To import a log file, perform the following steps:

1. Click the Start menu. Go to Programs ➤ Windows NT 4 Option Pack ➤ Microsoft Site Server Express 2 ➤ Usage Import. NT will open the Usage Import program.

2. In the Usage Import main screen, you will see a message indicating that there are no sites configured in the database. Click OK. Usage Import will display the Log Data Source Properties dialog box.

3. Select the log file type that you specified in IIS. Click OK. Usage Import will display the Server Properties dialog box.

4. Select the service you want to view the log from (WWW or FTP). You may also specify the IP address you want to view the log from. You must specify a site URL in the Local Domain field. Click OK. Usage Import will display the Site Properties dialog box.

5. Enter the home page path (URL) in the Home Page URLs field. Click OK. Usage Import will close the Site Properties dialog box and return you to the Usage Import main screen.

6. In the Log File Manager dialog box, click the Browse button to select the log file you want to import. After you have selected the log file, click the green arrow on the tool bar to import the log.

You can examine the contents of the imported log files using the Site Server Express Report Writer.

> **WARNING**   If you select a file and click the green triangle to import it and nothing comes up, it is probably because the log file format you selected in Site Manager is different than the log file format of the files themselves.

Site Server Express Report Writer requires setup before you can view log documents. First, you must create a report definition file. To do so, follow these steps:

1. Click the Start menu. Go to Programs ➢ Windows NT 4 Option Pack ➢ Microsoft Site Server Express 2 ➢ Report Writer. NT will open the Report Writer application.

2. Report Writer displays the Report Writer dialog box requesting a report document. You can choose either the Report Writer catalog (predefined reports), or you can create a report from scratch. We will assume that the predefined reports option was selected. Report Writer displays the Report Writer catalogs.

3. Select either a Detail or a Summary report. Under each report type, there are several individual reports. Click Next. Report Writer will advance to the next screen.

4. Select the time frame that you want to analyze. Click Next. Report Writer will advance to the Filters screen.

5. In this screen, you can create custom filters to alter your information queries. Click Finish. You have created a report definition file.

To create an actual report, perform the following steps:

6. In Report Writer, go to File ➢ Create Report ➢ Document. Report Writer will display the Report Document dialog box.

7. Enter a filename in the File Name field. From the Format drop-down list, select a file format for the output. Click OK. Report Writer will generate the report, open the application associated with the file format you selected, and display the report.

ODBC Log Files

Even though Site Server Express is capable of providing detailed reports, you may want to use the ODBC file format to log data. With this format, you can create custom reports in database applications, such as Microsoft Access or SQL Server.

Object Database Connectivity (ODBC) is an industry standard for linking database applications with data input. Using the ODBC file format, the data is continually written to the database. You can perform queries at any time on the current data in the log database.

To configure IIS to send log data to an ODBC database, perform the following steps:

1. From the MMC, select the site you want to configure to use ODBC logging. Right-click it and select Properties.

2. From the Properties dialog box, click the Web Site tab. In the Enable Logging section, click the Active Log Format drop-down list and select ODBC. Click the Properties button. IIS will display the ODBC Logging Properties dialog box.

3. Specify a Data Source Name (DSN) table and a valid username and password. Click OK. You have configured IIS to use the ODBC database.

After IIS logs data to your database, you can use any query format you want to view the IIS data.

Monitoring IIS

As the administrator of an IIS computer, one of your main concerns is performance. If your site performs poorly, users will look somewhere else for the services or information that your site provides. Sometimes it is difficult to determine what is causing poor performance, or to determine if you have a performance problem at all. You must first know what type of performance to expect before you can judge whether or not your performance is suffering. If you do have performance issues, you must then figure out what is causing your problems.

There are many sources of performance problems that can occur with IIS. For example, you could have a performance problem due to a lack of a specific resource, such as memory; or you could have content issues, such as large pages in your site.

Recently, I was asked to take a look at a company's site because they suspected a performance problem. Any time I examine a server with a suspected performance problem, I run Microsoft Performance Monitor to help me determine if there is a problem and what it might be.

I always run the following general Objects and Counters for IIS:

Internet Information Services Global Object

Objects   This Counter shows the total number of cached objects, including files, directory listings, and tracking objects.

Measured Async I/O Bandwidth
Usage   This Counter shows the total amount of bandwidth that your Web service is consuming.

The Web Service Object

Files Received/Sec   This shows how many files per second your server is receiving.

Files Sent/Sec   This Counter shows how many files per second your server is sending.

Total Files Sent   This Counter shows the total number of files that your server has sent since it started.

After viewing the Performance Monitor log file, I saw that there were not a large number of objects being cached. However, the bandwidth usage was substantial (close to 100%). Using the Web Service Counter, I noticed that a significant number of files were being transferred. The Performance Monitor data showed that there was a performance issue, but it did not tell me specifically what it was.

I decided to use Site Server Express to help diagnose this problem. I used the Site Server Express Content Analyzer to generate a report on the site. In the report (that comes up as an HTML document in your browser), in the object statistics, I noticed that the average page size was 1.3MB. This is very large.

Upon further investigation, the administrator admitted that he used large graphics on the site pages because he thought there was sufficient bandwidth available. The quick-and-easy solution was to compress all of the graphics, using a utility that is easily downloaded from the Web. I also recommended that he remove many of the graphics. Remember to always avoid graphic clutter. Graphics should enhance your site content, not slow down your site's performance.

24seven **CASE STUDY**

13

Troubleshooting IIS

Basic troubleshooting methodology is the same no matter what the problem source is. A methodical approach is what is important. Troubleshooting is a process of elimination. This is not to say that you don't have to be familiar with the item you are troubleshooting; on the contrary, the better you understand the mechanics of the problem, the better your troubleshooting results will be.

In order to troubleshoot any type of computer problem, you must be familiar with the basic process that your system uses to perform a specific function, such as a system logon. If you know what specific things must happen for NT to log a user on to the system, it's not difficult to figure out why the logon is not happening the way it should.

The best way to troubleshoot a system problem is to carefully perform a series of steps to accomplish the following:

Identify the type of problem.   The first step in successful troubleshooting is finding out what the problem's symptoms are. During this step, try to find out if anything has recently changed in the system. If you're trying to diagnose a problem involving a user, ask a lot of questions.

Identify the system's process.   After identifying the problem's symptoms, consider what resources the system requires to perform this function, as well as what specific steps the system goes through to perform it.

Track possible approaches to solving the problem.   Once you have diagnosed your problem and have figured out the system's process to perform the function, figure out what the most likely cause of the problem is and work from there. Try the simplest solution first.

Perform the most reasonable approach.   At this stage, you have already identified the system resources and the steps that the system requires to perform the specific function. Now, select the most reasonable approach to fix the problem. Usually, this is the easiest approach.

Check for success.   Once you think you have solved the problem, check to see that all of the system symptoms are gone. For IIS, check the site from a client computer. Be sure to check out all links and applications.

Log the problem.   If you have solved the problem, log the problem and its solution in a central location so that others can benefit from your experience. This is particularly important in large organizations.

IIS@Work: A Common IIS Problem

For IIS, one of the most common problems is resource access. Problems usually occur when resource permissions have changed on a file in a virtual directory or on the directory itself. Typically, your users will see Access Denied error messages when they attempt to load certain pages.

The best way to solve this type of problem is to troubleshoot it from the NTFS side first, and work your way out to IIS. Check to see if file permissions have been recently changed. Remember, if the IUSR_*server* account permissions have changed on any resource, your Internet users can have file access problems. After checking your NTFS permissions, examine the IIS access permissions. Make sure that the Read permission is turned on.

Resource access is the most common IIS problem that administrators have. Luckily, it is also the easiest type of problem to solve.

The Client Process

Some problems that you encounter are centered around network client-server connections. In order to troubleshoot a client-server problem, you must have basic networking knowledge. Let's examine the actual process of a client connecting to a server. Although the client process is slightly different between protocols, we will only examine TCP/IP because the focus of this book is on Internet network traffic. Let's begin with how a TCP/IP host connects to a Web server.

Before any connection with a server can be established, the client computer must have a way of identifying the destination computer from all other hosts on the Internet. The first step in identifying and connecting to a destination computer is a process called *name resolution*. Name resolution occurs when the client computer specifies the destination host and domain name in the Web browser; for example, www.companyx.com. After the client specifies the destination computer name, the name is resolved into an IP address that the client uses to address network packets to the destination. Host and domain name resolution is provided by a Domain Name System (DNS) server. We will discuss DNS troubleshooting later in this chapter.

Once an IP address for a destination computer is known, the client uses the IP address of the destination computer to contact that server. However, prior to any data being transmitted to the server, the client must resolve another type of address.

There are actually several ways that computers on networks distinguish each other. At the core of network client identification is the Ethernet Media Access Control (MAC) address. A MAC address is a unique 32-bit identifier for each network card. It is also referred to as the physical Ethernet address.

The only way that data can pass from one network card to the other is by using the MAC address. In order for a client computer to send data to another computer, the destination computer must be on the same TCP/IP subnet. If a client must use a MAC address to connect to another computer, and the client can only use the MAC address to connect to local computers, how do client computers connect to machines in other subnets? The answer is quite simple. Client computers use the MAC address of the router in their subnet to connect to either the destination computer or the next router on the network.

Before a client computer can use the destination computer's MAC address, it must determine what that address is. This process is called *MAC address resolution*. MAC address resolution works in the following manner: The client sends something called an Address Resolution Protocol (ARP) packet to the server (if it is on the same subnet) or to the local router (if the server is on a remote subnet). If the server is on a remote subnet, the router continues the same process of sending an ARP packet to the server, or the next router on the network, until the destination is reached.

After MAC address resolution, the client computer needs to establish a session and send an HTTP GET request to the server. This request is sent over TCP to port 80, unless an alternate port is specified by the client. The server processes the request. If no specific file is requested, the IIS service sends the default document to the client.

> **NOTE** If your IIS machine is using NTFS security, this process is slightly different in that the client is denied access on the first request. The server sends a request for a username and password to the client. When the client sends the requested information back, the server checks the client's credentials against the Windows NT Server directory database.

TCP/IP Issues

In this section, we will examine the various TCP/IP-related issues that you may encounter while administering your IIS environment. For example, you may experience problems with host name resolution or IP address configuration. Whatever type of problem you encounter, using sound troubleshooting methodology will have you up and running in no time.

Host Name Resolution

This is one of the easiest of the TCP/IP-related issues to solve. First, let's discuss how name resolution occurs in a Microsoft intranet environment. Understanding host name resolution greatly increases your odds of quickly troubleshooting problems with Internet access.

When a Microsoft client attempts to connect to a remote server, the name resolution method depends on two things: what application is requesting the name resolution and how your client machines are configured. Microsoft networks use two types of names to represent computers on the network: host names and NetBIOS names. In reality, most applications in Microsoft networks use NetBIOS names to establish connections. This is also called Microsoft name resolution. The administrator can configure this type of name resolution. The default NetBIOS name resolution occurs in the following order:

1. First, the client computer checks its local NetBIOS name cache. This is a cached area of memory where all recently acquired names to IP address resolutions are stored.

2. Next, the client broadcasts a name resolution query. This packet is sent to all computers on the local subnet.

3. If the broadcast packet for name resolution is unsuccessful, the client checks its LMHOSTS file. The LMHOSTS file is a text file containing the NetBIOS names to IP address resolutions. This file is manually administered.

4. Finally, the client resorts to host name resolution methods.

The other type of application is a WinSock application. WinSock applications use host names instead of NetBIOS names. All Internet applications are WinSock applications. Their name resolution process is similar to NetBIOS, but not identical.

When a client computer using a WinSock application enters a host and domain name for a remote resource, the client computer performs a series of host name resolution steps. The following describes the host name resolution process on your Microsoft hosts:

1. The client computer checks to see if the destination is the local host name. This is the host name of the client computer sending the request.

2. The next step is to send a name query request to a DNS server. (You will learn about DNS later in this chapter).

3. If the DNS server cannot resolve the host name, the client checks the local HOSTS file. This is a text file containing host names and IP address resolutions.

4. If the client is still unsuccessful after checking the HOSTS file, the client resorts to Microsoft-specific methods of name resolution. These methods include the LMHOSTS file, local broadcast, and WINS. WINS, LMHOSTS, and broadcasting are not host name resolution methods. Microsoft clients only resort to using non–host name resolution methods when all other options fail.

> **NOTE** Sometimes the combination of host and domain name is referred to as the Uniform Resource Locator (URL).

Address Resolution

There are instances where a client computer is not able to access a particular host, even when other computers are having no problems. If the network card is changed on a particular computer that has already been accessed by a client, the client is unable to connect to the destination computer for a short time.

The reason is that the client has cached the MAC address of the remote machine. This entry remains in the client's ARP cache for 10 minutes. During this time, if the destination computer's network card is changed, the MAC address is also changed. Since the client thinks it already has the MAC address of that destination, it will not ARP for it again until the entry is flushed from the cache. This is one problem that will solve itself, but knowing why this happens can save you from wasting time troubleshooting a problem that does not require your assistance.

IP Address Configuration

One of the most common problems in a TCP/IP network is improper configuration of IP addresses or other related configuration parameters. As with most of the problems you will encounter, this is not difficult to solve.

With TCP/IP configuration errors, you typically see one computer that cannot communicate with the other hosts in your network. If this configuration error is on the IIS computer, no one will be able to access the server. The best way to troubleshoot this type of problem is to identify which computers cannot communicate.

If you find that none of your client computers can communicate with the server, see if you can establish a connection to any other computer from the server. Check the configuration of your server. You are looking for an IP address that is within the range of your subnet. Remember to check the subnet mask and default gateway, as well. If this does not solve your problem, examine the physical links in your network.

Just like a server configuration error, if a particular client cannot see the Web server, perform the basic troubleshooting steps on the client.

Using IPCONFIG and Ping

For TCP/IP, there are two main tools that you can use to diagnose network problems: IPCONFIG and Ping. Both of these tools come with Windows NT Server and Windows NT Workstation. Both are for diagnosing TCP/IP errors only; you cannot use them to solve any other type of system problem.

IPCONFIG

When you want to know if TCP/IP is installed and how it is configured, you can use IPCONFIG. IPCONFIG is a command-line utility that displays the following information about IP address configuration:

- IP address
- Default gateway
- Subnet mask
- DNS server
- Host name
- NetBIOS node type
- Network adapter card identification
- MAC address of the network adapter card

- DHCP server
- Primary and secondary WINS addresses
- Other configuration information

To use IPCONFIG, type **IPCONFIG** from the command prompt. When no switches are used, you only see the IP address, subnet mask, and default gateway. To view more detailed information, add */ALL* to the end of the IPCONFIG line. This will activate the optional configuration items.

The purpose of IPCONFIG is to show you information about your current IP address configuration. This will let you determine if you have any configuration problems.

Ping

The other major tool for troubleshooting TCP/IP problems is Ping. Like IPCONFIG, Ping is also a non-graphical utility that runs from the command line. While IPCONFIG shows you what your configuration is, Ping allows you to test that configuration to see if there are any other problems. Ping sends out a series of packets to a destination computer that you specify. When the destination computer receives the packets, it responds with a series of replies. You can use these replies to determine if your network is working properly.

To use Ping from the command prompt, type **Ping** and the IP address or the host and domain name of the destination computer. For example:

```
Ping 207.49.189.12
```

Ping shows you if the physical cable, network cards, and basic TCP/IP configuration are correct and working properly. Ping will not let you determine if you can establish an actual session. After successfully using Ping, you should attempt to establish a session by using an application, such as Internet Explorer.

DNS Issues

Another area that you may encounter problems with is DNS. Once you solve a DNS problem, it is unlikely that you will ever have that specific problem again.

Since DNS is a distributed database of host name resolution records and related information, about the only problems that you can have are an incorrect host name entry or no entry record at all.

The symptom of a DNS problem is that you can establish a connection by IP address but not by host name. Since most Web site developers use Fully Qualified Domain Names

(FQDNs) to refer to graphic images in their Web content, you may be able to connect to a Web site and see text, but you will not be able to see graphics.

The easiest way to diagnose a DNS problem is to use the industry standard NSLOOKUP utility that comes with Windows NT Server. NSLOOKUP is a command-line utility, like IPCONFIG and Ping. It sends a query to a DNS server to see if specific DNS records exist. One difference between IPCONFIG, Ping, and NSLOOUP is that NSLOOKUP has its own command prompt.

To use NSLOOKUP, open the NT command prompt and type **NSLOOKUP**. At this point, you will start the NSLOOKUP command prompt.

NSLOOKUP supports many commands. The following commands are the ones you will use most often:

Name You can type a name, such as `www.sybex.com`, and NSLOOKUP will query the DNS server to see if it has a record for that host. NSLOOKUP only queries one DNS server, so you must know which DNS server is supposed to have a particular record.

Server If you need to change to a specific DNS server, you can use the `Server` command. At the NSLOOKUP prompt, type **`server IP address`**, and NSLOOKUP will change the default DNS server to the one you specify.

LS The LS command is very useful. You can use it to view multiple files at once. This command uses switches to alter the query output. For example, the switch–*d* lists all records on the DNS server that is queried. The switch –*t* and a specific record type that you are looking for, such as Alias, returns all records of the specified type.

Troubleshooting

Some problems are outside of your control. However, you must go through all of the standard troubleshooting steps to determine the problem's origin.

The Problem

About a year ago, a client was complaining that he had no Internet access. He blamed the problem on a tenant who had leased space in the building. The tenant owned the ISDN connection that my client used to access the Internet. When the tenant moved, he left the line and router for the landlord (my client), who also occupied space in the same building and was using the same ISDN connection.

When the tenant left, he took his IIS computer with him. The landlord thought that he needed the tenant's server back in order to access the Internet. I assured him that he did not need the old IIS machine to access the Internet.

The Solution

The first step in troubleshooting a problem like this one is to see if you can get a connection to any other computer in the building. This is done using the Ping utility. After pinging to see if I could get to any other computers in the building, I found that there

was no apparent problem with TCP/IP on the server or on any of the workstations.

The next step was to ping something outside the building. I pinged a remote site, using the IP address of that remote site. I received error messages indicating that the connection could not be made. So, I pinged the IP address of the router on this network. I did receive a positive response, indicating that everything was working properly.

The next step was to connect to the router and check its status. I found that the router was dialed up and connected to the ISP.

Summing It Up

Given my troubleshooting results, I made this deduction: Since I could see the IP devices in the building, including the router, but could not ping outside the building, the problem was on the other side of the router (the ISP). I contacted the ISP and explained the problem. They checked and found that when the tenant left the building and switched the service over to the landlord, somehow the messages got mixed up and the ISP turned off the connection, instead of switching it over to the landlord. So the ISP turned the connection back on, and the problem was solved.

Part 2

Proxy Server 2

Topics Covered:

- Architecture and deployment of Microsoft Proxy Server 2
- Different proxies and their usefulness in the Enterprise
- Using Proxy Server to manage outbound connections to the Internet
- Using Proxy Server to create internal and external security
- Using Proxy Server as a firewall product
- Managing cascading Proxy Servers
- Troubleshooting and maintaining Proxy Server installations

14

Proxy Server Overview and Architecture

In recent years, the Internet has grown from being a relatively small network into a global system of information distribution that links all types of users. Today, businesses, universities, government agencies, and private individuals all use the Internet in growing numbers. The Internet has become as important to some users as their own private LANs (Local Area Networks). As the Internet grows in its number of users and its scope, more people are looking for simple, cost-effective ways of linking their own LANs to the Internet.

Installing a full-fledged connection to the Internet can cost quite a bit. Even though hardware costs for Internet routers and CSU/DSU (Channel Service Unit/Digital Service Unit) units are decreasing, proper Internet connections are still beyond the reach of many small businesses and private users. This being the case, people have been searching for solutions that will provide LAN-wide access to the Internet through a smaller connection, which does not require all the fancy hardware that installing a large connection (such as a T1 line) does. ISDN (Integrated Services Digital Network), ADSL (Asynchronous Digital Services Line), shared T1 (Frame Relay), cable modem, and many other high-speed solutions (which still do not provide the performance of a T1 line) have taken hold as standards for data communication. These forms of data communication are far cheaper than installing a T1 line and are used by millions of people.

The nature of a TCP/IP network also makes it impossible for a private, non-sanctioned LAN to have a legitimate connection to the Internet with typical dial-up connections. The addressing scheme used requires all IP addresses to be unique. Many private networks using the TCP/IP protocol are set up using IP addresses that may already be in use by other Internet sites. Connecting a private network with IP addresses that are already in use on the Internet causes serious problems. There is also the issue of routing. Unless the entire Internet is aware of a block of addresses (known as a *subnet*), data will not be routed correctly to a site. That's where the InterNic comes in. The InterNic governs the Internet and, together with Network Solutions and other domestic groups unique to each country, issues addresses to sites wanting a legitimate presence there. Once a site has a valid set of addresses, the core routers are informed of the new addresses, and data flows correctly to and from the new site.

The process of getting a valid subnet and a connection can take many weeks, can cost several thousand dollars in hardware, and can cost between $1000 and $2000 a month in access charges. In contrast, a single-user dial-up connection to an ISP (Internet Service Provider) through a cable modem takes no time to obtain, averages about $50 a month, and requires little more than a cable modem (generally supplied by the ISP). ISDN access to a provider is about $20 to $70 a month plus metered charges, and about $300 for hardware. If a high-speed, company-wide connection to the Internet is beyond your price range right now, you're in luck. Microsoft has developed Microsoft Proxy Server, an NT Server application that makes it possible for an entire LAN with non-sanctioned IP addresses to have access to the Internet through a typical dial-up link to an ISP. Microsoft Proxy Server works with any valid link to the Internet: Analog Dial-Up, ISDN, T1, and beyond.

In some situations, using Microsoft Proxy Server is a better choice than granting full access to the Internet to workstations with valid IP addresses having context on the Internet (that is, workstations with IP addresses having meaning outside the local network). Microsoft Proxy Server is easier to set up and has security features that make it easy to control the type of Internet access client workstations have. Controlling access to the Internet on a LAN with a legitimate connection is tough to do because each workstation on the LAN can have its own valid presence on the Internet. When workstations connect through a Microsoft Proxy Server, they rely on its presence on the Internet for their connection. Proxy Server also provides many security benefits, including the firewall support in Proxy Server 2, which makes it a valuable tool in your enterprise.

Proxy Server Is an IIS Sub-Service

In order for Microsoft Proxy Server to be installed, the Microsoft IIS service must be installed first. The only element of IIS that must be enabled is the Web server element. The Microsoft Proxy Server Web proxy runs as an aspect of the IIS Web server and uses the IIS Web server to listen to TCP port 80 traffic. It determines if the traffic is to be serviced remotely by a Web or other server outside the proxy, or whether it is to be locally serviced by the IIS Web server (or another Web server operating on the local LAN). HTTP, FTP, and Gopher requests can all be handled through port 80. Microsoft Proxy Server is actually two services in one. The first part, the Web Proxy, handles CERN-compliant proxy requests through port 80 on the TCP/IP protocol. CERN, which stands for Conseil Europeen pour la Recherche Nucleair (European Laboratory for Particle Physics), developed many UNIX-based Internet communications standards. Among these standards was a proxy service protocol that allowed for remoting Internet requests through a dedicated connection point.

The CERN-compatible proxy server element of Microsoft Proxy Server supports communications through port 80 of HTTP, FTP, and Gopher requests. These services all obtain data through the Internet using similar means. In order for CERN-compatible proxying to function correctly, clients must be able to interact with a proxy server. This approach is fine for compliant applications, such as IE (Internet Explorer) and Netscape; but there are many other Internet applications that do not have built-in proxy capabilities.

Many Internet applications communicate with the Windows Socket interface (WinSock), which in turn communicates with the rest of the internal and external network. For these applications, another proxy method must be used to gain access to the outside Internet. The second element of Microsoft Proxy Server is known as the WinSock Proxy Server. For those applications that do not support CERN-compliant proxying, the WinSock Proxy Server can intercept their WinSock calls and remote them to Microsoft Proxy Server for external processing. This requires the installation of special WinSock Proxy client software, which can intercept a client's WinSock call and redirect it correctly.

The SOCKS Proxy Server (new to Proxy Server 2) supports SOCKS version 4.3a and most SOCKS 4 client applications. By nature, the SOCKS protocol functions as a proxy. It enables hosts on one side of a SOCKS server to gain full access to hosts on the other side of the server without requiring direct IP accessibility. This is done through two operations: *connect* and *bind*. The connect operation establishes separate sockets to each host. It then issues a bind operation to affiliate the two connections internally, effectively letting the SOCKS Proxy act as a bridge between the two sockets.

The differences between the Web Proxy, the WinSock Proxy, and the SOCKS Proxy are covered later in this chapter.

Proxy Server 2

PART 2

Understanding What a Proxy Server Is

Proxy servers have been around in the UNIX world for awhile, but Microsoft Proxy Server is Microsoft's first attempt at creating a proxy server for the NT environment.

The actual definition of a proxy server is a server that performs an action for another computer that cannot perform the action itself. A real world analogy for a proxy can be seen at high-priced art auctions. Many bidders at art auctions do not attend the auction themselves, for whatever reason. Some of the actual bidders at the auction are the *proxies* for the real buyers. The proxy acts for the buyer and relays the status of the proceedings to the buyer over the telephone. If you watch CNN coverage of important art auctions, you'll see proxies all over the bidding hall talking to their buyers. The proxy acts only when instructed to do so. Anything that the buyer can do in person can be done through the proxy.

In the world of computers and the Internet, workstations behind the proxy do not have valid Internet connections and, therefore, cannot talk to the Internet on their own. The proxy sits at the juncture of the Internet and the local LAN connection, which is typically an NT machine with two network interface cards (NICs) or with one network card and a RAS connection to the Internet. The proxy routes local LAN requests to the Internet as though the Microsoft Proxy Server itself was requesting the information. On LANs that do not have valid subnets issued from the InterNic, workstations cannot route data through an NT machine to the Internet.

Figure 14.1 diagrams a typical small network running over a Proxy Server.

Figure 14.1   A simple network taking advantage of a proxy server

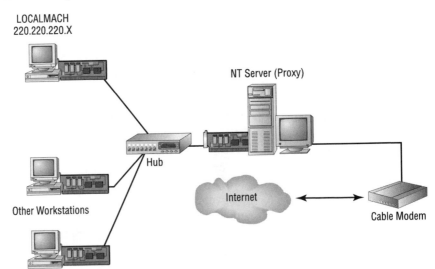

In the diagram, a user is working on the machine named LOCALMACH. The IP addresses given to all of the workstations and server are on the 220.220.220 subnet. This selection of a subnet was a fairly random process. It was selected for the graphic because it falls within the Class C subnet range and is easy to remember. Most network administrators implementing the TCP/IP protocol on a non-Internet connection LAN select a subnet in a similar manner. When a LAN is not connected to the Internet, network administrators have few restrictions when selecting the addressing scheme that is used. If a LAN is to be legitimately connected to the Internet, the LAN must be configured with IP addresses issued by the InterNic, Network Solutions, or another licensed addressing body.

There are sets of private IP subnets that private LAN administrators can use for their own internal TCP/IP networks. These private subnets were set aside by the InterNic and will never be used openly on the Internet. These addresses should be the ones given to private TCP/IP networks that will not be directly participating on the Internet. The addresses in the 220.220.220 subnet are actually poorly chosen. When a private LAN uses addresses for the Internet that are already taken, the Microsoft Proxy Server keeps all of the traffic directed to those addresses local. So, this particular subnet cuts off a large chunk of the Internet from your LAN users. The Microsoft Proxy Server determines what is local and what is external. When the internal addresses overlap external addresses, the Microsoft Proxy Server keeps the traffic as local-only.

The diagram in Figure 14.1 shows a simple 10-BaseT network of three Windows 9X workstations and one NT Server. The server is connected to the LAN via a standard NIC, and is connected to the Internet through a cable modem. When Microsoft Proxy Server is installed on the NT Server and properly configured, all workstations can connect to the Internet through Microsoft Proxy Server as though they are themselves connected. Of course, each workstation must be specially configured to connect to the proxy server rather than to the Internet. Setting up a proxy requires a little more effort that just installing and setting up the software on the server. Client-side configuration is very simple because all Microsoft Internet applications rely on a centralized configuration point in the Control Panel for proxy settings. Most non-Microsoft Internet applications can be easily configured to communicate through a proxy.

Because the use of proxy servers has become more common in recent years, most Internet application programmers are incorporating the ability for their software to communicate with the Internet through a proxy server. Currently, the vast majority of Internet applications have the ability to use a proxy server for their connection, and this trend is likely to continue. Even if an Internet application does not have the ability to communicate through a proxy, special client-side software can be installed that allows nearly all Internet applications to talk properly with Microsoft Proxy Server.

Understanding How Microsoft Proxy Server Serves a Network

The primary use of the Internet is World Wide Web (WWW) access. Whether users on your network use Internet Explorer or Netscape Navigator, LAN users will be able to "surf the net" through Microsoft Proxy Server as though they are connected directly to the Internet. If you have ever tried other proxy servers, such as WinGate or NetProxy, you'll find that Microsoft Proxy Server's performance typically exceeds their performance if you have sufficient hardware to run the product correctly. (We will discuss the hardware requirements in Chapter 15.)

Microsoft Proxy Server supports nearly any type of Internet client—from WWW, to FTP, to Newsgroup. Windows 9X Workstations work best through Microsoft Proxy Server; but almost any TCP/IP client, such as OS/2 and Windows for Workgroups, can access the Internet through an NT machine running Microsoft Proxy Server.

> **WARNING** There are some limitations to 16-bit clients using Microsoft Proxy Server. You will learn more about these later.

Users of a LAN can access the Internet through a personal dial-up account connected by RAS on the NT machine that is running Microsoft Proxy Server. This means that users on a LAN will not have personal e-mail accounts on the ISP providing the connection. Most ISPs only give one e-mail account for each dial-in account. Most companies in this situation opt to use the provided e-mail account as a company-wide account. Privacy is one of the concessions that you have to make when using Microsoft Proxy Server through a dial-in account.

Proxy Server's purpose is to provide LAN access to the Internet, not vice versa. Outside Internet users cannot access LAN workstations through Proxy Server. Proxy Server only listens to internal network requests for outside information.

> **NOTE** This concept is crucial to appreciating the benefits of Proxy Server. The fact that machines inside the proxy cannot be accessed directly from the Internet helps plug a huge security hole inherent in the TCP/IP networking model.

Proxy Server also provides a very high level of security for controlling which LAN users have access to the Internet connection and exactly what those users can access. Because Proxy Server is an integrated NT application, it draws on NT's internal security systems for LAN user authorization. All Internet protocols can be separately configured for different security levels. Different users or groups of users can be authorized for each type of Internet connection, such as HTTP, FTP, and NNTP. Microsoft Proxy Server also has the ability to limit the sites that LAN users can connect to. If you need a secure Internet access point, Microsoft Proxy Server is your best choice.

Considering the Three Proxy Types

As previously mentioned, Microsoft Proxy Server consists of three separate servers: the Web Proxy Server, the WinSock Proxy Server, and the SOCKS Proxy Server. All three are installed when Microsoft Proxy Server is installed, and each runs as a separate service under NT. Each service can be controlled and configured through the MMC, which is found in either the Microsoft Proxy Server folder or the Option Pack folder in the Programs group on the Start menu.

Basics of TCP/IP as It Relates to the Proxies

As you have learned in previous chapters, all communication that takes place over the TCP/IP protocol is done through ports. The IP address combined with a port number is known as a *socket*. Servers that communicate via TCP/IP do so through predefined ports, depending on what type of server they are. For example, the WWW server communicates using the HTTP protocol. This protocol uses port 80. FTP servers listen to port 21 for their traffic. Telnet communications take place over port 23. The NNTP protocol (Newsgroup communications) uses port 119, while SMTP (Mail) uses port 25. These ports are virtual channels of communication between servers and clients using the same protocol.

The most confusing part of this discussion is the term *protocol* because it is used to describe so many different levels of networking. Protocol is used at every level of networking to describe the procedure two applications (server/client) or devices (network interfaces) use to talk to one another. Network protocols are used by two network cards to communicate, while server and client applications communicate using software protocols. Take the following arrangement of protocols, for example:

- PPP is used to transport network protocols over an asynchronous link, such as a modem.
- A network protocol, such as TCP/IP, can be carried by PPP.
- An Internet protocol, such as HTTP, is carried by the TCP/IP protocol along TCP port 80.

TCP/IP packets have a header. This header has information, such as destination IP address and destination port. Two types of packets can pass over the TCP/IP protocol: TCP and UDP (User Datagram Protocol). The primary difference between TCP and UDP packets is that TCP packets contain header information that indicates the sequence of the packets, and UDP packets do not. Most Internet protocols use TCP packets to communicate. Because *sequencing* (making sure the order of received packets is the same on the receiving end as it was on the sending end) requires slightly more overhead, UDP communication is used by servers requiring the highest level of efficiency, but at the slight cost of data integrity. Servers, such as Real Audio and VDO Live, use UDP communications because their data is transmitted in real time and requires the fastest possible communication.

TCP packet transmissions are *stream-oriented*. UDP packet transmissions are *datagram-oriented*. Both use the TCP/IP protocol and are nearly identical, except for the differences mentioned earlier.

The Web Proxy Server

The Web Proxy Server element of Microsoft Proxy Server is a CERN-compliant proxy server that operates by listening to TCP/IP port 80 for traffic. It must use the IIS Web server as its listening mechanism because port 80 is the WWW port. The Microsoft Proxy Server Web Proxy Server is incorporated into the IIS Web server once it is installed.

The Microsoft Proxy Server proxy consists of two parts: the filter and the application. Clients properly set to talk to a proxy server send their requests out on port 80 in a different request format than they would if they were communicating with the destination server on their own. This alteration of request format is done so that the proxy server knows exactly what kind of request is being sent: HTTP, FTP, or Gopher. When browsers are not set to talk to a proxy, they make the correct type of request to the destination server, depending on the format of the user-entered request.

For example, when a non-proxy enabled browser gets a user request for a Web site, such as `http://www.klsent.com/index.htm`, the browser knows that the protocol to be used is HTTP from the format of the command. The browser sends the following request to the WWW server `klsent.com`:

```
GET ./index.htm
```

GET is a standard command for obtaining Internet objects, such as files, HTML documents, and imbedded objects. This command is implemented in different ways, depending on which protocol is using it.

If a browser that is not configured for proxy use sends `GET ./index.htm` to a proxy server, the proxy server does not know which protocol to use, nor does it know the location of the object to get. Therefore, when browsers are configured to send proxy formatted commands to a proxy server, the requests look like this:

```
GET http://www.klsent.com/index.htm
```

The browser assumes that the proxy server will correctly parse the command and issue it to the correct site in the correct format. Keep in mind that FTP clients configured for

CERN-compliant proxy interfacing use the same format and port (80) as Web clients, even though FTP clients use port 21 when talking to servers on their own.

Once the proxy server receives the properly formatted request, it sends the request to the destination in the same format that the browser would had it not been configured for proxy interface. If the request for data is an FTP request, the proxy server initiates communications to the destination FTP server on port 21. Once the proxy server receives a reply from the destination, it sends the data to the requesting workstation on the LAN, and the cycle is complete.

The job of the proxy filter is to determine if the received HTTP request is in proxy format or in local request format. If the filter determines that the HTTP request is in standard format (that is, GET ./index.htm), it assumes that the request is handled by the local WWW server. If the HTTP request is in proxy format, it passes the request to the proxy application where it is reformatted and re-issued to the correct destination.

The proxy application performs many operations on the request before it is sent out. The proxy application is responsible for looking in the local proxy cache to see if the data requested is already present. If the data is present, and its Time To Live (TTL) has not expired, and the object has not been changed on the destination server, the proxy application will pull out the object from the cache and send it to the requester without having to go to the Internet to get it. This process of holding a certain amount of information in a local cache can greatly increase Microsoft Proxy Server's perceived performance, especially when a small connection to the Internet is being used by many people. (Caching is discussed in greater detail in later chapters.)

The proxy application is also responsible for authenticating the requester and ensuring that there is authorization to use the protocol and to obtain information from the requested destination. Client authentication takes place before any other action.

Once the requested information has been obtained, either from the local cache or from the Internet, the proxy server sends the information to the requester via the HTTP protocol on port 80.

The WinSock Proxy Server

The WinSock Proxy Server works quite differently than the Web Proxy Server. In order for the WinSock Proxy Server to function correctly, special WinSock Proxy client software must be installed on each workstation that needs WinSock Proxy support. When Microsoft Proxy Server is installed, a special network share is created that contains the WinSock Proxy client installation files. Workstations can link to this shared resource and run the setup file found there to correctly install the WinSock Proxy client software.

When Internet clients, such as Eudora (a popular e-mail client), request data from a TCP/IP network, they make WinSock calls to the local WinSock DLLs (Dynamic Link Libraries). The WinSock DLLs process the request via the TCP/IP protocol. In order for applications such as Eudora (which has no special proxy configurability), to work correctly in a proxy environment, the WinSock layer on a workstation must be able to forward or remote the request to the WinSock Proxy Server that performs the action on behalf of the requester.

For this to happen, the client WinSock DLLs must be renamed, and the new WinSock Proxy DLLs must be put in place. In a 16-bit environment, the WinSock DLL is WINSOCK .DLL. In a 32-bit environment, such as Windows 9X, the WinSock DLL is WSOCK32.DLL. These original DLLs are not overwritten by the new DLLs, they are renamed and the new DLLs are copied in their place. Once the WinSock Proxy client software is in place, all Internet clients on workstations function as they always did for local LAN traffic.

During installation, Microsoft Proxy Server will examine your private LAN and determine which set of local addresses is used by your network. These addresses are contained in the LAT (Local Address Table). This information is kept in the file \MSP\CLIENTS\ MSPLAT.TXT. This is a very important file and will be discussed momentarily.

Once the WinSock Proxy client software is installed, any Internet application that is requesting data does so through the new WinSock Proxy DLLs. Once the WinSock Proxy DLLs get a request, they open a control channel to the WinSock Proxy Server on port 1745 and download a copy of the LAT. The address of the requested destination is compared against the contents of the LAT. If the address is found to be local, the WinSock Proxy DLLs relay the request to the local-capable WinSock DLLs on the workstation, and the request is processed like any other local request. If the request is found to be an external request, the WinSock Proxy DLLs remote the request to the WinSock Proxy Server for processing. The WinSock Proxy Server establishes a link on the client's original request port (for example, port 119 for news clients) to both the client and the Internet destination. From that point on, the WinSock Proxy client DLLs simply forward all data to the original WinSock DLLs for standard processing.

At this time, the original DLLs communicate on a given port and not to a specific IP address. Because the WinSock Proxy Server has been initialized by the WinSock Proxy client, the WinSock Proxy Server responds on that port for the client. The client sees the WinSock Proxy Server as the final destination, and the WinSock Proxy Server talks to the originally requested destination and relays information to the client. Several clients, such as FTP clients, send out their local IP address in a handshaking packet so that the Internet server that they are attempting to connect with is able to open a connection back to the requester. The WinSock Proxy Server is responsible for removing the local IP address used by the client and replacing it with the Internet IP that the WinSock Proxy Server has. This means that the contacted server opens a backward connection to the WinSock Proxy Server rather than attempting to open a connection with the originally indicated IP address. Keep in mind that the local IP addresses used on a private network are not valid, and the WinSock Proxy Server must use the IP issued to it from the ISP giving the Internet connection.

Once the Internet server correctly establishes a return connection to the WinSock Proxy Server, the WinSock Proxy Server establishes a return connection to its own client on the same port. The client lets the WinSock Proxy Server know that it is expecting a return connection by listening to the proxy server's IP address for a return connection. When the client makes a connection, it actually makes it with the IP address of the WinSock Proxy Server. The WinSock Proxy DLLs determine if the original request was local or remote. If local, the request was already passed to the real WinSock DLLs. If the request is remote, the WinSock Proxy WinSock DLLs instruct the client to talk to the WinSock Proxy Server IP, as though it was the final destination. If the client is listening for a return connection to come from the IP of the WinSock Proxy Server, the WinSock Proxy Server knows to expect a return connection from the destination Internet site. Figure 14.2 shows this sequence.

Figure 14.2   The connection process between client and WinSock Proxy Server

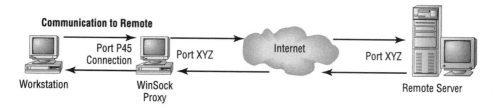

IP-Less Listening   There are some rare situations where a client application issues a TCP/IP listen command to the WinSock DLL without having a destination IP address. When the WinSock Proxy DLL cannot determine if the listen request is local or remote to the Internet, the request remains local. This is done for security reasons.

Web Proxy and WinSock Proxy Working Together

The combination of the Web Proxy Server and the WinSock Proxy Server allows Microsoft Proxy Server to service nearly any WinSock 1.1-compliant client application. Clients that have the internal ability to talk directly to a CERN-compatible proxy have this ability, and clients that do not can still get Internet access via the WinSock Proxy Server.

The WinSock Proxy Server can handle the traffic of Web browsers, SMTP clients, and FTP clients on its own if those browsers do not have the ability, or are not set, to use a proxy server. There are no drawbacks to using WinSock Proxy with these types of clients. The primary benefit that the proxy server has over the WinSock Proxy Server is that no special client software must be installed in order for it to work. This means that non-Windows operating systems can take advantage of a Windows NT Microsoft Proxy Server Web Proxy Server via the TCP/IP protocol.

The SOCKS Proxy

The SOCKS Proxy works in a manner identical to the WinSock Proxy. However, there are some implementation-level differences between the WinSock protocol and the SOCKS protocol—mostly in the low-level calls that bind the sockets together. The SOCKS Proxy is useful in situations where users may be coming from or accessing non-Windows platforms, and you are not sure that the computer communications are completely CERN-compliant. In such situations, the communications can be handled by the SOCKS Proxy, presuming that both the client and the server communicate using the SOCKS version 4.3a protocol.

Using IPX/SPX

It is possible to use the IPX/SPX protocol as the only protocol installed on workstations and still be able to access the Internet with clients via the WinSock Proxy Server. The WinSock Proxy client software has the ability to use IPX to transport Internet requests and responses to and from clients to the WinSock Proxy Server. This ability allows a network administrator to have full control over Internet traffic.

When IPX is used as the only network protocol on a LAN, any request made by a TCP/IP client is considered a remote request. The replacement WinSock Proxy DLLs remote the request to the WinSock Proxy Server, which uses IPX to respond to the client.

The TCP/IP protocol must be installed on the NT Server that is connected to the Internet in order for a legitimate TCP/IP connection to be established between the NT machine and the ISP.

The Microsoft Proxy Server performs a protocol translation between TCP/IP and IPX. The IPX protocol is similar in nature to the TCP/IP protocol in that each workstation on the LAN has a unique node ID, and IPX packets can be routed to specific destinations.

Proxy Server, IIS, and Windows NT

Microsoft tried to design NT 4 to be the platform of choice for all types of Internet servers and applications. Microsoft Proxy Server is part of a global package of Internet-oriented applications—although it does not come with IIS and is an add-on item. Because of its close integration with the operating system, Proxy Server utilizes NT sub-services, such as security and network channels, to work together with IIS and other server products to create seamless applications.

The NT Internet Interface

Access to the Internet can be gained in several different ways with NT. The two most common ways are as follows:

- Multiple NICs (network interface cards) where at least one card is physically linked to an Internet line, such as an ISDN line or a T1 line
- RAS (remote access services) via a modem

NT treats each form of connection the same way, although at a substantial difference in connection speed. Installation and use of Microsoft Proxy Server to facilitate global LAN access to the Internet is a pretty straight-forward process. However, no two LANs are ever set up identically, so it can get confusing when trying to describe certain scenarios.

Historically, there are two common network arrangements for private individuals and companies who use NT and need Internet access: an isolated LAN with periodic dial-up connections to the Internet, or a permanent connection for the Web server (for site hosting) and limited outbound traffic for workstations along this connection.

Either arrangement meant that Internet users on a LAN needed to have a separate phone line and a modem to each computer that needed Internet access. In such an environment, each individual LAN user also needs separate dial-in accounts with a provider. However, this is not always true because some providers do allow multiple simultaneous dial-ins on the same account. This can be expensive if a LAN has many users who need Internet access. There are ways to work around this, such as using a modem pool on a central server to eliminate the need for individual phone lines, or using modems at network workstations. These solutions can also be expensive because most modem-pooling software isn't cheap.

Modem pooling can also be inconsistent and can place extra overhead on network workstations. It still does not eliminate the possible need for individual ISP accounts for each LAN user that needs Internet dial-out access. Modem pooling does reduce the number of individual dial-out lines and modems, though. However, modem-pooling software for NT is $300 on average for a five-user license. The cost goes up for each additional line added to the system. If you are thinking about Microsoft Proxy Server for your LAN, one of the main reasons for this is to keep the cost of Internet access as low as possible. Of all Internet access scenarios, using Microsoft Proxy Server is the cheapest and offers the highest performance for multiple users.

Whether you are using modems, shared T1 access, Frame Relay, ISDN, or some other connection (even if you are using a T1), a Proxy Server is an important tool for controlling and directing access to the Internet and keeping bandwidth usage down and manageable.

NT Server Access to the Internet

The most convenient way for NT to access the Internet is to use a dedicated line. However, if a LAN has access to a dedicated line, it is most likely that all network workstations are already set up to access the Internet without the need of Microsoft Proxy Server. Figure 14.3 diagrams a typical network with LAN-wide Internet access.

Figure 14.3 A LAN with a permanent Internet connection and direct client access to the Internet

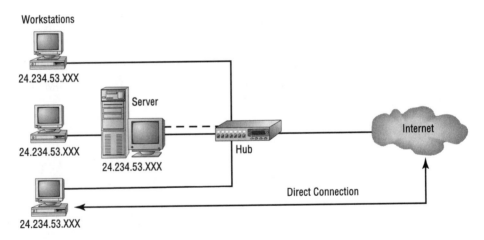

Under this scenario, network workstations can have direct access to the Internet. Full LAN access to the Internet requires more than just the correct hardware. The second element necessary for full Internet access is a valid set of addresses for each workstation on a network. If a LAN has a dedicated line, such as a T1 or higher, the provider giving such access will almost certainly have allocated a subnet of valid Internet addresses for the LAN. Therefore, it is unlikely that a LAN in this scenario will absolutely *need* the services of Microsoft Proxy Server. However, it is possible that, for some strange reason, workstations in this type of LAN are prevented from having fully qualified Internet addresses. If, for example, the private LAN only operated via the IPX or NetBEUI protocols, access to the Internet is not directly possible. Microsoft Proxy Server can provide access to the Internet if the TCP/IP protocol is not supported or is not used on the workstations, but the IPX protocol is. Microsoft Proxy Server can use IPX as a transport protocol when TCP/IP is not available or supported.

However, there are a host of modern-day issues that surround such permanent connections to the Internet, including the potential security risk that such connections pose to the network, as well as the lack of administrative control over access. Implementing a Proxy Server gives you a central point of control for Internet access by users behind the proxy, as shown in Figure 14.4.

Figure 14.4   A LAN with a permanent connection and a Proxy Server, which provides a central point of administration

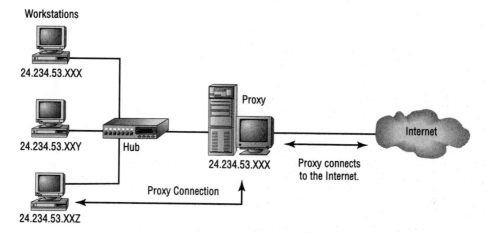

It's important to have a clear understanding of possible future needs of a LAN when setting one up. It's also important to understand some of the vital NT services, such as WINS and DHCP, if you're planning on adding Internet-type services to an intranet. WINS is similar in action to DNS, except its main purpose is to resolve NetBios names to IP addresses, as opposed to resolving Internet names to IP addresses. When used in conjunction with DHCP, the dynamic addresses that the DHCP server passes out to new machines on a network are automatically registered with WINS. Therefore, an up-to-date database of local IP addresses and their NetBios machine names is available for network use. This ensures continued proper network operation when IP addresses for a LAN change (among other possible changes).

Internet Servers

In recent years, many companies have begun to use Web servers to manage internal company information. The point-and-click nature of the Web makes it very simple for employees to perform their jobs, even if they are computer novices. Also, a Web interface is the perfect environment for disseminating information. It is a tricky task to open a Web server, or any Internet server (such as FTP and Telnet), to the outside world when the network that the server resides on does not have valid Internet addresses.

The purpose of Microsoft Proxy Server is not to grant outside Internet users access to the resources of a private LAN. Therefore, unless Internet servers are on the NT machines with the Internet connections, access to these servers is not possible from the outside. Even though general access to a LAN is not normally possible from the outside through Microsoft Proxy Server, it is possible that experienced hackers could gain access in rare situations. Microsoft recommends disabling IP forwarding on the Microsoft Proxy Server to ensure that the NT machine does not propagate outside packets into the private LAN.

Keep in mind that Microsoft Proxy Server does not require any form of IP forwarding on the server on which it is running in order to function normally. Microsoft Proxy Server handles its own delivery of IP packets to and from the outside connection. Disabling IP routing is covered in greater detail in later chapters.

Most arrangements have Microsoft Proxy Server running on the same machine as the Internet server applications. This poses no problem as long as the Web server in use is the Microsoft IIS Web Server. The Microsoft IIS Web Server is the only application that is required by Microsoft Proxy Server. This is because Microsoft Proxy Server "piggybacks" on the listening services of the IIS Web Server on port 80 in order to pick up LAN requests that are destined for the outside world. Any other Internet server applications can be run on an NT machine that also runs Microsoft Proxy Server. Microsoft Proxy Server's Web Proxy and WinSock Proxy services are implemented so that port conflicts are not an issue on the server.

Microsoft Proxy Server circumvents port conflicts in two ways. With standard proxy requests (HTTP, FTP, and so on), the IIS Web Server fields all traffic through a special filter DLL that determines if the traffic is local or destined for the outside. If the traffic is not to be picked up by the WWW server itself, Microsoft Proxy Server takes over the traffic and passes it outside. TCP/IP traffic that is not covered by the Proxy Server's Web Proxy Server (any traffic on a port other than 80) is handled by the Proxy Server's WinSock Proxy service or SOCKS Proxy service.

The WinSock Proxy Server works in tandem with the WinSock Proxy client on the workstations. The WinSock Proxy client software fields any local TCP/IP requests, translating the traffic to the port that the WinSock Proxy Server is listening to. This means that the

WinSock Proxy Server can handle nearly any type of TCP/IP client—such as SMTP, NNTP, and Telnet—without having a conflict with other Internet server software that may be running along side Microsoft Proxy Server.

NT Security

As with all IIS applications, Microsoft Proxy Server directly utilizes NT's network security systems for its own security needs. Unlike other Internet server applications, Microsoft has designed Proxy Server to use NT's security system to deal with outside users wanting access to a LAN. Microsoft Proxy Server also uses NT's security systems to deal with internal LAN users needing access to the outside.

Microsoft Proxy Server takes full advantage of the network security features of an NT-based network. When a LAN user attempts to access the Internet via Microsoft Proxy Server, whether by Web Proxy or WinSock Proxy (both types of servers can have their security configured independently), Microsoft Proxy Server authenticates their access against the NT user database.

When a user starts a Windows 9X Workstation and logs in, that user can do so in one of two ways. A standard Windows login requires the user to indicate a name and a password. This information is not immediately validated by a domain controller (primary or backup), but is stored by Windows. This form of login to a workstation is a *basic login*. If a user attempts to access a secured network resource, such as a server disk or a service (such as Proxy Server), the Windows Workstation will present the login information to an available domain controller for validation. If the user information is not in the NT database of users, or if the user is present but does not have sufficient access to use the requested resource, the server will deny access to the resource.

Windows Workstations can also have a login name and password that is immediately validated by a domain controller if the workstation is configured for such a log in.

Proxy Server has a wide range of security options. As already mentioned, the three proxy services can be configured independently. Each type of connection can also have independent security limitations placed on it. For example, Proxy Server can permit only a certain network group to access WWW servers, while allowing another network group to only have access to FTP servers. Microsoft Proxy Server can even permit or deny individual LAN users access to Internet servers.

Microsoft has devoted a great deal of development to the high-end security features of Proxy Server. In most cases, the functionality of Microsoft Proxy Server far exceeds the needs of most private individuals and small to medium companies. Microsoft Proxy Server does offer a great deal of control to the outside Internet via a central authority, while a great deal of control is lost when workstations have their own valid Internet access. For many companies, Microsoft Proxy Server is a better solution for Internet access than extending a valid Internet presence to individual workstations.

As well as controlling who can have access to the Internet, Microsoft Proxy Server can also control which sites on the Internet are accessible to LAN users.

Microsoft Proxy Server also has outstanding logging features that help to track misused Internet access. When workstations have their own valid Internet presence, users have less restricted access to the outside, and the logging features of NT are not nearly as thorough at tracking that kind of activity. In the long run, it may be better for some companies (and, as we have argued many times, most companies) to use Proxy Server rather than allowing workstations full Internet access.

NT Gateways

Access to the outside Internet is possible through more than just one point. A LAN can have several gateway points through which the Internet can be accessed. Workstations can be configured with a list of available network gateway points, which are each tried when the workstation needs outside access until the workstation successfully obtains such access.

If a single gateway point is not sufficient to handle the amount of Internet traffic a LAN has, multiple gateway points can be used. However, most networks simply increase the capacity of a single connection. Multiple gateways can also be used as a form of fault tolerance in case one connection fails.

The same approach can be used with multiple Microsoft Proxy Server gateways. Keep in mind that Microsoft Proxy Server gateways can be used just like normal gateways. Because most Microsoft Proxy Server gateways are using smaller connections, such as analog modems or ISDN modems, scenarios involving multiple Microsoft Proxy Servers are more common than gateways on LANs having valid Internet gateways.

An arrangement of which workstations access which Microsoft Proxy Server is a configuration element that is set up on each workstation. After installing Internet Explorer 3 or higher, a new control icon is placed in the Control Panel of Windows 9X machines. This icon is the access point to configuring all vital Internet settings for a Windows 9X workstation, including proxy settings. Figure 14.5 shows the Internet control applet of the Control Panel. The Connections tab is selected. This is the tab for controlling whether Windows 9X will use a proxy for its Internet connections.

The LAN Settings button of this area allows for the specification of proxy server locations, as shown in the Local Area Network (LAN) Settings dialog box in Figure 14.6.

Figure 14.5 The Internet applet in the Control Panel

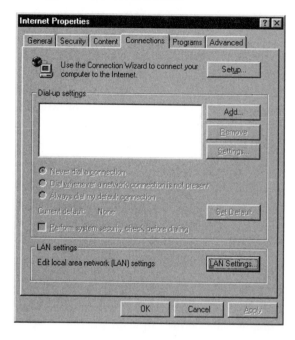

Figure 14.6 The LAN Settings area of the Internet Control Panel applet

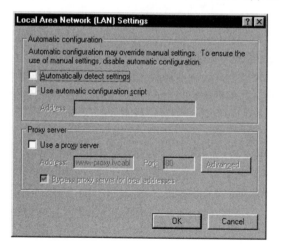

As you can see, Microsoft Proxy Server operates identically for WWW, FTP, and Gopher clients—passing all requests for such servers through port 80. The flexibility exists to configure each type of service differently if a different type of proxy server is used. Because the Microsoft Proxy Server Web Proxy listens for all requests on port 80, configuration is a simple task.

The WinSock Proxy portion of the client side is a little trickier than the Web Proxy side. With the Web Proxy side of things, configuration consists of only a few settings in the Control Panel. The WinSock Proxy client-side configuration requires installation of special client software. Enabling or disabling WinSock Proxy redirection is controlled via the system registry.

To spread out the Internet access load on LANs with many Internet users, multiple Microsoft Proxy Server gateways should be used. The organization of such an arrangement depends on a network administrator's need. Each Microsoft Proxy Server on a network can be dedicated to trafficking only a certain type of connection (FTP, for example). Another distribution method sets different groups of LAN users to use different Microsoft Proxy Servers. Keep in mind that FTP access is a more demanding of a connection than WWW access. Not only does FTP access involve lengthy file transfers, but the data that is transmitted is not stored in the Microsoft Proxy Server cache, as it is with WWW information. Caching information greatly improves the performance of Internet access through Microsoft Proxy Server.

Common Control Interface

When Microsoft Proxy Server is installed, it attaches itself to the same control interface that is used by other IIS servers—the MMC. All Microsoft Internet servers attach themselves to this common control interface. The Web Proxy Server, the WinSock Proxy Server, and the SOCKS Proxy Server show up as independent servers when you install Proxy Server. From this common interface, Microsoft Internet servers can be configured, stopped, started, or paused. As with most NT control interfaces, the MMC can be used to view and control the status of Internet servers running on other NT machines.

Using Proxy in a Dial-Up Environment

Several years ago, we were working with a small company (about $1.5M in revenues annually) that was very security conscious. The company wanted to display its own Web site, but didn't want to host the Web site on a remote server because they wanted complete control of the site's content. They also wanted to provide limited access to the Internet for users on their LAN. They didn't want to grant individual users unrestricted access to the Internet because of their security concerns. Because the environment was small, modem pooling was a viable solution; but their phone calls were metered, so the risk of individuals attaching to the Internet, remaining attached all day, and running up large phone bills was also a substantial concern.

The Problem

The challenge was to find a way to take advantage of their existing configuration, while being sensitive to their overriding security concerns. The fact that their internal network used NetBEUI as its protocol was also somewhat of a challenge. We knew that we could change their structure, obtain IP addresses from their provider, and link to the provider through a DHCP connection from the server. But that solution seemed clunky, particularly since the only reason they needed Internet access was for e-mail and the occasional Web research project.

The Solution

Instead, we opted for a Proxy Server installation, using the existing dial-up connection from the Web server as the Internet link. This allowed the administering and monitoring of all Web site access from that central point.

Summing It Up

Proxy Server provided us with a simple, cost-effective solution, while addressing the client's concerns about security and being able to limit employee Internet access. The company subsequently moved to a permanent Internet connection for the Web server, but maintained the Proxy installation to protect and defend their network against outside intrusion and internal misuse.

24*seven* CASE STUDY

15

Planning the Proxy Server Installation

While Microsoft has gone out of their way to make installing Proxy Server 2 as simple as possible, there are some important considerations to make during the pre-installation process. The minimal hardware and software requirements for a successful installation vary greatly, depending on the number of users that are behind the proxy in your network. In addition, the power of the hardware for the machine that serves as the proxy is critical. As the number of users increases, the proxy machine requires more processing power. In this chapter, we discuss the minimal requirements for a successful Proxy Server installation in the most common environments. We also discuss some of the common configurations and their recommended minimum hardware requirements.

System Requirements and Preparation for Microsoft Proxy Server

We will consider the most common connection configurations for modern-day networks and how differences in those configurations can result in differences in the Proxy Server installations themselves. We will also consider the differences in hardware requirements for situations when you use Proxy Server as your network's firewall, in addition to using it as a distributor of IP addresses.

> **NOTE** In general, you will not find that the hardware and software require-
> ments of Microsoft Proxy Server are much more demanding than the
> requirements of NT 4. While the minimums are often slightly higher, most admin-
> istrators configure their NT Server machines at a level consistent with the needs
> of Proxy Server 2.

Hardware Requirements

If your machine runs NT 4, it will run Microsoft Proxy Server—though, in all fairness, it may not do so well. Keep in mind that the more services that run on an NT machine, the stronger that NT machine has to be to keep up with network traffic. The nature of a Microsoft Proxy Server machine is to handle the traffic of multiple LAN workstations through the LAN's connection to the Internet—although, in some cases (particularly with dial-up accounts), you may be using Proxy Server as your network's sole connection to the Internet. When considering the design of the hardware for the machine that implements Proxy Server and the design of the network itself, the most important items that you should focus on are the amount of RAM in the server, the processor speed of the server, the hard drive space on the server, and the connection speed to the Internet.

Microsoft generally divides Proxy Server installations into three categories, depending on the number of users that the Proxy services. Microsoft also provides a minimum configuration for each of these three categories. In the following lists, we will consider the minimum configuration specifications for each of these categories.

No matter how many users will be accessing the Proxy Server, the required software configuration is the same. You must have three basic pieces of software installed before you can perform a successful installation of Proxy Server:

- Microsoft Windows NT Server 4
- Microsoft IIS 3 or greater (As a general rule, unless you have a specific reason for doing otherwise, we would recommend that you use IIS 4.)
- Windows NT Server 4 Service Pack 3 or greater (Service Pack 3 is included with Proxy Server 2.)

As mentioned previously, you need to make sure that your hardware meets certain minimum levels, depending on the number of clients served by the Proxy. For an environment where the Proxy Server is servicing up to 300 clients, the requirements are as follows:

- The server should have an Intel 486/66 DX2 chipset at a minimum, with a Pentium 133 MHz chipset recommended by Microsoft.

- The server should have a minimum of 24MB of RAM, with 32MB of RAM recommended. While the server will run with this much memory, performance is generally sub-standard. As a general rule, you should have at least 128MB of RAM in your NT Servers, whether they are Proxy Servers or not.

- The server should have a minimum of 10MB of free hard drive space, with a suggested minimum of not less than 250MB of free hard drive space (for the Windows NT swap file). You are best served by having at least 500MB, and as much as 2GB or more, of space reserved for the NT swap file.

For an environment where you are planning to use Proxy Server with between 301 and 2,000 clients, the hardware requirements are slightly increased, as detailed here:

- The server should have an Intel Pentium 133-MHz chipset at a minimum; we recommend at least a 200-MHz Pentium.

- The server should have a minimum of 64MB of RAM. Again, while the server will run with this much memory, performance is generally sub-standard. As a general rule, you should have at least 128MB of RAM in your NT Servers, whether they are proxy servers or not.

- The server should have a minimum of 2GB of space reserved for the NT swap file. In this environment, Proxy Server can easily make use of as much as a 4-GB swap file.

Finally, for an environment where you are planning to use Proxy Server with more than 2,000 clients, the hardware requirements increase again, particularly at the chipset, as detailed here:

- The server should have an Intel Pentium 166-MHz chipset at a minimum. We recommend at least a 300-MHz Pentium II. Depending on how much your clients are accessing the areas outside the proxy, multiple processors may be particularly appropriate in this environment.

- The server should have a minimum of 64MB of RAM. Again, while the server will run with this much memory, performance is often sub standard. As a general rule, you should have at least 128MB of RAM in your NT Servers, whether they are proxy servers or not. For a Proxy Server installation of this size, 256MB, or even 512MB, is often appropriate.

- The server should have a minimum of 2GB of space reserved for the NT swap file. In this environment, Proxy Server can easily make use of a 4-GB swap file. If your users' Internet access is heavy, a 6-GB or larger swap file may be most appropriate.

The requirements discussed in this section are minimum requirements. Performance can always be improved by adding additional hardware to your machine in the right places. The following section discusses some of the most common hardware improvements that you can make to your intended proxy server machine.

Optimal Hardware

Because of the way that Proxy Server 2 is designed, the biggest benefits to system performance occur if you spend money on hardware improvements in two specific areas. These areas are common to most high-volume (in terms of network usage) server products. Any time you have a piece of software whose job includes managing large numbers of users and connections, software benefits are typically found in RAM and hard drive space. Furthermore, as with many modern-day products, the addition of a second or multiple processors can result in large benefits, depending on your usage.

One of the best things that you can do to improve the performance on any NT Server is to add more RAM to it. Though NT can get by with as little as 12 or 16MBs of memory, Proxy Server, even in its most limited implementation, requires at least 24MBs. That said, any proxy server that you will use to maintain a significant number of connections to the Internet should have a minimum of 128MBs of RAM. Larger installations, those running 1,000 clients or more, often require 512MBs of RAM or more to perform at an acceptable level. If your proxy server performs any other server-based activities—for example, if it doubles as a Web server—you will want to have sufficient additional memory to support both the incoming and outgoing transmissions.

The number of internal connections Microsoft Proxy Server must support is also a factor in the amount of memory NT needs. The more connections that Microsoft Proxy Server must maintain, the more memory that is required. This is true for all forms of network connections. The TCP/IP protocol is a very memory-demanding protocol. Because Microsoft Proxy Server requires that the TCP/IP protocol be installed on the NT Server on which it is running, you will want to make sure that you have sufficient memory to provide adequate performance.

If the NT machine running Microsoft Proxy Server is only doing that, the minimum processor configuration discussed previously is sufficient; though, improving the processor power will ensure that your performance remains acceptable. One factor in deciding CPU requirements is the speed of the Internet connection that Microsoft Proxy Server is using. If the connection is a smaller one (such as an ISDN link or a 128Kb feed) and the number of clients being served is small, Proxy Server can get by with a lower-speed processor. If the CPU does not have to channel a large quantity of data between a few internal workstations and external Internet sites, a slower CPU generally works fine. If the CPU will have to channel large amounts of data between many internal workstations and external Internet sites, a slower CPU will be over-taxed, no matter how much memory the system has.

Microsoft Proxy Server can cache most WWW objects (graphics, sound bytes, and HTML documents for example). This means that Microsoft Proxy Server can draw from a local hard drive to serve out Internet data that it has already handled. This improves performance to workstations and reduces the use of the outside link. The larger the cache, the more data Microsoft Proxy Server can maintain. If your LAN has many users accessing many different sites throughout the day and your cache is small, Microsoft Proxy Server may be expiring cached data too soon for the cache to be of any use.

While there are several algorithms for determining the appropriate amount of cache space, Microsoft Proxy Server should use a cache of at least 250MBs. However, this is a dynamic cache and can be expanded if it is too small. As a rule, the vast majority of installations require a larger amount of cache space. In some installations that serve a large number of clients, caches of 8GBs or more are not uncommon. Typically, you should expand the Microsoft Proxy Server cache to be as large as possible. This ensures that cache objects are not expired because of an influx of new objects. If many users will be using Microsoft Proxy Server to access a multitude of different Web sites, objects in the cache could be flushed before they are ever called on again. This nullifies the function of the cache and adversely affects Proxy Server performance.

If you are using Proxy Server on the same machine as another server product, often, you are best served by adding another physical drive to the system (large or small, depending on your implementation, but typically at least 4GBs) and making that drive the sole storage location for the Proxy Server cache. This lets you maintain a large cache and also helps to minimize the impact that the regular caching and related activities have on the other software products that are running.

You can use either IDE or SCSI hard drives in your NT Server. Both IDE drives and SCSI drives can be found in sufficient sizes to fulfill your needs. SCSI drives are slightly more expensive than IDE drives, but have greater flexibility, access speed, and transfer rate—considerations that impact the performance of the server. Installing a large drive with plenty of free space allows Microsoft Proxy Server to have a sufficient cache to prevent possible future problems.

An additional consideration to keep in mind whenever you analyze your Proxy Server installation is whether you will also be using Proxy Server as a firewall product. If Proxy will be serving as your network's firewall as well, the demands on the server are substantially increased. The hardware that you use for the server should also be improved to match the demands.

Your Proxy Server implementation specifics are a function of the number of clients in your environment, their amount of Internet usage, whether your LAN uses IP addresses granted by Proxy Server for internal traffic, and so on. The guidelines specified by Microsoft and the additional suggestions found in this section are intended to provide you with a starting point. As you work with Proxy Server, you will be in the best position to evaluate its performance and also to determine what additional hardware you might need.

The Internet Connection

Microsoft Proxy Server can use any valid connection method that is supported by NT to talk to the Internet. Depending on the size of your organization and the number of users accessing the network, you will use, at a minimum, an ISDN connection. No matter which of these connection methods is used, RAS is the software portion of the equation. If an NT machine already has a permanent connection to the Internet, it is most likely that the LAN that the NT machine is connected to already has workstation-level access to the Internet. However, there are some situations when using Microsoft Proxy Server is preferable to letting workstations have valid Internet connections on their own; and you may want to change the settings for workstations with existing Internet connections to use Proxy Server, depending on your goals for the Proxy Server installation.

Proxy@Work: External vs. Internal Connection Devices

We can't stress enough how important it is to use external connection devices over internal devices. While external analog modems and ISDN modems are slightly more expensive than their internal counterparts, the flexibility external devices have over internal devices far outweighs the cost factor. In the vast majority of full-level access cases, the required serial modem needs to be external. If you are using an analog or ISDN modem to get to the Internet, keep in mind the following short list of benefits that external devices have over internal devices:

- External devices do not consume independent system resources. External devices connect to existing ports. Internal devices require their own I/O ports and IRQ assignments. If an external device is hooked up to an existing serial port, no additional system resources are used.

- External devices can be independently switched off and on should they lock up. If an internal device locks up during operation, the entire machine must be switched off and rebooted. The nature of network servers makes it difficult to find a free moment to reboot because they are always being accessed. In a busy office, the NT machine running Microsoft Proxy Server might also be performing other vital network services, such as serving shared resources (disks, printers, and fax modems) or acting as a DHCP or WINS server. In these environments, it may not be possible to reset the machine until the end of the day.

Proxy@Work: External vs. Internal Connection Devices *(continued)*

- External devices have the ability to accurately monitor device activity. Granted, RAS and Dial-Up Networking under NT provide simulated modem activity lights in the system tray, but these simulated lights are only partly accurate when displaying device activity. If you need to immediately see if a modem is experiencing activity, the simulated modem lights in the tray are all but useless. The simulated lights have a small lag time that makes them worthless for error debugging.

- External devices offer you the ability to replace defective or outdated devices without having to take the entire machine down. As a rule, network administrators always want to have the fastest hardware for LAN users that they can. External devices can be upgraded *much* more easily than internal devices. However, if a modem or a device is flash-upgradable, the device will require no hardware replacement; a simple software patch will do.

The one drawback (aside from price) in using external devices instead of internal devices is that the ports that external devices are connected to must be adequate to maintain the data passing through them.

Serial Port Hardware

Unfortunately, the device most computer manufacturers scrimp on is the serial port. Many serial ports installed in pre-made systems are sub-standard ports that are not suited for reliably passing large amounts of high-speed data. The primary element of concern when dealing with serial ports is the generation of its *UART chip*. A UART (Universal Asynchronous Receiver Transmitter) chip controls the flow of data passing through the port and also ensures that data from the outside gets to the CPU in the same form that it came in (from the device connected to the port). Older UARTs are 8250 or 16540 generation, while newer UARTs are 16550AFN or 16650 chips.

Advanced UART chips are very important because they handle the flow of serial data over very high-speed connections. Port speeds of 115Kbps are now standard for analog modems. The importance of a high port speed cannot be stressed enough. Many people get confused about the difference between port speed and connect speed. Port speed is often referred to as DTE (Data Terminal Equipment) speed. This is the speed at which the computer talks to the serial device or modem. The speed at which the modem connects to another modem is known as the DCE (Data Carrier Equipment) speed. Figure 15.1 shows the speed relationships.

Figure 15.1   Port and device speed relationships

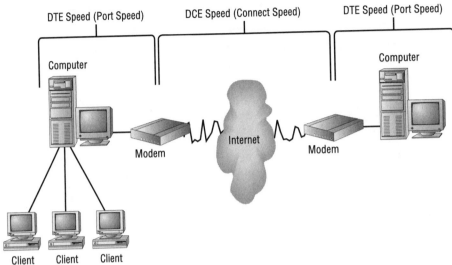

The main reason for needing a higher port speed than connect speed is the increasing use of hardware data compression techniques. Nearly all modems used today employ some form of data compression to increase the amount of data that can be passed through the connection. The same principle used with compressing data for storage in archive files, such as ZIP or LZH files, applies to passing data between modems. Because modems used in a Microsoft Proxy Server scenario or for dial-up networking generally deal with non-compressed data, a high port speed is essential.

Proxy@Work: Why High Port Speed Is Essential

Consider the following scenario: A Proxy Server client is requesting a large HTML text document from a Web site. The connect speed being used is a 33.6-Kbps connection. The sending end, which performs hardware data compression, achieves a compression ratio of 3:1. This ratio is not out of the question. Sometimes even higher compression ratios can be achieved on certain types of data. So, in essence, 100.8Kbps worth of data (33.6 × 3) is passing between the modems.

When the data arrives at the receiving end of the connection, the receiving modem expands the data to its original size. Basically, the receiving end is getting data at a rate of 100.8Kbps. The receiving end must be able to offload that data as quickly as the modem can spit it out (or, hopefully, more quickly). This explains the need for a

Proxy@Work: Why High Port Speed Is Essential *(continued)*

high-speed modem port. If the port speed is not sufficient to handle the stream of data being received, the sending end has to wait for the receiving end to process it. That means a drop in performance and efficiency.

The same principles apply in reverse. If the sending end is unable to feed data to the sending modem fast enough, the data stream is not as full as it could be; therefore, the performance is not as high as it could be.

Hardware data compression is not very useful in increasing the speed at which data that is already compressed can be transmitted. For example, images in JPG format are already very highly compressed; and archive files, such as ZIP, ARJ, and LZH files, are also already tightly compressed. Hardware compression done by modems achieves very little, if any, additional compression. However, much of the data transmitted from Web servers is not compressed.

Without advanced UART chips maintaining data integrity, high-speed data may be corrupted as it passes through the serial port. Because NT is a multitasking environment, the CPU is not constantly monitoring the serial ports and offloading the data as soon as it arrives. The data may have to wait a nanosecond or two before the CPU cycles around to the serial port. *FIFO* chips refer to 16550 and 16650UARTs. FIFO stands for First In/First Out. It's a reference to the manner in which UARTs ensure data integrity. The 16550 chip has an 8-byte buffer, and the 16650 chip has a 32-byte buffer. These buffers are used to hold data until the CPU can cycle back around to the serial port to offload the data. Some non-standard UARTs may have expanded buffers, but the principles of data integrity are the same. UARTs prior to the 16550 did not have buffers.

As you can see, it is very important to have a port that is capable of supporting the amount of data that a high-speed modem sends. When ISDN modems enter the picture, port speeds of 345Kbps and 460Kbps are necessary to ensure reliable data transfers. Special serial port hardware can be purchased that supports these tremendously high speeds, but most of these ports are not based on 16*xxx* UART technology. Without a sufficient port speed, the performance of a modem will not be what it could be, and workstation users will not get the fastest performance that they could and should get.

Port Speed with Internal Devices

Internal devices do not hook up to a serial port. Internal analog modems and ISDN modems have their own onboard UART chips that handle the data that passes between the modems and the CPU. Internal devices, like external devices, have separate speeds at which they talk to the CPU. The same terminology of port speed and connect speed applies to internal devices as it does to external devices.

If you are looking at Microsoft Proxy Server as a possible LAN Internet solution, you are most likely looking at it for its cost-cutting capability. Don't make the mistake of not optimizing your connection. An inefficient connection can make your online time increase. Depending on the ISP you use, online time may be an expensive part of the access equation.

Considering ISDN Feeds

ISDN is a digital interface. Digital is a faster and more reliable connection method than standard modems, which communicate over analog links. Comparing analog to digital is like comparing vinyl albums to compact disks. The quality and capability of compact disks far exceeds that of old vinyl records. ISDN as a connection format is available in two forms. The first is known as Basic Rate Interface ISDN (BRI ISDN) and is the most common form of ISDN. The second form of ISDN is known as Primary Rate Interface (PRI ISDN) and is harder to find.

BRI ISDN is a digital connection consisting of three channels. The first is a 16-Kbps controller channel that the ISDN modems use to talk to each other (the D channel), and the second and the third are two 64-Kbps channels, that are used to carry data (the B channels). The B channels can be used together to reach a throughput of 128Kbps, or they can be used separately as outbound or inbound data or voice lines. ISDN is handled much like regular telephone connections in that an ISDN line is assigned a telephone number and can be dialed up just like a regular telephone. The B channels can be used independently for bi-directional communication. They can be used for standard voice communication, as well. Many providers have various pricing schemes for utilizing ISDN channels together or one at a time.

PRI ISDN is equivalent in bandwidth to a full T1 line, but still has the flexibility of a periodic connection. PRI ISDN is broken up into 24 64-Kbps channels, 23 of which are used to carry data, and the 24th is reserved for communication between the two ISDN units. Hardware for PRI ISDN connections is different than BRI ISDN and is much more expensive, usually costing from $1,000 to $1,200 for an ISDN unit. PRI ISDN cannot be carried over standard copper lines as BRI ISDN can, but instead requires fiberoptic lines, making the installation costs much higher. If finding a provider for BRI ISDN is hard, finding a provider that offers PRI ISDN service is nearly impossible. Most people who use PRI ISDN are doing so for connections that transmit a high volume of data between set points rather than using PRI ISDN to link to the Internet.

If you are considering using PRI ISDN as your Internet connection, the better choice is committing to a T1 line. T1 access is a dedicated, 24-hours-a-day line of access that is not metered. Therefore, any amount of data can pass over the line at one set cost.

Some providers can handle obtaining ISDN service for you, and others can't. You may need to work through your phone company to get BRI ISDN service if you want to go that route. If you are setting up an ISDN connection that is far away from a phone company junction, you may be required to pay extra for the connection because the phone company will need to put in a special high-speed loop from your office or home to the nearest junction. In this way, ISDN is similar to a T1 line in that it needs a local loop to get to the nearest hookup point.

Dedicated Access (T1)

Getting dedicated access usually means that all the pieces are available for providing normal LAN-wide access to the Internet for all workstations on a network. This is usually the job of Microsoft Proxy Server through a smaller connection. However, there are ways of using Microsoft Proxy Server with a dedicated connection that provide greater control over how network users access the Internet. Also, the firewall support in Proxy Server is another compelling reason to use the product, regardless of the Internet connection your organization is using.

Dedicated access usually involves working directly with a provider to get a dedicated digital line of some kind (such as a DDS, Fractional T1, or a Full T1). A set of valid addresses to distribute to all workstations on the network usually comes with dedicated access so that each workstation can have a valid presence on the Internet and route correctly through the connection point. Figure 15.2 shows a diagram of a possible dedicated connection using a T1 line.

Figure 15.2   A possible dedicated connection arrangement

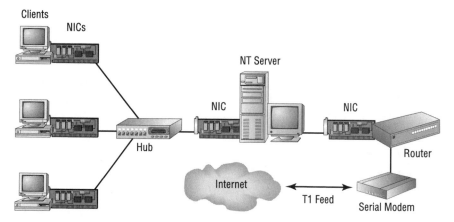

Proxy Server 2

PART 2

A CSU/DSU unit is a termination unit that converts the digital signal that passes along a T1 line into an Ethernet compatible signal. A router is also capable of communicating via an Ethernet signal. Routers can cost as little as $1,500 and as much as $15,000 or more, depending on the router use. CSU/DSU units can cost between $1,000 and $1,500. Installation charges can also be fairly expensive for T1-level access, costing anywhere from $900 to $1,500.

Generally, a T1 line costs at least $1,200 per month. That includes the charge for a local loop connection from your location to your provider's location and the charge for the bandwidth that you will use for the connection from your provider's site to the Internet.

A subnet of addresses comes with the connection and hardware. These addresses can be used by all machines on a network for authentic Internet access through the connection point. A subnet consists of up to 254 addresses. Microsoft Proxy Server can be used in the place of issuing valid addresses to all workstations. Microsoft Proxy Server can sit at the connection point and route local non-valid Internet addressed traffic through the connection point. This offers a level of control over the traffic passing through the connection point that a network administrator cannot get if all workstations on the network are valid Internet workstations—not to mention the security benefits of this model, which we will look at more closely in later chapters.

Software Requirements

There are two major software requirements that must be met in order for Microsoft Proxy Server to run correctly. The first is that IIS must be running. The only component of this service that must be installed is the Web server. The second software requirement is that a connection method must be used. This usually comes from one of the methods discussed in the previous section. There are a couple of other minor setup points, which will be discussed in the following sections.

The IIS Web Server

The IIS Web Server is required for Microsoft Proxy Server to operate properly. Microsoft Proxy Server relies on the IIS Web Server to provide its listening capabilities for LAN requests for outside connections. Microsoft Proxy Server Web Proxy runs as a sub-service of the IIS Web Server and has no ability to operate on its own. Installation of the IIS Web Server can be done after the installation of NT 4, by installing the server from the Windows NT 4 Option Pack CD-ROM.

> **NOTE**   Proxy Server 2 requires IIS 3 or greater. Generally, it is best to install IIS 4, which can be found on the NT 4 Option Pack CD-ROM.

Remote Access Service

RAS can be installed during the installation of NT, or it can be installed later as a standard network service. It is sometimes difficult to install RAS during the original installation of NT if the modems that RAS will use are connected to non-standard serial ports. At no time during NT's original installation does the administrator have the ability to configure RAS to talk to non-standard serial ports. Non-standard serial ports must be configured after NT has been successfully installed. If all modems that RAS will use are on standard serial ports, RAS can be installed with NT without too much trouble. However, because RAS relies on so many other NT services, most administrators tend to install it after NT is up and running.

To install RAS as an NT service, complete the following steps:

1. Open the NT Control Panel.
2. Select the Network icon.
3. Select the Services tab.
4. Select the Add button. A list of NT services will appear.
5. Select the Remote Access Service and click OK.
6. NT will ask for the location of the setup files. Enter the drive letter of your CD-ROM and **\i386** (for example, **e:\i386**). Setup will install RAS service.
7. If you have already setup modems under NT via the Modems icon in Control Panel, these modems will be available as possible RAS devices. However, if there are no modems installed, NT begins the Modem Installation Wizard and allows you to search for modems that are connected to the computer.
8. Once modems have been installed, they can be added to RAS as RAS devices. Once at least one device has been installed for RAS to use, the Remote Access Setup dialog box appears.

The primary purpose for RAS is to provide a dial-in feature for outside users of a network. However, it can also operate as a dial-out service for local users to connect to other networks. RAS can also be used to dial out and connect to the Internet. Under NT 4, the outbound capability of RAS is found in the Accessories folder as Dial-Up Networking. This was done to more closely parallel the look and feel of Windows 95.

By default, all RAS devices are set as inbound-only devices. To set a RAS device as an outbound and/or an inbound device, highlight the device in the RAS list and select Configure. The resulting dialog box allows you to set which direction(s) the RAS device is capable of operating in.

Selecting the Network button allows you to configure which network protocols are bound to RAS for both inbound and outbound traffic. For Microsoft Proxy Server, RAS only needs to be enabled for outbound traffic. On the RAS service, only the TCP/IP protocol needs to be active.

If any of the RAS devices are set for inbound connections, the dialog box you will see for setting up the Network options of RAS will be an expanded version of what you see otherwise. The inbound setup of RAS is not the focus of this section and will not be covered in this book. Deselect all protocols except TCP/IP. Select OK.

Once the TCP/IP protocol is set as the only protocol for outbound use, select OK at the Remote Access Setup dialog. The installation of RAS will be finalized. The NT Server needs to be restarted before a dial-out connection can be made.

NOTE   Because of the firewall features supported by Proxy Server 2, the installation program automatically disables IP forwarding on the server. Installing RAS re-enables IP forwarding on the server. As you will learn in Chapter 18, there are network security considerations involved with IP forwarding that you should be aware of.

Dial-Up Networking

Once RAS is installed and the system is rebooted, a new item will be available in the Accessories folder. This is the Dial-Up Networking applet. With this application, a valid Internet connection to an ISP can be achieved if you have an account with the ISP.

The first time you start the Dial-Up Networking applet, it prompts you to create a new entry to dial. A wizard will start and prompt you for all the entry items that are needed to complete the dialing directory entry. If you are familiar with dial-up networking settings, you can enter them manually.

The important items for a dialing directory entry are as follows:

Basic Tab—Entry Name   This is the name that you assign to the entry, for example, *ISP Connection.*

Basic Tab—Phone Number   This is the data phone number of the provider that you use.

Basic Tab—Use Telephony Dialing Properties   This check box determines whether Dial-Up Networking consults the internal NT telephony settings for controlling how the phone number is dialed. If it is unchecked, Dial-Up Networking dials the number exactly as entered.

Server Tab—Dial-Up Server Type   Indicates what type of server Dial-Up Networking will be calling for this entry. Most providers use a standard PPP protocol connection, so the default will work for most providers.

Server Tab—Network Protocols   Indicates which protocols this entry requires. Only TCP/IP should be selected.

Security Tab—Authentication and Encryption Policy   Most providers are UNIX systems and, as such, may only accept clear text authentication attempts. Select the first option, "Accept any authentication including clear text," to ensure that you can log in to the provider.

On the Server Tab, next to the TCP/IP Protocol check box, there is a TCP/IP Settings button. This allows you to manually enter an important number your provider may have given you: an IP address for your Proxy Server installation.

Most providers assign an IP address to you dynamically. This means that you are given a different IP address every time you log in to the provider. If you are lucky enough to have (or have requested) a static IP address, select the "Specify an IP Address" option and enter the IP address that your provider has given you.

The next section of the dialog box, concerning DNS resolution, may need to be filled in. Depending on the version of UNIX OS that your provider is running, it may pass DNS location information out when logging on. If it does not, you need to know what the address of the DNS server is that your provider uses to perform name resolutions. If the provider's system passes DNS information out at login, leave the default name resolution alone; it is Server Assigned. WINS resolution is a NetBios name resolution service that is only applied under an NT network and is, therefore, not necessary for NT-to-UNIX connections.

The remaining two options can be left alone because if they are not options with your provider, they will not be correctly negotiated at connect, but will not interfere with the process of connecting.

Once the vital elements of an entry are set, select OK. The entry is saved and ready to dial. Select the Dial button to begin a dial out to the provider.

By default, NT pulls up the username that you are logged in to NT with. This name is rarely the name your provider needs you to log in with. Enter your ISP login name and password. The domain field is only needed for connecting to another NT machine and should be cleared. NT will not correctly connect to a UNIX-based ISP if there is an entry in the domain field. Check the Save Password check box if you do not want to continually enter the password before dialing this ISP.

Click OK and Dial-Up Networking should dial the ISP and connect. From this point on, the NT machine has a valid connection to both the local LAN and the Internet. When Microsoft Proxy Server is running on the NT machine, it will be able to route local traffic to the Internet.

Connection Inactivity

Many providers disconnect a connection if there is no activity for a certain amount of time. This is usually 10 or 15 minutes. In order to keep a connection alive when there may not be activity for a long time, you need a program that passes a small amount of data through the connection at regular intervals, just to keep the connection alive. Many of these types of programs exist and can be found on various Internet sites.

Auto Dial

Microsoft Proxy Server has the ability to automatically dial a provider if the Internet connection is not currently available when a proxy client requests a connection. This is known as Auto Dial. Configuring Auto Dial is done through an external application found in the Microsoft Proxy Server folder. This application can be used to configure which ISP is dialed and what times of the day the ISP can be dialed. By default, Auto Dial is not enabled. The administrator is responsible for making the connection from the Microsoft Proxy Server to the Internet. You will learn more about Auto Dial later in this book.

Disabling the RAS Time Out

Just as ISPs have time-out periods, NT also has its own time-out period. By default, if a RAS connection is not used within 20 minutes, NT shuts it down. If your ISP does not have a time-out value, you can turn off NT's time-out value so that you will not need a utility, such as Ponger32, to keep the NT side of the connection alive. The NT time-out value can be disabled by editing a key in the registry.

To start the NT registry editor, open a command prompt and enter the command REGEDT32.EXE. Locate the HKEY_LOCAL_MACHINE\ System\CurrentControlSet\ Services\RemoteAccess\Parameters\Autodisconnect key. The Autodisconnect key is a hexadecimal key and is set to 14 (14 in hexidecimal notation is 20 in standard decimal notation). Editing this value and setting it to 0 disables the time-out value for RAS connections. Be careful when editing the registry. Making incorrect changes can render NT unbootable, and only a reinstallation of the system will take care of the problem.

Network Protocol Requirements

Microsoft Proxy Server requires that the TCP/IP protocol be installed on the NT machine on which it is running. Obviously, to make a successful connection to a TCP/IP UNIX host, the TCP/IP protocol must be installed first. Connections to LAN workstations do not have to be through the TCP/IP protocol. Microsoft Proxy Server WinSock Proxy will function via the IPX/SPX protocol. The Web Proxy portion of Microsoft Proxy Server will only function correctly via the TCP/IP protocol. When IPX is the transport protocol between workstations to Microsoft Proxy Server, all Internet requests from workstations are handled as though they are external requests, and WinSock Proxy Server will manage them all.

In order for IPX/SPX to be successfully used as the primary workstation transport method, the WinSock Proxy client software (provided with Microsoft Proxy Server) must be installed on all workstations wanting access to the Internet. Applications that would normally use the Web Proxy Server (such as Netscape, Internet Explorer 3, CERN proxy-compatible FTP clients) have to use the WinSock Proxy Server instead in such environments because the Web Proxy Server can only communicate with clients via a direct TCP/IP link.

> **NOTE**   You can install the TCP/IP protocol stack on top of the IPX/SPX protocol stack to avoid this issue.

Other than those minor points, Microsoft Proxy Server is very flexible when it comes to operating via either the TCP/IP or IPX/SPX protocols.

Disabling IP Forwarding

Under rare conditions, it is possible for outside packets to slip into a LAN that is connected to the Internet. This opens up the possibility for outsiders to have access to resources within the network. The following conditions have to be met before LAN security is compromised:

- Outsiders have to send directed packets into the LAN and know ahead of time the actual IP address of the system in order to connect to it.

- The target system must be running a server application that the outsider is attempting to connect to. Remember that Windows 95 is a network server that can serve out connections to valid Microsoft Networking clients.

- Network security must be breached. If the resource that is attempting to be accessed has a password assigned to it (in the case of a Windows 95 or Windows for Workgroups system), the outsider must know the password. If the target resource is an NT resource, the outsider will be challenged to provide valid NT security credentials.

- IP Forward on the NT machine connected to the Internet must be enabled.

Keep in mind that this issue has nothing to do with Microsoft Proxy Server's proxy-only services because the proxy services only direct internal traffic outward. (Though it does have to do with the firewall capabilities of Proxy Server.)

As you can see, it's not very likely that a breach of security will ever occur.

Proxy Server 2

PART 2

The last item in the list can be the total stopping point for all inbound TCP/IP accesses to the LAN. When IP Forwarding is disabled, the NT machine connected to the Internet and the LAN does not pass IP packets between NICs. To disable IP Forwarding, complete the following steps:

1. Open the Control Panel.
2. Select the Network icon.
3. Select the Protocols tab.
4. Select the TCP/IP protocol.
5. Select Properties.
6. Select the Routing tab.
7. Uncheck Enable IP Forwarding.

Now your LAN is ultimately secure (provided, of course, that no one "hacks" the Proxy Server and re-enables IP Forwarding). Restart your NT machine for the change to take effect.

Don't think that by disabling IP Forwarding you are preventing Microsoft Proxy Server from doing its job. Microsoft Proxy Server does its own separate secure routing of LAN traffic to the Internet.

Planning Your Installation and Configuration

Designing a network architecture for a LAN that uses Microsoft Proxy Server as its primary Internet gateway is one of the most important steps you will take. Microsoft Proxy Server can be easily reconfigured; but once the topology of a network is set, it is sometimes very difficult and time-consuming to change. This is especially true of medium or large networks. If you have the luxury of designing your network before it is used by hundreds of users, you will be able to carefully plan most of the foreseeable situations you might encounter. Unfortunately, most network administrators do not have the luxury of building a network before users are active on it. In most cases, the network is "mature" and has been in place for some time.

Most networks come into being one piece at a time, and the design process is an ongoing chore, which is more an issue of problem solving than actual topography design. Most network administrators inherit a network from a previous administrator. This means that the new administrator not only has the job of trying to understand what has already been done, but also must figure out how to improve the network and upgrade it to current standards. Networking is one of the fastest growing segments of computer technology. With the growth of the Internet as a daily business tool, learning how to properly integrate the two will ensure that your network has the capabilities that are needed in business.

In the remaining sections of this chapter, we discuss the issues of setting up a network for use with Microsoft Proxy Server and how to best implement Microsoft Proxy Server. This chapter cannot cover all of the scenarios that a network administrator will encounter. We hope that this chapter presents enough information to enable you to efficiently and effectively deal with most situations.

> **NOTE**   In the remaining sections, we will deal almost exclusively with Microsoft networking architecture and tools. If Novell servers and NDS (Novell Directory Services) are used on a network that is partly Microsoft in design, they should not conflict with anything related to NT Servers. In reality, NT Servers and Novell servers get along quite nicely on a network when they are properly configured. Windows 9X machines can simultaneously utilize both Microsoft Networking client software and Novell Networking client software to access both types of servers.

Proxy Server 2

PART 2

Designing the Network

This section discusses how a network should be designed if a network administrator could have every wish granted. The topics discussed here can be optionally implemented or implemented in an alternative manner to suit the specific needs of your network. There are always multiple ways of getting something done, and not everyone has the same opinion on the best way to do a task. However, having installed more than our fair share of networks over the past few years, we believe that we have an understanding of effective network design. The discussion presented in this chapter is our own personal opinions and should be taken as such.

The first decision that must be made is what network protocol will be used as the primary transport method for Microsoft Proxy Server. Microsoft Proxy Server can use either TCP/IP or IPX between workstations and the NT Server running Microsoft Proxy Server. The NT Server that runs Microsoft Proxy Server must have TCP/IP installed and working properly, but the workstations can use IPX exclusively.

Using TCP/IP or IPX

The TCP/IP protocol is the native protocol used on the Internet and has some advantages over just using IPX. Keep in mind that there are three proxy components to Microsoft Proxy Server: the Web Proxy, the WinSock Proxy, and the SOCKS Proxy. The WinSock Proxy requires special client software to be installed on each workstation that will allow nearly any windows socket application to communicate with the Internet through Microsoft Proxy Server. This client software simply renames the existing WinSock DLLs and replaces them with new ones that are designed to forward TCP/IP traffic to the WinSock Proxy Server if the TCP/IP traffic is destined for the outside world. If the traffic is local, the original WinSock DLLs take over, and the WinSock Proxy Server is not hampered by routing local traffic. Figure 15.3 shows a possible network architecture with TCP/IP.

Figure 15.3 A network with TCP/IP and Proxy Server

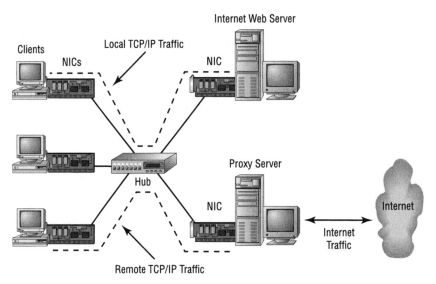

The figure shows that local TCP/IP traffic is routed directly to any local Web servers that are accessible by users of a network. Many businesses today are using intranet Web servers for a wide range of business needs. Operations (such as information distribution, database searching, and forms processing) can all be handled via a well-set-up Web server.

If IPX is the only network protocol available to the workstations, the WinSock Proxy is required to handle all WinSock traffic, both local and external. Even if a workstation is connected to a local Web server, the WinSock Proxy is required to act as an intermediary between the workstation and the Web server. The Web server and the WinSock Proxy Server communicate with each other via the TCP/IP protocol, but the workstations communicate with the WinSock Proxy Server via the IPX protocol. This adds more stress to Microsoft Proxy Server if any local intranet servers are accessed frequently by LAN users.

A huge drawback to using only the IPX protocol as the transport method between workstations and Microsoft Proxy Server is that the Web Proxy portion of Microsoft Proxy Server is completely unused. The Web Proxy requires workstations to use the TCP/IP protocol. If only IPX is used, the WinSock Proxy handles all traffic. The WinSock Proxy can handle all of the traffic that the Web Proxy can, but it does so through other methods. Keep in mind that, unlike the Web Proxy, the WinSock Proxy does *not* cache any information passing through it. This means that a greater amount of work is placed on the WinSock Proxy because it has to go out to the Internet for all data requests. The Web Proxy caches information that passes through it and uses this cached data whenever possible to cut down on the amount of time that it has to go to the Internet for information.

A benefit to using only the IPX protocol is enhanced security and less configuration time. Admittedly, the TCP/IP protocol requires more network configuration than does the IPX protocol. Also, when IPX is used, network administrators can be certain that all LAN Internet traffic is being handled through one service (the WinSock Proxy). If you have a high-speed connection to the Internet and do not need to provide caching services to workstations, using the IPX protocol between workstations and Microsoft Proxy Server will eliminate your need for configuring two proxy services.

It also allows you to prevent LAN users from doing things such as setting up their own FTP or WWW servers. Many large companies want to restrict LAN users from setting up their systems to operate as servers, even though this is a built-in feature of Windows 95. Imagine a network with 500 or more computers all showing up in the Network Neighborhood when users go browsing. Network performance would drop dramatically, and users would be swapping files without having to go through a network server. A new generation of semi-literate computer users is evolving who have the knowledge to circumvent network security by doing things such as running their own FTP servers or WWW servers. By using only the IPX protocol, you can prevent clever LAN users from getting around company policies.

The benefits of the caching services built into the Web Proxy are hard to let go of if your connection to the Internet is a small one compared to the number of users accessing the Internet from your LAN. Our advice is to use the TCP/IP protocol, which enables the use of both the Web Proxy and WinSock Proxy Servers. A network will always have security problems from internal network users. Vigilant monitoring of network activity is the best way to ensure proper use of network services. As a network administrator, you can always limit problem users to the IPX protocol. There is no configuration issue that limits the entire network to just one of the transport methods that Microsoft Proxy Server supports. The two can be used in concert to achieve the desired results.

Private vs. Registered IP Addresses

The next most important issue to discuss when dealing with network setup is what IP address range should be used with a network. This discussion is only relevant when the TCP/IP protocol is used.

The InterNic has set aside several address ranges that can be used by private networks for their own TCP/IP configuration. These address ranges are never found on the Internet because they were set aside so that private networks could use the TCP/IP protocol without conflicting with other sites. The private addresses are as follows:

Class A subnet   10.0.0.0

Class B subnets   172.16.0.0 to 172.31.255.255

Class C subnets   192.168.0.0 to 192.168.255.255

Class A subnets are subnets of 16 million addresses. Any IP address starting with a number between 1 and 126 is a class A subnet. These subnets are all taken by large companies, such as IBM. A *Class B subnet* contains 65,000 addresses and is any IP address starting with a number between 128 and 191. Class B subnets are also spoken for. *Class C subnets* contain 254 addresses and include any IP address starting with a number between 192 and 223. It has been estimated that the InterNic has enough class C subnets to hand out for another four or five years. After that, the addressing scheme of the Internet will have to be altered to handle the Internet's increasing growth rate.

NOTE   For a more extensive discussion of TCP/IP addresses on the Internet, refer to Chapter 2, where we consider subnets and addressing in detail.

The 127 subnet range is a special subnet range reserved for local addressing only. The IP address 127.0.0.1 is always a reference to the local host computer. If you perform a ping on 127.0.0.1 and TCP/IP is configured correctly on your network, the local workstation should immediately respond to the ping request.

Most people thinking about using Microsoft Proxy Server to service the Internet needs of their network have either a dedicated connection or rely on a periodic dial-up link via a modem (or set of modems) or ISDN. These periodic connections do not provide a permanent subnet of valid Internet IP addresses, so you will need to set up your network with one of the previously mentioned subnets. If you do have a dedicated connection of some kind, you have, most likely, been given a valid class C subnet (or multiple subnets) address from the InterNic. If you have a dedicated connection and know how to correctly configure an NT Server to act as the official gateway between your LAN and the Internet, each workstation on the network can have a valid presence on the Internet and will not need to go through Microsoft Proxy Server for its connection. Or all of your IP addresses can be assigned to the Proxy Server and used by the Proxy Server for outside accessing.

When each workstation on a network has a valid Internet address, you lose a great deal of access control. Workstations with their own valid Internet presence have a virtual free reign over Internet access. NT is not designed to monitor or restrict TCP/IP access in valid network arrangements. Microsoft Proxy Server, on the other hand, is heavily designed to monitor and restrict the activities of clients to the Internet. It is for this reason that Microsoft Proxy Server is sometimes the best choice for network clients to use to access the Internet. Note that, with DHCP and Proxy services working in tandem, you can grant IP addresses to workstations without assigning permanents to those addresses. Note further that, with firewall support installed, this issue becomes even more important.

If you do have a dedicated connection to the Internet and have been given a valid class C subnet or subnets, it is a good idea to shelve those addresses and use a reserved address, as listed previously in this chapter. A huge advantage to this approach is that you can use the class A subnet, or one of the class B subnets, if your network needs to support more than 254 network workstations. Large networks that are forced to use multiple class C subnets to cover the number of workstations on the network are much more difficult to administer due to the routing problems that isolated class C subnets cause. When you have the ability to use a larger subnet, administering a large network becomes much easier.

Other NT Services

In addition to the defaults, there are several other NT services that you will want to consider deploying in your Proxy Server network. The following sections discuss these common services.

Deploying a DHCP Server   Once you have decided what protocol and IP subnet to use (if you will be using TCP/IP), the next step is to decide whether DHCP (Dynamic Host Configuration Protocol) will be used and what form of name resolution (if any) will be used on your network.

DHCP is an NT service that is designed to hand out IP configurations to workstations on a network. If workstations are set to use DHCP for their IP configuration, they broadcast a datagram requesting configuration information from the network when they start up. DHCP servers are designed to hear these datagram broadcasts and respond with setup information that is pertinent to the network architecture. DHCP greatly cuts down on the amount of administration work that must be done for each workstation on a network. Imagine having a 200-workstation network and having to manually configure the IP address for each workstation. It would not only be time-consuming but also very inflexible. Should something change on the network, it would be a huge task to alter the IP address scheme. Using DHCP gives the network administrator the ability to centralize the TCP/IP configuration of all workstations. Should the TCP/IP arrangement of a network change, only the DHCP server needs to be reconfigured.

The Microsoft DHCP service is an NT service that can run on any NT Server. It does not have to be running on the primary domain controller or a backup domain controller. It

Proxy Server 2

PART 2

cannot be separated from a portion of the network by a router. Routers do not forward broadcast packets. Therefore, new workstations that are booting up and looking for a DHCP server that happens to be across a router will never find the server because the router does not forward the broadcast information that they generate.

There is a great deal of help on the Microsoft DHCP service in the internal NT help system. By default, it is not installed as a service. There should be only one DHCP server for a network segment.

Setting Up Name Resolution Services   Another network element that must be considered is a name resolution mechanism. In NT 4, two name resolution mechanisms are available: WINS (Windows Internet Naming Service) and DNS (Domain Name Service). WINS is a Microsoft-only name resolution service that performs both NetBios name resolution and Internet-style name resolution, but only to Microsoft clients. WINS is only supported by Microsoft operating systems. It is not supported by UNIX, MAC, or OS/2 systems. These systems must rely on the globally-accepted DNS resolution method.

The ability to resolve Internet style names to an IP address is a function that adds a high level of flexibility to your network. When Internet clients attempt to contact Microsoft Proxy Server (either the Web Proxy or WinSock Proxy services), they can do so either directly, by IP address, or by NetBios or Internet-style name resolution. If all workstations are set to address Microsoft Proxy Server via a static IP, changing the location of Microsoft Proxy Server can be a tough task. In these cases, all workstations have to be manually altered to address the new IP address. On large networks, this can be a very time-consuming task.

When clients are set to access Microsoft Proxy Server via a name, the location of Microsoft Proxy Server can be easily changed by altering the IP address that is resolved to the name in question. For example, a static mapping in the WINS server can be established for the name *PROXY* at 192.168.10.101. Should the location of Microsoft Proxy Server change, the static mapping for PROXY can be edited to point to the new IP location. All workstations would immediately begin to resolve the name *PROXY* to the new address.

If your network must support workstations of other platforms, such as UNIX or Macintosh, you will need to provide DNS resolution capabilities. NT 4 does ship with an available DNS service that can run alongside of the WINS service without conflict. By default, Windows Workstations attempt to access a WINS server before they attempt to contact DNS servers (if workstations are configured to look for both types of name servers). Their basic functionality requires little extra networking knowledge and their presence on a network can greatly enhance the functionality of services, such as Microsoft Proxy Server or other Internet-style servers.

Use Web Proxy, WinSock Proxy, Socks Proxy, or All Three

By now, you understand that Microsoft Proxy Server is actually two separate services running alongside one another. The Web Proxy Server is a CERN-compliant proxy server that provides cross-platform proxy services to any client that is capable of interacting with a CERN-compliant proxy. The Web Proxy can handle HTTP, FTP, and Gopher traffic from clients all through TCP/IP port 80 (This is a default, but this port can be changed). Clients, such as Internet Explorer and Netscape Navigator, all have the built-in ability to communicate with a CERN-compliant proxy server. Other Internet clients, such as WS or FTP, also have the ability to communicate via CERN proxy standards.

The WinSock Proxy is very new and is currently only supported by Windows environments. The WinSock Proxy involves special client software, which takes traffic destined to the outside Internet and redirects it through the WinSock Proxy Server. When the WinSock Proxy client software is installed on Windows systems, almost any WinSock application can have access to the Internet, even if it does not have built-in CERN proxy communication ability.

Benefits of using the Web Proxy are as follows:

Cross platform support   Mac clients, UNIX clients, and OS/2 clients can all access the Microsoft Proxy Server Web Proxy via the TCP/IP protocol without any special software.

High-level data caching services   Most information that passes through the Web Proxy gets cached to be used later to help cut down on the amount of external traffic generated by the Web Proxy.

Support by the major Web browsers   95% of all the Internet activities that LAN users do is through a Web browser, such as Netscape Navigator and Internet Explorer; so the Web Proxy Service may be all that you need for your network.

The benefits of using the WinSock Proxy are as follows:

Support for nearly any WinSock 1.1-compliant client application   Some workstations may need support for Internet applications, such as a Newsgroup Reader, a mail client, or RealAudio. The WinSock Proxy provides support for these protocols.

The ability to manually configure support for a protocol that is not currently configured   The WinSock Proxy comes preconfigured to support a wide range of Internet protocols, such as NNTP, SMTP, and Telnet. If you need to add client support for another protocol, the WinSock Proxy has this flexibility.

Both servers can be configured for security and site restrictions. If you do not want to provide support for any client other than a Web browser, you do not need to worry about dealing with the WinSock Proxy. This will cut your configuration chores down by at least half. Using the Web Proxy also ensures that the special WinSock Proxy client software does not cause any configuration problems on workstations. We have not seen the WinSock Proxy client software cause any problems to date, and we have put it through its paces enough to be quite comfortable with it. However, the networks that we have tested it on do not encompass all possible scenarios.

Most small networks need the services of both servers. We can say this with conviction because most small networks do not have high-end NT services, such as an Exchange gateway, available to them. The only major thing lacking in the Web Proxy is the ability to support mail clients. If your network users use a mail program, such as Eudora, to retrieve mail from an Internet host, the Web Proxy alone will not give them this access. On medium or large networks, it is more common to find an Exchange server available or to use the SMTP services provided by IIS, as discussed in earlier chapters.

An Exchange server is another Microsoft product that provides network and Internet mail services to LAN users. The mail server—whatever type it may be—is usually accessed from the client using Outlook, Outlook Express, or some other third-party software program. When an Exchange server is available, the only part of Microsoft Proxy Server that is usually needed is the Web Proxy. However, some WWW functionality may be lost if only the Web Proxy is used. It is becoming more common for Web browsers to execute hidden client applications, such as Shockwave and the RealAudio player, without the knowledge of the user. These kinds of clients do require the WinSock Proxy because they do not communicate via CERN standards.

Again, it may be better to not support these kinds of clients because they are exceedingly high bandwidth consumption clients. Shockwave and RealAudio involve high-volume data transfers of sound, video, and animation information. These kinds of clients can quickly drag down the performance of an entire network's Internet connection, presuming that the network connection is one of the slower connection types. On a T1 feed, clients such as this can only cause significant performance problems if many, or most, of the users of the proxy are running them.

> **WARNING** Nevertheless, a concern for many network administrators is the amount of outside content, such as Shockwave content, that users (knowingly or unknowingly) bring into the organization through Web access. Using Proxy Server's firewall capabilities, it is possible (and sometimes wise) to block user access across the proxy to specific content types. You will learn more about these features later—for now, simply recognize that security or bandwidth considerations may require you to block access to such content.

Physical Distribution

If you have only one large dedicated connection that Microsoft Proxy Server is using, the physical setup is simple. However, if you are using multiple smaller connections, you have some decisions to make as to how Microsoft Proxy Server will be used on each connection.

A WINS server or a DNS server can be used to daisy chain multiple Web Proxy Servers together. Don't confuse this with multiple Web Proxy Servers working together as one unit. A WINS server can be easily configured to resolve names for a multi-homed group. A static mapping can be added to a WINS database that represents all available Web Proxy Servers on the network. For example, a multi-homed group, called WEBPROXIES, can be added to the WINS database. This group would list the IP addresses of the participating members of the group. When referenced by a client, the WINS server would select an IP of a member of the group to resolve the name to. The selection criteria is based on the proximity of the group member to the client asking for name resolution. Members of the group within the same subnet as the client are resolved to the name before groups outside the subnet are. If there are no close candidates within the group, the WINS server selects a member at random.

Through this method, you can set up a group of Web Proxy Servers that will be used by network users to address a proxy server named WEBPROXIES, for example. Figure 15.4 shows this arrangement.

Figure 15.4   Multiple Web Proxy Servers cascaded by a WINS server

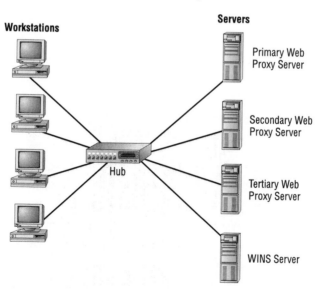

Proxy Server 2

PART 2

In this example, we can assume that a multi-homed group, called WEBPROXIES, has been set up on the WINS server. In this group, the IP addresses for Alpha, Beta, and Gamma have been established. When any of the workstations attempt to address WEBPROXIES, the WINS server will pick the best candidate out of the group and resolve the name request to that IP address. If the requesting workstation had been outside of the subnet, the WINS server would have resolved the address to a randomly selected member of the group.

Through this name resolution method, you can set up a group of cascading Web Proxy Servers for a network so that the workload of Internet traffic is spread out among multiple Web Proxy Servers. However, you are not required to use a WINS server. You can manually configure each workstation to access a specific Web Proxy Server. If you have multiple Internet channels, you should do your best to distribute the workload equally among them.

WinSock Proxy Servers should not be arranged in this manner. A workstation should be specifically configured to access one WinSock Proxy Server. If a group of WinSock Proxy Servers are arranged in a cascading group, Internet clients will not function properly. WinSock Proxy clients must have a constant connection to a single WinSock Proxy Server to operate correctly.

User Groups vs. Task Groups

When you are configuring members of your network to access specific Web Proxy Servers, you have two choices to consider. In the proxy configuration area of the Internet Control Panel, you can specify the address to be used for the HTTP proxy, the FTP proxy, and the Gopher proxy. To spread out the traffic load among multiple Web Proxy Servers, you can opt to divide your LAN users into groups assigned to each available Web Proxy Server, or you can set all users to access a separate Web Proxy Server for each type of connection they need to make.

Since FTP traffic causes the most stress on a connection, you might want to assign all Web Proxy users to access a dedicated FTP Proxy Server and leave another Web Proxy Server dedicated to only serve HTTP connections. The Web Proxy serving FTP connections should have the largest available connection. This approach may help increase the contentment your network users have with your proxy arrangement. Because access to the Web is generally more interactive than downloading files via FTP, make sure your users are not staring blankly at their screens waiting for an HTML document to pop up.

Unfortunately, the protocols supported by the WinSock Proxy Server cannot be split up like the protocols supported by the Web Proxy Server. When a workstation is configured to access a WinSock Proxy Server, that server will be used for all protocols supported.

This being the case, you to have a thorough understanding of what activities your network users will be doing through the available WinSock Proxy Servers. Users who will be accessing a WinSock Proxy Server just to retrieve e-mail cause far less of a workload on the server than those users drawing a RealAudio feed. Spread users out evenly based on the amount of traffic they will generate for each WinSock Proxy Server.

Site Filtering

By far, the most powerful feature Microsoft Proxy Server has for controlling the amount of Internet traffic caused by LAN users is the ability to filter out access to specific sites on the Internet. Both the Web Proxy and the WinSock Proxy can be set to filter out access to all, or just some, sites on the Internet. By default, there is no filtering policy set for either server. However, it is a simple task to add a filter for certain sites, or you can set a general no-access policy for the entire Internet and set exceptions to the rule.

There are many distractions on the Internet. One of the biggest problems a company has once network users have desktop access to the Internet is wandering minds. One of the more popular office distractions is a software package known as the Pointcast screen-saver. The Pointcast screen saver is a Windows 9X screen saver that goes out to the Internet to the Pointcast site and transfers news and information back to the user's machine, where it is displayed throughout the day whenever the screen saver kicks in. When you have hundreds of LAN users all generating Internet traffic for a screen saver, your Internet bill can be an ugly thing. The Pointcast screen saver operates through the Web Proxy Server so the information that comes into the network is cached and usable by other network users. However, the range of information that the Pointcast screen saver can retrieve is very wide, and the information is updated many times a day. While the caching element of the Web Proxy Server will help, LAN users will still generate a lot of Internet traffic. In this example, the network administrator can filter access to the Pointcast site, `pointcast.com`. This eliminates the traffic problem entirely.

Unfortunately, site filtering is still rough around the edges and does not support many filter options. Site filtering is done on a yes or no basis only. Perhaps in future releases of Microsoft Proxy Server, site filtering will be able to filter for time of day and specific users. Currently, the Web Proxy can only globally permit or deny access to sites.

If you really need to restrict access to the outside Internet, a global "deny" policy can be set, and a few exceptions to this rule can be defined. This basically controls which Internet sites your network users have access to. Unfortunately, Microsoft Proxy Server does not have the ability to filter sites based on a user-by-user approach. This means that you cannot define filters for specific users. Perhaps this will be a feature in later releases of Microsoft Proxy Server.

Granting Internet Access

One of the strongest elements of Microsoft Proxy Server is its ability to utilize the internal security system of NT. You have to decide which of your network users will have access to the Internet and which ones will not. You should become familiar with the User Manager for Domains. This utility controls the user database of NT and can be used to define new security groups and set user access rights.

Before you set up Microsoft Proxy Server, you should take some time to decide how you are going to configure security groups. Working with groups of users who share common needs is far easier than trying to configure individual user access for each protocol supported by both the Web Proxy and the WinSock Proxy. Once you have defined a group or set of groups for Internet access, you can readily configure security for the Web and WinSock Proxy Servers.

Unfortunately, Microsoft Proxy Server does not have the ability to configure access for specific times of day. If you have a large network of users but a relatively small link to the Internet, it would be nice to have the ability to separate a morning group and an afternoon group of Internet users. This would go a long way to more evenly distribute the traffic load that the Internet link sustains throughout the day. We have been in large network environments and have found that the Internet connection is slowest about an hour after everyone arrives in the morning.

Perhaps later releases of Microsoft Proxy Server will have a wider range of time-driven access controls. For right now, you'll have to make due with security groups defined in User Manager for Domains.

The Decision Process

The following is a suggested list of decisions you need to make when setting up Microsoft Proxy Server:

1. Which network protocol will be used to transport data between workstations and Microsoft Proxy Server—TCP/IP or IPX? If IPX is the protocol used, you do not need to worry about configuring the Web Proxy Server, only the WinSock Proxy needs to be installed.

2. What IP address range will your network be using? Will the addresses fall within the reserved ranges, or will you use a set of valid addresses?

3. Does your network have all the desired services up and running to support name resolution (through WINS or DNS) and dynamic host configuration (through DHCP)?

4. Will you be using the Web Proxy Server, the WinSock Proxy Server, the SOCKS Proxy Server, some combination, or all three? Small networks will probably need to use at least two, while larger networks may only need to use the Web Proxy.

5. How will the physical layout of your proxy server(s) be set? If you will be using more than one Web Proxy, will you arrange your users into groups to access each Web Proxy, or will you set each Web Proxy to perform transport for a specific protocol?

6. If you have multiple WinSock Proxy Servers, make sure to distribute the traffic load equally. Don't just spread your users out numerically.

7. If you have multiple Web Proxy Servers, will you be using name resolution to cascade access to them?

8. Will you allow any access to the Internet, or will you filter access to certain sites? Will you deny access to the Internet as a general rule and then set exceptions to that rule?

9. If your Internet connection is relatively small for the number of users you have on your network, which users truly need Internet access and which ones simply want Internet access? Use the User Manager for Domains to configure security groups.

Installing Proxy Server

Unlike many other Microsoft Internet products, Microsoft Proxy Server is not being distributed for free. It's estimated retail price is $996 per server, with no connection licenses required. Microsoft Proxy Server only runs under Windows NT 4 and may be obtained through many channels. The most common channel is to purchase it on a CD-ROM or together with Microsoft BackOffice.

Installing Microsoft Proxy Server

Once an NT machine is ready for Microsoft Proxy Server, it can be installed by running MSP.EXE from the root directory of the Microsoft Proxy Server installation CD-ROM, or by running the MSP.EXE application that was downloaded from Microsoft.

An initial licensing dialog box is displayed. Select Continue to proceed to the first installation dialog box.

At this stage, you can alter the directory that Microsoft Proxy Server will be installed to. If you need to install Microsoft Proxy Server into a directory other than C:\MSP, select the Change Folder button and locate the directory where you want to install Microsoft Proxy Server. If the default directory is acceptable, selecting the Installation Options button will continue the installation procedure.

The next stage lets you select whether or not to install the Server and Client files, the Administrative tool, and Microsoft Proxy Server documentation. Microsoft has started a new approach to online documentation. The documentation for Microsoft Proxy Server is in HTML format and requires a Web browser to read. This is a very handy form of documentation because cross-references from one section to another can be easily embedded in the text.

The Install Microsoft Proxy Server check box allows you to set the installation of the Server and the Client share. Figure 15.5 shows the detailed view of the options in the dialog box. If any client files are installed, the installation routine will create a new network shared resource, called MSPCLNT, on the server. This shared resource contains all the necessary files for installing the WinSock Proxy client software onto workstations. The WinSock Proxy client software is required for non-CERN proxy-compatible software to function in a proxy environment. To determine which platform client files are installed on, highlight the Install Microsoft Proxy Server option and select Change Option. The dialog box shown in Figure 15.5 is displayed.

Figure 15.5   The Install Server and Client Installation Share options

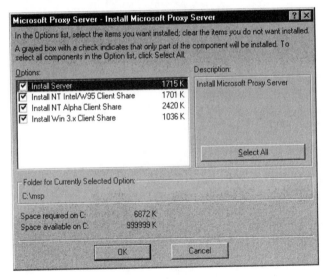

You can cut down the amount of disk space used by the client share files by unchecking the systems architectures that do not apply to your network. The Alpha, MIPS, and PPC clients are NT-only clients. Microsoft only makes an NT OS version for these system architectures. Windows 9X is an Intel-only operating system. The Install Server check box controls whether or not the actual server software is installed. If you only need to install the

WinSock Proxy client software, uncheck the Install Server check box. Uncheck all unneeded system architectures, select OK, and you will return to the main options dialog box.

You can always add support for clients of different platforms at a later time by re-running the installation routine and selecting platforms again.

If you only want the HTML documentation portion of Microsoft Proxy Server, clear the other two options and leave the HTML Documentation checked.

The Administration tool is actually the IIS Manager (for IIS 4, the tool is the Proxy Server plug-in to MMC). This application is the gateway for accessing all control interfaces for Microsoft Internet server applications, such as the IIS Web Server and the Microsoft Proxy Server. You can install the Administration tool application on other NT machines that will need to access the Microsoft Proxy Server for configuration needs. Since the IIS Manager is installed at the same time as the IIS Web Server, installing the Administration tool is not needed on the server that will be running Microsoft Proxy Server. This option is mainly for adding the IIS Manager to other NT machines that might need to control the Microsoft Proxy Server.

Once you have selected all the appropriate options to install, select Continue to proceed with the installation. The Microsoft Proxy Server Cache Drives dialog box is displayed.

This dialog box allows you to indicate which local hard drives should be used to hold Microsoft Proxy Server cached information. As a guideline, the Microsoft Proxy Server cache should be set to at least 100MBs, plus 1/2MBs per supported proxy client. Allocate as many hard drives as you feel you can to hold Microsoft Proxy Server cached information. If one cache drive becomes too full, Microsoft Proxy Server uses other allocated drives for cache data. Controlling the cache is discussed in greater detail in later chapters. Select the desired drive(s), indicate the cache space to allocate to that drive, and select the Set button. Try to arrange at least 100MBs of cache between drives. Once you have indicated the cache arrangement, click OK to continue. The Network Configuration dialog box is displayed next.

This dialog box allows you to enter the IP addresses that should be considered as local addresses for the private LAN. This should include the IP address of any NIC installed in the NT Server, even NICs that are connected directly to the Internet. Contacting all addresses entered here will be handled by the internal WinSockets of each workstation and will not be forwarded to the Web Proxy or WinSock Proxy Servers for outside remoting.

Addresses are entered in pairs and indicate a range. If you wish to enter a single address, enter the same address as the From and To address. Selected button to add the new address range to the Local Address Table (known as the LAT). Highlight an entry in the LAT side of the dialog box and select Remove to remove the address.

Select the Construct Table button and the installation routine will examine the routing table information stored by the NT Server. This should adequately set up the LAT with the correct values for your network. The Construct Table button will set the range of the subnet(s) that the NT Server is on into the LAT. This will also automatically set into the LAT the range of private addresses that the InterNic has set aside for private networks. You should set up the IP subnet for your LAN from one of the reserved addresses, as outlined earlier in this chapter.

Click the Construct Table button to bring up the Construct Table dialog box. You can indicate whether or not to include the known private subnets in your LAT by checking the first option. The Load From NT Internal Routing Table check box allows the installation routine to pull from the internal routing table maintained by NT. This routing table controls TCP/IP traffic between all networks interfaced on the NT Server. You can pull subnets from all known interfaces or just from a single interface card. The default is to pull from all interfaces. NT supports multiple NICs and can be part of several different subnets. You should let the installation routing construct the table from all the subnets that the NT Server is part of. Click OK to return to the main LAT Table dialog box.

If a LAN uses both IPX/SPX and TCP/IP between workstations and servers, you can choose to have no addresses considered local. This forces the WinSock Proxy client software to utilize IPX as a transport method, and all TCP/IP traffic is handled through Microsoft Proxy Server, even if the destination is within the private LAN. If IPX/SPX is the only protocol used between client and server, the addresses entered here as local IP addresses do not matter because WinSock Proxy has to pass all TCP/IP packets to Microsoft Proxy Server for processing.

Once you have added all necessary IP ranges, select OK to continue the installation routine. The next stage allows you to indicate how client workstations access Microsoft Proxy Server.

When the WinSock Proxy client software is installed on LAN workstations, the settings you indicate here will be used by clients. The top portion of this dialog box allows you to indicate how WinSock Proxy clients will access the WinSock Proxy Server. When set to Computer or DNS Name, the name you indicate in the entry field is used by clients to access the WinSock Proxy Server. This requires your network to have some form of name resolution capability available, such as WINS or an internal DNS server. If you do not use any internal name resolution service on your network, you have to use the IP Address option to indicate the IP address where the Microsoft Proxy Server is running.

> **WARNING** NT or Windows 9X machine names do not usually have a period (.) or a space in them. Using these characters causes problems with client setup. This can be fixed with a little manual editing, though. In order to alleviate client installation problems, it is best that the server name be a single word or a valid Internet-style name with no space.

If a WINS server is running on the LAN, a static name entry, such as MSP, can be added to the name database to represent the Microsoft Proxy Server. If the machine name indicated at this point contains a space, the WinSock Proxy client software may only pick up the last part of the name. This requires WinSock Proxy clients to be manually configured for the correct machine name after installation.

One way around this problem, is to use the IP address of the Microsoft Proxy Server. This is the only choice if the LAN has no name resolution capability. It does cause extra configuration effort if the Microsoft Proxy Server is ever moved to a different machine because all client workstations will need to have their addresses modified. If Microsoft Proxy Server is accessed via a machine name, client workstations will simply resolve the name to a new address if the location of Microsoft Proxy Server changes (provided the machine name can follow the Microsoft Proxy Server to a new machine.) This is where a WINS server comes in very handy. If a static entry is added to represent the Microsoft Proxy Server, this is the only element that must be changed if the Microsoft Proxy server changes IP locations and clients are set to look for Microsoft Proxy Server via a network name.

The Enable Access Control check box controls how the WinSock Proxy Server grants Internet access to clients. If this box is checked, the WinSock Proxy Server follows the access restrictions placed on individual protocols controlled by the WinSock Proxy. If this check box is unchecked, any WinSock Proxy client is granted a connection to the Internet. If internal security is not an issue for your network, unchecking this option will save you some time in configuring access permissions. By default, no one has permission to use any protocols through the WinSock Proxy Server.

The bottom portion of this dialog box allows you to indicate whether the workstation proxy settings should be altered. The Web Proxy element of workstation connections to Microsoft Proxy Server do not require any special client software, as WinSock Proxy connections do. However, they do need to have the proxy settings enabled in order to work correctly via proxy. The WinSock Proxy client installation routine can make these settings during installation if the "Set Client setup to configure browser proxy settings" check box is marked. The WinSock Proxy client set-up routine can configure internal Windows 9X Internet settings for Web Proxy use, as well as older versions of Internet

Proxy Server 2

PART 2

Explorer and Netscape, which do not rely on the internal Internet settings maintained by Windows 9X.

The Proxy To Be Used By Client entry field allows you to indicate the proxy name or address that the WinSock Proxy client installation routine should set the Web Proxy clients to communicate with. Again, the same precautions taken with naming conventions with the WinSock Proxy Server name should be taken with the proxy server name.

The Clients Connect To Proxy Via ## Port field is unchangeable. It indicates the TCP port that Microsoft Proxy Server listens to for proxy traffic. This can only be changed by altering the port that the IIS Web Server listens to and is done through the Web Server Properties dialog box.

When the Enable Security check box on this dialog box is checked, the Web Proxy will follow the security settings for client access. When this check box is not marked, any Web Proxy client is permitted access. If you do not have need for high security, you can uncheck this box.

Once these options are set, select OK. The Microsoft Proxy Server installation routine installs all necessary files. Once all files are copied and installed, the IIS server and Microsoft Proxy Server should be restarted. Microsoft Proxy Server will now run and listen for LAN traffic that needs to get to the Internet. The NT Server does not need to be restarted in order for Microsoft Proxy Server to run correctly.

How to Read the Documentation

The default location of Microsoft Proxy Server is C:\MSP. Two sub-directories branch off of this directory. These are the C:\MSP\DOCS and C:\MSP\CLIENTS directories. The DOCS directory contains all of the HTML documentation files for Microsoft Proxy Server. Microsoft Proxy Server documentation can be read by selecting the Microsoft Proxy Server Documentation entry in the Microsoft Proxy Server folder (under Start, Programs, Microsoft Proxy Server folder).

In order to read the documentation, you must have a Web browser installed on the NT machine that Microsoft Proxy Server is installed on (typically IE 4). The Microsoft Proxy Server Documentation entry starts up the default Web browser on the system and loads TOC_CAT.HTM. This is the Table of Contents document that links all chapters of the Microsoft Proxy Server Documentation.

The *mspclnt* Share

The Microsoft Proxy Server set-up routine, if allowed, creates a new shared resource on the NT Server, called mspclnt. This is where the shared resource workstations should connect in order to install the WinSock Proxy client software. Workstations do not need to map a network drive letter to this shared resource in order for the WinSock Proxy client installation software to run correctly. Some applications cannot be executed over a UNC (Universal Naming Convention) link. Instead, they must run from a valid drive letter. Most software created by Microsoft does not fall into this category. This means that the Network Neighborhood or the Windows Explorer can be used to run the Win-Sock Proxy client installation program.

The Microsoft Proxy Server installation routine sets the `mspclnt` share to be accessible to everyone on the network. Unfortunately, the share is also set to grant everyone full control over this resource, which means that workstations can modify or delete files contained in this share. It's advisable to modify the access permissions for this share on the NT Server to make the share accessible to everyone, but only in read-only mode. This can be done through the NT Explorer by following these steps:

1. Open the NT Explorer.

2. Locate the `C:\MSP\CLIENTS` directory and right-click it. A pop-up list will be displayed.

3. Select the Sharing option.

4. Select the Permissions button. Change the "Type of Access for Everyone" for the `mspclnt` share from Full to Read. This ensures that no client workstation on your LAN will inadvertently modify or delete files in this shared directory.

5. Select OK until you return to the main NT Explorer display.

If you reinstall Microsoft Proxy Server for some reason, check to see if the installation routine has reset the permissions for the MSPCLNT share.

Altering Microsoft Proxy Server after Installation

The Microsoft Proxy Server can be reinstalled to modify some of the installation settings when needed. `SETUP.EXE`, found in the `C:\MSP\SETUPBIN` directory, can be run to alter the installation settings of Microsoft Proxy Server. Running the installation routine again will preserve all settings that do not change. This is a simple way to alter things such as the location of the client share and which client platforms are supported.

Altering Microsoft Proxy Server Installation Settings

Running setup one more time allows you to reconfigure the options you originally set during the first installation. This is an easy way to modify things, such as the Local Address Table and cache drive locations, without having to go into the NT Registry Editor. Some of these settings can only be modified by reinstalling Microsoft Proxy Server. Luckily, permissions are preserved during a reinstall.

Selecting the Reinstall button allows you to run through the installation process again and reset any option you need to change. If the Local Address Table is modified, the machine needs to be restarted before the changes take effect.

Adding/Removing Components

Components can be added or removed after the initial installation by selecting the Add/Remove button. If you need to reinstall components for WinSock Proxy clients because a network machine of a different architecture has been added, this is how to do it.

Removing Microsoft Proxy Server

Microsoft Proxy Server can be removed by selecting the Remove All button from the Setup dialog box. Microsoft Proxy Server can be removed successfully without having to restart the NT Server that it is running on.

Reinstallation Problems

There may be situations where Microsoft Proxy Server will not reinstall after a crash or other problem. Sometimes either the WinSock Proxy Server or the Web Proxy Server (or for that matter, the SOCKS Proxy Server) will simply stop responding during startup, and a reinstallation will not fix the problem. In these situations, you may need to remove the IIS Web Server and reinstall it before reinstalling Microsoft Proxy Server.

Solving Security Policy Issues with a Proxy Server

Two of the biggest topics in the IS market-place today is the need for qualified security professionals and the need for system administrators, in even the smallest environments, to be more aware of security considerations and to address them appropriately. To that end, many companies have adopted the suggested government model of creating a network *security policy*, a document that specifies what types of actions are acceptable and unacceptable in a network environment. While such a document is a useful and powerful tool for system administration and rules enforcement, users often ignore specific considerations about the policy either through lack of knowledge or simply because they don't think those rules were meant to apply to them.

As administrators, one of our primary goals is to automate the network environment as much as possible—there is enough real work to do without creating more for ourselves. Unfortunately, security policy enforcement often requires a significant time commitment and seems, to many administrators, to be somewhat akin to police work and outside of the scope of their duties.

Recently, we worked with an organization that adapted a security policy for a number of reasons but, in part, because their Internet connection had limited bandwidth (128K) and they wanted to minimize the extent of their users' Internet access so as not to clog the pipe. Certain sections of the security policy dealt specifically with Internet downloads, maintenance of non-standard

programs on user machines (such as Point-Cast or ICQ), and other bandwidth-related issues.

The Problem

Despite the security policy's specific instructions to the contrary, many users were downloading custom content of a non-standard nature and placing it onto their local workstations. Though the company was not particularly large, the system administrator found herself uncomfortable about having to constantly speak with employees about their not using such software, and found herself wasting significant amounts of time removing it from their systems after installation.

The Solution

We addressed the problem by installing Proxy Server 2 and installing both the proxy and firewall capabilities. We also installed a DHCP server on the network. We left several computers that needed to be able to download software with permanent IP addresses and used DHCP to allocate the remainder of the addresses. All of the computers with DHCP addresses were set up to use the Proxy. We customized the firewall installation to block downloads, real-time communication (such as ICQ), and certain other types of MIME-based transmissions to the block of IP addresses managed by the DHCP server. The permanent IP addresses were granted permission to bridge the firewall to download and test software, as necessary.

24seven CASE STUDY

CASE STUDY

24*seven*

Summing It Up

Proxy Server, in conjunction with other NT Server products, is an effective solution to many network issues, including some issues that don't seem to fall under its umbrella of services. When a full deployment of Proxy Server is done (including firewall support) and combined with other standard NT solutions (such as DHCP and WINS services), the administrator can achieve a highly customized level of control over content going into and coming out of the enterprise. The addition of third-party products—for example, content-blocking products that prevent surfing to certain Web sites (such as adult sites), or virus-checking products that reside on the Proxy and examine all incoming content—are also simplified by a Proxy Server installation.

16

Managing Access to Resources and Configuring Proxy Server

Clearly, one of the two big reasons to use Proxy Server 2 is to control access to resources; that is, to control user access to the Internet and to the actual Internet connection itself. Configuring such access and managing how it works is a relatively simple process, though depending on the level you are configuring access to, it can get rather tedious from time to time. In this chapter, we will consider some of the specifics of Proxy Server 2 configuration, as well as some principles of proxy server configuration that apply to any proxy server product, not just Microsoft's.

Configuration Principles

For the complicated job Proxy Server performs, its setup is very easy and straightforward. The complicated part of Proxy Server is understanding the principle behind what it does. Proxy Server is actually two separate servers working together to perform similar tasks. These servers are separate services under NT but are both controlled through the IIS Service Manager. The first part of Proxy Server is the Web Proxy Server. This is a fully CERN-compatible Web Proxy Server, so any client that adheres to CERN Web Proxy standards can use the Proxy Server Web Proxy to talk to the Internet. Web Proxy clients do not just have to be Windows-based clients. There are no proprietary elements to the Proxy Server Web Proxy. In fact, there is no special software that must be installed on client workstations for them to be able to see the Proxy Server Web Proxy.

For example, UNIX-based systems connected to an NT server running Proxy Server by the TCP/IP protocol can run the UNIX version of Netscape and connect to the Internet through the Proxy Server Web Proxy Server. All flavors of Netscape can be internally configured to see any standard CERN Web Proxy via the TCP/IP protocol.

The second part of Proxy Server is known as the WinSock Proxy Server. It is proprietary to the Windows environment because special WinSock Proxy client software must be installed on workstations in order for them to access the WinSock Proxy Server.

WinSock Proxy works by replacing the local workstation WinSock DLLs with special DLLs that either keep TCP/IP traffic local or remote it over the WinSock Proxy Server for transport to the Internet, depending on the traffic's destination. Only WinSock version 1.1 communications are supported by the WinSock Proxy Server. Microsoft will be updating Proxy Server to support WinSock 2 communications as soon as it can. When support for WinSock 2 standards will be incorporated into Proxy Server is hard to say because the WinSock 2 standards themselves have not been set. It may be that Proxy Server 3 will still only support WinSock 1.1 standards if WinSock 2 standards have not yet been agreed upon.

By adding a new WinSock layer to a system, the WinSock Proxy client software communicates with the WinSock Proxy Server via a special control channel. This avoids TCP/IP port conflicts on the NT Server running Proxy Server. Any Internet server software can be run on the NT machine running Proxy Server because the WinSock Proxy Server itself does not perform broadband TCP/IP port listening as smaller third-party WinSock Proxy software, such as WinGate, does. With these third-party software packages, the server side runs by listening to all applicable TCP/IP ports for traffic. The Proxy Server WinSock Proxy Server communicates with clients via a single control channel. The WinSock Proxy client-side software is responsible for listening to specific TCP/IP ports.

By using WinSock Proxy on client workstations, nearly any Internet application (such as e-mail, Newsgroup reader, and FTP client) can operate locally, just as if it were directly connected to the Internet. Because the communication control takes place at the WinSock level, client applications using the WinSock Proxy interface normally need very little special configuration to work correctly.

The SOCKS Proxy works in a manner fundamentally similar to the WinSock Proxy, only inserting itself into communications when necessary because either end of a socket does not support the WinSock interface.

Once you have a grasp of the three faces of Proxy Server, you will know how to best make use of each element on your private LAN. Accessing the configuring controls for these elements is as easy as opening the MMC. While configuring SOCKS Proxy is important, you will only use it occasionally, so we will focus primarily on the configuration of the Web Proxy and the WinSock Proxy.

MMC and the Internet Service Manager

The major prerequisite for installing Proxy Server is to have the IIS server installed first. The Web Proxy part of Proxy Server runs as a sub-service of the WWW service and therefore requires it in order to function. Proxy Server also makes use of the IIS Service Manager to provide an interface for controlling both the Web Proxy and the WinSock Proxy. If you are running IIS 4, as we have suggested, then the IIS Service Manager can be found in the NT Option Pack Microsoft Internet Information Server folder. If you are running IIS 3, the Internet Service Manager can be located in the Administrative Tools (common) folder. You may have more Internet services running on your system. For example, our server includes the NNTP, SMTP, MTS, MSMQ, WWW, and FTP services, as well as the three proxy services.

> **NOTE** Whichever IIS version you are running, note that Proxy Server installs into its own folder and has its own service manager—in the case of IIS 4, another plug-in to the MMC.

Connecting to Other Servers

NT is a fantastic environment for being able to fully control services running on other NT machines. The IIS Service Manager can be used to control any valid Microsoft Internet service running on another NT machine on the local LAN or even over the Internet. In fact, the Proxy Server installation routine can be used on NT Workstations for just installing the Administration tool, which is just another name for the IIS Service Manager. By installing the Administration tool on an NT Workstation, that workstation can be used to control the Internet services running on NT Servers anywhere on the network. However, the WinSock Proxy cannot be used to remote NetBios traffic, although it is used to control remote NT services. This means that Proxy Server cannot be used to allow LAN workstations to perform network type activities, such as mapping drives or printing to systems on the Internet. Proxy Server does not currently remote NetBios traffic.

Proxy Server 2

PART 2

The first two buttons on the toolbar are Connect to Server and Search Servers. The Search button will only locate IIS servers running on other NT machines on the private LAN. It won't search the Internet.

The Connect button can be used to connect to other servers, either by machine name or by IP address. A NetBios machine name or the actual IP address to connect to can be entered here. Once connected, the service display area will list all services running on the other machine, as well as services running on the local machine. From that point, all services can be controlled in any way.

Configuring Service Properties

To configure service properties, highlight the service to configure, right-click, and choose Properties from the resulting pop-up menu. You can also choose Properties from the Action menu.

Authentication Principles

A large part of configuring both the Web Proxy and WinSock Proxy Servers deals with setting up security. This section will give a brief overview of how Proxy Server deals with security. For a full account of Proxy Server security, please see Chapter 17.

The Web Proxy service uses two levels of security, whereas the WinSock Proxy service uses only one.

The first level of authentication used by the Web Proxy service is login authentication. Since other operating systems can access a Proxy Server Web Proxy, don't rely on the internal Windows login security. CERN authentication is built into the Web Proxy standard. When a client attempts to use the Proxy Server Web Proxy service, it must send a standard HTTP request for access over port 80. Upon receiving this, the Web Proxy Server returns an authentication challenge to the client. Clients that adhere to CERN authentication (such as Netscape and IE 3 or higher) should see a login prompt displayed. Some clients may be configured to send an authentication name and password directly to the Web Proxy without prompting the user. The client must log in with an anonymous login (if that is permitted) or must provide a log in name and password that is present in the NT user database.

If the Web Proxy login is permitted, the authentication name and password used will also be further used by Proxy Server to determine which specific Web Proxy services the user can access (WWW, FTP, and/or Gopher). This is the second level of authentication: protocol-specific access.

The WinSock Proxy service, on the other hand, uses only protocol-specific authentication because the WinSock Proxy client can only run on a Windows platform. It's assumed that the network itself has already taken care of login authentication. Therefore, the WinSock

Proxy service can use the internal NT security layer to demand network identification from clients to find out exactly who they are. That information is used to determine protocol-specific access permissions.

Using the WWW Service to Provide Login Access

Because the Web Proxy service runs as a sub-service of the WWW service, the login configuration of the WWW server applies to the Web Proxy service. To examine the login setup of the WWW service, follow these steps:

1. Highlight the WWW service in the service list of the IIS Service Manager.

2. Click the Properties button. The WWW Properties dialog box is displayed.

3. If you want to alter which account controls anonymous login permissions, enter a new user account name in the Username field of the Anonymous login section. Even if a password is blank, NT displays a string of 14 asterisks for enhanced security. As you have learned in earlier chapters, when the IIS server is installed, an NT user account is created to handle the rights given to anonymous logins. The name of this account is usually *IUSR_computername* where *computername* is the name of your NT IIS server. This account should not be assigned a password. If this account is given a password, anonymous logins must provide this password for access. The nature of the anonymous login is to use the e-mail address of the requesting user for a password.

4. Note the TCP Port field of the WWW Properties dialog box. This is the field for indicating which TCP port the WWW server listens to. This also affects which port Proxy Server listens to and can be used to great effect when necessary. For example, if you want to run a completely separate WWW server, you can set the IIS Web server to listen to a port other than 80 for network traffic (for example, port 81). Another WWW server can be installed to listen to the traditional port 80. Proxy clients on the LAN can configure their software to talk to port 81, leaving the other Web server to handle available external connections on port 80. There is an option in the Web Proxy configuration for disabling external Web connections to the IIS server, though. When LAN workstations install the WinSock Proxy client software, they will automatically import the correct settings for whatever port you have set the IIS Web server to listen to.

Forms of Access   The WWW service supports three forms of login access, all of which you learned about in earlier chapters. Any single one of these forms can apply, or all three can be used simultaneously.

Anonymous   When anonymous logins to the WWW service are permitted, anyone can log in without providing any form of authentication. Unlike FTP anonymous access, which requires a login name of *anonymous* and a valid e-mail address given as a password, WWW anonymous access requires no credentials. If the WWW service does not receive any user information upon client connection, it is assumed that the connection should be extended anonymous login access permissions.

Basic (Clear Text)   When clear text logins are permitted, WWW clients can present their username and password in a standard, low-level encryption format. This form of authentication is fairly simple to break and should be avoided if possible.

Windows NT Challenge/Response   This option is the highest form of security that the WWW service supports. When a client attempts to access the WWW service, the WWW service demands the presentation of login credentials in NT security encryption and format (NTLM C-R). In order for this form of login authentication to be available, the WinSock Proxy service must be present, and the client must have the WinSock Proxy client software loaded. Windows 9X and NT support this form of authentication, but Windows 3.1 and Windows for Workgroups 3.11 do not. However, they can be upgraded to do so if you can still find the software.

The WWW service is designed to field access requests from the outside Internet, and Proxy Server is designed to field access requests from the inside. Keep in mind that a TCP/IP connection to the Internet is just another network connection. Login authentication can take place over a dial-up link just as it can over twisted pair cable.

Proxy Server and NT Security

Proxy Server runs as a standard NT service. As such, access by clients is controlled on a user-by-user basis. When a user attempts to connect, Proxy Server consults the internal NT user database. Both the Web Proxy and the WinSock Proxy Server grant access to Internet protocols. A protocol is a TCP/IP virtual port and a standard form of communication between two applications: client and server side. For example, the NNTP protocol is a form of communication between a newsgroup server and a newsgroup reader. By convention, this communication is carried out over TCP port 119. Proxy Server grants outside access on a protocol-by-protocol basis. All communication with the Web Proxy Server happens over port 80, no matter if the client is a WWW client, an FTP client, or a Gopher client. The Web Proxy Server determines the protocol request by the format of the data. The WinSock Proxy Server determines the protocol by the port the client attempted to connect to.

Each protocol handled by the Web Proxy and WinSock Proxy Servers has independent access permissions assigned to them. These permissions can be in the form of permission for specific users or permission for a group of LAN users. Proxy Server can take full advantage of local NT security groups for assigning access to protocols. Out of the box, neither the

Web Proxy nor the WinSock Proxy Servers have permissions assigned to any of the protocols they support. Therefore, no one can use Proxy Server until the administrator does some reconfiguring. The following configuration information will cover the basic steps needed. Chapter 17 covers the in-depth issues associated with Proxy Server security.

Configuring the Web Proxy Server

The first thing to do is open up the Web Proxy Server configuration dialog box. To configure the Web Proxy Server, follow these steps:

1. Open the IIS Service Manager.

2. Highlight the Web Proxy Server in the service list.

3. Click the properties button on the toolbar or choose the Properties option from one of the available dialog boxes. Figure 16.1 shows the Web Proxy Server configuration dialog box.

Figure 16.1 The Web Proxy Server configuration dialog box

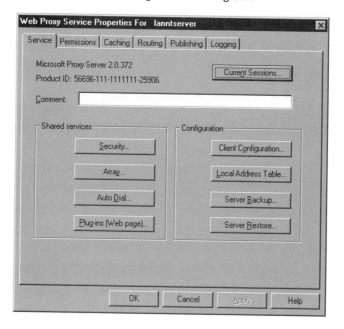

Conforming to the Microsoft configuration interface format, elements of the Web Proxy configuration are accessed via tabs at the top of the dialog box. The following is a basic description of the purpose of each tab.

Service A basic description of the Web Proxy service can be added on this tab. If only a specific group of users is permitted to access the server, some comment to that effect would be a good idea. A large environment of Internet servers is easier to manage if you know what each server does. This tab also allows you to access the LAT (Local Address Table) and edit it as needed.

Permissions Access permissions for each protocol handled by the Web Proxy Server are configured on this tab.

Caching This tab has settings that control the Proxy Server Web Proxy cache.

Routing This tab has settings that control how the proxy is routed outside the local network, including the aliasing that the proxy performs.

Publishing Computers downstream from the Proxy Server can use it to publish to the Internet. Enabling Web publishing allows you to control how such publishing works.

Logging This tab has settings that control how the Proxy Server Web Proxy logs activity information. Tracking access information is second in importance only to security.

To select a tab, click it. The following sections will consider each of the tabs.

The Service Tab

The Web Proxy Server comment will be displayed in the IIS Service Manager service display area. If there are many Internet services running on a network, using comments is important to keep things straight. This tab also allows you to view current connections and edit the LAT.

Viewing Current Sessions At the top, right-hand side of this tab, there is a button for viewing online sessions to the Web Proxy Server. Click this button to view current sessions. Figure 16.2 shows this dialog box.

Figure 16.2 The Microsoft Proxy Server User Sessions dialog box

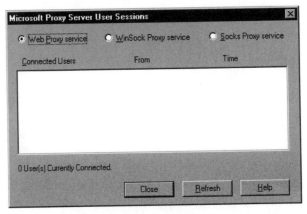

This dialog box shows the name of the connected user, the IP address that user comes from, and how long that user has been online. The username is *anonymous* if no authentication information has been exchanged between the client and Proxy Server. If anonymous access is not permitted, the username will be displayed. This dialog box does not dynamically refresh itself. To update the list, click the Refresh button. Click the close button to return to the Web Proxy configuration dialog box.

Editing the LAT   The LAT is the table that indicates which addresses are local to the network. This is a text file stored in the MSPCLNT share and is transferred to WinSock Proxy clients when the WinSock Proxy client software is installed. This file is named `msplat.txt`. The Edit Local Address Table button calls up an editor that will allow you to make changes to the LAT should your network arrangement change. The LAT is also dynamically sent to clients via the WinSock Proxy control channel.

You can make changes to the LAT in the same manner that you did when Proxy Server was installed. The Construct Table button in the LAT editor will call up another dialog box.

This dialog box allows you to import the values found in the NT routing table to create the LAT. The NT routing table contains all IP information about how to route TCP/IP packets between all network interfaces on the NT Server. There are also options on this dialog box for creating entries in the LAT for the reserved local IP subnets. Chapter 15 covers the details of configuring this dialog box when installing Proxy Server.

Note that the dialog box shows any existing RAS connection of your NT Server as a valid network interface, even though it will be grayed out near the bottom of the dialog box. If you have a static IP for your network connection to an ISP, that static IP address should be part of the LAT.

Once the LAT has been edited correctly, the NT Server should be rebooted in order for the changes to take effect.

The Permissions Tab

Configuring the permissions for the Web Proxy Server protocols is simple compared to configuring permissions for the WinSock Proxy Server. With the Web Proxy Server, only three protocols have to be dealt with. These three protocols also have nothing special to configure. With protocols handled by the WinSock Proxy Server, many more configuration elements are involved, so you have to be a bit more careful in making configuration decisions.

The Enable Access Control check box turns on and off all forms of access restrictions. When not checked, the Web Proxy permits any connections, regardless of the credentials of the client needing access. When checked, the permissions settings restrict client access accordingly.

Proxy Server 2

PART 2

The drop-down box allows you to select the protocol to configure permissions for. Three Web Proxy protocols can be configured: HTTP, FTP, and Gopher (even though Gopher support is deprecated in IIS 4). The display area shows which NT users or groups have permission to use the indicated protocol. By default, the display area shows no access. If you do not have a need for manual security associated with each protocol, assigning Everyone as a permission to a protocol opens the protocol up for LAN-wide use.

You can also assign the Everyone group to the Unlimited Access protocol to open the Web Proxy to unlimited access. Your Administrator group should be assigned to the Unlimited Access protocol. This ensures that users with administrator privileges will not be hampered in any way.

Clicking the Add button allows you to select NT users or groups who should have permission to use the protocol.

If the current domain is in a trust relationship with another domain, you have access to add users and groups from the other domain into the permission list for the protocol being configured. The List Names From drop-down list allows you to select the domain from which to draw users and groups. The default is the home domain of the Proxy Server.

To add a user or group to the permission list for the protocol, follow these steps:

1. Highlight the group to add to the permission list. If you want to add a specific user, click the Show Users button. Proxy Server pulls in a list of all users of the selected domain.

2. Click the Add button. The user or group selected shows up in the Add Names display area.

3. Repeat the process and select all users and groups to give permission to for this protocol.

4. Click OK. Those users and groups will now have permission to use this Web Proxy protocol.

The Show Members button allows you to display exactly which NT users are members of a highlighted group. This is very handy to view just who you are granting Web Proxy permission to when you are granting permission to a group.

The Search button allows you to search for a user or a group within the selected domains that can be contacted from the current domain. Multiple domains can be searched simultaneously. On large networks, this is a handy feature. Domains must be in a trust relationship before groups and users can be shared between them.

Back on the Permission tab, the Remove button removes a highlighted user or group from the permission list of a protocol.

You may consider creating an Internet group rather than relying on one of the existing NT groups for handling Internet access.

The Caching Tab

The Web Proxy service can cache objects that pass through it on their way to clients. These objects can be graphics, sound files, icons, anything that would normally be part of a Web page. Currently, only WWW objects are cached. Files transferred by the FTP protocol through Proxy Server are not cached, just as Gopher data is not cached. These stored objects can later be issued out to requesting clients on the private LAN if the right conditions are met (such as if the object has not expired or if the object is unchanged on the server). This reduces the amount of external traffic Proxy Server has to maintain. The Web Proxy cache settings are controlled through this tab, shown in Figure 16.3.

Figure 16.3   The Caching tab of the Web Proxy

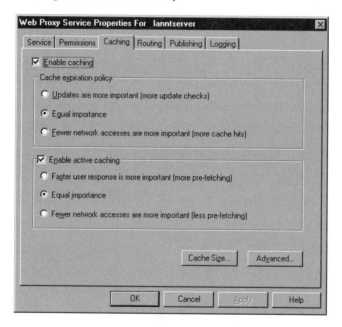

Caching can be turned on and off through the Enable Caching check box. Turning the cache off does not mean that Proxy Server will not serve out cached objects to clients. It means that it does not actively store any new incoming objects into the cache.

Modifying the Cache Expiration Policy   Objects held within the cache are set to expire after a certain time period. This is called an object's time to live or *TTL*. It is a value measured in seconds. Two things can happen to an object when it has expired:

- The object will no longer be issued out by Proxy Server from the cache to clients, and a new version of the object will be kept when a client requests the object from the Internet.
- Proxy Server will actively update the objects on its own if active caching is configured properly.

To access and control TTL information directly, you must click the Advanced button on the Caching tab. Otherwise, the input you provide to Proxy Server from the radio buttons on the tab only gives it direction in how to make decisions about the appropriate TTL for a given page or site.

Modifying the Active Caching Policy   Active caching causes Proxy Server to go out to the Internet and retrieve a fresh copy of an object without needing a client to prompt it to do so. This ensures that popular objects in the cache are always under their TTL and are synched with the originals of the objects on the Internet. This means that clients get HTTP objects locally and do not clutter up the Internet connection.

The Enable active caching check box turns active caching on and off. Proxy Server does not need to be restarted for any alteration in the active caching policy to take effect.

When you choose the first radio button, Proxy Server caches objects more actively. The active caching implementation is controlled by an advanced algorithm that factors in elements such as object popularity and Proxy Server peak access times. When the algorithm determines it to be the correct time to update an object based on these factors, Proxy Server refreshes the object from the Internet. When you choose the last radio button, the algorithm is adjusted so that active caching occurs less frequently, and the Internet connection is not crowded with Proxy Server caching activity.

Modifying Cache Size and Directories   As discussed in previous chapters, Proxy Server's available cache space should be at least 100megs plus 1/2meg for every proxy client that will be supported. If there are many users on a LAN accessing many different sites on the Internet, the suggested size may not be enough to provide adequate caching services. Click the Cache Size button to modify where the cache directories are and how large they should be.

By default, Proxy Server sets up five directories to store cache data. These cache directories are set up under the *URLCACHE* directory. They are named *DIR1*, *DIR2*, *DIR3*, *DIR4*, and *DIR5*. The reason Proxy Server uses multiple cache directories is to speed up access to objects. When a single large cache directory is used, searching the directory for the right object (in the Proxy Server) can be time-consuming. Cache directories should always be placed on a local hard drive, not on a network drive.

Setting the cache is as easy as indicating the drive for a piece, or all, of the cache. The URLCACHE directory will be created automatically on all selected drives. Each of the subdirectories within the main URLCACHE directory will be used equally by the Web Proxy. The Set button must be clicked to set any size alterations or additions before the changes take effect. Proxy Server does not have to be restarted for any cache change to take effect.

Advanced Cache Settings   The Advanced button on the Proxy Service Properties dialog box allows you to control elements, such as what protocols are cached and the maximum size of objects that should be cached, and to filter sites so that their objects are not cached. In Proxy Server's current version, only WWW objects are cached. The ability to enable caching of FTP and Gopher objects is not available.

The settings available on this dialog box limit the size of cached objects, return cache objects when the target site is unreachable, and set filters so that specific sites are not cached. The "Limit the size of cache objects" check box allows you to indicate a maximum size for cache objects. Objects above the size indicated in kilobytes will not be cached by Proxy Server and will always be retrieved from target Web sites. The default is to have all objects cached no matter what their size.

The Return Expired Objects When Site Is Unavailable check box controls whether or not Proxy Server will return objects in the cache if the target site is currently unreachable, but the object's TTL has expired. This allows Proxy Server to simulate a successful connection to a target site even when the objects returned are expired. This can be bad and good for obvious reasons. It's up to you how you want to handle this setting.

The lower portion of this dialog box displays any special filter considerations that you might have configured in Proxy Server. Filters can specifically include or exclude certain sites for or from caching. Sites can be set to Always cached or Never cached. It is possible to set a general never cache policy for a root domain but create a special always cache policy to cache certain sites within that domain. For example, you could set a never cache policy for *.microsoft.com, but create an always cache policy for www.microsoft.com. That way, only objects from www.microsoft.com will ever be cached from the microsoft .com root domain. Cache policies can be set for specific paths on a domain, as well.

You might set www.microsoft.com as a never cache site, but the specific path www .microsoft.com/proxy might be set as an always cache site. Append a site with an asterisk if you want all sub-paths from the parent path to be cached. Without the asterisk, only the specific path will be cached.

The Add button will present a dialog box for adding a site filter to the cache configuration. Simply enter a site name in the appropriate format, as indicated in the URL field, and indicate whether the site is to be Always or Never cached. Click OK after configuring a site's caching policy.

The Edit button allows you to edit existing cache policies in the same way that you add a new site policy.

The Routing Tab

You will use the Routing tab with arrays to direct client requests for Internet objects. Requests can be routed through an array to upstream Proxy Server computers or directly to the Internet. You use the Routing dialog box to configure routing for Web Proxy clients.

The Use HTTP Via header appends the name in the text box to the HTTP Via header for proxied requests. Typically, this entry should be the name of the computer on which Proxy Server is installed.

The Upstream Routing options determine whether a client request is sent directly to the Internet or to another Web Proxy Server or array. The default is to use a direct connection to the Internet; however, if you use a Web Proxy, you can also set a *backup route*. In the event that the primary upstream Proxy Server or array is inaccessible, you can specify a backup sequence that the Proxy should use to access the Internet.

The Publishing Tab

Computers downstream from the Proxy Server computer can use Proxy Server to publish to the Internet. Proxy Server supports reverse proxying and reverse hosting. These two features enhance security by allowing any computer on your internal network to publish to the Internet. All incoming and outgoing requests are filtered through the Proxy Server computer. In addition, Proxy Server can also cache incoming requests from the Internet, which provides safe, easy access.

To take advantage of these settings, you must enable Web publishing. Then, you can decide whether incoming Web server requests should be discarded, sent to the local Web server, or transferred to another Web server. If transferred to another Web server, you can specify the request path and the mapping it should use within the spaces at the bottom of the dialog box.

The Logging Tab

Proxy Server keeps a very good record of who uses the Web Proxy or WinSock Proxy services and exactly what sites they access. By default, Proxy Server logs data in a straight text format. Log files are stored in the \WINNT\SYSTEM32\MSPLOGS directory for Web Proxy accesses and in the \WINNT\SYSTEM32\RWSLOGS directory for WinSock Proxy accesses. By default, both services start a new log file daily. The filenames are YYMMDD .LOG where *YY* is the year, *MM* is the month, and *DD* is the day. These log files are prefixed with *WS* for Winsock and *W3* for the Web Proxy.

The following list is a description of each check box on the Logging tab:

Enable Logging   Controls whether the Web Proxy service logs information. Unchecked, the Web Proxy service will not keep track of accesses.

Regular Logging   Controls whether a full range of information is stored in each log file. If unchecked, only minimal information is stored in the logs. This cuts down on the size of log files.

Verbose Logging   Controls whether or not each Internet access is recorded. By default, Proxy Server Web Proxy will only keep information concerning who on the local LAN accesses the Web Proxy Server. Verbose logging will force Proxy Server to record what Internet sites were visited by each user.

Proxy Server can log to a text file or a SQL or ODBC database, provided that these services are present on the network. Checking the Log to File check box tells Proxy Server to log to a standard text file in the appropriate directory. The Daily, Weekly, Monthly, and When File Size Reaches check boxes tell Proxy Server how often to begin a new log file. If you have little Proxy Server activity, a longer logging period is best. The higher the activity, the shorter the turn-around time should be for opening new log files. Be very watchful of your log files. If a client has a great deal of trouble accessing Proxy Server, it will generate an error line for each bad attempt the client makes. Some of the log files on networks we have seen have easily reached and exceeded 250Mb in a single day due to continuous automatic client reconnection attempts. It's a good idea to archive your log files or delete them on a regular basis to conserve disk space.

If you have a need to change the location where Proxy Server stores Web Proxy logs, you can change the contents of the Log file Directory field.

If the Log to SQL/ODBC Database check box is marked, Proxy Server will attempt to connect to a database server to store its log information. This form of logging is slightly slower than writing to a straight text file, but data manipulation for reports and so on is much more powerful. Any installed ODBC (Open Database Connectivity) drivers can be used. Microsoft Access is a common application that installs a full set of ODBC drivers for external applications, such as Proxy Server, to use when attempting to save data in a database format. During installation, Proxy Server can install several types of current ODBC drivers. These drivers will allow Proxy Server to interface with associated database engines for saving log information in the database engine's own format. Proxy Server can log database information to any machine on the network.

The configuration information in this area of the Logging tab is defined as follows:

ODBC Data Source Name (DSN) This field contains the name of the DSN of the database engine to connect to.

Table This is the name of the table within the database that Proxy Server opens to store its log information.

Username This is the username associated with the database table.

Password If the table is password protected, this field contains the correct password to allow Proxy Server to have access to the table.

Once the SQL/ODBC logging fields have been completed, Proxy Server immediately begins logging to the indicated database table. The service does not have to be restarted.

Configuring the WinSock Proxy Server

Configuration of the WinSock Proxy Server is almost an identical process to configuring the Web Proxy Server. The Service, Logging, and Filters tabs are identical in purpose and configuration elements. Refer back to the tab definitions in the Web Proxy Server configuration section earlier in this chapter for details on the settings involved. The following differences in the three tabs apply:

- The Service tab of the WinSock Proxy configuration does not have a View Sessions button. The WinSock Proxy Server cannot view a list of sessions it is currently supporting; instead, you can view the sessions for the WinSock Proxy from the View Sessions dialog box that you saw figure 16.2.

- The Caching tab is not present in the WinSock Proxy configuration. No caching occurs with WinSock Proxy, so this tab does not apply.

- An extra tab is present. This is the Protocols tab and is used to add support for new protocols or edit settings for support on existing protocols.

A major difference in configuration between the WinSock Proxy Server and the Web Proxy Server is in the Permissions tab. Like the Web Proxy Server, each protocol support by the WinSock Proxy Server is assigned a different set of access permissions. Unlike the Web Proxy Server, administrators can define support for new protocols that do not come pre-configured in the WinSock Proxy Server. Remember that nearly any Internet application can communicate with the WinSock Proxy Server. The client software is responsible for listening to local port requests and establishing a link between the client and the WinSock Proxy Server. As long as a port is correctly configured in the WinSock Proxy setup, almost any Internet application can use the WinSock Proxy Server as though it was directly connected to the Internet.

Protocols the WinSock Proxy Server Supports by Default

By default, the WinSock Proxy Server comes pre-configured to handle all major TCP and UDP port communications. Support for TELNET, FTP (non-proxied), NNTP (Network News Transfer Protocol), SMTP (Simple Mail Transfer Protocol), POP3 (Post Office Protocol 3), Finger, RealAudio, VDO Live, and several other common Internet sockets is configured into the WinSock Proxy Server. This means that unless you have special Internet applications that communicate over an uncommon port, you will probably not have to do any special configuration on the WinSock Proxy Server to get all the commonly used client Internet applications running correctly.

The WinSock Proxy Permissions Tab

To open the WinSock Proxy configuration, do the following:

1. Highlight the WinSock Proxy service in the service list of the IIS Service Manager.

2. Click the Properties button on the toolbar.

The WinSock Proxy Permissions tab looks substantially similar to the Web Proxy Permissions tab but provides a greater amount of configurable options than the Web Proxy does. Figure 16.4 shows the WinSock Proxy Permissions tab.

Figure 16.4   The WinSock Proxy Server Permissions tab

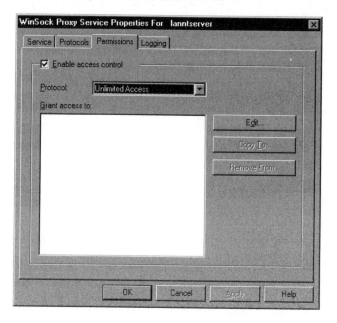

Proxy Server 2

PART 2

Assigning permissions to WinSock Proxy supported protocols is the same process as assigning permissions to Web Proxy protocols. Select the protocol to assign permissions to in the right drop-down list and click the Add button. For more information concerning granting users and network groups rights to use a protocol, refer to the Web Proxy Permission tab discussion earlier in this chapter.

The Copy To and Remove From buttons can be used to copy sets of groups and users from the currently selected protocol to groups of other protocols. For example, if a protocol has seven permission definitions in it, you could display this protocol, select five of these definitions in the traditional Windows select method (holding down CTRL and clicking the desired elements), and then click Copy To. A list of all available protocols would be displayed. You can then select a protocol (or group of protocols with the multiple select method again) and click OK. The selected groups and users are copied into the permission sets of the target protocols. Remove From works in the same way but in reverse. Selected groups and users will be removed from the selected protocols rather than added to them.

The Protocols Tab

The Protocols tab allows you to modify existing protocols or create new protocols that the WinSock Proxy Server will support. When you view this tab, you see the protocols that the WinSock Proxy Server supports listed in the Protocol Definitions area. From this dialog box, existing protocols can be edited or removed, and new ones can be added. The dialog boxes produced by the Add and Edit buttons are identical.

When adding support for a new protocol, the first thing you have to know in advance is what port the client application talks to its server on and what type of data packets (TCP or UDP) the application uses. Most clients initiate communication with a server over one port, but expect a response over another port. Some clients expect the server to set the return port number, while others expect a return over a consistent port. For example, under normal circumstances, FTP clients initiate communication with an FTP server over port 21 but expect a response over port 23. However, most good FTP clients can be set for something called Passive transfer (PASV Mode), which means that they instruct the server to set up a non-standard return port.

PASV mode is a security form. It is mostly needed to pass over routers and firewalls. The purpose of a firewall is to prevent access to a network over known ports, such as the return FTP port 23. When the server sets up a non-standard return port, the communication can pass over a firewall.

You must be familiar with how a client/server pair communicates before you can correctly set up the WinSock Proxy Server to connect the two. For example, an application might use UDP packets and initiate communication with conforming servers over port 2417. The application might expect a return channel from the server over a dynamically established port—that is, the return port will vary. The return port is not as important as knowing the initiating port. Most of the time, the WinSock Proxy client software will be able to tell the WinSock Proxy Server what port to expect a return response on from the way the actual client secures the return port on the workstation. The process happens like this:

1. The application initiates communication with a server over port 2417.

2. The WinSock Proxy client software intercepts this call and informs the WinSock Proxy Server about it over its control port—1745.

3. The WinSock Proxy Server begins to communicate with the application as though it was the actual site that the application is trying to talk to. Understand that the WinSock Proxy Server is not responding for the actual target server. It can't. It doesn't know what the application wants. The WinSock Proxy Server only receives the network connection as though it were the target site.

4. The application initiates a listen on a dynamic UDP port for return data from the server it is trying to contact.

5. The WinSock Proxy Server intercepts the listen and tells the WinSock Proxy Server what port the application is listening to.

6. The WinSock Proxy Server initiates a connection between itself and the target site over port 2417. At the same time, the WinSock Proxy Server begins to listen for a response over the UDP port that the application is listening to.

7. When the target site responds on the dynamic return port, the WinSock Proxy Server forwards the response to the application, as if it were the actual site.

In this process, the WinSock Proxy Server acts as the middleman. It pretends to be the target server when talking to the application, and it pretends to be the application when talking to the target server. As long as it knows what port to expect an initial connection on and what type of data packets to toss around, it should be able to handle any Internet client/server combo.

To add support for a new protocol, click the Add button in the Services (protocols) dialog box. The following list defines each element on the Protocol Definition dialog box.

Protocol Name   This is any name you want to assign to the protocol.

Initial Connection Port   This is the port the client will use when first attempting to contact a server.

Initial Connect Type   This can be either TCP or UDP. You must know what type of packets a client uses to initiate communications with a server. If you are not sure, try TCP. TCP packets are more commonly used than UDP.

Initial Connection Direction   This setting tells the WinSock Proxy Server which direction to expect the packets on this port. Since the application begins the communication in the model we have sketched, the direction is outbound. Outbound will be the direction for 95% of all protocols you set up.

Once you have the basics configured, you need to add information about how subsequent connections from the target server back to the client application will be made. With our sample application, we will need to indicate that any UDP port can be used for a return connection. Clicking the Add button (or the Edit button to edit an existing return port) will produce the Return Connection dialog box.

The return port number (or range) should be indicated in the Port or Range fields. A value of 0 indicates that any port may be used as a return port for this protocol.

The Type will set the packet type that is normally the same as the outbound packet type, in this case, UDP. The Direction will be inbound. The application will not send further outbound packets to the target server over a different port. Some protocols may need to send out packets over multiple ports once an initial connection to a server is made. If this is the case, you need to know which ports the client application is utilizing and create multiple subsequent connection entries, or create a range for ports.

Once you have indicated these elements, you can click OK to return to the primary protocol definition dialog box. Those should be the only configuration elements you need to set. For most protocols you will configure, you can set all subsequent connections for any valid port. Once the protocol has been completely defined, click OK to return to the Protocols tab. Don't forget to add permissions to new protocols you configure.

Multiple Proxy Server Gateways

More than one Proxy Server gateway can be used on a network. The Web Proxy and WinSock Proxy Servers behave slightly differently in a network environment where more than one Proxy Server is used.

Multiple Web Proxy Servers

Clients can access multiple Web Proxy Servers in a cascading fashion. Web Proxy Servers can be grouped and accessed in a chain to provide the best possible performance for clients. In order for this to be possible, some form of internal name resolution ability must be present on the network. Either a DNS or WINS server must be available to perform name resolution on behalf of the clients and then provide resolved name information to the clients.

All Web Proxy Servers can be put into an Internet group. This group is defined as an entity by a DNS server or a WINS server. When the group is accessed, either the DNS server or the WINS server serving out the name resolution functionality for the network will sequentially choose a member from the group and resolve the group name requested as the IP of one of the members of the group. The name server is responsible for tracking which member of the group is up for the next resolution request.

Under a WINS environment, a multi-homed, static database entry is created to list all of the Proxy Servers. The WINS server chooses a representative from this list differently from how the DNS server chooses its representative. The WINS server first matches a client's request with the client's IP. The WINS server then tries to find a Proxy Server from the list that has the same subnet as the client. Failing to do that, the WINS server attempts to locate a Proxy Server on the same net as the client. If none of these searches finds a proper candidate, the WINS server picks a member of the group at random and resolves the request to that member's IP address.

Multiple WinSock Proxy Servers

WinSock Proxy Servers cannot be cascaded like Web Proxy Servers can. In order to make best use of multiple WinSock Proxy Servers, network clients should be evenly distributed among all WinSock Proxy Servers to make sure that no one WinSock Proxy Server becomes overloaded. You need to have a good understanding of which Internet protocols demand the most out of a connection. Knowing that will allow you to separate client access correctly. Internet applications, such as RealAudio and VDO Live, consume huge amounts of connection bandwidth and can bring the Internet applications of other network users that are running through the same connection to a stand still.

Configuring Proxy Server Security and Authentication

Proxy Server security relies directly on the internal security found in NT's architecture. When NT Servers are used in a workgroups-based network, the user information provided on each server is separate and independent. Each server or NT workstation system can maintain a full database of users and groups. These user and group definitions only apply to accessing the particular server on which they are kept.

Arranging a network into a domain takes a little more effort to manage, but the benefits of less confusion and tighter security far outweigh the extra management effort. NT Servers in a workgroup are like islands of independent security. The security credentials needed to access resources or services on one NT Server may not be the same as those needed for a different NT Server.

Login Process

As you should know, several things happen when a workstation logs on to a network. If the workstation is set to logon as a workgroup member, the workstation itself performs user authentication with its own user database of information. If the workstation is set to logon as a domain member, the workstation machine will consult the primary domain controller for user authentication. A login proceeds in the following manner:

1. The domain controller must be found before the logon when the system is started. This process is called *discovery* and is only done when a workstation is set to log on to a domain. The actual method of discovery depends on the protocol(s) the network uses. To discover a PDC (primary domain controller), a workstation must perform a network broadcast, which triggers the PDC of the network to perform its own broadcast to indicate with a directed datagram where the PDC can be found. Once the workstation receives the broadcast response from the PDC, which lets the workstation know exactly where it can find the PDC so that the workstation can correctly direct its *own* datagrams, the next step of logging on can proceed.

2. Once the PDC is found, the workstation attempts to establish a secure channel between itself and the PDC, or the BDC (backup domain controller) if it responded in place of the PDC. This secure channel consists of datagrams directed back and forth between the workstation and PDC. Each side must prove to the other that they are who they say they are. This process is called Secure Channel Setup.

3. Once the workstation and the PDC have found each other and set up a secure channel, Pass-Through Authentication can occur. In this process, the workstation sends the login username and password to the PDC (or a BDC) in encrypted format. If the user information is correct, the PDC sends back an OK for the workstation to permit the login.

4. After authentication is complete, the system and user are given a security token by the controller that performed the authentication. This token is the actual network item that is passed around to network servers accessed by the client workstation. Any target server will use this token to consult a controller to find out if it is valid and if the associated user should be granted access to use whatever resource the user is attempting to access.

A Proxy Server is like any other resource on the network. Accessing it takes proper network validation. The Proxy Server service is fully capable of utilizing the internal NT security process.

Domain Controllers and Their Impact on Proxy Server

On an NT-based network, the central authority figures are known as *controllers*. There is one primary domain controller and any number of backup domain controllers. These systems are responsible for fielding all Microsoft Network Domain logins and granting or denying access to secured network resources. PDCs and BDCs are always NT Servers and, as such, all share information. User data stored on the PDC is replicated to all BDCs across the domain. The network administrator determines which NT systems are to be BDC machines when these systems are installed. The job of the BDCs is to share some of the workload of the PDC. On medium or large networks, a single authority figure might quickly become overloaded with network traffic. BDCs help to ensure that network performance is kept as high as possible.

Administration of user data can be done from any NT machine, Server, or Workstation, as long as the logged-in user has administrator rights. The main application for modifying user data is User Manager for Domains, which is found in the Administrative Tools folder. When systems are not members of a domain, this application only modifies user information stored in the local user database. When an NT system is a member of a domain, this application links to an available controllers and modifies the domain-wide user database.

When talking about user information concerning Proxy Server authentication, note that we are discussing a domain-wide database of user information. While a Proxy Server machine can be a completely isolated server, not part of any domain, the task of managing separate authorization for network users and Proxy Server users in such an environment becomes far more time-consuming and counterproductive.

In general, most NT installations deal exclusively with a domain-based network. To that end, we will focus on implementing Proxy Server within an NT domain model.

Creating a Global Security Group   To create a global group, follow these steps:

1. Click the File menu in the User Manager for Domains.
2. Click the New Global Group selection.
3. The Create Global group dialog box will appear.
4. The name of the group should appear in the Group Name field. In this example, you might name it something like *Proxy Users*.
5. The Description field can be any description you want to give this group.
6. Next, indicate which users should be members of this group. The Not Members list shows all users who are not currently members of this group. Because this is

a new group, the Not Members list shows all NT users. Select all users who should be allowed general proxy access and click Add.

7. Click OK. The Proxy Users group is created and a set of users are defined.

WARNING Make sure you do not add the IUSR_*servername* user to the group. If this account is added to the group, anonymous users will be granted access to whatever features you assign to the Proxy Users group. This account should only be dealt with on an individual basis and never assigned to any global group.

Once the group is created, it can be used within Proxy Server to define access to various protocols. If this group needs to have special NT network permissions granted to it, the group can be nested within an existing local group that already has the permissions assigned to it. This approach is a simple way of cutting down some of the management time spent on security. If a group of users needs to have certain access permissions in more than one domain, two groups should be created: one that is local and one that is global. Both can have the same name. Users can be assigned to the global group, and the global group can be nested within the local group. The local group can then be granted whatever permissions are needed, and those permissions will filter down to the global group users.

The next step is to grant this group access to a supported protocol, either in the Web Proxy or the WinSock Proxy.

Granting Proxy Permission to the New Group

Open the IIS Service Manager and open the properties for the Web Proxy. Once you have opened the properties of the Web Proxy, select the Permissions tab. By default, no permissions are configured for any protocol in Proxy Server. Therefore, no users have access to get to the Internet through the Web Proxy or the WinSock Proxy. In order to grant access permission to the new Proxy Users group, do the following:

1. Select the protocol you wish to grant access to in the Protocol drop-down list. For example, you will often use the WWW (HTTP) protocol.

2. Click the Add button. This opens a dialog box for adding groups or users to the access list for this protocol.

3. The List Names From drop-down list allows you to select any domain you currently have access to. Access to foreign domains can be through a trust relationship or from having a parallel account in other domains. By default, you can select users and groups from the local domain.

4. The Default Only drop-down list has both local and global groups. However, you can list users by clicking the Show Users button. This displays the users of the domain, as well as the groups. Configuring individual users is fine for small

networks or special cases, but this can be a management nightmare for medium or large networks. You should always work with groups whenever possible.

5. Scroll down the name list until the Proxy Users group is displayed.

6. Highlight the Proxy Users group and click the Add button. This adds the Proxy Users group to the Add Names list.

7. You can select any additional groups or users to grant WWW access permission to if necessary.

8. Click OK to return to the Permissions tab. The group appears in the Grant Access To list area and has access to use the WWW protocol.

The Members button on the Add Users and Groups dialog box displays a list of users for the currently highlighted group. If more than one group is selected, this button is not available. The Add button at the bottom of this dialog box will add the group to the Add Name list on the Add Users and Groups dialog box. It is not for adding additional users to the group. This function allows you to view which users are members of the group.

The Search button on the Add Users and Groups dialog box will let you search for users or groups on the local domain or on domains that you have access to, either through a trust relationship or by having a parallel account on the other domain(s).

In this dialog box, you can indicate which domains to search and the name of the user or group you want to search for. You can search in the local domain or in all available domains. By default, all domains will be searched. Search results will be displayed in the lower area. Elements of the search result can be selected. Click the Add button to add the user or group to the permissions list.

Once you have added the Proxy Users group to the permission list for the WWW protocol, the users of that group will be able to use Web browsers through Proxy Server Web Proxy to access WWW sites on the Internet.

Complete this process for all of the protocols (WWW, FTP, Gopher, or Secure) you need to grant users permissions to. The process for adding permissions to WinSock Protocols is very similar, but the WinSock Proxy has special universal access settings that make it easier to grant global protocol permissions for a group of users.

Controlling Inbound Access from the Internet

When Proxy Server is installed, two elements of NT are altered so that security is enhanced. The first element that is altered is IP Forwarding. IP Forwarding is found within the TCP/IP settings. It is turned off by default. It controls whether or not NT will forward IP packets between network interfaces in managers (such as a network card and a RAS connection to an Internet Provider). Under conditions where a dedicated, full-time Internet connection is available to a network and each workstation on the LAN is configured for its own direct Internet access, IP forwarding must be enabled for workstations to pass their packets to the Internet and vice versa. This in itself will halt all inbound traffic at the NT Server, which is connected to the Internet.

To further restrict access to the NT Server from clients connecting from the Internet, Proxy Server disables listening on all TCP/IP ports which do not have permissions set for them. This means that any Internet server application (such as an FTP server, a telnet server, or a POP3 server) running on the connected NT Server will be unable to hear any external inbound traffic until permissions are set for the associated protocol in the WinSock Proxy. The Web Proxy only listens to port 80 for traffic. If permissions are set for any of the supported protocols in the Web Proxy, port 80 will be listened to for inbound traffic.

Isolating Proxy Server on Its Own Domain

If you want to set your network security at a very high level for proxy access, one approach is to set up the NT Server running Proxy Server as a primary domain controller of its own domain. A one-way trust relationship can be established between the Proxy domain and the network domain. The Proxy domain would be set to trust the network domain, but the network domain would not trust the Proxy domain. This arrangement will further limit the access that can take place between the proxy server and all other systems on the network domain.

This arrangement also works well when the network is not set as a domain but rather as a workgroup. The NT Server running Proxy Server can be set on a primary domain controller of its own domain, which will give greater security control and allow easier expansion for future growth.

Using Proxy as Part of a Proxy Array

Often, companies find that they have to divide their network into several local groups, using routers and bridges to divide it up. This reduces the amount of traffic that transits certain parts of the physical network.

In such an environment, building a Proxy Server array can be a useful technique, particularly if the users in the different subnets tend to access substantially different pages. In such a case, building a Proxy Server array can speed user access without substantial impact on the network as a whole.

The Problem

Assume for the moment that a company has five divisions, each of which works closely with extranets of vendors and other related organizations. However, none of the different divisions overlap on access to any of these particular extranets. Instead, these only overlap on generic Web site surfing.

The Solution

By configuring a proxy array and setting individual routing tables, you can set up each individual Proxy Server to cache the information appropriate only to its department, while accessing a central Proxy Server for generalized Internet access. Such a construction will speed departmental access to common sites, reduce network traffic, and still maintain our Proxy Server goals of providing central points of management accessible by the administrative staff.

Summing It Up

While Proxy Server lends itself to simple Internet access distributions, using it in a complex environment with a multiple-server array model can help you effectively manage Internet access, as well as network bandwidth.

17

Integrating Proxy Server
with the Network

This chapter details how client applications gain access to Microsoft Proxy Server services. Both the Web Proxy Server and the WinSock Proxy Server are discussed independently because security is handled differently by each server. Understanding how client applications gain access to the Proxy is a crucial part of setup because, once the Proxy is in place, client applications should not be able to gain access to the Internet *except* via the Proxy. In other words, once you install the Proxy, there should not be a way for client applications to access Internet resources unless the Proxy exposes that access.

Client Security

When any entity on a network attempts to access a secured resource, it must present the right credential to the controller of that resource in order to gain access. This includes access to network printers, shared directories, and server services (such as Microsoft Proxy Server). Presentation of credentials can be a very subtle process, completely hidden from the user and requiring no user interaction. Or it can be a totally interactive process where the network user must indicate a valid username, password, and (in the case of NT-based networks) the network domain to present the credentials to. Netware-based networks with Netware Directory Services are similar in nature to NT-based domains in that there is an overriding authority for servers, called the Tree. For the security discussion in this chapter, we will focus only on NT-based networks.

The two dominant components of Microsoft Proxy Server can be set to follow security settings, or they can be set to ignore security settings and permit access from any client regardless of what credentials they present. In fact, when no security is used by Microsoft Proxy Server, no credentials will be demanded from clients.

When a user starts a Windows machine (for this particular discussion, Windows 9X or NT), Windows prompts the user for logon information if the system is configured correctly. Logon information can be obtained through a standard Windows logon or by a domain logon. Of the two logon methods, a domain logon is by far the most secure and useful in a complete network environment.

Windows Logon

Windows 9X Workstations can be set to perform a standard Windows Logon through the Network Control Panel. By default, when a network card is present in a Windows 9X computer, all available network clients are installed. This includes the Microsoft Networking client and the default Novell Netware client. For this chapter, the Novell Netware client will be ignored. The Windows 9X operating system requires the installation of special network client software if the workstation will be accessing servers of that network type. A standard Windows logon will not be sufficient to gain access to secured NT Servers. The Microsoft Networking client must be installed before Windows 9X will be able to present credentials to an NT Server in the correct format.

Setting a Windows 9X computer to perform only a standard Windows logon without the presence of the Microsoft Networking client only provides local machine security. Access to NT Servers that are part of a domain is not possible. Access to any Windows workgroup server isn't possible either. The Microsoft Networking client controls network access to all Microsoft-based servers.

However, a Windows Workstation can be set to perform a standard Windows logon and still have access to network resources when the Microsoft Networking client is present. When a standard Windows logon occurs, a network user is presented with a Logon dialog box that asks for a username and a password. Once entered, Windows checks for a password list for the given name. If found, the password the user has given is checked against the stored (and encrypted) password in the password list file. If the two match, Windows permits the logon, and the user continues into the operating system. If the two passwords do not match, Windows prompts the user for a new password, or the user can enter a new username and password. If there is no password list for the username given, Windows prompts for confirmation of the given password, and a new password list is created.

Note that this logon process does not involve authentication by a central security agent, such as an NT domain controller. After a user logs in with a standard Windows logon, the user is still unknown to the network. The workstation is forced to present the logon credentials to the security agent, requiring them only if the user attempts to access a secured network resource. However, if the Microsoft Networking client is configured to perform a domain logon, immediate network authentication is attempted (to the default domain indicated in Microsoft Networking client properties) using the username and password given at the Windows Logon dialog box. If these are not valid in the default domain, a second Domain Logon dialog box that requires a valid domain username and password is presented. This means that to Windows, a user can be known by two (or even more) identities. To Windows itself, the user is known by his or her Windows logon. To NT Servers, the user is known by the network credentials that are presented or by the credentials that were automatically presented. If Novell Netware servers are participating on the network, a user may be known by a *third* identity, that of his or her Netware logon.

If a Windows logon is used as the primary logon, all subsequent client logon credentials can be stored in the password list created by Windows. This means that subsequent logons will proceed without the user needing to enter a username and password for each network client that is installed in Windows. Changing secondary network client passwords can be done through the Password icon in the Control Panel; or the password list can be deleted, and the logon process can be redone. This approach is often the easiest way of changing a password for a secondary client.

If a standard Windows logon is used, and the Microsoft Networking client is not set to log on to a domain, no immediate network authentication is performed. Network authentication will be done when a network resource is accessed (for example, attempting to view a resource list of an NT Server listed in the Network Neighborhood). When this is the case, the password list is consulted for domain logon information. If none is found, the current Windows logon name and password are presented to a domain controller in the domain of the server that is being accessed. If the Windows logon username and password are not valid in the domain being consulted, permission to access resources in that domain are not granted, and the user is not prompted to enter new credentials.

A standard Windows logon is very low in security because the password list files can easily be deleted or modified on the local machine.

Domain Logon

The second type of Windows logon that can be performed is known as a domain-based logon. This type of logon is similar to a standard Windows logon, except that the credentials entered by the user are immediately presented to an NT domain controller for authentication. The Logon dialog box is nearly the same, except that an additional field for indicating the logon domain is present.

In order for this type of logon to be used, the Microsoft Networking client must be selected as the Primary Network Logon. Further network configuration to indicate a domain logon should be performed. Once the primary network logon has been set to the Microsoft Networking client, the properties need to be altered. This is done by high-lighting the Microsoft Networking client entry in the Components list, clicking the Properties button, and entering the domain name.

The settings for controlling domain logon and the domain to log on to are checked. Once the Log On To Windows NT Domain check box is marked and a domain name is given, all logons from that machine are authenticated by a controller in the indicated domain. This provides immediate network authentication. Microsoft Proxy Server needs network authentication for its own validation purposes.

When a domain logon is performed at startup, a password list is created for the user that is logging on to the system. This is done in case a domain controller cannot be found in the future. This permits a user to log on to a Windows machine based on the validation data contained in the password list, even when a domain controller cannot be found (for example, when the network is down). In this logon scenario, the Windows logon name and password match the domain logon name and password. When a standard Windows logon is performed first, the logon information between the Windows logon and the domain logon may be different.

Suggested Logon Method

The easiest way of setting a Windows machine to logon to a network is to set it to perform a domain logon. This provides the highest security and allows immediate network authen-tication. This approach requires a domain controller to be present somewhere on the net-work to field all logon attempts.

If your network does not contain any domain controllers, you need to set workstations to perform standard Windows logons; but this necessitates that the logon information be unverifiably correct. Unverifiable means that users can log on with bogus credentials and this will not be known until they attempt to access a network resource and get an Access Denied error. However, problems other than a bad username and password can cause Access Denied errors. Troubleshooting this error without a central domain authority can be quite difficult.

When there is no central domain authority for a network workgroup, each NT Server on the network is an island that follows its own security database. Usernames and passwords configured on NT Servers that are set up as workgroup machines are not shared among other NT Servers, even when those servers are members of the same workgroup. When a user attempts to access an NT workgroup server, the workstations present network credentials directly to that server. That server permits or denies access to the requested resource or service based on its own security database.

As long as the username and password are valid for a domain resource that a network user is attempting to access, permission is granted. This means that if a user gains validation in one domain and his credentials are valid in another, access to the second domain is permitted. This process of having parallel accounts in multiple domains is difficult to manage from a network administrator's point of view, but it does overcome certain difficulties.

Another arrangement, known as a trust relationship, can be established between two or more domains to allow users from one domain to have access to resources in another domain using only a single account that has access to both domains. If your network has multiple domains, you should read up on the benefits of creating trusts between domains for the purpose of allowing users to access both domain resources.

When deciding what the best logon method is, use a domain logon when a domain controller is present and use a standard Windows logon when a domain controller is not present. For standard Windows logons, be sure that the logon information used by network users is correct for the servers they need to access. Multiple simultaneous workgroup logons are not supported under Windows, so parallel accounts must exist on all workgroup servers that network users must access.

> **TIP** As a general rule, all networks should have a domain controller (or a Novell logon server) to verify user credentials before granting access to network resources.

Web Proxy Authentication

Now that we have reviewed how a network user is known on a network, let's discuss how the Web Proxy side of Microsoft Proxy Server grants or denies access to its services. The first element of the Web Proxy that needs to be covered is how it accepts authentication requests.

Remember that the Web Proxy is a fully CERN-compliant HTTP proxy and, as such, can be accessed by operating systems other than Windows. Any operating system that supports the TCP/IP protocol can run applications that talk to the Microsoft Proxy Server Web Proxy. This being the case, the Web Proxy has to have a way of finding out who is attempting to access its services when the standard Windows network security layer is not usable.

The WWW service is the security-controlling mechanism that is used by the Web Proxy. Because the Web Proxy runs as a sub-service of the WWW service, the security mechanisms configured in the WWW service also applies to the Web Proxy service. The Service tab of the WWW Service Properties dialog box contains the configuration elements that control which security mechanisms are permitted.

The Password Authentication portion of the Service tab contains the configuration for the permitted security mechanisms. There are three forms of security negotiation that the WWW service (and therefore the WWW Proxy) can perform:

- Anonymous
- Basic (Clear Text)
- Windows NT Challenge/Response

Checking each security method enables it. While we have considered these concepts extensively in the context of the Web server, it is worthwhile to review them again in the additional context of the Proxy Server. The following sections discuss each security method in detail.

Anonymous

If the Anonymous security method is enabled, any client can have access to the WWW Proxy service without providing a valid username and password that can be found in the NT security database. In most cases, anonymous access is gained by entering a username of *Anonymous* at a username prompt, and then entering an e-mail address as the password. When Anonymous security is enabled, all non-Windows clients will access the WWW service and the Web Proxy Server as anonymous clients. This will override Basic security.

When Anonymous security is enabled, clients don't see an authentication dialog box pop up in their browser or FTP client when attempting to access the Web Proxy. For Web Proxy anonymous access, no username or password is required. This is unlike standard anonymous FTP access where a user is prompted to enter the name *Anonymous* and an e-mail address as a password.

If your goal is to allow all of your network users unlimited access to the Web Proxy, allowing only Anonymous security is not the best approach. The Anonymous security mechanism is primarily used with the actual WWW service and not with the Web Proxy Server. Microsoft has created a double-edged sword. On the one hand, if your NT Server runs the WWW service alongside the Web Proxy for external Internet users, you will want to enable Anonymous security so that external Internet users are not required to enter a name and password to access your Internet site. However, enabling Anonymous security opens up the Web Proxy to any non-Windows network client wanting external Internet access.

There are other ways to permit any valid network user access to any protocol supported by the Web Proxy without enabling Anonymous security. These security issues will be discussed later in this chapter. It's a tough decision to make. Enable Anonymous security if you have no need to control internal access to the Web Proxy and want external Internet users to freely access your Web site. Disable anonymous access if you want to control internal access to the Web Proxy but want to require external Internet users to provide a valid username and password. For Web Proxy control, you should disable anonymous access.

Basic (Clear Text)

When this form of security is enabled, clients pass their credentials to the Web Proxy via a low-level encryption method. This is done in a very simplistic encoding format that can be easily intercepted and decoded by devoted hackers. However, it is the only form of authentication available to non-Windows clients.

When Windows clients access the Web Proxy Server with a browser, such as Netscape or Internet Explorer, and Basic security is the only enabled security, an authentication dialog box appears that allows you to enter a username and password.

This name and password combination is checked against the NT user security database for authentication. Microsoft Proxy Server is the service that initiates the authentication request to the system. Once the user is validated, the Web Proxy consults its own security configuration to find out what protocols the user has access to. Remember that once a user has been authenticated, Microsoft Proxy Server knows which NT security groups that user has access to.

> **NOTE** This means that clients under other operating systems, such as Macintosh, are also able to use Basic security to gain access to the Web Proxy, even though they may not have a full Microsoft Networking client connection to the NT Server running Microsoft Proxy Server.

The current versions of Netscape are only capable of performing Basic proxy authentication. In the case of a stand-alone NT Server, credentials submitted through a Basic security connection are checked against the current NT user database. In the case of an NT Server participating in a domain, the credentials are checked against the domain security database.

Referencing an account in an external domain requires a Trust between the current domain and external domain. Microsoft Proxy Server does not have the ability to pass authentication requests to another domain unless the authentication name contains a reference to where the credentials should be presented. A trust relationship must exist between the two domains in order for the client to be granted access.

NT Challenge/Response

This is the highest form of authentication that the Web Proxy can perform. It is only available between clients that support NT Challenge/Response and the Web Proxy. This is a proprietary Microsoft form of authentication and is used by standard Windows Workstations and NT Servers. The only current client that supports NT Challenge/Response is Internet Explorer. Understand that all authentication discussed in this chapter is negotiated between the Internet client and Microsoft Proxy Server. At no time is the operating system itself performing any negotiation with Microsoft Proxy Server. An Internet client may be able to draw on existing logon information, but the client itself is passing the information to Microsoft Proxy Server and receiving its responses. It is for this reason that the client application must support NT Challenge/Response in order to utilize its advanced security.

This form of authentication utilizes the existing user logon information for validation to the Web Proxy. When a client attempts to access the Web Proxy, it sends an authentication demand back. If NT Challenge/Response is enabled, this is the first authentication form that is demanded. If the client supports NT Challenge/Response, it automatically responds with the current domain logon information that was presented when the user first logged in to the Windows operating system. The username and password given during a standard Windows logon are used if there has not yet been a domain logon.

Clients running on other operating systems can use NT Challenge/Response. It is not a feature that is necessarily embedded in the operating system itself. Clients running on other operating systems may not have any default user information they can automatically send to the Web Proxy. In these cases, the user is presented with a dialog box for entering the username, password, and logon domain.

In such a case, the user is prompted to give a username and password, and to indicate which domain to present the credentials to. If the domain is a domain other than the one that the Web Proxy is running on, a trust must exist between the other domain and the Web Proxy domain, or access is denied, even if the credentials are valid on the other domain.

When a network client authenticates to the Web Proxy with NT Challenge/Response, a much higher level of username and password encryption is used. This greatly decreases the chance that an intermediate hacker might steal vital information. Another aspect of NT Challenge/Response is party verification. When the negotiating process begins during

NT Challenge/Response, each side attempts to prove to the other that they are who they say they are. A client that supports NT Challenge/Response attempts to ensure that the target party who is requesting logon credentials is a valid server.

Anonymous Security with Basic Security

If Anonymous and Basic security are enabled but NT Challenge/Response is disabled, some clients are permitted anonymous access, while others are required to perform basic logon to the Web Proxy. Some clients support password-less proxy access. This means that they can talk to a CERN-compliant proxy, but do not recognize the authentication demand that the proxy may respond with. In cases where the client does not initially respond with an acknowledgment to an authentication demand, the Web Proxy permits the client to continue with anonymous access. However, if the client acknowledges the demand response, the client is required to provide valid logon credentials.

Anonymous Security with NT Challenge/Response

When Anonymous and NT Challenge/Response security are enabled but Basic security is disabled, any client that is not capable of performing NT Challenge/Response authentication is granted anonymous access to the Web Proxy. Those clients that do support NT Challenge/Response are required to provide valid logon credentials through NT Challenge/Response.

If you establish an Internet Explorer-only policy in your company, you can force network users to adhere to the security configuration you create under the Web Proxy. Enabling anonymous logon does not mean that anonymous logons have any rights in the Web Proxy. In order to fully utilize anonymous logons, the permissions for the Web Proxy protocols must be set for anonymous access.

Basic Security and NT Challenge/Response Security

When Anonymous security is disabled but Basic and NT Challenge/Response security are enabled, no anonymous access is permitted to the WWW service or to the Web Proxy. Clients have to provide some form of authentication before they are granted access to the Web Proxy. Obviously, this also passes through to the WWW service. In most cases, this is not good. Most network administrators want their Web sites to be accessible to everyone on the Internet. If you have the luxury of running your Web server from a different machine than the one running Microsoft Proxy Server, this problem is not a factor.

Using the Anonymous Account

When IIS is first installed, a user account, called IUSR_*computername*, is created on the domain or in the local NT user database if the NT Server is a stand-alone server. Here, *computername* refers to the name of the NT Server. For example, the account created on our office network's primary domain controller was IUSR_KLSENT. This account was created when we initially installed IIS on the machine. In our network, this user account controls the level of access given to anonymous logons for all Microsoft Internet server applications.

NOTE The anonymous account in your environment will be different and will correspond to the computername for each server providing Web services on your network.

Remember that the WWW server and the Web Proxy Server present authentication requests to the NT security layer as they would any normal user logon. If you have a password assigned to the anonymous account, be sure to indicate that password in the Anonymous Account field, or the WWW server and the Web Proxy Server will be unable to gain anonymous authentication when necessary. Normally, the anonymous account can have no password assigned to it because it doesn't have rights to normal network resources.

By default, the presence of this account grants anonymous users access to the WWW service without needing any further configuration. However, this is not true with the Web Proxy and WinSock Proxy services. In order to grant anonymous access to the protocols supported by the Web Proxy or the WinSock Proxy, protocol permissions must be granted to the IUSR_*computername* account, just as permissions for any other network users are granted. This is covered in more detail later in this chapter.

WinSock Proxy Security

In the current version of Microsoft Proxy Server, only NT Challenge/Response is used between the WinSock client software and the WinSock Proxy Server. Because the WinSock client software runs under a Windows-based system, the underlying architecture is only present for NT Challenge/Response security negotiation.

In order for WinSock clients to access the WinSock Proxy, special client software must be installed. Client software is available for all flavors of Windows, but no other operating systems are supported. NT Challenge/Response authentication is built into the WinSock client software. The WinSock client software automatically grabs the current username and password from the system logon information and passes it correctly to the WinSock Proxy, where a WinSock client attempts to make external Internet contact.

When the WinSock client software is installed, two new security DLL files are added to the \WINDOWS and \WINDOWS\SYSTEM directories. These files are SECURITY.DLL (\WINDOWS) and SECUR32.DLL (\WINDOWS\SYSTEM). These libraries control WinSock client authentication to the WinSock Proxy Server. Without these files, WinSock clients are unable to access the WinSock Proxy.

IPX under WinSock Proxy

One of the best security features of WinSock Proxy is its ability to utilize IPX as the transport protocol from WinSock Proxy to the network client. Only the NT Server running the WinSock Proxy needs to have the TCP/IP protocol installed for communicating with the Internet. The WinSock Proxy can use the IPX protocol for communicating with network clients. This ensures that any network intrusion attempts stop at the NT Server that is running the WinSock Proxy because the TCP/IP protocol does not extend beyond the server itself.

Enabling and Disabling Access Control

All of this discussion about how security is handled is essentially useless unless Access Control is enabled. On the Permissions tab for both the Web Proxy and the WinSock Proxy, you'll note a check box entitled Enable Access Control. When this check box is marked, the permission structure you set for either of the servers is followed. If this check box is not marked, any user is granted access to any protocol supported by the respective server.

This does not mean that anyone can log in to the services. The logon security methods defined for the Web Proxy must be met before access to the actual service is permitted. However, once a successful logon is performed, no further access restrictions are applied to the user who is accessing the service. For WinSock Proxy accesses, clients must meet the NT Challenge/Response logon requirements before being allowed to proceed.

The following sections will give you a step-by-step definition of how a logon to the Web Proxy Server proceeds. This will give you a better idea of how all of these pieces fit together.

An Anonymous Logon

This example of an anonymous logon assumes that Netscape Navigator/Communicator is used to access the Internet through the Web Proxy, and that Anonymous security is the only security method that can be used.

1. The browser attempts to contact an Internet site through the Web Proxy. If Basic security is disabled, the browser has to rely on Anonymous security because it cannot perform NT Challenge/Response security.

2. The Web Proxy receives the Internet request.

3. The Web Proxy sends an NT Challenge/Response authentication demand to the browser.

4. The browser receives the authentication demand but does not respond to it because it does not understand it.

5. Upon receiving no response to its authentication demand, the Web Proxy permits the browser to have anonymous-level access to its services.

6. If the target site is an HTTP site and the HTTP protocol in the Web Proxy does not permit anonymous access, the Web Proxy responds with an Access Denied message. If anonymous access is configured in the HTTP protocol under the Web Proxy, the Web Proxy retrieves Internet data from the target site.

7. The Web Proxy begins acting as an intermediary between the browser and the target Internet site.

A Basic Logon

The following example assumes that Netscape Navigator/Communicator is used and that Basic security is enabled. In this example, all three forms of security can be enabled. Because Netscape supports Basic security, it responds to any Basic authentication demand. The operating system for this example does not matter.

1. The browser attempts to access an Internet site through the Web Proxy.

2. The Web Proxy receives the access request and issues an NT Challenge/Response authentication demand from the browser. The browser does not respond to this initial authentication demand because it does not understand it.

3. The Web Proxy sends a Basic authentication demand that is received and responded to by the browser.

4. The browser displays an Authentication Request dialog box for the user to fill out. This dialog box asks for a username and password.

5. After completing the necessary data and selecting OK, the browser forwards the authentication data to the Web Proxy.

6. The Web Proxy presents the logon credentials to the NT security layer for verification.

7. NT checks the credentials against the NT user database. If there is a match, the logon proceeds. If there is no match or if the user does not exist in the user database, the Web Proxy receives an invalid logon response from the NT security layer and prompts the browser to attempt the logon again.

8. Once a valid set of credentials is presented by the browser, the Web Proxy examines its own permissions database to see if the authenticated user has permission to access the requested protocol.

9. If the user does not have access to the requested protocol, the Web Proxy responds with an Access Denied message, and the logon process is halted.

10. If the user does have permission to use the requested protocol, the Web Proxy begins acting as an intermediary between the browser and the target Internet site.

Many services are involved with a Basic authentication. The NT user database is referenced and then the internal permissions settings of the Web Proxy are applied.

An NT Challenge/Response Logon

If a client supports NT Challenge/Response authentication, this form of authentication is attempted first. In this example, assume that the browser is the Windows 9X version of Internet Explorer 4.

1. The browser attempts to access an Internet site through the Web Proxy Server.

2. The Web Proxy Server issues an NT Challenge/Response authentication demand to the browser.

3. The browser receives the authentication demand and acknowledges it.

4. The browser references the existing logon information given at system startup and passes the username and password to the Web Proxy. The browser also sends information about which domain to present the credentials to.

5. The Web Proxy receives the data and passes it to the necessary domain for validation. If it is the local domain, no trust relationship is required. If it is an external domain, the external domain must be trusted by the local domain.

6. The NT security layer of the target domain processes the logon request and accepts or denies it, depending on the username and password combination.

7. If the logon is permitted, the Web Proxy begins to act as the intermediary between the browser and the target Internet site.

If the authentication attempt is originating from a non-Windows operating system, the user needs to provide on-the-fly logon information (username, password, and logon domain) when the browser demands credentials.

This process also applies to WinSock clients accessing the Internet through the WinSock Proxy because the WinSock client software supports NT Challenge/Response authentication.

Setting Protocol Permissions

Once primary authentication has been gained, the user accessing either the Web Proxy or the WinSock Proxy must have permission to use the requested protocol. The Permissions tabs of both the Web Proxy and the WinSock Proxy are utilized in the exact same manner. Each proxy controls a certain set of protocols. Users and/or groups of users are granted permission to use these protocols. Unless permissions are configured for the necessary protocols, access is still denied, even if the user trying to gain access presents valid network credentials.

The supported protocols are listed in the Protocol drop-down list. The Add button allows you to select a user or group of users to grant permission to access this protocol to, as you learned in Chapter 16.

There is a special Protocol setting that you can configure in the WinSock Proxy Permissions that is not present in the Web Proxy. This protocol is the Unlimited Access protocol. Any group assigned to this protocol is granted access to use all other protocols under the WinSock Proxy. If you do not want to worry about which network users are accessing which protocols, you can add the Everyone group to the Unlimited Access option. However, this can be dangerous because it opens the WinSock Proxy to almost any request generated by an external Internet client. It might be a good idea to follow the instructions given in the previous chapter for setting up an NT security group for users who need some form of proxy access. That group can be added using the Unlimited Access option.

Once you have set the necessary protocol permissions, network users have the ability to use the two proxy servers to access the Internet from their desktops.

Domain Filtering

Setting filters for controlling which sites can or cannot be accessed is a straightforward process. By default, Microsoft Proxy Server does not filter which sites users have access to. However, from the Security dialog box (which you can open by clicking on the Security button on the Services page of the Properties dialog box for any of the Proxy Servers), you can add Domain Filtering to protect against internal user access to outside Web locations. Figure 17.1 shows the Security dialog box with the Domain Filters tab selected.

To begin the filter assignments, you must first determine what approach you need to take. If you want to allow LAN users to access only a handful of sites on the Internet, all access to all sites should be denied. If you want to deny access to certain sites but leave the rest of the Internet accessible, all sites should be granted access by default. Click the appropriate radio button for the default permission you want to grant. (You must first enable filtering by checking the appropriate check box at the top of the form.)

Once you have determined the default permission for sites, you can begin to set the exceptions to that rule. Exceptions can be indicated as single computers designated by IP address, groups of computers designated by IP address, or entire domains. Choose the Add or Edit buttons to add a new exception or to edit an existing one.

Exceptions can be indicated in the following manners:

Single Computer   This option allows a single Internet site to be excepted from the default rule (in this case, denied access to). The IP address of the computer should be indicated in the IP Address field.

Figure 17.1 The Security dialog box with the Domain Filters tab selected

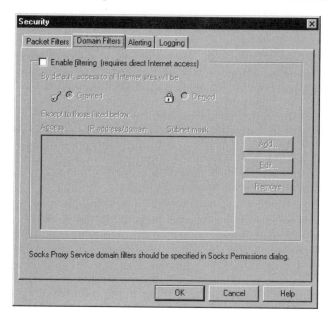

Group of Computers This option allows you to indicate by IP address a group of computers to except from the default rule. Enter an IP address in the IP Address field, and then enter a subnet mask. The subnet mask controls the range of addresses excepted from the default rule, based on the single IP address given. For example, if an IP address of 234.176.58.5 is indicated and a subnet mask of 255.255.255.0 is indicated, any site with an address beginning with 234.176.58 is excepted from the default rule.

If a subnet mask of 255.255.0.0 is indicated, all sites with an address beginning with 234.176 are excepted from the default rule. A subnet mask of 0.0.0.0 nullifies the entire filter process because it contradicts the default rule by excepting all addresses. Indicating a subnet mask of 255.255.255.255 is the same as indicating a single computer as an exception to the default rule. Moreover, ranges of addresses may also be included here. The ranges of addresses are based on the incremental value of the subnet mask. For example, a subnet mask of 192 will permit or deny access to up to 64 addresses.

Domain This option allows you to indicate verbosely the name of a domain to except from the rule. This is probably the most usable option in this dialog box because most people know Internet sites by their domain names. Indicate the name of the domain to except from the default rule in the Domain field. An asterisk can be used to indicate multiple domains based on one domain name. For example, *.netscape.com excepts all domains, such as home.netscape.com and www.netscape.com, from the default rule.

Once you have set all necessary options, click OK to return to the Services tab. The Edit button is used to change an existing entry. The Remove button is used to remove an entry from the filter list.

Filtering can be very useful and is the one of the major advantages that using Microsoft Proxy Server has over giving all workstations on a LAN full access to the Internet. Let's face it, there are a lot of distractions on the Internet, and LAN users have a tendency to be easily lured away from their jobs.

Using Proxy Server to Control Internet Access

While the Internet is a powerful tool for work and play, occasionally, there are situations where you want to prevent users from accessing some sites on the Internet. For example, recent legal decisions have made companies culpable for employees traveling to Web sites that are sexual in nature and that by creating a hostile work environment violate sexual harassment laws. Protecting against such accesses is a long process. In fact, so many new sites go up each day that the administrator's job is nearly impossible. However, good management can limit the number of undesirable sites that users can surf to.

Limiting Internet access is an especially important issue for small businesses, where a single lawsuit can spell the end of the company. We worked on just such a situation not too long ago and found Proxy Server to be an excellent tool for controlling access. First we wrote an additional program (a *robot*) to travel around and gather lists of sites for us. We found that the administrator was unable to keep up with the number of new sites being created. But we were able to block access to hundreds of the most commonly hit sites.

The Problem

An organization has a high-level employee who is viewing and downloading porno-graphic material from the Internet. No employees have complained about the downloads. Nonetheless, this activity is a violation of company policy. A person in a less crucial position would have been fired for similar actions. The company needs to stop the user from downloading this material, but doesnt want a confrontation because the user and the owner have a long personal relationship.

The Solution

After some discussion, we implemented Proxy Server in the client's location. In addition to our robot searching out new sites, we created another quick-and-dirty custom application to review the pages and graphics coming into the cache and to add any questionable material to the list of sites that need to be blocked. In this way, the user was not able to access any questionable site more than once.

Summing It Up

Proxy Server provides excellent tools for blocking user access to Web sites and domains. The only thing lacking in the server implementation is an ability to automatically add additional domains to the blocked content by dropping them into a text or INI file.

24seven **CASE STUDY**

18

Optimizing and Tuning the Proxy Server Installation

Proxy Server allows a network of local users to access the Internet through one nexus point, which is also known as the gateway computer on which Proxy Server is running. Depending on how large your network of users is and how often they access the Internet, the stress on the Microsoft Proxy Server may require you to optimize in order to effectively handle data from 10 to 100, or perhaps even more, connections. Evaluating and tuning your Proxy Server to ensure that its performance is at the highest possible level is a key issue in the ongoing administration of your installation.

Proxy Server Performance Issues

The majority of LANs in use by everyday people and businesses are 10-Mbps (megabits per second) networks. By comparison, a T1 line (the most common line used by businesses to bring in Internet access to an office LAN) is only a 1.54-Mbps channel. Though this speed is very fast by Internet standards (compared to a standard dial-up connection at 33.6Kbps or 0.0336Mbps), a 10-Mbps network can quickly overload a T1 line. With the growth of newer 100-Mbps networks, a T1 line seems almost puny by comparison.

It's important that the Microsoft Proxy Server on a LAN be set up as efficiently as possible to handle outbound and inbound Internet traffic. There will be inevitable hiccups in

Internet-related traffic if the outside channel is overloaded. As the network administrator, it is your job to ensure that there are no network hiccups due to server inefficiency.

NT Network Priority

Even though Windows NT Server is designed as a network-oriented system, user applications can still be executed on it while background network services are being performed. Novell servers do not permit any execution of normal applications on the server itself. This is one of the major differences between NT Servers and Novell servers. Different people prefer one type of server or the other, depending on their needs.

By default, NT gives quite a bit of CPU attention to any task that may be executing in the foreground on the server. If no user tasks are being executed, the priority NT gives to foreground execution is not an issue. However, if the computer running Microsoft Proxy Server is also used as a network workstation, the application performance boost time should be lowered in order to ensure that Proxy Server traffic is not slowed down. It is rare to see such a deployment. However, if your Proxy server is installed in this manner, be aware of the implications.

To alter the boost time NT gives to foreground applications, complete the following steps:

1. Open the Control Panel.

2. Select the System icon. The System applet is executed, and the System Properties dialog box opens.

3. Select the Performance tab. You can adjust the Boost Slider as needed. By default, the Boost Slider is set to the maximum value. This gives a great deal of extra CPU time to any foreground application. Moving this slider to the left decreases the boost time. As you will encounter in most server situations, decreasing the foreground application boost time—to the point where there is no boost for foreground applications—is the correct setting since the operative programs are all running as services.

4. Moving the slider all the way to the left (None) forces NT to handle background and foreground tasks equally. The best value here is None because Proxy Server is never a foreground task.

5. Once the Boost Slider is adjusted, select OK. The NT Server must be restarted in order for the new settings to take effect.

Screen Savers

While screen savers may look nice and can also increase server security, the high-end screen savers of NT 4 can be real CPU hogs. Although they are very impressive, the Open GL screen savers can drain server performance. High-end screen savers should not be used on an NT Server that is responsible for a significant amount of network traffic. If a password-protected screen saver is used on an NT Server to prevent unauthorized access, be aware that logging off of the server will accomplish the same thing without placing any additional overhead on the duties that the server must perform. In fact, NT Servers perform better when no one is logged on because resources are not consumed by the Explorer shell.

Unbinding Services from the Internet Gateway

When new NICs (Network Interface Cards) are set up under NT, NT automatically binds all appropriate installed services to the cards. These services range from actual protocols to services, such as WINS (Windows Internet Name Service). NT assumes that all NICs are destined to be full network interfaces. Because the purpose of Proxy Server is to establish Internet connections to the outside world for LAN workstations, certain protocols and services can be unbound from the NIC that Proxy Server will use to channel network data that is destined for the Internet. Unbinding these services improves network performance over the Internet channel.

> **WARNING** Unbinding base elements from a NIC may cause higher level services to fail. When a base element (such as protocol) is unbound from a NIC, make certain that no dependent services are still bound to that NIC.

If a base-level service is unbound and some network services do not start on the next boot, rebind the service/NIC in question to remedy the situation. Unbinding network services should not prevent NT from starting. Such actions might simply stop the NT Server from seeing or being seen on the network.

If RAS (Remote Access Services) is the primary Internet channel, special care must be taken to ensure that RAS is not adversely affected when unbinding elements. The primary NIC that connects the Microsoft Proxy Server machine to the rest of the LAN should also not be touched, alter only the bindings of the NIC that give Proxy Server its Internet connection.

Alteration of network bindings is done through the Control Panel via the Network icon. To access the bindings dialog, complete the following steps:

1. Open Control Panel.
2. Select the Network icon.
3. Select the Bindings tab.

The Show Bindings For drop-down list can be used to change how the bindings are displayed. Bindings can be displayed from the top down (to see which NICs are bound to what services), or from the bottom up (to see which services are bound to which NICs).

Depending on how the bindings need to be altered, the view of the bindings can be adjusted. To alter the way bindings need to be changed, it is best to view the protocol bindings. This will display a list of the protocols and the base elements they are bound to.

In the Show Bindings For drop-down list, select all protocols. All bindings on the Internet NIC that are not related to the TCP/IP protocol can be disabled (unbound). RAS channels can be treated like regular NICs for binding purposes. If RAS is used for dial-in access to a LAN, make certain that inbound callers can get by with just the TCP/IP protocol. If RAS callers need other protocols and services on the RAS channel, the bindings can still be adjusted to the TCP/IP protocol that is high in the priority chain.

For example, to unbind the NetBEUI protocol from the RAS channel (or from a dedicated NIC), complete the following steps:

1. Select the + sign to the left of the NetBEUI protocol. This expands the binding details of the NetBEUI protocol.

2. Lower elements (network NICs and RAS Wrappers) that are bound to the NetBEUI protocol are displayed. Highlight the first reference to the Remote Access WAN Wrapper.

3. Select Disable.

All channels that have their bindings disabled from a protocol are denoted as such by a universal No sign (a red circle with a slash through it).

Complete this procedure for all references to the specific NIC card or RAS channel to be streamlined for the TCP/IP protocol. In order to ensure network stability, only unbind the Internet NIC from the NetBEUI and IPX/SPX protocols. All other bindings should remain intact, unless you are very familiar with altering bindings. Services, such as WINS and DHCP, are related specifically to the TCP/IP protocol and should not be altered.

Changing the NIC Hierarchy in Bindings

The hierarchy of network interfaces can be adjusted to give the Internet NIC the highest priority when dealing with TCP/IP data. Rather than selecting the Disable button to unbind a NIC from a protocol, the Move Up button is used to raise the selected NIC or RAS channel in the binding hierarchy. If all bindings must be kept intact but the performance of the Internet NIC still needs to be improved, moving the Internet NIC up in the binding hierarchy does just that.

Removing Unneeded Network Services

Another way of streamlining an NT Server for Internet gatewaying is to remove all non-essential services or move the services to another NT Server on the network. Many NT administrators make the mistake of overloading an NT machine with all network services simply for the ease of having all services in one centralized location. An efficient network is one that has network services (such as WINS, DHCP, gatewaying, DNS, WWW servers, and RAS) spread out over as many NT Servers as possible.

Converting to NTFS

NT 4 supports two types of hard disk formats: traditional FAT and NTFS (NT File System). Because a large amount of Internet information will be stored in Proxy Server's disk cache—and page caching is not possible without a corresponding disk cache—it is a good idea to convert all hard disks on an NT Server to the NTFS format. NTFS format has several major advantages over FAT:

- True 32-bit file system
- Advanced, network-oriented security options for files and directories
- Quicker access time
- Less wasted space

The major disadvantage to NTFS is that it is not supported by MS-DOS. NT Servers can be multi-boot systems, allowing an administrator to reboot the machine to another operating system, such as MS-DOS. (Alternately, you can use NTFS-DOS to access a hard drive, if necessary.) When a hard disk is converted to NTFS, only NT Server and NT Workstation operating systems can read these volumes. If the boot disk of a system is converted to NTFS, the system can only be booted to an NT operating system (for all intents and purposes).

Initial setup of NT allows the administrator to select which disk format the NT installation target disk should be. NT does have the ability to convert FAT hard disks to NTFS hard disks while still maintaining the data integrity of the disk. FAT hard disks can also be converted to NTFS at any time, not just during installation of NT. This can be done safely and without much effort or system downtime.

To convert a disk from FAT to NTFS, run the program CONVERT.EXE with a parameter indicating which disk to convert. If the boot disk is being converted, the NT Server must be restarted. Conversion of a boot disk to NTFS must be done before the full operating system is started; therefore, it must be done during the boot process.

Determining How Many Users Can Share a Given Bandwidth

The majority of people who need Proxy Server have a periodic network connection, such as a dial-up connection to an ISP (Internet Service Provider), and would like to offer the rest of the users of a LAN the ability to connect to the Internet without having to have their own dial-up accounts. Or they are people with limited Internet connection bandwidth, wanting to share that bandwidth among multiple computers without giving those computers a permanent connection to the Internet.

By far, the most bandwidth-consuming Internet activity is downloading large files from the Web, such as RealAudio or Streaming Video files. Proxy Server allows a great deal of flexibility when it comes to limiting which types of outside connections are permitted. For example, if a LAN only has a small 28.8- or 33.6-Kbps connection to the Internet, it is wise to prohibit the use of FTP in order to prevent serious outside-connection performance issues. One FTP user can quickly drag down the normal performance of three or four WWW users.

Another disadvantage to FTP users on a network is that Proxy Server does not cache FTP files. If a user downloads a file via FTP and has to download it again later, the file must be completely downloaded again from the Internet. Microsoft Proxy Server does cache WWW objects, such as graphics and sound bytes. If those objects are referenced again, the Microsoft Proxy Server can issue them to the requesting client without having to pull them from the Internet again. Caching greatly speeds up performance and allows more users to access the Proxy Server channel without performance problems.

The numbers given here are our own estimations, based on our experience with Internet traffic and NT Server. Table 18.1 shows how many WWW clients should be able to use various bandwidth Internet connections through Proxy Server.

Table 18.1 The Average User-to-Bandwidth Ratio

Bandwidth Speed	Number of WWW Users
28.8 or 33.6Kbps	23
64Kbps	57
128Kbps	1,214
1.54Mbps	5,075

These numbers take into account some cached data, as well as non-concurrent accessing of large blocks of data, such as graphics or sound bytes.

Under normal network conditions, Proxy Server's performance will allow LAN clients to experience no appreciable network lags. Network clients should see the same performance from Proxy Server as they would if they were actually dialed into an ISP on their local machine. Proxy Server's performance level is very impressive, even when serving data to multiple LAN clients.

Making certain that Proxy Server has a large cache for WWW objects also helps to ensure that connections to the Internet are as fast as possible. For its cache, Proxy Server should be configured for 100 megabytes plus 1/2meg per disk space user. If you have many LAN clients accessing different places in the outside world, it is a good idea to increase Proxy Server's cache so that it can maintain local copies of most outside objects.

Packet Latency

When the Proxy Server connection to the Internet becomes heavily used or overloaded, clients begin to see errors, such as the "Unable to Resolve Host Name" error or the Connection Timed Out error. These errors occur when packets are delayed in transit so long that the client believes that the connection has been broken.

If these errors are cropping up on a network and the Proxy Server connection is not overloaded by LAN clients, the ISP may be overloaded. We have tried many ISPs and know that just because they claim to be the biggest and the fastest, this does not always mean that they are not overloaded. The late afternoon and early evening are normally when ISPs experience their highest volume of users. During these times, you may find the most problems with outside connections. Most of the time, attempting a connection again will prove successful. However, there are some cases when an ISP is too overloaded to be of any use. In these cases, a dedicated channel is very useful.

Multiple Proxy Server Gateways

If the only connections to the Internet are modem-based dial-up connections, it is wise to look at installing multiple Microsoft Proxy Servers. When communicating with the Internet through RAS, Proxy Server only uses the latest connection. Installing two or three modems on a single server and connecting all of them to an ISP does not yield any higher data throughput than connecting just one.

When connecting an NT Server to another NT machine, multiple modems *can* be used to gain a larger channel. This is called *multi-link* and is a RAS option that allows multiple server connections to act as a single connection. Since NT is not yet the preferred choice of ISPs for their dial in service systems, multi-link is not an option for Internet connections. When routing under TCP/IP, NT uses the first available gateway to the outside world that it finds. This means that only the latest RAS connection is used for outbound Internet traffic from the LAN. If RAS is used to offer separate inbound traffic a connection method, you may want to use two or more connections.

In order for similar situations to work correctly, the Proxy Server connection must be made last. Remember that Proxy Server always uses the last connection made to the Internet. In order to leave the domain connection to itself, it must be connected to first. In this arrangement, the modem connected to the ISP that maintains the domain connection is not overloaded with both incoming Internet traffic and outbound traffic from LAN users.

If the last connection is broken, Proxy Server automatically uses other connections to the Internet. This can be used as a form of redundancy to ensure that the Internet connection is not severed if one of the modems accidentally hangs up.

Many ISPs have inactivity time-out periods for dial-in connections. If there is no activity on a dial-in connection for a certain amount of time, usually about 15 minutes, the ISP disconnects. There are many shareware applications available that are designed to keep a dial-in connection open by pinging a server at preset intervals.

Of course, the AutoDial feature of Proxy Server can be used to make an Internet connection if the ISP's connection is down. However, making a connection can sometimes take a full minute. Some client applications time out with an error before Proxy Server can establish a RAS connection to the Internet. In most environments that use a dial-up account, the administrator simply leaves the NT Server connected to the ISP via RAS.

Splitting Up LAN Users between Multiple Proxy Servers

If one Microsoft Proxy Server is not enough to service the needs of the users on a LAN, multiple Microsoft Proxy Servers can be set up on different computers. Different permissions can be granted to different LAN groups, giving only certain groups permission to use certain Proxy Servers. This gives the network administrator the ability to evenly spread out the load that LAN users place on Microsoft Proxy Servers.

Because each network workstation is told which proxy address to communicate with, any number of Proxy Servers can be on a LAN. Proxy Server also has the ability to deny access to certain sites on the Internet. If LAN users are misusing the Proxy Server connection, it is possible to indicate which IP addresses are allowed to be connected to. Administrators can filter out sites with inappropriate material and prevent users from connecting to these sites.

If the network resources are available to dedicate multiple machines to outside connections, it's a good idea to have a plan of action for Proxy Server's organization. It is possible to dedicate one Proxy Server to WWW connections and another to FTP connections. However, it might make more sense to arrange separate groups of users who are authorized to connect to certain Microsoft Proxy Servers.

Using the Performance Monitor

The NT Performance Monitor can examine such things as CPU usage, RAS port usage, and other important bits of information that can help to track down bottlenecks on a Microsoft Proxy Server.

Performance Monitor is located in the Administrative Tools folder on the Start menu. When started, no Counters are shown, so it appears that the Performance Monitor is displaying nothing. Like most Windows applications, Performance Monitor has a top toolbar of command buttons. The middle area of the display shows performance information when Counters have been added. Information is displayed in a percentage of usage line chart. The display area ranges from zero percent usage (when chart lines are at the bottom of the display) to 100 percent usage (when chart lines reach the top of the display). The bottom of the display area shows the available Counters. Each new Counter added is represented by a different color and/or line thickness.

To add a Counter to the display, select the + icon on the toolbar. A dialog opens that allows a specific Counter to be added. A wide range of Counters can be added to the display. Once the IIS servers and Proxy Server are added to an NT Server, a specific set of Counters are used to display pertinent data concerning these applications. The following is a description of each of the major elements of the Add to Chart dialog:

Computer   Indicates the computer whose performance data will be monitored. Any NT computer across the network can be monitored, not just the local machine.

Object   Indicates the class of Counters that can be selected from the Counter list box. For example, the processor is an Object that can be monitored in various ways. Running applications, such as the WWW server, are also considered Objects.

Counter   This list box shows the various Counters that can be added to the monitor display for the currently selected Object.

Instance   If a Counter is shown in more than one instance, this list box shows the available instances. For example, some Counters display data concerning disk usage. When these Counters are selected, the Instance list box shows the available disks on which the Counter can display data.

Color   This is the color of the chart line for the selected Counter.

Scale   This is the scale used for the selected Counter. Depending on how in-depth the Counter needs to be, the scale can be adjusted up or down from its default to see greater detail in the chart line.

Width   This is the width of the chart line for the selected Counter.

Style   This is the line style of the selected Counter. This can be a solid line, a dashed line, a dotted line, and so on.

The Add button adds the selected Counter to the display. The Explain button expands the Add To Chart dialog box to include a Counter Definition area that shows a description of the selected Counter. This is very handy for visualizing the relevance of each Counter.

Proxy Server 2

PART 2

Table 18.2 lists some of the Counters that are useful when tracking the performance of a Microsoft Proxy Server:

Table 18.2 Microsoft Proxy Server Performance Counters

Object	Counter	Description
Processor	Percent Processor Time	This Counter is one of the most useful. It tracks the amount of busy time experienced by the CPU. If this Counter is indicating a consistently high CPU load of 70% or more, this may indicate that the computer that Microsoft Proxy server is running on is not strong enough to do an effective job. Or it may indicate that too many other services are being run on the NT machine, and that some services should be removed and/or moved to other NT Servers on the network.
Processor	Percent Interrupt Time	This Counter tracks the amount of CPU time devoted to servicing hardware interrupts (IRQs). If this Counter is showing a consistently high chart line (more than 70%), this may indicate that a piece of hardware is demanding too much CPU time. Serial ports may cause performance problems if their DTE (data terminal equipment) speed, also known as port speed, is not high enough to handle the actual connect speed of the modems that are attached to them. A 33.6-Kbps modem should have a port speed of at least 57.6Kbps. If the hardware supports it, a 115.2-Kbps port speed should be used. If the port speed is too low, the serial port has to constantly interrupt the CPU to offload incoming data from the modem. Improving a serial port to a 16550 UART, or to the 16650 UART, can also help relieve interrupt problems.

Table 18.2   Microsoft Proxy Server Performance Counters *(continued)*

Object	Counter	Description
HTTP Service	Bytes Total/sec	This Counter tracks the total in and out bytes of data that the HTTP server is handling. Because Proxy Server uses the HTTP server for most proxied WWW, FTP, and Gopher data, this Counter is a good indication of the workload of the Microsoft Proxy Server. However, it also tracks HTTP requests to the local WWW server. If the total-bytes-per-second Counter is consistently showing a near maximum number for the speed of the Proxy Server connection to the Internet, the connection is being overused and should be upgraded if possible. Another option is to cut down traffic in some way.
Inet Proxy Service	Inet Bytes Total/sec	This Counter is almost identical to the previous Counter, except it shows only the amount of data being passed to and from the Internet by the Proxy Server.
Inet Proxy Service	Maximum Users	This Counter indicates the number of users that are, or have been, connected to the Proxy Server over the displayed time period.
RAS Port	*	These Counters are extremely useful in tracking the performance of RAS connections. Many of the Counters for this Object deal with connection errors and port overruns. These types of Counters can help find physical problems with a connection. If error Counters run high, the problem may be the quality of the connection line or the port hardware itself. Other Counters of this Object can show the exact amount of data being passed through a RAS port. The Instance list box of the Add to Chart dialog allows each RAS port to be shown as an independent Counter.

Proxy Server 2

PART 2

Table 18.2 Microsoft Proxy Server Performance Counters *(continued)*

Object	Counter	Description
LogicalDisk	*	These Counters allow disk performance tracking information for the logical disks to be displayed. Don't get confused by another similar Object, PhysicalDisk. The LogicalDisk Object allows Counters to be displayed for logical drive letters, such as C:, D:, and E:. The PhysicalDisk Counter only displays information on actual hard disks. More than one logical disk can be held on one physical disk. The percent Disk Time Counter is very useful in tracking how busy the selected disk (in the Instance list box) is. A busy disk is better than a busy connection to the Internet. A busy disk indicates that the Microsoft Proxy Server is pulling a large percentage of data from its cache and is not having to go to the Internet to get the information. A very high percentage of disk usage might mean that there are far too many Proxy Server users for Proxy Server to handle. It is also possible that the NT Server that Proxy Server is running on is also serving out shared resources, such as hard drive space. A high percent Disk Time Counter may mean that the NT machine is very busy serving out shared resource data. Disk accessing is the single most common process that causes Proxy Server to hiccup when transferring data. All other processor tasks are paused until data from a disk is read or written.

Once the desired Counters have been added to the display, select Close to exit the Add To Chart dialog. The display area of the Performance Monitor will show the added Counters.

By default, the display area shows data for the past 100 seconds of system activity. The tracking bar jumps at 1-second intervals, though this can be increased if more than 100 seconds of data must be displayed. The Options icon on the toolbar (the last one on the right) can be used to alter some of the chart settings, such as interval time and grid line options.

By default, the chart is periodically updated each second. This can be changed to a manual update if desired. A manual update is handy to use if random, user-initiated snapshots of system activity are desired. The periodic interval can be adjusted to any desired interval. The display chart is broken down into 100 segments, so the overall time displayed in the chart is 100 times the interval that is selected in this dialog box. If the interval is 5 seconds, the overall chart time will be 500 seconds.

The vertical scale can also be adjusted. If lowered, more detail will be shown for Counters with smaller scales, but it may show other Counters as constantly maxed out. If raised too high, the display may not show enough detail to be of any use. Trial and error is the best way to find the correct vertical scale for your system.

For example, you might construct a view of the Performance Monitor that displays three Counters: percent Processor Time, RAS Port COMX Bytes Transmitted/Sec, and RAS Port COMX Bytes Received/Sec. Note that in such a case, the Counters for the RAS Port information max out for short periods. Because these Counters are not percentage Counters and their data goes beyond 100, you may see this result. To fix this "error," the scale of these Counters should be decreased to a value that allows the Counter data to fit within the display area. RAS Port COM3 is a 28.8-Kbps modem, and its bytes per second in either direction (transmitting or receiving) rise as high at 3,200 bytes per second. Setting the scale for these Counters to 0.01 (or 1/100th-scale view) allows the data to fit within the display nicely. At a 0.01 scale, a normal maximum value for this RAS data ranges from 0 to 32.

Charts can be saved and later reloaded. From the File menu, the Save Workspace command saves the chart in its current view. Chart settings can also be saved by using the Save Chart Settings command from the File menu.

The Performance Monitor is the best tool to use for indentifying problems in your system. The wide range of Performance Monitor data keeps you informed about how well a Microsoft Proxy Server is operating and which parts of the system are overworked. Become familiar with Performance Monitor and use it frequently.

Specific Proxy Server Objects and Counters

Once Proxy Server is installed, several new Objects and Counters are available to the Performance Monitor. These Objects and Counters are specifically intended to show vital information on how Proxy Server is servicing the needs of LAN users for outside Internet access. The following Objects deal specifically with Proxy Server:

Web Proxy Server Cache   This Object has Counters for tracking the status of the Web proxy cache. Such things as how full the cache is, how often it is accessed, and the number of URLs cached can all be tracked with Counters in this Object.

Web Proxy Server This is one of the most important Proxy Server Objects. These Counters track many things, including the traffic that passes through the Web Proxy, the number of each type of request (HTTP, FTP, or Gopher), the number of users denied access, and the number of sites granted access. All of these Counters deal only with the Web proxy. The WinSock Proxy Server has its own Object.

WinSock Proxy Server Service This Object has Counters that track data similar to the way that the Web Proxy Server Service Object tracks data, but for the WinSock Proxy instead. Because each service is independent, each has its own Performance Monitor Object.

You can use the Counters from these Objects to design performance monitoring charts to track all activity on the Proxy Server. Microsoft has created a basic chart, and it is included with Proxy Server.

Built-in Proxy Server Chart

In the Proxy Server folder, you'll find a premade chart that details the basic performance Counters that pertain to Proxy Server's operation. This chart is loaded by clicking the Monitor Proxy Server Performance link found in the Proxy Server folder. This link runs Performance Monitor and automatically loads the chart, MSP.PMC. This chart is found in the C:\MSP directory, along with the other Proxy Server files.

The following Counters are part of this chart:

HTTP Server/Connections per Second This Counter tracks the number of HTTP connections per second that are made to the HTTP server. Because Proxy Server runs as a sub-service of the main HTTP server, this Counter is useful in seeing the stress load of the HTTP server in general.

Processor/percent Processor Time: INETSRV This Counter tracks the percentage of processor time devoted to the INETSRV process. The INETSRV process is the general process that drives the HTTP server.

Processor/percent Processor Time: WSPSRV This Counter tracks the percentage of processor time devoted to the WinSock Proxy Service process.

WinSock Proxy Server/Active Sessions This Counter tracks the number of active connections maintained by the WinSock Proxy Server over the tracking period.

Web Proxy Server Service/Cache Hits Ratio percent This Counter tracks the percentage of cache hits to extra data retrieval. The more data that comes from the cache, the higher the Counter percentage.

Memory/Available bytes   This Counter tracks the amount of memory used by the system. The lower the available memory, the lower the performance of the system as a whole.

These Counters provide all the necessary tracking elements to see the basic Proxy Server performance, as well as the performance of the entire system. Feel free to add or subtract from this included chart to track Counters that you consider important.

Proxy Server Performance Issues

Without a doubt, one of the most common complaints that we hear about Proxy Server is that it is slower than accessing the Internet directly. While this can occasionally be the case, if you install the product in accordance with Microsoft specifications and have sufficient memory and cache space, you should not see any substantial performance drop with Proxy Server.

A friend of ours owns his own company. Not too long ago, he installed Proxy Server in his organization to control Internet access from his internal network and also to protect his network from outside encroachment. Though he has not had much experience with NT, he performed the installation himself. About a week later, he asked us for help. His performance on Internet connections had dropped to a third of what it had previously been. He was quite irate and convinced that he had wasted the $1,000 that he paid for the product. He wanted to know if there was anything we could do to help his performance.

The Problem

He installed the Proxy Server on the oldest machine in his network, a little 486/66 with a 400-Mb hard drive. By the time he had NT and Proxy Server installed (as well as some other services, such as IIS), he was left with only about 75Mb of available space for the Proxy Server cache. In addition, he only had 32Mb of physical memory in the machine.

The Solution

With Performance Monitor and the MMC, it didn't take long to figure out his problem. We suggested that he move up to a more expensive server, and pointed him in the direction of a Pentium II 300 with 256Mb of memory and lots of hard drive space. The hardware cost was approximately $1,500. Once he upgraded his equipment, his system performance was comparable to what it had been before the original installation. In fact, in some cases, his performance was vastly improved.

Summing It Up

While Proxy Server is not a particularly huge program, it does require substantial amounts of storage space to function correctly, as well as a fast processor and a decent amount of memory. If you are having performance problems with Proxy Server, analyzing and meeting the hardware requirements is often the best place to begin to address these issues.

19

Troubleshooting the Proxy Server Installation

Throughout the previous chapters, you have learned about the various concerns that you must keep in mind when working with Proxy Server. This last chapter covers some basic scenarios you might encounter when working with Proxy Server and the troubleshooting issues surrounding both installing and maintaining Proxy Server. Keep in mind that it is impossible to write troubleshooting instructions for every conceivable system design. For the most part, Proxy Server is a very smooth-running service, requiring very little, if any, administrator intervention once the service is installed and properly configured.

In general, you can almost always find all the information you need by asking fellow network administrators for help on the Proxy Server newsgroup. This is a private newsgroup supported only by Microsoft and can be found by linking to their newsgroup server at `msnews.microsoft.com`. The name of the Proxy Server newsgroup is `microsoft.public.proxy`. Microsoft operates a private newsgroup server that does not share its newsgroup feed with the rest of the Internet on a global basis. However, the public is free to access their newsgroup server and on it will find a large number of newsgroups dedicated to various Microsoft software topics. In other words, you can obtain access to these newsgroups, but you must access the Microsoft Newsgroup servers directly to do so.

Error Messages

Both the Web Proxy and the WinSock Proxy generate different kinds of errors. The Web Proxy communicates more easily with the client through return HTTP documents when an error is encountered. When the WinSock Proxy encounters an error, it is often impossible to determine the exact cause of the error because the WinSock Proxy has no direct way of communicating with the client.

The errors listed for the Web Proxy are displayed in a client's browser window unless otherwise noted. The errors listed for the WinSock Proxy can also be seen in the display area of client browsers if the browser is not set to perform CERN proxy communication and must rely on the WinSock Proxy for its Internet connection. Errors may also be logged through the Event Viewer on the NT Server running Proxy Server.

Obviously, not all possible error messages are listed in this chapter. We have instead chosen the ones that you are most likely to encounter. If you would like to view a complete list of error messages for Proxy Server, you can do so through the online documentation for the program.

Most error messages are given as a verbose string and a numeric error code. The error code will be listed at the end of the verbose string. Obviously, most network administrators prefer reading a verbose string to a cryptic error code.

Web Proxy Messages

Table 19.1 is a short list of common error messages you might see as pop-up dialogs displayed on the NT Server running Proxy Server. These are server-based messages, not user-based messages.

Table 19.1 Common Error Messages with the Web Proxy and Their Descriptions

Error Message	Definition
The server was unable to load ODBC32.DLL for SQL logging due to the following error: number. The data is the error code.	Most likely, ODBC is not properly installed on the NT Server running Proxy Server. Reinstall a valid ODBC32 driver into the system or check to ensure that ODBC32.DLL is present in the c:\winnt\system32 directory.

Table 19.1   Common Error Messages with the Web Proxy and Their Descriptions *(continued)*

Error Message	Definition
The server was unable to log on the Windows NT account *accountname* due to the following error: *number*. The data is the error code.	This error occurs when a client is attempting to pass a username to Proxy Server that is not present in the NT user database or is present but the password is incorrect. This is a standard logon error message. Double-check to make sure that the client has submitted the correct credentials.
The server was unable to open ODBC Data Source *sourcename*, Table: *tablename*, under User Name *username*. The ODBC Error is: *number*. The data is the error code.	This error occurs when one or both of the proxy servers is configured to log active information to a database, and Proxy Server cannot find the correct DSN entry for the given database. Double-check the ODBC Control Applet in the system Control Panel to make sure that the DSN name has been correctly configured.
W3PCache corrected a corrupted or old format URL cache by removing all or part of the cache's contents.	If a disk error occurs on your NT service, you may see this error message. It indicates that at least some portion of the cache has become corrupt. It is unlikely that an old format URL will be present because the Web Proxy qualifies all cache data as valid before it stores it in the cache. Scan the system hard disk for physical errors that hold the cache directory.
W3PCache failed to initialize the URL Cache on disk.	This message indicates that the Web Proxy cache has become extremely corrupt. Because the Web Proxy stores cache items in a coded format, corruption of the reference file may result in the entire contents of the cache being wasted. Delete the cache directory or attempt to reset the cache defaults from within the Web Proxy properties. The Web Proxy Server will not start when the cache is corrupt. You will need to restart the NT Server after correcting the problem or manually start the Web Proxy Server on its own.

Table 19.1 Common Error Messages with the Web Proxy and
Their Descriptions *(continued)*

Error Message	Definition
W3PCache initialization failed due to incorrect configuration. Please use the administration utility or manually edit the registry to correct the error and restart the service.	It's unlikely that the NT registry will become corrupt; however, it does occur once in a while. If this error occurs, examine the registry settings involved with Proxy Server and see if they look OK. It's often difficult to tell correct registry settings from bad ones. Refer to the registry entries/settings section later in this chapter for details on registry entries that might help.

Table 19.2 is a list of error messages the user might see when attempting to connect to the Web Proxy Server. These messages will be shown in the display area of the user's browser.

Table 19.2 Common Web Proxy Errors Received by Browser Clients

Error Message	Definition
A connection with the server could not be established.	If clients are receiving this message, it means that the proxy server could not be contacted. Check to see if the Web Proxy service is running and/or if the workstation can see any other server resource or service. If no other server service can be seen, check the actual network cabling or setup.
Access is denied.	This message is by far one of the most common error messages. This message indicates that the client is requesting access to a site or protocol that they do not have access to (as defined in the permissions list of the Web Proxy). Alter the permissions list or explain the security restrictions to the user. This is also referred to as HTTP error 5.
The access code is invalid.	This error usually means that there is an error in the LAT file. Copy the server version of the LAT down to the workstation having trouble and see if that takes care of the problem. Try using another browser and see if the same error occurs. If it does not, reinstall the first browser that was having trouble. If the error does occur, check to make sure the network connection between the workstation and server is stable.

Table 19.2 Common Web Proxy Errors Received by Browser Clients *(continued)*

Error Message	Definition
The connection with the server was reset.	This error means that the client lost connection with the proxy server and then regained the connection. The server may have rebooted or the service was shut down and restarted.
The connection with the server was terminated abnormally.	This error means the client's connection with the proxy server has died and has not been regained. This does not mean that the connection with the outside Internet host has been terminated. Check to see if there is an operational problem with the NT Server or the Web Proxy Server.
The login request was denied.	This error means that a client workstation was trying to present logon credentials to the Web Proxy and the credentials were not accepted. This will only occur when authentication is required. Check the NT user account to make sure the workstation is presenting the correct information. Also check to make sure the account is not disabled.
The operation timed out.	This is the most common user error. It means the target Internet site did not respond to the Web Proxy Server's access request. The target name was resolved to an IP, but the IP did not initially respond or has stopped responding. This error could mean that the Web Proxy's connection to the Internet has been suddenly disconnected after an initial contact to the target site has been made. This error will not be received if the connection to the Internet is down before initial contact because the target name will not have yet been resolved into an IP address. Check the Web Proxy Server's connection to the Internet or try contacting the site directly from the NT Server running Proxy Server. It is unlikely that there is a problem with the Web Proxy Server.

Proxy Server 2

PART 2

Table 19.2   Common Web Proxy Errors Received by Browser Clients *(continued)*

Error Message	Definition
The server name is not resolved.	This error means that the client is referencing a Web address over Proxy Server with a name that cannot be found in the name resolution server's database. If you want clients to reference the Web Proxy Server by a name, some form of name resolution on the network must exist. If name resolution services are available on the network, check to see if the workstation's TCP/IP settings are correct.
The URL is invalid.	The URL entered by the client is not formatted correctly. Re-submit the request in the correct manner.

By far, the previously listed client errors will be the ones most commonly received by clients. Most of the time, errors will be related to a down Internet connection. Keep in mind that ISPs lose their Internet connections too. Just because your NT Server is connected to the ISP does not mean you still have a valid connection to the rest of the Internet. If workstations cannot connect to target sites, yet the NT Server is connected to an ISP, check with the ISP to inquire about their situation.

WinSock Proxy Messages

Table 19.3 is a list of server-based WinSock Proxy error messages. These messages will be displayed as pop-up dialogs on the server itself or can be found through the Event Viewer. They are not user-based messages.

Table 19.3   The Server-Based WinSock Proxy Error Messages

Error Messages	Definition
Incorrect network configuration. None of server's addresses is internal.	This error means that the LAT file is not constructed properly. The WinSock Proxy cannot determine which addresses are local and which are remote. Reconstruct the LAT manually or by letting the WinSock Proxy (or Web Proxy) do it automatically. This is done via the Edit LAT Table button on the General tab of either proxy property sheets.

Table 19.3   The Server-Based WinSock Proxy Error Messages *(continued)*

Error Messages	Definition
User *username* at host *hostname* has timed-out after *number* seconds of inactivity.	This error means that the client did not respond to the WinSock Proxy within the time-out period defined through the RAS connection settings. RAS connections can have inactivity periods defined for them on the NT side. If clients do not keep the connection active for the required period, RAS will close the Internet connection. To fix this error, extend or disable the time-out value for the RAS connection to the Internet.
WinSock Proxy Server failed to determine network addresses.	This error generally means that the workstation copy of the LAT does not match the server copy of the LAT. Make sure both LAT files match.
WinSock Proxy Server failed to initialize. The data (if any) is the error.	This is one of the most irritating error messages. It means almost anything could be wrong. Reinstall the WinSock server to ensure that all necessary data and application files are present on the server.
WinSock Proxy Server failed to initialize because of bad registry. The data is the error.	The registry entries for the WinSock Proxy are incorrect. Have you been messing with them? Feel free to edit the registry but always export the branch you are working on to a saved file before making any changes. If you can't remember how to reset the registry settings for the WinSock Proxy to the correct values, you will need to reinstall the WinSock Proxy.
WinSock Proxy Server failed to initialize the network. The data is the error.	Something is wrong with the network on the NT Server running the WinSock Proxy. Reset the server or try stopping all network services and restarting them through the Service Manager. Many times the NT Server will come back to life after a bum service is restarted. Make sure you know what order to stop and restart services in, though.

Proxy Server 2

PART 2

Table 19.3   The Server-Based WinSock Proxy Error Messages *(continued)*

Error Messages	Definition
WinSock Proxy Server failed to load security DLL.	In order for the WinSock Proxy to be able to communicate with the NT security layer, the file `security.dll` must be present in the `c:\winnt\system32` directory. Without this file, the WinSock Proxy cannot submit logon credentials to NT. Make sure this file is present. If not, reinstall the WinSock Proxy.

Table 19.4 shows some possible WinSock Proxy errors users may see. These error messages may be displayed as pop-up dialog boxes generated by the WinSock Proxy client software, or the user's Internet client application(s) may report the numeric version of a given error. For example, if a client cannot connect to a target Internet site, it may simply report error 10060.

Table 19.4   Possible WinSock Proxy Errors Users Might Encounter

Error Message	Definition
Connection refused.	This is a common error encountered by many Internet clients, especially FTP clients. It usually means that the target site has no available connections and the user will have to retry the connection later.
Connection timed out.	This error means that there is a DNS entry for the site name the user is trying to connect to, but the site itself is not responding to the access request. The target site could be down, or the Internet connection between your network and the target site could be severed. This is error 10060 in standard Internet parlance. It is unlikely the error is with the WinSock Proxy. Wait and try the connection later.
Current version is not supported.	This is a WinSock Proxy client software-generated error, and it means that the workstation Internet client application has made a WinSock call that does not fall in the WinSock 1.1 standards. Find a client application that is WinSock 1.1 compliant if you want to use the current version of Proxy Server.

Table 19.4   Possible WinSock Proxy Errors Users Might Encounter *(continued)*

Error Message	Definition
Host was not found.	This error means that a workstation client has submitted a DNS request that could not be resolved by any known DNS servers. Check the address and try again.
Permission denied.	This error indicates that the workstation client does not have permission to access the requested protocol. Check the WinSock Proxy permissions list to ensure that the affected user has permission to use the protocol desired.
System is not ready.	This error means that the workstation client has attempted to contact the WinSock Proxy during startup or shutdown. If the NT Server running Proxy Server was just restarted, retry the operation in a few minutes. This error will not be reported in the Proxy Server's logs.

Since the WinSock Proxy client software runs as a service on workstations, it can also report errors related to normal network operation. If things seem error prone between the workstation and the WinSock Proxy, check to see if the workstation's network settings are correct.

Using the WinSock Proxy Status Program

Located in the `c:\mspclnt` directory created by the WinSock Proxy client software installation routine is a small program for testing the WinSock Proxy connection between the workstation and the WinSock Proxy Server. This application is `chkwsp32.exe`. Run this application through a DOS shell, not by using the Run command on the Start menu. You will need to see the results it displays. Run `chkwsp32.exe` with the `-f` parameter to see a detailed report about the status of the WinSock client software and the server status.

Keep in mind that the WinSock Proxy client software must match the WinSock Proxy Server version running on the NT machine. If you upgrade Proxy Server, all network workstations using the WinSock Proxy client software will need to be updated accordingly.

The `chkwsp32.exe` utility will tell you if the WinSock Proxy Server can be contacted and/ or if the WinSock Proxy client files are installed correctly.

Proxy Server 2

PART 2

> ***WARNING*** We have found that changing almost any network settings on workstations when the WinSock client is installed will make it so the WinSock Proxy Server cannot be contacted, even if every configuration setting is correct. After altering network settings for such things as protocols and network clients, the WinSock Proxy client software just seems to die. If you have to alter workstation network settings, uninstall the WinSock Proxy client software, make the necessary network changes, and reinstall the WinSock Proxy client software.

Installation Errors

As with any piece of software, installation errors can occur. Most errors are minor, but some will prevent you from installing Proxy Server and the WinSock Proxy client software. The following sections detail some of the errors you might encounter.

Server Installation Errors

One of the most common errors you may encounter when installing Proxy Server is the presence of two or more of the same DLL files in the \WINNT and \WINNT\SYSTEM directories or along the system search path. This will affect both Windows NT and Windows 9X client workstations. If the system finds a DLL in more than one place in the system, you will experience buggy performance and possible corruption of data. Many TCP/IP applications these days want to do things their own way. Applications such as the America Online client for Windows 9X might decide to add their own directories to the search path and add their own `winsock.dll` and `wsock32.dll` files into the Windows system area. This could cause more problems than you even want to imagine.

Another common problem encountered when installing Proxy Server is the need to have Administrator privileges on the NT Server you want to install the software on. In order to correctly install Proxy Server you must be logged on with a user account that has Administrator privileges.

Locked files are another common problem. Sometimes it is impossible to install the server software because another application has locked open the system files Proxy Server needs to overwrite. When installing the server software, make sure all extraneous software is shut down. Default NT service applications should not cause any files to be locked open.

If you have an NT 4 Server installation that came right out of the box, you should install Service Pack 3 (at a minimum) and also the Option Pack. Proxy Server's installation routine will check to ensure the service pack has been applied and will not continue unless it has been.

Client Installation Errors

Client workstations will normally install the WinSock Proxy client software by connecting to the shared resource named MSPCLNT on the server running Proxy Server. This shared resource is created and shared by default and should be used for all client installations.

In the field, we have a lot of problems getting the WinSock Proxy client setup to run correctly over the network. Most frequently, we encounter errors related to the setup routine being unable to open the necessary files. In some cases, we even have to go so far as to copy the entire contents of the MSPCLNT share and all sub-directories down to a temp directory on the local workstation and run the WinSock Proxy client setup from that temp directory. So far, this has not caused any configuration problems on the client side and is a relatively easy fix.

If you find you are having similar problems, your only alternative may be to copy the setup files to the local workstations and run the setup routing from there. In theory, you should be able to run the WinSock Proxy client setup routine directly from the Network Neighborhood without even having to map a drive letter to the shared resource. If the "in theory" approach doesn't work for you, try mapping a drive letter to the resource and then running the setup routine from the mapped drive. If that still fails, your only alternative may be to copy down to the local workstation.

As already mentioned, making changes to workstation network settings while the WinSock Proxy client software is installed may render the WinSock Proxy client unusable. If you find your workstations are suffering from this apparent bug, follow the uninstall routine for the WinSock Proxy client, reboot, and then make any necessary network setting adjustments.

If you have set the WinSock Proxy client setup routine to automatically set workstations for Web Proxy interface, you should already have Internet Explorer 3 or higher installed on all target workstations. Remember that the Internet Control Applet is not present in the Windows 95 Control Panel until Internet Explorer 3 or higher is installed. In order to reduce the amount of setup work you may have to do to workstations later on, it is best to have the Internet Control Applet present in Windows 9X for the WinSock Proxy client setup routine to adjust. The WinSock Proxy client setup routine will also make automatic proxy changes to stand-alone clients like Netscape (all versions).

If the NT Server running Proxy Server has a space in its name, you might find that the WinSock Proxy client installation routine does not correctly set up Web Proxy clients if you have indicated clients should reference the Web Proxy Server by name, rather than IP address. Clients may only reference the first or last part of the server name. To try and remedy this, edit the MSPCLNT.INI file in the \MSP\CLIENTS directory on the NT Server and enclose any server name references in double quotes (as in "My Server" or "\\My Server\MSPCLNT"). This should take care of the problem. If it does not, create a static mapping in the WINS server database (for example, PROXY) to reference the Proxy Server running Web Proxy and then edit the MSPCLNT.INI file on the server to reference this static mapping name (edit only the WWW-Proxy= line to reference the Web Proxy Server name; do not alter any NetBios names (names starting with \\)). This is often the best approach because you can segregate the name used to reference Proxy Server Web Proxy completely from any specific server name. This WINS database entry can then be easily adjusted, if the location on Proxy Server Web Proxy changes.

When the WinSock Proxy client software is installed, you should understand how DNS is affected. Any TCP/IP traffic that originates from a workstation will automatically be routed to the WinSock Proxy service if it is destined for the outside world. This generally means that DNS resolution will take place on the NT Server running the WinSock Proxy.

LAT file errors can cause parts of the Internet to become inaccessible. All addresses found in the LAT file will be referenced as though they were part of the local network. This means that if your network IP subnet is not one of the reserved subnets set aside by the InterNic, you may be unable to contact the sites on the Internet that validly have IP addresses used by your own private network.

Registry Settings

It's unlikely you will have to edit registry settings for Proxy Server yourself (well, OK, maybe not *unlikely*, but at the very least uncommon), but just in case, this section discusses some of the most important ones. On NT there are two registry editing utilities. You should always use the RegEdt32 editor when working with the NT hive. To that end, this section will only cover the use of the native NT version of the registry editor.

Most of the Proxy Server registry settings can be found off the following registry trees:

WinSock Proxy Settings
HKEY_LOCAL_MACHINE\SYSTEM\CurrentControlSet\Services\WSPsrv

Web Proxy Settings
HKEY_LOCAL_MACHINE\SYSTEM\CurrentControlSet\Services\W3Proxy

Web Proxy Cache Settings
HKEY_LOCAL_MACHINE\SYSTEM\CurrentControlSet\Services\W3PCache

WWW Service Settings
HKEY_LOCAL_MACHINE\SYSTEM\CurrentControlSet\Services\W3Svc

SOCKS Proxy Settings
HKEY_LOCAL_MACHINE\SYSTEM\CurrentControlSet\Services\SOCKSProxy

When making changes to the registry through the registry editor, keep in mind that the changes you make might not take effect immediately. You should always stop and restart any service after making changes to its registry settings. Changes made through the Internet Server Manager, however, will be immediately effective.

And, as always, edit the registry at your own risk. Making changes to the wrong settings could make it impossible to start Windows NT, and only a reinstallation will remedy the situation. However, none of the settings dealing with Proxy Server should affect how NT itself starts up. The wrong settings may cause the service to not start, but not NT itself.

Keep in mind also that most of the key values are set by hexadecimal notation, which is base 16 notation. If you are not familiar with hex notation, it's a pretty simple thing to grasp. For example, hexadecimal 20 equals 32 in standard notation (2 x 16 = 32). The hexadecimal value of 14 equals 20 in standard notation (16 + 4 = 20).

Most of the registry settings are simply the configuration settings you set on the property sheets of both the Web Proxy and the WinSock Proxy. Site filtering settings are common between both the Web Proxy and the WinSock Proxy. These settings are held in the registry branch:

```
HKEY_LOCAL_MACHINE\SYSTEM\CurrentControlSet\
Services\W3Proxy\Parameters\DoFilter
```

Table 19.5 shows a list of useful keys in this branch:

Table 19.5   Useful Filtering Keys in the Registry

Key	Definition
FilterType	0 = No site filtering enabled 1 = General site deny policy set 2 = General site grant policy set
NumDenySites	Can be set to any number. When set to a non-zero value, Proxy Server will deny access to the first x number of sites listed in the DenySites key (not created by default). Sites will be separated by a space.
NumGrantSites	Can be set to any number. When set to a non-zero value, Proxy Server will grant access to the first x number of sites listed in the GrantSites key (not created by default). Sites will be separated by a space.
DenySites	Can be set to any string value, for example, www.klsent.com ftp.xyz.com *.netscape.com. The sites listed here will be excepted from the general site grant policy and access to them will be prohibited through Proxy Server.

Proxy Server 2

PART 2

Table 19.5 Useful Filtering Keys in the Registry

Key	Definition
GrantSites	Can be set to any string value, for example, www.klsent.com.ftp.xyz.com *.netscape.com. The sites listed here will be excepted from the general site deny policy and access to them will be granted through Proxy Server.

A short list of important Web Proxy registry keys is shown in Table 19.6. These keys are found in the Parameters folder off the main Web Proxy branch (as shown in the section "Registry Settings").

Table 19.6 Important Web Proxy Registry Keys

Key	Definition
DnsCacheSize	Can be set to any hex number in the range of H12c–H7530. The default is Hbb8. This refers to the cache size in bytes. This key sets the DNS cache size for Proxy Server. When clients access the outside Internet, Proxy Server stores the most recently accessed IP addresses. Increasing this value on busy networks may speed up name resolution somewhat.
DnsTTLInSecs	Can be set to any hex number in the range of He10–H8ca0. This refers to the Time to Live in seconds. The default is H5460 (24 hours). This sets the Time to Live value for DNS cache entries. When their Time to Live expires, cached DNS entries will be flushed.
MaxFtpThreadsFactor	Can be set to any hex number in the range of H08–H24. The default is H08. This refers to the number of processor threads Proxy Server will start for FTP sessions. Once the thread limit has been reached, Proxy Server will begin sharing threads for FTP sessions.
RequestTimeoutSecs	Can be set to any hex in the range of H10–H1000. This value is in seconds. The default is H3c. Determines what the time-out factor is when Proxy Server is attempting to contact an Internet site.

Table 19.7 shows a list of important registry key values that affect Web Proxy caching. These keys are found in the Parameters folder of the Web Proxy Cache primary branch (as shown in the section "Registry Settings").

Table 19.7   Table 19.7 Important Registry Key Values Affecting Proxy Caching

Key	Definition
CleanupFactor	Can be set to any hex number in the range of H0–H64. The default is H19. This number represents the cleanup percentage. When a cache cleanup is performed, this key determines what percentage of the cache is cleaned up. By default, only the oldest 25% of the cache is cleaned.
CleanupInterval	Can be set to any hex number in the range of H0–H93a40. The default is H15180. This number represents number of seconds. This determines how often the cache is cleaned. By default, it is set to 86,400 seconds, or once every 24 hours.
CleanupTime	Can be set to any number in the range of H0–H23. This number indicates the hour of the day. By default it is set to 0 (12 A.M.). This key determines when cleanup occurs (by default at midnight).
Persistent	Can be set to 0 or 1. By default it is set to 1. Determines whether the cache is cleared when the Web Proxy service is stopped. A 0 value indicates the cache will be completely cleared every time the Web Proxy service stops (which will happen when NT shuts down to reboot).

Some important registry keys that control how the WinSock Proxy Server operates are shown in Table 19.8. They are found in the Parameters branch off the main WinSock Proxy Server branch.

Proxy Server 2

PART 2

Table 19.8   Registry Keys Controlling the Operation of WinSock Proxy Server

Key	Definition
Authentication	Can be set to 0 or 1. By default it is set to 1 (authentication enabled). If this key is set to 0, the WinSock Proxy will not demand NT Challenge/Response Authentication from workstations, which will essentially grant access to everyone.
TcpBufferSize	Can be set to any hex number H600 or higher. By default it is set to H800. This number refers to number of bytes. By default, this key defines the number of buffer bytes allocated to each TCP/IP connection.
UdpBufferSize	Can be set to any hex number in the range of H600–Hffff. By default it is set to H1000. This number refers to number of bytes. This key determines the largest UDP packet size that will be passed through the WinSock Proxy Server. UDP packets that exceed this size will not be passed from client to server and vice versa.

Obviously, there are many other keys involved with each element of Proxy Server; however, these other keys are more easily set through the property sheets of both proxy servers. Remember to stop and start the proxy servers after making changes to their registry settings.

Troubleshooting Tips with Proxy Server

When trying to figure out a problem that seems to involve Proxy Server, try to first determine if it is a general network problem or specific only to clients trying to access Proxy Server. For what it does, Proxy Server is a very simplistic service.

If clients are having trouble connecting to Proxy Server, check to see if the TCP/IP protocol is loaded correctly. Many times workstations are set to receive their IP setup from a DHCP server, but sometimes they can't contact the DHCP server on startup. If workstations have disabled the DHCP server error message, they may never know they do not have an IP address. To test to see if this is the case, try pinging the name localhost. If TCP/IP is loaded correctly, Windows 9X will respond to the local ping request. If TCP/IP is not loaded correctly, the ping command will display an error message.

If workstations are set to use DHCP for their startup IP configuration, but they are not getting it and you are certain there are no physical errors with the network or the DHCP server itself, try deleting the following folder out of the Windows 9X registry:

HKEY_LOCAL_MACHINE\System\CurrentControlSet\Services\VxD\DHCP

When a Windows 9X workstation first contacts a DHCP server, the workstation logs the server's location for future reference. Sometimes Windows 9X seems to get confused about where the DHCP server can be found and no longer broadcasts a DHCP location request. This prevents it from obtaining an IP address even after it has booted many times and successfully contacted a DHCP server. Deleting the folder mentioned will force Windows 9X to rebroadcast a DHCP location request on the next boot up. This folder will be recreated once a new (or possibly the same) DHCP server is located (or relocated, as the case may be).

If you are using IPX as your exclusive network protocol, the Web Proxy Server will not be used at all. Only the WinSock Proxy client and server can communicate over an IPX connection. If workstations are having trouble contacting the WinSock Proxy over an IPX link, make sure the frame type defined for IPX on both the NT Server and workstation(s) match. Do not trust Windows 9X to automatically determine the frame type used by a network. This rarely works, and you'll therefore likely save yourself a lot of headaches by manually indicating which frame type to use.

The ping utility can be used on workstations to attempt to ping a server on the Internet through the WinSock Proxy Server. Only the first half of the ping command will work, though. Ping should be able to get as far as resolving the host name to an IP address; however, the ping negotiation after that point takes place using ICMP, which is not supported through the WinSock Proxy. Ping can therefore be used to simply test to see if workstations are getting proper name resolution through the WinSock Proxy Server.

If you are using RAS to make the Internet connection from your NT machine running Proxy Server to an ISP, but the connection keeps timing out, you might need to find a utility that can run on the NT machine to simulate network activity through the RAS connection to the ISP. Most ISPs will disconnect after so many minutes of non-activity.

Troubleshooting Proxy Server in Complex Deployments

As you have seen in previous chapters, effective troubleshooting is often as central to the long-term administration of a server product as correct installation of the product is. Proxy Server is an especially important example of where troubleshooting is key for successful deployments.

In general, you will most often have Proxy issues with Proxy Server from a WinSock client connecting to the WinSock Proxy. Even though Microsoft has greatly improved their implementation of WinSock in version 2 of Proxy Server, it can still tend to be a difficult administration task to deploy it throughout the environment.

In most Proxy Server deployments we have been involved in, the WinSock Proxy has been the most difficult part of the administration process. However, in one recent job, we found that users were unable to reach the Internet from behind a specific Proxy Server. The server was part of an array of servers; all the other servers in the array were able to reach the Internet, and we were able to ping the Proxy Server, so it was live. Moreover, we were able to ping the Internet from the Proxy Server, so that was working as well.

The Problem

Other servers in the organization were able to access the Internet without a problem, and everything seemed to physically be in order on the Proxy Server itself. It was time to go to the setup properties of the server. Close examination revealed the mapping table into the array had incorrect values in it, and the net result was a communications loop.

The Solution

Fixing the mapping table information corrected the problem. After fixing it, we had to further stop and restart the service so that the new mapping table information would be reflected in the service's execution.

Summing It Up

While troubleshooting a Proxy Server stand-alone installation is generally a straightforward process, working with Proxy Server in more complex installations can cause some headaches. Taking the troubleshooting process carefully, one step at a time, makes solving the problem much simpler.

Appendix

Topics Covered:

- What Is a Resource Kit?
- What's in the Microsoft IIS Resource Kit?

Microsoft IIS Resource Kit

Throughout this book, you have heard about the Microsoft IIS Resource Kit as an additional resource or to supplement documentation that you already have. Therefore, this book would not be complete without giving you a basic understanding of what the IIS Resource Kit is. In this appendix, we will discuss the features and utilities that are part of the Microsoft IIS Resource Kit.

Understanding Microsoft Resource Kits

Before we discuss the particulars of the Microsoft IIS Resource Kit, let's review what a resource kit is. Some Microsoft products have complimentary books with CD-ROMs that help administrators and end-users better operate and manage the products. These books with CD-ROMs are called *Resource Kits*.

Resource Kits contain valuable information to supplement the reference materials that you already have. You will usually find information such as how to configure security, performance optimization, and capacity planning. In short, these books contain information that you will not find in any other book.

In addition to the information that you will find in the Resource Kits, you will also find their companion CD-ROMs very useful. They contain utilities that can improve performance, provide better security, and help you manage the product that the Resource Kit pertains to.

What's in the IIS Resource Kit

The Microsoft IIS Resource Kit book has ten chapters, three appendices, and one companion CD-ROM. This appendix explains what information is in each chapter, as well as the three appendices and the companion CD-ROM.

Chapter 1: Internet Information Server Overview

This chapter is an overview of the whole Resource Kit. It takes you through the basics of what IIS 4 has to offer, including a brief description of each component and service, and what they do. It also covers the basics of IIS 4 architecture.

Chapter 2: Managing Content

This chapter gives you insight into how to manage an IIS computer. It includes the following:

- A description of content management
- Helpful hints on what to put in your Web site
- A description of the content creation process
- The steps an administrator goes through to publish content
- The role of the administrator site publication
- Site creation tools
- How to test site content
- How to use the Web Capacity Analysis Tool (WCAT), which allows you to test and monitor your site's performance response to a simulated load

Chapter 3: Capacity Planning

This chapter covers how to plan for the future growth of your IIS system. Capacity planning is the job of all system administrators; it involves determining what your current resource load is and planning what type of future improvements you might need. In this chapter, you learn the tools to use to monitor your system's performance. It contains valuable information, such as how long it takes to download a given file size, and how to use Microsoft Clustering for fault-tolerance.

You will also find recommendations on hardware such as hard disk controllers, memory, and processors. This chapter also includes a description of RAID fault-tolerant levels.

Chapter 4: Performance Tuning and Optimization

One of the most important jobs a system administrator performs is analyzing system performance and tuning the system to improve performance. This chapter discusses the four main system bottlenecks—memory, processor, network, and disk—and how to resolve them.

It also specifically describes Windows NT Performance Monitor objects and counters that you can use to monitor your IIS server's performance.

Chapter 5: Developing Web Applications

Although most administrators are not directly involved with site development, this chapter discusses site architecture theory so that an administrator can better understand the process of site development. You will find topics such as:

- Building on client/server technology
- Three-tier site design
- Design patterns for Web applications

Chapter 6: Data Access and Transactions

The majority of Web sites today are client front-ends used for accessing databases. Without the ability to access a database, your site will simply be an electronic billboard. This chapter also deals with linking your site content to external database sources, such as SQL or Microsoft Access. This chapter contains information on the following:

- Web database access
- Client-side data access
- Accessing data from ASP pages
- Transaction processing

Chapter 7: ISP Administration

Some administrators manage small single-site servers, while others manage IIS computers that host several sites. Companies that provide Web hosting and dial-in access to the Internet for end users are called Internet Service Providers (ISP).

This chapter provides essential information for administrators of ISPs, including:

- Site management
- Customization
- Applying other Microsoft technologies within an ISP

Appendix

Chapter 8: Security

IIS relies heavily on the existing security of your Windows NT Server. However, there are some built-in security features that you may want to implement, such as IP address restrictions. This chapter discusses all the aspects of IIS security, including the built-in and external (NT) security features. The following is a list of some of the security topics discussed in this chapter:

- Guidelines for creating a security policy
- Using built-in NT security
- Defending against malicious attacks
- Auditing access

Chapter 9: Accessing Legacy Applications and Data

Some companies still use older database applications, such as applications written in Common Business Oriented Language (COBOL). This chapter deals with linking your Web presence with these older applications.

The topics covered in this chapter include:

- Identifying strategies
- Integrating IIS and legacy applications
- Gaining access to legacy file data
- Replicating legacy databases
- Migrating transaction processes

Chapter 10: Migrating Web Sites and Applications

Although it is not something that an administrator must do often, there are times when you migrate a Web site from one server to another. This can be required for a variety of reasons. One of the most common is that the Web server product is being replaced with a different product, such as IIS.

Migrating Web content can be a big job, depending on how your content was developed. This chapter deals with all the intricacies of moving a site from one type of server to IIS, including:

- Migrating CGI applications
- Migrating from Netscape Enterprise Server
- Migrating from Lotus Domino

Appendix A: Using the IIS Resource Kit CD

The Microsoft Internet Information Server Resource Kit comes with a companion CD-ROM that has many useful tools on it. This chapter describes the Resource Kit tools and what they are used for. Here is a brief list of what you will find on the Resource Kit CD-ROM:

- ISAPI filters
- ISAPI applications
- Counters
- A content rotator
- A permission checker
- Utilities to manage your IIS computer

Appendix B: ASP Standards

This chapter contains information for Web developers on how to create Web content that takes advantage of the Microsoft Active Server Pages (ASP). You will find information on how to properly structure your scripts to run on browsers.

Appendix C: Debugging Applications and Components

The last appendix in the IIS Resource Kit is dedicated to debugging your Internet applications. Debugging refers to finding and correcting errors in applications. This appendix focuses on the basics of application debugging, and also on specific problems to watch for in applications on IIS. This chapter covers:

- Active Server Pages (ASP)
- ASP performance tips
- Using the Microsoft Script Debugger
- Debug tracing
- Script management
- Running IIS as a process

The Internet Information Server 4 Resource Kit is essential if you intend to continually manage a Windows NT Server running the IIS service. The IIS Resource Kit is a powerful combination of information, components, and utilities to increase the functionality of your IIS server, as well as enable you to manage your server in diverse environments.

Appendix

Index

Note to the Reader: Throughout this index **boldfaced** page numbers indicate primary discussions of a topic. *Italicized* page numbers indicate illustrations.

Index

Index

Index

Index

From the Experts...

Who bring you Mark Minasi's #1 best-selling *Complete PC Upgrade & Maintenance Guide,* Sybex now presents...

Nearly a million copies sold!

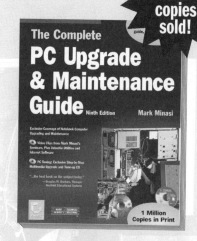

The Complete Network Upgrade & Maintenance Guide
BY MARK MINASI, JIM BLANEY, CHRIS BRENTON

The Ultimate Networking Reference—this book is a practical and comprehensive guide to implementing, upgrading, and maintaining networks, from small office LANs to enterprise-scale WANs and beyond.

ISBN: 0-7821-2259-0
1536 pp., $69.99

The Complete Website Upgrade & Maintenance Guide
BY LISA SCHMEISER

Destined to be the industry's ultimate Website reference, this book is the most comprehensive and broad-reaching tome, created to help you turn an existing site into a long-lasting sophisticated, dynamic, effective tool.

ISBN: 0-7821-2315-5
912 pp., $49.99

The Complete PC Upgrade & Maintenance Guide, 9th edition
BY MARK MINASI

After selling nearly <u>one million copies</u> of its previous editions, the 9th edition carries on the tradition with detailed troubleshooting for the latest motherboards, sound cards, video boards, CD-ROM drives, and all other multimedia devices.

ISBN: 0-7821-2357-0
1600 pp., $59.99

www.sybex.com

©1998, Sybex Inc.

SYBEX

SYBEX BOOKS ON THE WEB

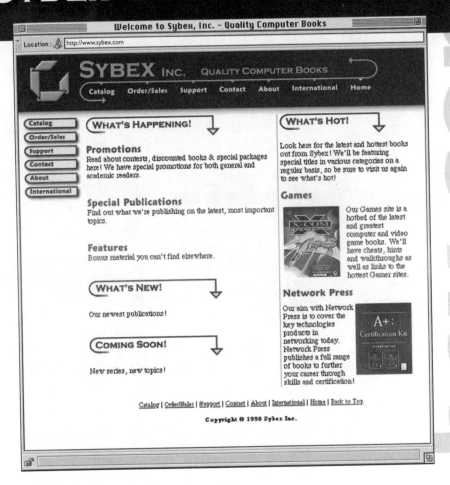